Contents

To

PINTER

London and Washington

First published 1997 by
Pinter, *A Cassell Imprint*
Wellington House, 125 Strand, London WC2R 0BB, England
PO Box 605, Herndon, VA 20172

Reprinted in paperback 1998

British Library Cataloguing in Publication Data
A catalogue record for this book is available from the British Library.

ISBN 1 85567 417 3 (hardback)
ISBN 1 85567 567 6 (paperback)

Library of Congress Cataloging in Publication Data
Tourism and economic development in Asia and Australasia/edited by
Frank M. Go. and Carson L. Jenkins
　　p.　cm. — (Tourism, leisure, and recreation series)
　　Includes bibliographical references and index.
　　ISBN 1–85567–417–3 (hardcover)
　　ISBN 1–85567–567–6 (papercover)
　　1. Tourist trade—Asia. 2. Tourist trade—Australasia.
I. Go. Frank M. II. Jenkins. Carson L. Series. III.
G155.A74T655 1996
338.4'791504429—dc20　　　　　　　　　　　　　　　　96–23789
　　　　　　　　　　　　　　　　　　　　　　　　　　　　　CIP

Typeset by York House Typographic Ltd, London
Printed and bound in Great Britain by Biddles Ltd, Guildford and King's Lynn

List of Figures

List of Tables

List of Contributors

Frank M. Go is Professor in Tourism Management at The Rotterdam School of Management, Erasmus University, Rotterdam, The Netherlands.

Carson L. Jenkins is Professor in International Tourism at The Scottish Hotel School, University of Strathclyde, Glasgow, Scotland.

Jong-yun Ahn is Professor at the Department of Tourism, College of Social Science, Hanyang University, Seoul, Korea.

Tom Baum is Professor of International Hospitality Management at The Scottish Hotel School, University of Strathclyde, Glasgow, Scotland.

Nicolette Boele is Tutor in Tourism Management at the School of Leisure and Tourism Studies, University of Technology, Sydney, Australia.

Michael V. Conlin is Dean at the International Australian Hotel School, Canberra, Australia.

Simon Darcy is a Lecturer at the School of Leisure and Tourism Studies, University of Technology, Sydney, Australia.

Tony Griffin is Senior Lecturer at the School of Leisure and Tourism Studies, University of Technology, Sydney, Australia.

Toh Mun Heng is at the Department of Business Policy, National University of Singapore, Singapore.

Vincent C.S. Heung is Assistant Professor at the Department of Hotel and Tourism Management, The Hong Kong Polytechnic University, Hong Kong.

Zainab Khalifah is a doctoral student at The Scottish Hotel School, University of Strathclyde, Glasgow, Scotland, and Lecturer, University Teknologi, Malaysia.

Lan Li is a Lecturer at the Department of Hotel and Tourism Management, The Hong Kong Polytechnic University, Hong Kong.

Zhen-Hua Liu is Senior Lecturer at the Faculty of Tourism, Hospitality and Food, Cardiff Institute of Higher Education, Wales.

Linda Low is Senior Lecturer at the Department of Business Policy, National University of Singapore, Singapore.

Stan McGahey is Assistant Professor of International Tourism and Co-Director of the International Business and Tourism Institute at the University of Guam.

Stephen Morris is Assistant Professor of English at the Faculty of Political Economy, Yachiyo International University, Chiba, Japan.

Douglas C. Pearce is Associate Professor at the Department of Geography, University of Canterbury, Christchurch, New Zealand.

Hailin Qu is Associate Professor at the Department of Hospitality Management, College of Business, San Francisco State University, California, USA.

Ludwig C. Rieder is President of the Asia Pacific Tourism Development Corporation, Philippines.

Catherine Robinson is Principal Lecturer at the Centre for Professional Development, Auckland Institute of Technology, New Zealand.

Irene Vlitos Rowe is a Management Consultant, London, England.

David G. Simmons is at the Department of Parks, Recreation and Tourism, Lincoln University, Canterbury, New Zealand.

Shaharuddin Tahir is a doctoral student at The Scottish Hotel School, University of Strathclyde, Glasgow, Scotland, and Lecturer, University Utari, Malaysia.

H. Leo Theuns is a Senior Lecturer at the Department of Development Economics, Faculty of Economics, Tilburg University, The Netherlands.

Geoffrey Wall is Professor at the Department of Geography, Faculty of Environmental Studies, University of Waterloo, Ontario, Canada.

Jordan G. Yee is Information Specialist at the Pacific Asia Travel Association, San Francisco, California, USA.

Hanqin Qiu Zhang is an Assistant Lecturer at the Department of Hotel and Tourism Management, The Hong Kong Polytechnic University, Hong Kong.

Wei Zhang is a Lecturer at the China Tourism Management Institute, Tianjin, People's Republic of China.

Acknowledgements

This project was originally conceived by Dr H. Leo Theuns of the University of Tilburg, The Netherlands. Unfortunately, due to other professional commitments, Dr Thuens was unable to continue the project. The editors are grateful for Dr Theuns' input and especially for his contribution of the Chapter on Vietnam.

Our gratitude also goes to Sandra Miller and Ms Zhang Wei who were responsible for the preparation of the manuscript and the many associated texts. Without their assistance, this project would never have been completed.

Preface

The focus of this volume *Tourism and Economic Development in Asia and Australasia* is an exploration of critical issues facing the evolution of the economies in the world's most buoyant tourism region. The volume approaches the topic in an analytical manner and from an international perspective. It is a first attempt to lay a foundation for tourism studies in the region.

Defining Asia and Australasia, also often referred to as Asia–Pacific, is not an easy task. Largest of all continents, Asia covers nearly one-third of the earth's land surface and stretches from the frozen wastes of the Arctic in the north to the rain forests of Indonesia south of the Equator. In the west, Asia's boundary with Europe is defined by the line that may be traced from the Ural Mountains via the Caspian Sea to the Mediterranean. About 9,655 kilometres to the east, Asia ends in the archipelago of Japan and to its north the Sakhalin archipelago.

Hence the reader shall observe that the tag 'Asia' in the title of this volume is plainly too broad. More properly the focus of this volume is on those countries in East and South-east Asia, many of which follow a value system that can be classified under the rubric of Confucianism.

The spectacular economic performance of Japan since the 1960s and the more recent emergence of the South-eastern and Far Eastern Asian countries have given rise to the popular image of Asia as a region of frantic growth. However, this popular image masks the reality in 40 Asian countries, home to more than half of the world's people, which have many problems in common. Feeding a continually increasing population is one of the most pressing problems, and poverty and strife cause millions to migrate from rural areas into cities that are already crowded.

The economies in South-east Asia and the Far East have managed an annual average growth of 5 per cent or more, from 1973 to the present, whilst Gross Domestic Product (GDP) in the USA and Western Europe have grown at an average rate of 2.3 per cent over the same period. The resulting shift of the world's centre of economic gravity to Asia is perhaps one of the most significant events of the past three decades.

Australasia, also referred to as Oceania, is comprised of Australia, New Zealand and the islands of the Pacific east of Indonesia and the Philippines. In contrast to East and South-east Asia, the population in Australasia is small, under 30 million. In Australasia, there is little pressure on resources and its economic growth has been relatively slow.

Thus, the Asia and Australasia sub-region contains a great diversity of physical environments, cultures and levels of development of the world's continents. The expansion of the economies and tourism in the region may be characterized as 'explosive'. But the results of the rapid growth have been a collapsing infrastructure that is hardly able to respond to further tourism demand; a shortage of semi-skilled human resources; and an ecological crisis that in certain destinations is turning visitors away.

Whilst tourist flows in Asia/Australasia have shifted from predominantly North–South to intra-regional, the existing hospitality industry in the region reflects the Western model. However, the fundamental aim of economic and tourism development should be to enhance the functioning of the tourism sector and improve the host society's living standard. In order to redress the present situation, especially in Asia, 'need led' priorities should direct economic and tourism development rather than the traditional 'market led' approach (Theuns and Go, 1991).

These pronounced issues form the backdrop against which researchers attempt to answer two broad questions:

- How are the individual countries of Asia changing and what are the implications these changes may have on tourism and economic development?
- What are the major challenges facing the development of Asian economies, specifically from a tourism perspective?

Contributors from Asia, Europe and North America, representing various disciplines reflecting the interdisciplinary nature of tourism, including economics, sociology, geography, business administration and management, examine tourism development within Asia and Australasia in all its geographical and economic complexity. Each chapter focuses on current tourism developments in a specific country. Within this contextual framework, the present anthology surveys 14 countries that have been grouped according to their level of economic development:

1. Industrial countries, such as Australia, New Zealand and Japan.
2. Three newly industrialized countries: Hong Kong, South Korea and Taiwan.
3. Six South-eastern Asia nations: Brunei, Singapore, Malaysia, the Philippines, Thailand and Indonesia.
4. Two low-income communist countries namely the People's Republic of China and Vietnam which are increasingly turning to the (socialist) market system.

PART I

Analysis of Tourism and Economic Development

Asian and Australasian dimensions of global tourism development

FRANK M. GO

Introduction

International trade and tourism activity has grown significantly in recent decades. Nowhere is this more apparent than in Asia and Australasia, where international trade and tourism are key reasons for the region's current economic prosperity. This chapter examines the significant aspects of tourism development in Asia and Australasia in a global context. It is therefore important to identify the key dimensions of appropriate tourism development. The essence of formulating and implementing tourism development is 'to attain broader and environmental goals' (Singh *et al.*, 1989: 13).

Whether one agrees with this statement or not, it is relevant in this context because it can be broken down into three parts that reflect three crucial dimensions of tourism market development:

1. The first part of this statement, 'The essence of formulating and implementing', indicates that there must be a process at play. Whether formal or informal, rational or irrational, tourism development proceeds through a number of stages and is driven by a myriad of variables, such as demand, supply and capability. This dimension of tourism, which considers how tourism developed, may be referred to as the tourism process.

    The 'emergence' of Japan, and thereafter the Newly Industrialized Countries, and 'open regionalism' are viewed in this chapter as ever-growing factors in the shift towards East and North Asia assuming a major and growing role in global tourism. This shift, in conjunction with changes in the long-haul travel market, especially the greater emphasis on special interest travel, can be expected to have a chain reaction forcing market reforms, to varying degrees, in the tourism process throughout the region.

2. The second part of this statement, 'tourism development', indicates that the tourism process should result in 'output' or 'products'. This output of tourism activity is a course of action to be followed by a destination that will allow for

the attainment of national and/or regional goals in the face of competitive pressures. This dimension of tourism development is concerned with the content (what) of tourism, including the products the tourist comes to experience.

3.   The final part of this statement, 'to attain broader and environmental goals', indicates that policies should be developed to suit varying contexts. It hardly needs to be argued that Asia/Australasia comprise a very heterogeneous region in terms of their level of development, factor endowment and national cultures.

Asia's primary allure for visitors has always been its other-worldliness, which is underpinned by divergent national cultures. However, the convergence towards commercialization and service quality threaten to spoil some of the most idyllic places and the concept of sustainable tourism is probably the central issue (Hall, 1994: 14) in Asia/Australasia tourism. This dimension of tourism is referred to as the tourism *context*.

The present Chapter attempts a three-dimensional view of tourism development by paying attention to each dimension (process, content and context). In this chapter the terms Asia and Australasia, the Orient, Asia Pacific will be used interchangeably.

Data are drawn for this chapter from various sources as indicated throughout the chapter. Particularly useful sources, as far as this chapter is concerned, are the holiday market analysis of European tourists by Aderhold (1995) and a study of Asia–Pacific tourist destinations by Baldwin and Brodess (1993). Finally, the section on marketing in this chapter is derived from an earlier publication (Go, 1989).

Evolution of Global Tourism

Since the early 1950s international tourism has grown rapidly, particularly after the liberalization of foreign exchange and travel restrictions which characterized the years following World War II. In the early 1960s international tourism, which in Europe had been mainly limited to neighbouring countries, began to spread more widely and grow in developing countries (Theuns, 1988).

From 1950 to 1970 international tourist arrivals in all countries grew from 25 million to 168 million, an average annual growth rate of 10 per cent. At the same time, international tourism receipts rose from $2.1 billion to $17.4 billion. The introduction of wide-bodied planes, such as the Boeing 747 and the DC-10, increased worldwide airline capacity and caused airlines to offer lower fares. The arrival of the big jet airliners, capable of ferrying hundreds on a single flight, made Pacific travel not only swift and convenient, but also affordable. 'The formerly vast expanses of the Pacific which deterred travel now became manageable, so that far away places – which had until then been only dreams out of adventure novels – now became a reality' (Gee and Lurie, 1993: 3).

Until 1967, foreign travel from Japan was severely limited. But with the easing of restrictions in subsequent years, Japan's outbound travel grew very rapidly. This event caused two important developments: the world's major tourist generating areas expanded to three – North America (United States and Canada), Western Europe and Japan; it signalled the beginning of the ascend of 'mass tourism' in the Far East.

The energy crisis in 1973/74 and in 1979 and the economic recession in 1981 in the developed countries dampened travel demand. The latter event caused international tourism growth to slow, on average, to 4.4 per cent per year in the 1980s. Between 1986 and 1990, the growth in international travel resumed and international arrivals increased at an average rate of 7.6 per cent per year whilst receipts rose at an average rate of 16.1 per cent per annum.

The Persian Gulf War in 1991 renewed travellers' concerns of safety and fears of terrorism and thus international tourism was depressed in many parts of the world including the Far East and Australasia. At the same time the Western world was affected by an economic recession causing declines in many European countries. For example, international tourist arrivals in both Italy and Germany declined by 15 per cent whilst arrivals in France fell by 20 per cent.

Of all World Tourism Organization (WTO) macroregions the growth of tourist arrivals in the East Asia/Pacific region has been most dramatic. Between 1980 and 1990 the index of total tourist arrivals rose from 100 to 250, that of total tourist arrivals rose from 100 to 250, that of youth tourist arrivals surged to 386. The latter is of considerable significance as youth tourism seems to be the forerunner in redirecting the growth in tourist arrivals towards new destinations in the Third World.

Definition and Typology

Contemporary tourism may be described as a temporary migration stream. In Theobald's (1994: 3) view, tourism is 'distinctly a twentieth-century phenomenon', because people in earlier periods tended to travel for purposes other than leisure. Many different definitions of tourism exist, and thusfar there is no uniform definition that has been adopted. It is therefore a field which is ill-understood by policy-makers and the public at large. For purposes of this discussion tourism is defined as the study of humans away from their usual habitat, the industry catering to their needs while they are travelling and their social, economic, ecological and cultural impact on the host community (Mathieson and Wall, 1982).

Tourism by definition implies travel. People engage in tourism for different purposes such as: pleasure, recreation, holiday, sport, business, visiting friends and relatives, missions, meeting, conference, health, studies, religion (Chadwick, 1987), and different forms of travel including foreign independent tours (FIT), group travel and backpacking. Because there exists a variety of tourism purposes it follows that tourism is heterogeneous rather than homogeneous in nature. In order to gain an understanding of the major issues affecting economic and tourism development throughout Asia and Australasia it is important to be familiar with the main features and types of tourism in a regional and worldwide context.

Smith (1977) distinguishes different types of tourists, ranging from 'explorer' to 'charter tourist'. The former's impact in terms of number of tourist arrivals is very limited both on a world scale and in Asia and Australasia. In contrast institutionalized tourism, including both 'mass tourism' and 'charter tourism', is much more pronounced in the region and worldwide. The introduction of Smith's tourists typology is important in the context of regional tourism development because of its significant implications on sustainable economic development. We shall return to this notion later in this chapter.

An alternative approach to understanding tourism is to define it as an industry. The term tourism industry might be considered a strange appellation, since in the literal sense of the term an industry in tourism has never materialized. Rather fragmentation in tourism has been the rule and no single concept has been developed and accepted, universally, on what tourism precisely constitutes. Gee *et al.* (1989: 4) have raised several arguments that fuel the debate whether a tourism industry exist at all:

- The term industry is commonly identified with manufacturing and production-based enterprises.
- The tourism industry consists of a collection of businesses selling travel-related services. The general public is likely to be more familiar with each component such as the airline industry, the hotel industry, or the entertainment industry.
- The individual industries do not necessarily act together as an integrated group and very often have conflicting views amongst themselves.
- There are businesses involved that serve both travellers and residents with regard to 'dining out', 'shopping' and 'recreation'.

From the above four observations it follows that tourism represents a part of the economy with a relatively low degree of integration. However, tourism is interdependent in the sense that 'poor performance by one business affects the tourism industry as a whole. By the same token when tourism operators produce quality goods and services, their quality work brings both them and the industry success.' (Jafari, 1983: 73).

In order to advance the notion of its 'interdependence', Burkart and Medlik (1974) explain tourism as an 'amalgam' of economic activities, whilst Gunn (1988) refers to the functioning tourism system which consists of four major parts:

- A market of people who travel.
- An attraction, representing part of the supply side of tourism, in the destination to which people travel.

- A series of linkages comprised of services such as telecommunications, transportation, banking/finance that facilitate information and people flows between the market and the destination.
- A destination infrastructure comprised of a set of services that cater to the requirements of travellers, including hotels, foodservice, retail and other services.

For any tourism system to function effectively it has to be able to meet demand, contribute economically, socially and environmentally to the host community, and ensure a reasonably profitable tourist trade. In order to achieve this goal, much depends on the way tourism is handled in the host society, specifically in Asian countries, which have traditions that are much different from Western ones.

The Pacific Asia Travel Association (PATA), a not-for-profit travel industry association, has been instrumental in promoting the Pacific–Asia tourist destinations and contributing to the growth, value and quality of travel to and within the Pacific Asia area on behalf of 2,200 worldwide travel industry organizations. PATA membership includes 76 government, state and city tourism bodies, 60 airlines and cruiselines serving the Pacific–Asia area, over 600 hotel operators, 500 travel agencies, 400 tour operators and tourist attractions, and over 16,000 individual travel industry representatives in over 40 countries on five continents.

Specifically, PATA plays an important role in developing tourism in the Pacific–Asia region on behalf of its membership by:

- Augmenting and assisting local promotion and development efforts of member destinations by organizing task forces of industry experts who analyse their tourism products or services and make recommendations on how to improve them.
- Carrying out advertising, promotional and publicity efforts that focus attention on the member destinations in the Pacific–Asia area.
- Promoting the practice of environmental ethics that support responsible conservation and restoration of the Pacific–Asia region's unique combination of natural, social and cultural resources.
- Conducting statistical and research work relating to travel trends and tourism development.

PATA's Annual Conference serves as the Association's Annual General Meeting where resolutions are adopted by the general membership and delegates and chapter leaders discuss subjects of common interest and form resolutions.

Asia/Australia: Convergence Versus Divergence

A second point that requires clarification, in terms of context, is the definition of Asia and Australasia. The World Tourism Organization divides Asia and Australasia into two a priori regions: South Asia and East Asia/Pacific. The Asia-Pacific region, with its vast population base, rapid general economic growth, and rich natural resources, is one of the most important tourism and trade regions in today's global market. Any attempt to cover tourism development in the vast Asia and Australasia sub-regions within a chapter or a volume is risky, due to the vastness of the area, the great distances between countries, and the diversity of cultures that are found in the countries within the region.

In this chapter Asia and Australasia are taken to mean the East Asia Pacific region, excluding the Americas and Asian part of Russia. The countries in Asia and Australasia may be divided in several geographic areas:

- South-east Asia, which includes the high growth countries of Singapore, Thailand, Indonesia, Malaysia, Brunei and the Philippines.
- South Asia, or the area often referred to as the Indian subcontinent.
- North Asia, which includes Japan, South Korea, Taiwan and the People's Republic of China.
- The South-west Pacific area, including Australia, New Zealand and the Pacific islands (Wise, 1993: 52).

Asia and Australasia is not a homogeneous region because it lacks the definition of 'a set of objective, internal similarities' (Smith, 1989: 163). Rather, the Asia–Pacific region is the most heterogeneous among the different regions of the world, in terms of level of development, factor endowment, and trade structure. For example, regarding level of economic development between the countries in Asia and Australasia, the 'Four Dragons' Hong Kong, South Korea, Singapore and Taiwan have expanded to an economic level in two generations that took Europe and North America about four generations. Nevertheless, at present many nations such as China and Vietnam, despite the opening up of their economies and rapid expansion, remain economically backward nations.

In future, international trade is likely to give impetus to the convergence of the level of development, trade structure and cultural traditions. Recently, the concept of 'open regionalism' has emerged in East Asia, which implies that countries in the region seek to reduce the intra-regional barriers to economic exchange of goods and services (Chan, 1995), in the framework of the worldwide trend towards a multilateral trading system. Lee provides an example of such successful sub-regional cooperation without the gaps in level of development showing up.

ASEAN's open and liberal policy regimes constitute a necessary, though not sufficient condition, for growth triangles to proliferate and flourish. For example, the Singapore–Johor–Indonesia southern growth triangle positions Singapore as a linchpin for the area's economic development. Singapore's surplus capital and lack of land (made up for by its two neighbors) were the driving forces when the triangle was introduced in 1989. Indonesia also provides lower cost labour while Singapore's supporting infrastructure also zeroes in on transportation, skilled labour, telecommunications and access to the world market. Further up, the south China triangle of Guangdong in China, Hong Kong, and Taiwan is perceived as the most developed of sub-regional zones, complementing China's low land cost and land availability with the skilled labour, marketing and services infrastructure of its neighbours. (1995: 10)

The concept of growth triangles, the major purpose of which is to facilitate economic exchange, is relevant to tourism development in general (Arroll, 1993), and the development and marketing of facilities such as marinas, golf courses, and beach resorts, in particular. It also offers the potential to develop 'international circuit tourism' (Ayala, 1993: 66). For example, Menezes and Chandra (1989) indicate that close to 70 per cent of US visitors bound for the Far East visited more than one country in the region.

Whilst the Orient may seem intriguing and exotic to some, an ethnocentric 'market led' approach has resulted in 'institutionalized' tourism development. The institutionalization of tourism within the region is reflected in, for example, the resort facilities, hospitality activities and travel organizations. In particular, the metropolitan economic hegemony in tourism development has led to the convergence of global quality standards in many of the existing industry facilities and services and implies a certain level of homogeneity in the travel experience of visitors. The emerging homogeneity of tourism stands in stark contrast to the rich diversity of cultures the countries in the region possess. Most of the countries in the region are each noted for their own arts, crafts and traditions. And reference is often made to this vast diversity in the cultures between countries and sub-regions of Asia and Australasia. For example, the Republic of Indonesia alone has four main ethnic groups: The Melanesian, the proto-Austronesian, the Polynesian and the Micronesian. These races are again subdivided into hundreds of ethnic population groups, each with its own cultural and social heritage.

Destinations should capitalize on the cultural diversity as a potentially important source to cultivate a competitive edge in the global tourism marketplace. To some extent and in certain facilities, the convergence in the region towards global quality service may seem a prerequisite for destinations to compete internationally. However, the loss of vernacular architecture, heritage and culture in conjunction with the convergence of global quality poses a danger that, in the mid- to long-term, places might lose their uniqueness, and therefore their attractiveness.

In view of the fundamental changes that are taking place in the market (Krippendorf, 1987; Poon, 1989) and in order to redress the situation, 'need led' priorities, rather than the traditional 'market led' approach, should direct tourism development in Asia and Australasia. It is becoming increasingly apparent that the challenge of tourism and economic development in Asia and Australasia can only be successful if both contribute simultaneously to the advancement and it improves the host communities' livability, service quality and sustainable development in a balanced manner.

Demand Determinants

Tourism demand is determined both by exogeneous variables and by market forces. Exogeneous variables are found in the external environment that influence the scale and scope of tourism demand. Market forces refer to the demand for and the supply and distribution of tourism products and services. The exogeneous factors include social structure, educational levels, changing life styles, the degree of urbanization, political stability and regulatory developments, technological innovations, and safety and health developments (Cleverdon, 1993).

The following section examines, to some extent, demographic trends, the changing economic landscape, the shift towards the service sector, relative price changes, and the political and regulatory environment. Examples of several exogeneous and market variables, both positive and negative factors, that are shaping international tourism in East Asia and the Pacific are captured in Table 1.1

Demographic trends

Demographic and social trends in both the developed and developing countries have given the international tourism market a distinct new flavour. In particular, the aging of the population of the industrialized countries combined with a rising middle class in the developing countries shall result in more people with discretionary money, time and desire to travel. The major demographic changes that will affect tourism destinations around the world include:

- An aging population that has more discretionary income, better health and more leisure time than any other age group. For example, in 1970, only 7 per

Table 1.1   Factors shaping international tourism in East Asia and the Pacific

Positive factors	Negative factors
• Intensive and successful marketing and promotional efforts by National Tourism Organizations of most countries of the region.	• Insufficient air seat capacity and airport congestion.
• Opening of international gateways and increased flight frequencies.	• Slowdown of the Japanese economy resulting in slight reduction of outbound travel.
• Modernization and expansion of tourist facilities and infrastructure.	• Political instability in some countries of the region.
• Increase in personal disposable income in the new industrialized countries in the region.	• Natural disasters in selected tourism destinations.
• Growth in private sector activity, business and finance.	• Increased competition among countries of the region.
• More frequent short duration trips.	
• Important ethnic ties between countries.	

Source: WTO (1993b: 11)

cent of Japan's population was over 65 years old, but by 1995 this proportion will have risen to 14 per cent (WTO, 1993a). A similar trend is shaping the travel markets of other industrialized countries. For example, the American market aged 55–64 will grow by 78 per cent by the year 2015.

- Level of urbanization. The rise of manufacturing and service industries have caused the rapid growth of urbanization. At present, more than 70 per cent of the total population in South Korea, Japan, Hong Kong, Singapore and Australia live in urban areas. The increasing urbanization of the Asia–Pacific population is likely to result in the demand for open spaces and clean air in resort and rural areas. Perhaps as a consequence, beach resorts in Thailand, Indonesia, Malaysia and Australia have become increasingly popular both amongst European and Asian visitors, of late.
- Leisure. The big rise of a burgeoning middle class in Asia Pacific has caused leisure travel to expand. In Seoul, Bangkok, Hong Kong, Taipei and Singapore the number of working hours have decreased and paid holidays increased. However, by comparison, workers in Copenhagen (Denmark), Dusseldorf (Germany), Madrid (Spain) and London (UK) work considerably less hours and enjoy substantially more paid holidays (Table 1.2)

Changing economic landscape

Until the 1960s world economic activity and international tourism were firmly concentrated around the North Atlantic. Europe and the United States of America were the major centres of industrial growth and international tourism. But since the 1970s Asia and Australasia have achieved a higher rate of growth than the other parts of the world and maintained its economic performance during the 1980s (Schwab and Smadja, 1994). As a comparison, the economic growth of the countries in Eastern and South-eastern Asia has measured at around 8 per cent annually since 1983, whilst the economies in Europe and North America grew 3–4 per cent per annum (UN, 1993).

The relatively high growth rate of Asia–Australasia makes it an attractive region for investment. Foreign direct investment to the region has increased dramatically over the past years. For example, between 1985 to 1988 world investment increased by 290 per cent while investment in Asia–Australasia

Table 1.2 Number of working hours and paid holidays in selected Asian and European cities

City	Working hours per year	Paid holidays
Seoul	2,302	7.8
Bangkok	2,272	8.8
Hong Kong	2,222	12.1
Taipei	2,136	17.0
Singapore	2,044	17.7
Copenhagen	1,669	25.0
Dusseldorf	1,682	30.5
Madrid	1,721	32.1
Frankfurt	1,725	31.2
London	1,880	22.1

Source: Far Eastern Economic Review (1994: 43)

increased by 520 per cent. As a consequence, Asia-Australasia's share of world investment rose from 3.9 per cent in 1987 to 10.7 per cent in 1990 (UN, 1993).

The rise of Asia–Australasia is anticipated to continue into the next century. The long-term dynamism, especially in East Asia and South-east Asia 'has its roots in various combinations of export-oriented policies, pragmatic interrelation between the State and the private sector in support of growth, active diversification towards manufacturers, human resource development, and high levels of national savings' (UN, 1993). A possible result of the long-term dynamism of the region is that Asia's share of world trade may reach 40 per cent by the year 2015, largely at the expense of Europe's market share (CPB, 1994).

Shift towards service sector

In East Asia, minimal government intervention and low taxes have encouraged corporations to expand and create ongoing industrialization, and have also encouraged a rapidly emerging middle class with steadily rising incomes, which, in turn, implies opportunities for various products. As countries in the region change from developing nations to industrializing countries, there has been an increase in business activities and the expenditure on services (Heath, 1993). Consequently, the demand for both business and pleasure travel has been increasing and caused the rapid growth of tourism throughout the region.

At the same time, there has been a pronounced shift throughout Asia from agricultural-based economies to manufacturing and from manufacturing to service economies. The shift toward the service economies has caused the number of affluent Asians who earn more than US$30,000 and lead consumption trends in Asia to become the fastest growing segment across Asia, expected to grow from 33 million households in 1992 to 51 million households by the year 2000 (Laurent, 1993). These affluent households are highly likely to increase their spending on leisure-related products and services and business activities involving travel and tourism to neighbouring countries and destinations outside the region.

However, tourism may still be considered a 'luxury' for most Asians who, for whatever reasons, cannot, as yet, partake in it. One major constraint is that the number of paid holidays Asian workers receive are limited. For example, the number of paid holidays in Asia ranges from a low of 7.8 in Seoul to a high of 17.7 holidays in Singapore. In contrast, employees in Europe work less hours and enjoy more paid holidays. For example, as Table 1.2 indicates, the number of paid holidays in Western Europe ranges from a low of 22.1 in London to a high of 32.1 paid holidays in Madrid (Leger, 1994: 43).

Comparative prices

Ease of mobility, cost of transportation, changing consumer tastes and preferences have a synergistic effect and determine the aggregate effect on the demand of international travel in a given outbound market area. Fluctuations in the economy such as exchange rates, inflation rates and transportation costs significantly affect travel patterns and hotels catering to international markets (Arbel and Geller, 1983).

Edwards (1987) indicates that shifts of exchange rates tend to be more important in the short term, while in the longer term differences between the rates of inflation and the declining costs of air travel are of greater importance. Middleton (1988) observes that 'the concept of comparative prices is highly complex in practice and the effects are far from easy to predict with any precision, partly because customers' perceptions may differ from reality'. It is the strongest influence on demand in the holiday sector. For example, the soaring exchange rate of the yen, even before the Kobe earthquake, caused the number of tourist arrivals in Japan to decline. In contrast, the weak US dollar contributed to stronger tourist arrivals in Hong Kong, the currency of which is pegged to the 'greenback'.

Political and regulatory environment

Until recently, business travel was restricted by the closed economies of Japan, China, South Korea and Taiwan and they also imposed restrictions on outbound pleasure travel. Since 1987 Taiwan citizens have been allowed to visit mainland China for family reasons. Most Taiwanese travel to mainland China via Hong Kong, because Taipei insists that its citizens enter China from a third jurisdiction (Guangrui, 1993). Taiwan's liberalization of pleasure travel in 1988, reflects Japan's early travel development in the period 1968–72. The currency restrictions in China and advances in transportation and telecommunications have reduced regional and international trade barriers. Nevertheless, the constraints imposed on Asian nationals remain in certain source countries. For example, outbound travellers have to pay departure taxes ranging from a low of US$6 in Indonesia and Singapore to a high of US$15 in Japan and Sri Lanka. Furthermore, all Asian countries, except Hong Kong and Malaysia, impose currency restrictions on outbound travellers that limit the potential to travel (WTTC, 1991).

The collapse of communism, the rise of capitalism, and more active government involvement in tourism planning have caused Asia to change considerably and enhanced tourism growth in the region. At the same time, economic unions such as the European Community, North American Free Trade Agreement and ASEAN are expected to result in more competition between trading blocs. The limited expansion opportunities in 'slow growth' industrialized economies will cause companies to look outward for new markets. Dynamic regional development will drive business and conference travel in Asia and Australasia although independent business travel may not grow as fast as the meetings, incentives, conferences and exhibitions market segments through the 1990s.

Presently, there remain at least five areas of potential political instability in the region, namely China's take-over of Hong Kong in 1997, China's own political future, the intentions of North Korea and the potential of Korean unification, uncertainty in Indo-China as a result of rebel attacks, and the forces at work in India aiming to undermine its democracy. Throughout this decade and into the Third Millenium the interface between dictatorship and democracy in the region will be a challenging one.

Tourism Demand

The concept of tourism demand has been comprehensively explained, for example, by Cooper *et al.* (1993) and Bull (1995). The following section shall examine the distinctive formations of tourism demand in Asia and Australasia.

There are two salient factors that underpin, in particular, the tourism 'boom' in Asia and Australasia. First, the region's rapid economic growth, triggered by economic reforms and entrepreneurship. Second, the more active government involvement in tourism planning and the slow dismantling of political barriers.

These two factors have caused a considerable shift towards the predominance of intra-regional tourism in Asia and Australasia, and away from the long-haul travel market. Though statistical data may be incomplete, the broad pattern of present and prospective tourism developments are fairly clear. The bulk of tourism in the region, like elsewhere, is over relatively short distances within and between Asian and Australasian countries. Over long-haul distances there are still substantial numbers of visitors from Europe, North America, and other markets. And within many countries in the region domestic tourism is emerging.

Therefore, the region's tourism market mirrors the European in the sense that it is segmented and includes a number of 'distinctive formations' (Williams and Shaw, 1988: 17–19). As such, destinations in Asia and Australasia are drawing visitors from three major sources: domestic markets, (sub)regional markets, and intercontinental-long-haul markets. The mainstay of today's Asia–Pacific travel market is intra-regional tourism, as opposed to long-haul tourism, which used to be the dominant market up to the 1970s. This shift toward intra-regional tourism is causing a chain reaction, forcing market reforms, to varying degrees, in tourism destinations throughout the region. Australia and New Zealand especially stand to benefit considerably from Asia's economic growth both in terms of trade and tourism.

Domestic tourism

Although international tourism, involving border crossing, is on the rise it only represents an estimated 17 per cent of all global tourism movements (Jenkins, 1992: 2). By deduction, domestic tourism, or travel undertaken in the country of residence involving a stay of at least one night in a collective or private accommodation in the country visited, accounts for 83 per cent of worldwide tourism movements. Domestic tourism is more difficult to measure than international tourism because domestic tourists do not cross borders or have to exchange money for foreign currency, and there are, therefore, 'few regular records kept of domestic travel' (Pearce, 1987: 95).

Domestic tourism demand in Asia and Australasia varies according to the country and may be very substantial. For example, in 1992 an estimated 330 million locals travelled in China generating RMB 25 billion in tourist receipts (Wei Xiaoan, 1993). And the promotion of domestic tourism is a priority in certain countries in Asia and Australasia. For example, in Malaysia domestic tourism plays a role in engendering 'a local awareness of cultural matters and national identity and heritage, and to enhance national pride and commitments' (King, 1993: 109).

Intra-regional market

The nature of travel in the Asia Pacific region has changed considerably during the past 20 years. At present, tourism flows in Asia and Australasia are predominantly intra-regional in nature, with Japan, after the launch of its 10 million programme in September 1987 (Polunin, 1989; Nozawa, 1992), remaining the most important and influential outbound travel market in Asia.

Edwards (1990) cites five features that differentiate the Asian travel market from those in Europe and North America:

- Relatively few people travel as family groups in South-east Asia. Even when taking holidays, more men than women travel and few children travel.
- Nearly all travel is by air. There is a high proportion of medium- and long-haul trips.
- Most travellers primarily visit major cities. Many also visit more than one country in a given trip.
- Shopping and eating out are major attractions.
- Seasonal fluctuations in overall demand are mild.

There is another major difference in tourism demand between Asia and Western Europe. The travel propensity in the eight Asian countries listed in Table 1.3 amounts to only 1.4 per cent. By comparison, the proportion of the population of Western European countries who travel abroad range from a high of 69 per cent for Germany, 67 per cent in Belgium, 65 per cent in the Netherlands and a low of 35 per cent for the UK, 8 per cent for Spain and 7 per cent for Greece (Burton, 1994).

Table 1.3 Travel propensity in eight Asian countries

Country	GNP US$ (billions)	Population (millions)	Potential travellers (millions)	Outbound travellers (millions)
Japan	4.255	124	62	14
South Korea	306	44	9	3
Malaysia	55	19	10	4
Taiwan	181	21	11	5
Thailand	79	59	9	2
China	547	1,200	12	4
India	272	860	9	2
Indonesia	120	189	9	1

Source: WTTC (1995: 1)

In other words the average propensity of the population in these six European countries to travel abroad is roughly 33 times greater than that of the population of the earlier identified eight Asian countries. The scale of European tourism may be explained by the proximity of countries, an excellent infrastructure, which facilitates car and rail travel, relatively easy entry of countries, and high standards of living and leisure time.

During the 1980s, package holidays dominated the outbound travel patterns in major markets such as Japan and South Korea. However, there are signs of change as an increasing number of Japanese and South Korean tourists prefer individual itineraries. As the travel market in the industrialized markets such as Australia, New Zealand and Japan and the newly industrialized economies of Korea, Hong Kong, Taiwan and Singapore have become more sophisticated, they have also become more segmented. For example, niche markets, such as adventure tourism and eco-tourism, are beginning to develop. Single individuals, younger, senior, health conscious, better educated individuals and double income travellers, all have different expectations. In general, consumers in the region are becoming better informed and demanding with respect to the quality of travel experience they seek, the information they require in making travel decisions and greater flexibility in flight times, itineraries and accommodation arrangements.

Long-haul tourism

In the 1960s and 1970s the demand for Asia Pacific tourism destination was primarily generated by markets in North America and Europe. Both these travel markets are characterized by 'mostly multidestination and stopover trips with relatively short average stays' (Yacoumis, 1989: 20). Although these long-haul markets have declined in proportion to the share of intra-regional travel, they remain important in many Asian destinations.

For many Europeans, Asia remains the second most popular long-haul destination after the USA (Chew, 1987: 84). However, the long-haul market will be characterized by changes in both the number and the nature of the travellers. For example, Aderhold (1995) found that out of 187.6 million holiday journeys made by European tourists in 1994, 5.2 million such journeys were to destinations in developing countries. Table 1.4 shows a general overview of the market dimensions for the actual and potential tourist arrivals in developing countries. The regions and developing countries covered by Aderhold's survey include Asia–Pacific (excluding Japan, Australia and New Zealand), Africa (excluding North Africa) and Latin America (including the Caribbean).

The data Aderhold collected, indicate that Germany represents the largest market for tourist destinations in developing countries, both actual and potential. For instance, German tourists accounted for 3.6 million holidays between 1992–94, or 35 per cent of the total number of such holidays accounted for by the eight European countries. France and the United Kingdom are the next two largest long-haul markets to developing countries, together these two countries account for 48 per cent of market share.

The projected number of potential tourists from the eight European countries listed in Table 1.4 amounts to more than 20 million. Importantly, Aderhold's survey reveals that Asia is likely to continue to be the most popular tourist destination in the Third World for European holidaymakers. Specifically, between 35–45 per cent of the 20 million potential tourists to developing countries cite Asia as one of the regions they are planning to visit in the 1995–97 period, of which about two-thirds of such trips will be realized.

The European long-haul travel market is not only changing in quantitative terms but also in qualitative terms, in particular with regard to motivations, expectations and behaviour. In view of these developments, Aderhold investigated tourists' motivations and preferences for different types of holiday. Potential holidaymakers to developing countries were asked to rank on a scale the importance of 26 different possible motives for going on holiday. Figure 1.1 shows the percentage of holidaymakers whose stated most important motivations for visiting destinations in developing countries during the 1995–97 period fall into five categories, which indicate preferences for different types of holidays clustered around 'experience'/'adventure', 'culture', 'nature', 'beach'/'relaxation' and 'sport'/'hobby' activities.

The survey findings, which are listed in Figure 1.1, indicate that half of all the potential tourists to developing countries perceive 'experience'/ 'adventure' as their most important motivator to travel to a destination in a developing country. A third of all such potential tourists selected 'culture' as the major motivator, whilst 31 per cent are motivated by the desire to enjoy 'nature', and 27 per cent by a 'beach'/'relaxation' holiday.

The relatively low score in the 'beach'/'relaxation' category should not be misinterpreted. The 'beach'/'relaxation' type of holiday is not going out of fashion, but other tourist motives, particularly 'culture' and 'nature', have become more important. Aderhold's findings regarding the greater popularity of special interest travel amongst Europeans, including cultural and heritage tourism, nature or eco-tourism, and adventure travel, appears to be a part of a worldwide trend, and has been cited, amongst others, in Australia by Weiler and Hall (1992) and in the USA by Read (1980) and Forbes and Forbes (1992).

The increasing significance of special interest travel has potential implications for destinations in developing countries. Specifically, in the future between 35–50 per cent of European tourists are likely to prefer different holiday types, that is non-institutional holidays, in Asia. This 'new tourist generation' will be characterized by more independent travel, preference for smaller hotels, interest not only in tourist attractions but also in the social and

Table 1.4　Market dimensions for the actual and potential tourist arrivals in developing countries

Countries in survey	Germany	UK	France	Switz.	Holland	Denmark	Sweden	Norway	Total
Population in millions (over 13 years of age)	62,7	44,7	45	5	12,5	4,2	6,3	3,5	183,9
Sample size (n)	7780	3879	4001	2926	4045	4072	4000	3206	33909
Holiday intensity in %	78	60	63	72	58	66	68	66	68
No. of tourists in millions	48,9	26,8	28,4	3,6	7,3	2,8	4,3	2,3	124,4
Travel frequency	1,4	1,6	1,6	1,5	1,4	1,5	1,7	1,6	1,5
No. of holidays in millions	68,5	42,9	45,4	5,4	10,2	4,2	7,3	3,7	187,6
Actual tourists 1994 to developing countries in millions	2,1	1	1,2	0,3	0,3	0,1	0,2	0,04	5,2
Actual tourists 1992–94 to developing countries in millions	3,6	2,2	2,7	0,5	0,6	0,2	0,3	0,1	10,2
Potential tourists 1995–97 to developing countries in millions	7	5	5	1	1	0,3	0,6	0,2	20,1
Potential tourists 1995–97 to Asia in millions	2,9	2,5	2,2	0,6	0,7	0,2	0,4	0,1	9,6

Source: Dr Peter Aderhold, Institute for Tourism Research and Planning. (Representative surveys in eight European countries based on 34,000 comparable face-to-face interviews in 1995.)

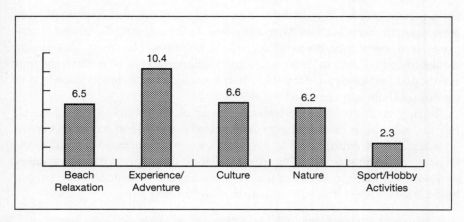

Figure 1.1 Potential tourist motivation for travelling to developing countries, in millions. *Source:* Dr Peter Aderhold, Institute for Tourism Research and Planning. (Representative surveys in eight European countries based on 34,000 comparable face-to-face interviews in 1995.)

political aspects of the host country, and contact with the host people. This shift should lead to changes in marketing policy for some destinations.

Tourism choices

Individual demand for tourism products involves generally complicated decision-making. Bull (1995: 30) refers to several choices consumers have to make, the outcome of which determines the demand for any tourism product, namely the overall type of tourism required, destination, travel mode, accommodation and attractions, easy access to information and booking series. These product and distribution variables are the subject of the sections which follow.

Types of tourism products

Generally the types of tourism products can be categorized under four broad headings: rural/resort, touring, city and outdoor/sport/adventure.

A resort vacation is a single destination trip typically to a rural area where the visitor is offered all vacation requirements, such as relaxation, sport and entertainment at one facility. The important elements of the resort product tend to be: water (oceans/lakes/rivers), beaches, high quality cuisine, night-life, entertainment, water sports, golf, tennis and shopping. In the Asia Pacific market there is a growing demand for resort products, that is the 'get-away-vacation' for relaxation and recreation. Baldwin and Brodess (1993) indicated 'that beach resort holidays are the top aspiration of Asian tourists'. With the exception of the Philippines, the appeal of beach resorts was among the top three holiday choices by tourists in all countries. But, at present, only developed markets such as Australia, New Zealand, Hong Kong and Singapore have significant demand for beach holidays. However, this strong desire among tourists in Asian and Australasian markets, other than the four mentioned, indicates a region-wide trend towards beach resort vacations in the future (Baldwin and Brodess, 1993).

Touring consists of a trip by car, bus or train through areas of scenic beauty, cultural or historical interest. Typically, the tourist comes to experience a different culture and to see well-known landmarks. Therefore, the important elements of a touring trip are historic sites, national parks, scenery and wildlife, cities, and cultural attractions such as museums and art galleries. Baldwin and Brodess indicate that sightseeing activities

> dominate the other major holiday aspirations of Asian tourists. The most preferred type of sightseeing is touring natural/scenic locations followed by visiting historical places and experiencing cultural attractions. Sightseeing has strong existing and potential appeal across all markets, irrespective of their stage of development. It is a top priority of both inexperienced tour groups tourists, looking for value in a full touring itinerary, and of well travelled, independent tourists looking for new and different experiences. (1993: 13–14)

Cities can be destinations in and of themselves, part of a tour or a stopover to break a long trip. The city product includes a variety of sightseeing, entertainment, a full range of accommodation, quality restaurants, nightlife, theatre, concerts, spectator sporting events, historic sites, museums, galleries, zoos and shopping (Ashworth and Tunbridge, 1990). There are indications that the

> shopping oriented trip is gradually declining in popularity, as Asia's retail markets rapidly evolve in tandem with national economic development and market liberalization. While the travel industry indicates that shopping remains a major holiday motivator in less developed countries where access to a wide range of foreign goods is still limited (India, Indonesia, Thailand and the Philippines), it is less of a priority for tourists in the more developed markets. (Baldwin and Brodess, 1993: 14)

Within Asia and Australasia the major urban gateways include Bangkok, Beijing, Hong Kong, Shanghai, Singapore, Sydney and Tokyo.

Outdoor/sport and adventure travel involve a single destination trip to a natural area to engage in activities such as hiking, rafting, kayaking, hunting, fishing or skiing. A large proportion of this market segment typically will camp or stay in budget accommodation, visit parks and participate in recreational activities. The largest proportion of this market segment tends to seek an easily accessible destination for a two- to three-day trip. The small wilderness and adventure market will usually take a longer trip and accessibility, in the accepted sense, is less of a factor. Baldwin and Brodess (1993: 14) indicate that 'Asian tourists have yet to develop a strong taste for active sporting holidays, but that there are emerging pockets of demand such as for water sports in Hong Kong and for golf in Korea' and Japan.

Destinations

Tourist destinations are dynamic and evolve and change over time. Table 1.5 lists the top ten East Asian and Pacific destinations in 1993 both in terms of international arrivals and international receipts, and shows the relative change in both variables over the previous year. 'This evolution is brought about by a variety of factors including changes in the preferences and needs of visitors, the gradual deterioration and possible replacement of physical plant and facilities' (Butler, 1980: 5). The life cycle of tourist destinations could become increasingly shorter due to the fickle nature of travellers, pollution, such as the discharge of sewage effluent into the bay at Pattaya, Thailand, and congestion, for example at Kuta Beach, Bali, Indonesia (Jenkins, 1992: 12). As a consequence, destinations have to constantly reposition and adapt themselves to the demands of the market and investors should be contemplating long-term investments more carefully. Baldwin and Brodess (1993) propose that Asian and Australasian destinations conform broadly to four categories: escalating first visit growth; undeveloped potential; steady repeat-visit growth; and static/declining appeal.

First visit growth
Australia is the most desirable holiday destination in the region. It is preferred by one of three tourists originating in all the major Asian markets. However, this alluring country has so far remained off the beaten track for the majority of tourists. As the region's developing markets mature over the long term, Australia's high visibility/image will enable it to capture an increasing share of outbound tourists. Following the rationale, Australia, New Zealand and the Pacific Islands are also 'dream' destinations, but these in absolute terms are far smaller markets. (Baldwin and Brodess, 1993: 14).

Undeveloped potential
The perception of Singapore is overall more favourable than for Malaysia and Indonesia, which can be characterized as having undeveloped potential; the latter two countries have yet to make a significant impact on travel patterns of the region's tourists. Indonesia, with 3 million tourist arrivals in 1992, provides an example of a country that has opted for slow-growth

Table 1.5 Top ten East Asian and Pacific destinations

Country	International arrivals 1993	% change 92/93
1. China	19,452,000	17.8
2. Hong Kong	7,898,000	13.2
3. Malaysia	6,800,000	13.0
4. Singapore	5,848,000	7.4
5. Thailand	5,714,000	11.3
6. Macau	3,888,000	22.3
7. Indonesia	3,400,000	11.0
8. Rep. of Korea	3,331,000	3.1
9. Australia	2,977,000	14.4
10. Japan	2,100,000	−0.1

Country	International receipts 1993 (in billions)	% change 92/93
1. China	7.8	28.6
2. Hong Kong	5.8	11.6
3. Malaysia	5.7	18.4
4. Singapore	4.7	18.3
5. Thailand	4.3	6.8
6. Macau	3.7	3.1
7. Indonesia	3.6	31.9
8. Rep. of Korea	3.5	7.0
9. Australia	2.8	23.1
10. Japan	2.4	−2.2

Source: World Tourism Organization (1994b: 3)

tourism development. The Indonesian government has turned tourism into an essential lever to enhance the national economy whilst making every effort to preserve cultural assets. It remains to be seen if Indonesia will be able to sustain tourism development along its intended direction as tourist arrivals have doubled since 1988.

Repeat-visit growth and declining appeal

A destination that has demonstrated 'steady repeat-visit growth' is Japan. Due to the appreciation of the yen against other currencies, Japan is a very expensive destination to visit. However, despite its high cost of living, Japan has been able to attract a steady stream of overseas visitors.

Although Singapore and Hong Kong are among the most visited holiday destinations in the region, both appear to be suffering a decline in appeal, as fewer tourists would like to holiday there in the future than have done so in the past. This development constitutes an especially serious threat to Singapore and Hong Kong where, in 1994, tourist earnings contributed 11.5 per cent and 6.5 per cent of Gross Domestic Product (GDP), respectively. In contrast, tourist earnings contributed 4.4 per cent in Australia, 4.2 per cent in Thailand, and 0.6 per cent of GDP in Taiwan, according to Hong Kong-based SG Warburg Securities.

Travel mode

Due to the region's geography, which consists, to a great extent, of islands and peninsulas, air transportation represents the bulk of the travel mode (85 per cent) used by tourists in Asia and Australasia. In many parts of Asia surface transport is generally inadequate. Consequently, transportation by sea accounts for 6 per cent and road transportation represents 8 per cent of the travel mode used by tourists in the region.

This condition has prompted a rapid growth in air transportation and Chew (1987) observed that the 'growing attractiveness of the Asia-Pacific region owes much to the technological improvements in air travel'. Currently, the sluggish airline industry in America and Europe has pushed major international carriers to offer bargain fares and concessions in order to survive. Though Asian airlines are performing well and are profitable, the global competition has increased pressures considerably and led to reforms in the regional market. In particular, Asian airlines are experiencing a transition period and are evolving towards a stage of cooperation that carriers in Europe and America experienced earlier on. For example, the introduction in 1993 of Asia's first frequent flyer programme entitled 'Passages' exemplifies such a cooperative relationship (Mak and Go, 1995). The general lack of infrastructure to support the expansion of trade and tourism presents one of the biggest challenges in Asia. For example, airport congestion is already apparent throughout Asia and Australasia. Therefore, with the anticipated doubling of the number of passenger traffic by the year 2010, the infrastructure of air navigation systems, airports, roads and other transportation systems will need to be increased dramatically.

The accommodation sector

The region is home to some of the world's leading hotels. The unprecedented growth in hotel demand in Asia combined with sound returns resulting from low overheads and high room rates, made hotels in the 1980s the diversification vehicle of choice for local real estate developers and financiers. They followed the path trodden first by Regent International, a company started in 1974 by American hotelier, Robert Burns, first with backing from Tokyu Corporation and more recently from Japan's EIE Development Company, before the Regent International was taken over by Canada's Four Seasons Hotels & Resorts. Regent moved quickly to establish five-star properties in key Asian and North American cities. Its approach to appeal to young business travellers with 'Asian quality' has been replicated by other Asian hotel chains such as Peninsula Hotels, Mandarin Oriental, Hilton International, Inter Continental, Sheraton, Hyatt and Holiday Inn and Shangri-La.

However, the developers have tended to build deluxe hotels and many countries in the region lack three- and four-star hotel facilities. Furthermore, the trend to ignore the mid-market has led to cases of insolvency in, for example, Thailand, where five-star hotels abound but often fail to deliver the internationally accepted standards. Australia has also seen a particular glut due to the rash of up-market hotel building. Reflecting the changes in travel patterns, particularly the shift towards the intra-regional travel market, many hotel companies in Asia have begun, of late, to pay greater attention to the building and operation of mid-market hotels and resorts.

Another important change in the hotel business has been the shift in the power position from operators to owners. During the 1970s and 1980s hotel operators tended to dictate the terms of the management agreement, because they had the required expertise, whereas the owners knew very little about hotel operations and management. Presently, owners in Asia Pacific tend to be much better informed because they have assembled their own team of management specialists and lawyers, and some have established their own hotel brands. Consequently, there are fewer investors and more competition for fewer contracts. Transnational hotel corporations, within this climate, have to perform much better than ever before to achieve a greater return on the owner's investment (Saunders and Renaghan, 1992).

Marketing attractions

Marketing and promotion campaigns have been conducted since the 1980s by individual Asian and Australasian countries promoting their own attractions. Australia, Singapore, Hong Kong and Thailand particularly have carried out large, international marketing campaigns during the past decade. These campaigns are designed to increase the awareness of each destination and its particular features. The Australian Tourist Commission's advertising campaign, which featured Paul Hogan, is one such example. More recently, Indonesia, Malaysia and South Korea have also started their own tourism marketing campaigns.

Tourism marketing during the past few decades has been based on the conventional marketing concept of catering to consumer needs and wants through the travel trade in order to maximize profits, while neglecting the interests of the host society. Britton (1981) has described this 'dependency' model, whereby tour wholesalers, based in metropolitan economies, purchase accommodation and related services in 'bulk' at a discount in a destination area in a peripheral economy, and sell the same directly or indirectly through retail agents to the public in metropolitan markets.

There are, however, symptoms that indicate the time may have come when the international travel industry must proceed on a new assumption, namely that it will be welcome only when it is willing to respect what the community is, that is 'to fit the fabric' of the host community. For example, West German tourists, who arrived in the Indian State of Goa per Condor charter airline, were prevented by the host population from travelling by bus to their hotel, because deluxe hotels 'rob our villagers of their land, the use of beaches, and their traditional way of life, to satisfy your demand for recreation and pleasure – with the full agreement of government' (Ram, 1987: 4).

Because destination areas that develop tourism along the conventional marketing approach stand to lose 'their uniqueness, heritage, and natural resources', beside economic returns (Mill and Morrison, 1985), and because 'fundamental changes are taking place in the tourism market scene' (Krippendorf, 1987), a new marketing orientation in tourism is not only desirable but necessary.

The societal marketing approach (Mill and Morrison, 1985), not only considers consumer wants, but also the long-term interests of the host society, before, during and after planning, development and marketing activities. Societal marketing is a marketing orientation which makes it possible to combine market-led and needs-led models as introduced by Firat (1987), providing the host society with the opportunity to participate in the exchange process – with consumers and the international travel industry – to assist in satisfying particular needs of the destination area.

Implementation: image and competitive position

Can tourist destinations be sold like soap? Some marketing experts believe that everything and anything can be sold by Madison Avenue. But what happens when all destinations sell 'sun, sea, sand and sex'?

Clearly they begin to look alike. Today, especially due to fierce competition, tourist destinations are forced to find a new basis for distinction. Some destinations have begun to realize that they cannot be all things to all visitors. Consequently, they have chosen to select a viable market segment and have 'positioned' themselves in the market. 'The terms "position" or "positioning" have recently been frequently used to mean "image", except that they imply a frame of reference for the image, the reference point usually being the competition' (Aaker and Myers, 1987).

However, the consumer may see competitive destinations as basically alike. For example, to the North American consumer, Asian countries are not easily distinguishable from each other. Sheldon and Boberg (1987) point to the need for each destination (either separately or jointly with a limited number of other destinations) to develop its own distinct image so that the potential traveller is able to distinguish between the numerous 'Asian experiences' on offer. Positioning aims to help customers know the real differences between competitive destinations so that they can match themselves to the destination that will be of most value to them. Since the travel market for most developing nations is invariably international and long-haul in nature, energy and resources should be devoted to the full exploitation of a 'handpicked' cluster of markets. This concentrated marketing strategy advocated by Majaro (1983) has the highest probability of yielding optimum results.

The image of a country is its most important asset for attracting visitors. Too often, however, there appears to be a disparity between advertised image and 'reality' in tourism. The persistence of distortion is clearly manifest in the surprise and dismay that international tourists frequently encounter when travelling in developing countries. The travel industry continues to portray these destinations as 'paradise', 'unspoiled', 'sensuous' or other distortions, presumably to compensate for obvious poverty beyond the hotel or sightseeing bus. This kind of information is not simply harmless propaganda, but adversely affects the visitor's quality of travel experience, and the host society in terms of social impact.

Anyone casually familiar with the consumer travel media or other publications that carry tourism advertising knows that tourist destinations, like manufactured goods, are portrayed in a highly favourable and glossy manner. Clearly, however, promoting a society, especially a developing one, is not the same as marketing soap, no matter how commoditized travel has become.

There are several reasons for the distortion and unreality of images. Firstly, the travel industry uses the shiny illustrations and flattering text to overcompensate for the poverty immediately evident in destinations. A related reason is that much mass tourism, particularly to tropical countries, is sold as an 'escape', and a vacation is not reckoned to be the time to consider new problems.

Secondly, growing competition between superficially similar destinations and the spatial elasticity of demand – too many warm places are readily substitutable – makes it unlikely that firms or governments will deviate from the 'bliss' formula. Finally, for many governments of developing nations, a precarious dependence upon tourism means that despite protests from constituents, they will do as the metropolitan establishment advises. Consequently, destinations seek to build an image in the traveller's mind as 'friendly' or 'sunny', making campaigns less than distinctive.

Positioning may be used to distinguish the destination from its competitors along real dimensions, outlined earlier, for example cultural assets, in order to be the preferred destination to certain segments in the market. For instance, Wafer (1988: 25) presents a strong case for the economic benefits that heritage travel can bring:

> Heritage tourism provides a means for countries to complement their established 'sun and surf' appeal while protecting their natural and cultural assets', including 'all those elements that make each place a unique destination: its flora, fauna, and physical terrain; its architecture, folklore, arts and crafts; and its colonial, and indigeneous roots'.
>
> The links between developing sound conservation strategies and building lasting tourism appeal are becoming more evident even to hard-nosed developers. If such developers can be persuaded to work in concert with local preservation groups, a strong appeal can be made to the traveller who will

promote sustainable growth in the islands while stimulating local interest in conservation of heritage.

Through properly managed marketing of and investment in unique habitats and heritage, it can be demonstrated that economic value can be derived from a balance of conservation and development.

Issues and Prospects

'Whether tourism is an appropriate activity for developing countries to encourage has been subject to controversy' (De Kadt, 1979: v). Nevertheless, it should be clear from the previous discussion that tourism development represents an important part of the region's economic development. The newly won prosperity in Asia has created a burgeoning outbound travel market, which represents both economic and tourism development opportunities.

In the near future tourism growth in the East Asia–Pacific region may profit from the opening of new destination markets in Vietnam, Myanmar, Laos and Cambodia. Although South Asia is somewhat lagging behind, it may soon catch up due to an increased emphasis on tourism as a vehicle for earning foreign exchange and income and employment creation. Together, according to the World Tourism Organization (WTO), the share of the East Asia–Pacific and South Asia regions in world tourist arrivals has grown from 8 per cent in 1980 to 12 per cent in 1990.

WTO forecasts indicate that there will be 100 million tourist arrivals in Asia–Pacific countries in 2000 and 190 million in 2010, four times the number of 1990. The emerging trends in the growth, pattern and characteristics of travel demand for Asia require the identification of appropriate tourism development and marketing strategies that countries in the region might pursue individually and collectively.

The challenges in tourism development in Asia and Australasia are complex and vary between geo-political regions and the time required to fully develop or manifest themselves. However, there are three overwhelming issues in Asia and Australasia that have to be addressed to ensure appropriate tourism development, namely infrastructure, human resources and the impact of tourism on the physical environment.

Infrastructure

Forecasts indicate that annual increases in air passenger traffic will rise by about 5 per cent annually until 2000 when annual passenger movements will be approaching the 2 billion mark. A Forecast by the Boeing Commercial Airplane Group indicates that between 1994 and 2013 the largest addition to increased air travel will come from within the Asia Pacific region. As shown in Table 1.6, an estimated 40 per cent of future growth will come from the combination of Trans Pacific, Asia–Europe and Intra Asia Pacific travel.

This 'unfolding fan' of opportunity has spurred airlines to expand to nearly every major gateway city in Asia–Pacific, to tap this growing market. Accordingly, in the 1990s the following features are likely to influence travel patterns in the region; it will see more air carriers connecting more Pacific destinations with generating markets, more frequently. Whilst the development of new aircraft such as the B 747-400 is expected to support worldclass resorts in Asia and Australasia, it may portend continuing instability to Pacific island destinations.

Presently, there are numerous international airports under construction in the region, including five facilities inside a 100-kilometre radius of China's Pearl River Delta including Hong Kong's Chek Lap Kok Airport, an addition to Shenzhen Huangtian airport, Macau International, Zhuhai, and a new international airport for Guangzhou. The new airport of Hong Kong will be capable of processing 80 million passengers per year. With the tunnels, bridges and highways required to link the airport, situated on an island in the Western harbour within the central business district, it is the largest construction project that has been undertaken in Hong Kong.

Human resources

The tourism industry has thus far been unable to factor out the human element in providing a quality product. This is in contrast to the automobile industry, which is increasingly producing cars with the input of robots. The labour intensive nature of tourism has created direct and indirect employment for an estimated 204 million individuals worldwide, or '1 in every 9 workers'. By 2005 growth is projected to add a further 144 million new tourism jobs (WTTC, 1991).

The human resources shortage is becoming increasingly accute in the 1990s as educational institutions and corporations are generally failing to meet the demand. For example, the planned tourism development in Thailand between 1995 and 1999 should require an additional 18–20,000 trained staff,

Table 1.6   Major air travel markets 1994–2013

Intra Asia Pacific	23.5
North America	22.7
Trans Pacific	13.3
Intra Europe	11.2
North Atlantic	9.8
Asia-Europe	8.8
North America–Latin America	3.8
Europe–Latin America	2.5
Intra Latin America	2.1
Europe–Africa	1.9

Note: Figures represent average annual incremental traffic measured in billions of Revenue Passenger Miles (RPMs).
Source: Boeing Commercial Airplane Group (1994) *Current-Market Outlook: World Air Travel Demand and Airplane Supply Requirements*, p.5

whereas the anticipated total output from private and public tourism training programmes will only amount to 3,500 (Gee, 1994: 36). Hong Kong and Malaysia face similar labour problems.

The region, which has been world famous for its high quality service of its deluxe hotels and national carriers such as Cathay Pacific Airways, Singapore Airlines and Malaysia Airlines, is facing a lack of appropriately skilled workers. One study (WTTC, 1993) indicated that 'more than half of the employers surveyed reported "moderate-to-serious" shortages of skilled and semi-skilled workers, especially in the hotel and resort industry'. The same study identified the following major human resource development issues which the region's industry will face in the years ahead. These are:

- The lack of tourism education facilities and qualified instructors to prepare workers for the field.
- The lack of national standards for tourism occupational programmes.
- A reluctance to supplement or replace conventional schooling in the face of a rapidly changing society.
- An emphasis on management education as opposed to training the 'rank and file' workers.
- An insufficient fit between educational programmes and the industry needs and the requirement of more integration of relevant human resource development activities and policies into the national plan of tourism development (WTTC, 1993: 4–6).

Another human resource management challenge is that the region's tourism industry reflects the Western culture, through the proliferation of transnational hotel and travel-related facilities. However, at present, tourism throughout Asia and Australasia is predominantly intra-regional in nature and industry 'offerings' may not match demand. Furthermore, if tourism education and training systems in the region aim to improve both the functioning of the tourism sector and the host society's living standard, they would require a 'need led' rather than a 'market led' approach (Theuns and Go, 1991: 335).

Physical environment

Given the need of countries within the region to earn foreign exchange, it is tempting to follow Thailand's 'fast-track' tourism development model. The rapid development of tourism along this scenario would be encouraged by foreign direct investment and the exploitation of sex tourism by an impoverished people. For example, prostitution, an unfortunate residue that was left by the succession of military interventions and foreign troops, has demonstrated the potential to attract countless numbers of 'tourists' to Thailand. However, the tourism boom in Thailand has recently faltered due to image problems, and a pessimistic outlook is indicated by the narrower base of interested potential tourists compared with previous visitors (Baldwin and Brodess, 1993: 14–15).

Whilst trade and tourism have been unfolding in the region at a pace unmatched at any time there is a threat that destinations serving hundreds of thousands of visitors may self-destruct. The very expansion of tourism poses an environmental challenge to the region, which could lead, in the absence of skilful management and purposeful action, to the stagnation or demise of traffic. Because the more visitors that come in search of a country's assets, the more those cultural assets are endangered and threatened with obliteration. This is a problem only beginning to receive attention from both governmental planning agencies and the international travel industry.

Increased travel in Asia Pacific has led to the potential increase in exposure to risk due to poor health conditions, the lack of adequate medical facilities, and the probability of accident or injury in places across Asia Pacific. The travel industry cannot ignore these travel health risks because they result in the ruining of the quality of travel experience, 'bad press' followed by a fall-off in visitation. It is therefore important that the travel industry promotes the travel health issue to preserve the health of its own business. In taking a pro-active role the travel industry should introduce health and welfare through educational and training programmes and promote the quality of the visitor experience.

Concluding Remarks

Despite the explosive growth, Asia and, to a greater extent, Australasia, to a lesser extent, remain relatively immature as a tourism region. This is primarily due to a lack of infrastructure, human resources, and knowledge and political will to confront environmental problems.

Fortunately, several of the countries in the Asia–Pacific region appear to be working in unison to optimize growth opportunities. For example, the Association of South-east Asian Nations, which includes the Philippines, Thailand, Brunei, Malaysia, Singapore and Indonesia, seeks to work towards political stability and encourages economic progress, setting the stage for sustainable tourism development.

As a general principle, host destinations should attempt to develop tourism on a scale, at a rate of growth, and in locations that avoid serious adverse social, cultural and/or environmental impacts on its society. Asia and Australasia represent an extremely diverse region, ranging from wealthy and advanced nations, like Japan and Singapore, to developing states, like Indonesia, Cambodia and Thailand with completely different economic, cultural, demographic, geographic and political dimensions. These different profiles have significant implications to what degree Asian nations should attempt to use tourism as a vehicle to diversify their economy and create employment.

Destinations in Asia and Australasia have arrived at the crossroads. They can continue to develop like in the past and risk stagnation and decline, or they can choose to reframe their environment by embracing change and give greater priority to sustainability, authenticity and quality. Asian and Australasian visitor destinations that wish to compete effectively in the global market should build tourism as a factor of economic development. Wise destination management will base tourism development on those features that make the countries of the region unique, in order to encourage and sustain variety and heterogeneity, both in the region's tourism and the global travel market.

Bibliography

Aaker, D. and Myers, J.G. (1987) *Advertising Management* (3rd edn). Englewood Cliffs, NJ: Prentice-Hall.

Aderhold, P. (1995) *The European Holiday Market for Developing Countries 1995*. Copenhagen: Dr Peter Aderhold Institute for Tourism Research and Planning.

Arbel, A. and Geller, A.N. (1983) Foreign exchange sensitivity: how a strong currency weakens hotel revenues. *The Cornell HRA Quarterly* **24** (3), 64–70.

Arroll, J. (1993) Tourism cooperation in the Asia Pacific region. *Tourism Management* **14** (5), 390–1.

Ashworth, G.J. and Tunbridge, J.E. (1990) *The Tourist – Historic City*. London: Belhaven Press.

Ayala, H. (1993) The unresearched phenomenon of hotel circuits. *Hospitality Research Journal* **16** (3), 59–73.

Baldwin, P. and Brodess, D. (1993) Asia's new age travellers. *Asia Travel Trade* **24** (5), 12–17.

Britton, Stephen G. (1981) Tourism, dependency and development: A mode of analysis. Canberra: ANU Press (Development Studies Centre Occasional Paper No. 23).

Bull, A. (1995) *The Economics of Travel and Tourism* (2nd edn). Melbourne: Longman.

Burkart, A.J. and Medlik, S. (1974) *Tourism: Past, Present and Future*. London: Heinemann.

Burton, R.C.J. (1994) Geographical patterns of tourism in Europe. In Copper C. and Lockwood A. (eds) *Progress, in Tourism, Recreation and Hospitality* Vol. 5. Chichester: Wiley.

Butler, R.W. (1980) The concept of a tourist area cycle of evolution: Implications for management of resources. In *Canadian Geographer*, XXIV.

Chadwick, R.A. (1987) Concepts, definitions and measures used in travel, tourism research. In Ritchie, J.R.B. and Goeldner, C.R. (eds) *Travel, Tourism and Hospitality Research. A Handbook for Managers and Researchers*. New York: Wiley.

Chan, K.S. (1995) Asia Pacific nations set example to world on benefit of treaties. *South China Morning Post*, 22 May, 8.

Chew, J. (1987) Transport and tourism in the year 2000. *Tourism Management* **8** (2), 83–8.

Cleverdon, R. (1993) Global tourism trends: influences, determinants and directional flows. In Ritchie, J.R.B., Hawkins, D.E., Go, F. and Frechtling, D. (eds) *World Travel and Tourism Review 1993* Vol. 3. Wallingford: CAB International, 81–9.

Cooper, C., Fletcher, J., Gilbert, D. and Wanhill, S. (1993) *Tourism Principles & Practice*. London: Pitman.

CPB (1994) Changing share of world trade. *De Telegraaf* 6 September, 25.

De Kadt, E. (1979) Introduction. In De Kadt, E. (ed.) *Tourism: Passport to Development? Perspectives on the Social and Cultural Effects of Tourism in Developing Countries*. New York/Oxford/London: Oxford University Press.

Edwards, A. (1987) *Choosing Holiday Destinations: The Impact of Exchange Rates and Inflation*. London: Economist Intelligence Unit.

Edwards, A. (1990) *Far East and Pacific Travel in the 1990s*. London: Economist Intelligence Unit.

Firat, A.F. (1987) Tourism marketing development: structural constraints facing underdeveloped countries. Unpublished manuscript.

Forbes, R.J. and Forbes, M.S. (1992) Special interest travel – creating today's market-driven experiences. In Ritchie J.R.B., Hawkins, D.E., Go, F., Frechtling, D. (eds) *World Travel and Tourism Review* Vol. 3. Wallingford, Oxford: CAB International, 128–34.

Gee, C.Y., and Lurie, M. (1993) *The Story of the Pacific Asia Travel Association*. San Francisco: Pacific Asia Travel Association.

Gee, C.Y. (1994) Presentation on strategic human resource development. Report from seminar on Challenges For East Asia and The Pacific Region Up to the Turn of the Century. (Kuala Lumpur, Malaysia, 7 July) Madrid: World Tourism Organization, 35–47.

Gee, C.Y., Makens, J.C. and Choy, D.J.L. (eds) (1989) *The Travel Industry* (2nd edn). New York: Van Nostrand Reinhold.

Go, F.M. (1989) Appropriate marketing for travel destinations in developing nations. In Singh, T.V., Theuns, H.L. and Go, F.M. (eds) *Towards Appropriate Tourism: The Case of Developing Countries*. Frankfurt: Peter Lang Verlag.

Guangrui, Z. (1993) Tourism crosses the Taiwan Straits. *Tourism Management* **14** (3), 228–31.

Gunn, C.A. (1988) *Tourism Planning* (2nd edn). New York: Taylor and Francis.

Hall, C.M. (1994) *Tourism in the Pacific Rim Development, Impact Markets*. Melbourne: Longman.

Heath, R. (1993) Services poised to become top sector. *South China Morning Post*, 26 August (Business).

Jafari, J. (1983) Anatomy of the travel industry. *The Cornell HRA Quarterly* **24** (1), 71–7.

Jenkins, C.L. (1992) Tourism in Third World development – fact or fiction? Inaugural Lecture. Glasgow: University of Strathclyde.

King, V.T. (1993) Tourism and culture in Malaysia. In Hitchcock, M., King V.T., and Parnwell M.J.G. (eds) *Tourism in South East Asia*. London: Routledge.

Krippendorf, J. (1987) *The Holidaymakers*. Oxford: Heinemann.

Laurent, C.R. (1993) Mid market hotels. Why and where are the Opportunities. Presented at *4th Annual Hotel Development & Finance Conference*. Hong Kong, 24–26 March.

Leger, J.M. (1994) The boom. How Asians started the 'Pacific Century'. *Far Eastern Economic Review* **157** (47), 43–9.

Majaro, S. (1983) *International Marketing: A Strategic Approach to World Markets*. London: George Allen & Unwin Ltd.

Mak, B. and Go, F. (1995) Matching global competition cooperation among Asian airlines *Tourism Management* **16** (1), 61–5.

Mathieson, A. and Wall, G. (1982) *Tourism: Economic, Physical and Social Impacts.* London: Longman.

Menezes D. and Chandra, S. (1989) The distant overseas U.S. tourist: an exploratory study. *Journal of Travel Research* **28** (2), 6–10.

Middleton, V.T.C. (1988) *Marketing in Travel and Tourism.* Oxford: Heinemann.

Mill, R.C. and Morrison, A. (1985) *The Tourism System: An Introductory Text.* Englewood Cliffs, NJ: Prentice-Hall.

Nozawa, H. (1992) A marketing analysis of Japanese outbound travel. *Tourism Management* **13** (2), 226–33.

Pearce, D. (1987) *Tourism Today. A Geographical Analysis.* Harlow: Longman.

Polunin, I. (1989) Japanese travel boom. *Tourism Management* **10** (1), 4–8.

Poon, A. (1989) Competitive strategies for a 'new tourism'. In Cooper, C.P. (ed.) *Progress in Tourism, Recreation and Hospitality Management* Vol. 1. London and New York: Belhaven Press.

Ram, M. (1987) Duitse toeristen zn niet welkom op de witte stranden van Goa. *NRC,* 19 November.

Read, S.E. (1980) A prime force in the expansion of tourism in the next decade: special interest travel. In Hawkins, D.E., Shafer, E.L. and Rovelstad, J.M. (eds) *Tourism Marketing and Management Issues.* Washington DC: The George Washington University.

Saunders, H.A. and Renaghan, L.M. (1992) Southeast Asia: a new model for hotel development. *The Cornell HRA Quarterly* **33** (5), 16–23.

Schwab, K. and Smadja, C. (1994) Power and policy: the new economic world order. *Harvard Business Review* **72** (6), 40–50.

Sheldon, Pauline and Baberg, Kevin (1987) Long haul travel from North America to Asia. In *Travel and Tourism Analyst* (April), 19–31.

Singh, T.V., Theuns, H.L. and Go, F.M. (eds) (1989) *Towards Appropriate Tourism: The Case of Developing Countries.* Frankfurt: Peter Lang.

Smith, S.L.J. (1989) *Tourism Analysis: A Handbook.* Harlow: Longman.

Smith, V. (1977) *Hosts and Guests.* Philadelphia: University of Pennsylvania Press.

Theobald, W.F. (1994) The context, meaning and scope of tourism. In Theobald, W.F. (ed.) Global Tourism: The Next Decade. Oxford: Butterworth-Heinemann.

Theuns, H.L. (1988) *Toerisme in Ontwikkelingslanden.* Tiburg, The Netherlands: Tiburg University Press.

Theuns, H.L. and Go, F. (1991) 'Need led' priorities in hospitality education for the Third World. In Bralton, R.D., Go, F.M. and Ritchie, J.R.B. (eds) *New Horizons in Tourism and Hospitality Education Training and Research Conference Proceedings.* Calgary: University of Calgary.

UN (1993) *World Economy Survey 1993. Current Trends and Policies in the World Economy.* New York: United Nations.

Wei Xiaoan (1993) *The Developing China Tourism, China National Tourism Administration.* Leaflet.

Wafer, Patricia (1988) Heritage tourism in the Caribbean. In *Place* **8** (1), 25–7.

Weiler, B. and Hall, C.M. (eds) (1992) *Special Interest Tourism.* London: Belhaven Press.

Williams, A.M. and Shaw, Gareth (1988) *Tourism and Economic Development: Western European Experiences*. London: Belhaven Press.

Wise, B. (1993) The Far East and Australasia. In Jones, P. and Pizam, A. (eds) *The International Hospitality Industry Organizational and Operational Issues*. London: Pitman.

WTO (1993a) Tourist numbers expected to double. *WTO News* No. 6. Madrid: World Tourism Organization.

WTO (1993b) *Tourism Trends Worldwide Series East Asia and The Pacific 1980–92*. Madrid: World Tourism Organization.

WTO (1994a) *Compendium of Tourism Statistics*. Madrid: World Tourism Organization, 236, 239.

WTO (1994b) Marketing, manpower and sustainability – top challenges for EAP. *WTO News* No. 4. Madrid: World Tourism Organization.

WTTC (1991) *Bureaucratic Barriers to Travel*. Brussels: World Travel and Tourism Council.

WTTC (1993) *Gearing Up for Growth: A Study of Education and Training for Careers in Asia–Pacific Travel and Tourism*. Brussels: World Travel and Tourism Council.

Yacoumis, J. (1989) South Pacific tourism promotion: a regional approach. *Tourism Management* **10** (1), 15–28.

Zhang, G. (1993) Tourism across the Taiwan Straits. *Tourism Management* **14** (3), 228–31.

2

The projection of international tourist arrivals in East Asia and the Pacific[1]

HAILIN QU
HANQIN QIU ZHANG

Introduction

International tourism is one of the largest sources of income and employment. Even after excluding international transportation, international tourism accounts for one quarter of the world trade in services and 7 per cent of the total value of world exports. In terms of employment, 1 in 14 workers is employed in the tourism industry, contributing about 5.5 per cent of the global Gross National Product. In 1992, international tourist arrivals totaled 476 million, accounting for over 279 billion in Gross Travel Receipts, excluding transportation payments. The World Tourism Organization predicts that 630 million people will be travelling annually by the year 2000, a substantial increase from the 476 million in 1992.

Tourist arrivals and receipts in East Asia and the Pacific have grown substantially during the last decade. It has shown the strongest increase in the world market share, rising from 7.3 per cent in 1980 to 12.3 per cent in 1992. According to a report from WTO in 1993, the actual tourist arrivals in East Asia and the Pacific increased almost three-fold between 1980 and 1990, from 21 million to 58 million, representing an average growth rate of 8.9 per cent annually, which is higher than that in any other region of the world during the period (Africa – 7.3 per cent; America – 4.3 per cent; South Asia – 3.6 per cent; Europe – 3.5 per cent; Middle East – 1.5 per cent). The growth of tourism receipts in the region was even more spectacular than tourist arrivals, rising from US$8 billion to US$43 billion in 1992, a five-fold increase and an average growth rate of 15 per cent annually. Almost 75 per cent of the growth rate occurred during the second half of the 1980s (WTO, 1993).

Europe has remained the main tourist destination in the world, with more than 60 per cent of world tourist arrivals, despite the loss of almost 6 percentage points in its market share between 1980 and 1992. The market share of East Asia and the Pacific increased considerably from 7.3 per cent in 1980 to 12.3 per cent in 1992. America maintained its one-fifth share of world tourist arrivals. In terms of world tourism receipts, the European share dropped by almost 8 per cent, from 60.4 per cent to 52.8 per cent. The East Asia and Pacific region almost doubled its share of world tourism receipts from 8.3 per cent in 1980 to 15.5 per cent in 1992. America performed better in terms of receipts than arrivals, with a gain of almost 4 per cent in its market share.

The ranking of total arrivals by destinations in the East Asia and Pacific region is presented in Table 2.1. In 1992, the top five tourist destinations (including Singapore, Hong Kong, Thailand, China and Malaysia) took 50 per cent of the total tourist arrivals in the region. These five main tourist markets have been relatively stable, especially the first three, Singapore, Hong Kong and Thailand. There have not been any changes in terms of their ranking, except that Hong Kong's number one position in 1981 was lost to Singapore and became number two in 1992. Thailand remained number three in 1981 and 1992. Japan dropped from position four in 1981 to position five in 1992. Taiwan suffered a tremendous loss dropping from position five in 1981 to position ten in 1992.

The rapid growth of the tourism industry in East Asia and the Pacific has been very much associated with the economic development in the region. It is the fastest growing area in the world and is characterized by the rapid emergence of middle classes and white collar employees enjoying steadily rising incomes. Growth in the dynamic Asian economies of South Korea, Taiwan, Hong Kong, Singapore, Thailand and Malaysia is projected to be about 6.5 per cent in 1993 and 1994, well in excess of the OECD (Organization for Economic Cooperation and Development). It is aided by the economic

Table 2.1   The ranking of international tourist arrivals in 12 tourist destinations in East Asia and the Pacific, 1981 and 1992

Ranking		Tourist	Tourist arrivals (000s)	
1981	1992	destinations	1981	1992
1	2	Singapore	2,829	5,990
2	1	Hong Kong	2,535	6,986
3	3	Thailand	2,016	5,136
4	5	Japan	1,583	3,582
5	10	Taiwan	1,409	1,873
6	6	South Korea	1,093	3,231
7	9	Malaysia	1,006	2,346
8	11	The Philippines	939	1,153
9	8	Australia	937	2,603
10	4	China[2]	714	4,172
11	7	Indonesia	600	3,064
12	12	New Zealand	478	1,056

Source: PATA Annual Statistical Report (1981, 1992)

recovery in the United States and continued economic expansion in China, which has become an increasingly important market for Asian exports. Many countries in this region are changing from developing countries into maturing business and manufacturing economies (Accor Asia Pacific, 1993). Therefore, the demand for both domestic and regional travel is increasing.

Infrastructure development must continue if tourism in East Asia and the Pacific is to prosper further. During the 1980s most governments in the region became aware of the need to improve and develop tourist facilities. Some examples are China's plan for 11 national resorts, the opening of Disney theme parks in Tokyo, the construction of a new airport in Hong Kong, and the construction of the third runway for the international airport in Sydney.

Despite the prosperous future of the East Asia and Pacific region, the Asian tourism industry still faces some problems, such as political instability, insufficient air seat capacity, airport congestion, the inaccessibility of scenery spots and resorts, skilled labour shortage, and intensive competition among the tourist destinations within the region. In order to maintain substantial growth rates, the countries in the region need to continuously restructure and liberalize their economies.

The tremendous growth of the tourism industry and the booming economies in East Asia and the Pacific have drawn some scholars' attention in forecasting tourism. The World Tourism Organization undertook a major study in 1990 entitled 'Global Tourism Forecast to the Year 2000 and Beyond'. Some of the main objectives of the project are to familiarize the countries in East Asia and the Pacific with regional and worldwide tourism trends, and with global tourism forecasts to the year 2000; to examine the overall growth prospects in the region; and to identify appropriate product development and marketing strategies for the destinations of the region to pursue in the 1990s. Mak and White (1992) studied tourism development in Asia and the Pacific and found that tourism development in East Asia and the Pacific would depend on continued economic growth and the willingness of governments to open their countries to the world and to allow their own nationals to travel freely abroad.

To date, few, if any, studies are found that deal with forecasting the demand of tourist arrivals in East Asia and the Pacific. The forecast of tourist volume in the form of arrivals seems to be the most important study since it can provide basic information for policy-making. Tourist flows have a bearing on basic elements such as the occupancy rate of hotels; investment in transportation and accommodation; the souvenir industry; and promotion and information (Van Doorn, 1984). Therefore, both the private sector and government bodies can use the basic data to plan their future operations and to foresee facilities and infrastructure development needs.

Fundamentally, the projection of international tourist arrivals in East Asia and the Pacific will contribute to answering three vital questions:

(1) How many international tourists will arrive at a destination in a given projected time period?
(2) What will the growing trend look like for the major destinations in the region by the year 2005?
(3) What will be the implications of those growing markets for the whole East Asia and the Pacific region?

Data

The data examined in this study are annual international tourist arrivals in 12 East Asia and Pacific tourist destinations from 1970 to 1992.[3] The destinations selected for the present study are Australia, China, Hong Kong, Indonesia, Japan, South Korea, Malaysia, New Zealand, the Philippines, Singapore, Taiwan and Thailand. The selection is based on data availability and the importance of these destinations in the region's tourism industry. There are 23 observations over this period in general, except that there are 11 for China and 21 for New Zealand. The data on international tourist arrivals used for the projection are from two sources: the Annual Statistical Report 1970–1992 published by PATA (Pacific Asia Travel Association), and the Yearbook of China Tourism Statistics 1986–1993 published by CNTA (China National Tourism Administration). Projections will mainly focus on international tourist arrivals from seven major originating markets: Africa, America, Asia, Europe, Middle East, Oceania and others.

Inevitably, there are data inconsistencies across the destinations in how international tourist arrivals are measured, classified and tabulated. Island destinations with limited access such as Indonesia, the Philippines, Japan, New Zealand, Taiwan and so on, with travel mainly by air, tend to have more complete data than those with wide open boundaries such as China. Destinations composing their data on the basis of arrivals and departure cards are more likely to have complete and accurate data than those composing their data on the basis of reports from hotels or other public sources, as the data from these sources are prone to be incomplete or duplicated.

The concept of international travel differs sharply between people living in small countries or regions or near international borders, and residents of large or rather isolated countries or regions. A one-day or weekend trip can easily encompass travel through Hong Kong or Macao to China; or through Singapore to Malaysia, but the same is not true in Australia or Japan. The differences in the underlying concepts, composition and comparability of the data among these 12 destinations have been noticed and special effort has been made, especially for China, to adjust and modify the arrivals data.

First, a special category of tourist arrivals, compatriot,[4] has been established in China's *The Year Book of China Tourism Statistics*. The percentage of compatriots in China's total arrivals ranged from 89 per cent to 94 per cent during the period 1981–92. For comparison purpose this category was omitted from the figures for China's international tourist arrivals in this study. Second, the number of tourist arrivals from the Middle East is not listed as a separate category in *The Yearbook of China Tourism Statistics*. It is classified into the category of 'others'.

Projection Model

A literature survey revealed that behavioural models, which include independent variables such as GDP (Gross Domestic Product), income, exchange rates, relative price and travel cost, have had quite limited success in forecasting the future international tourist arrivals. For example, the models developed by the Economic Intelligence Unit to project the level of tourism in major countries for 1980–86 greatly overstated actual travel (Edwards, 1988). The problems were due in part to the unpredictable recession in the early 1980s that was not anticipated in the projection models. The problems were also due in part to the types of models applied (Hiemstra, 1991). It was found that in some cases time series models have been shown to be equally or even more accurate when compared with behavioural models (Choy, 1984). A time series regression model selected by Choy to develop annual forecasts of travel to the East Asia and Pacific region generated relatively high accuracy when compared with other models. The results suggested that improvements in forecast accuracy can be achieved by using time series regression models for tourist arrivals. Martin and Witt (1989) also tested the accuracy of different forecasting models for tourist arrivals, and found that time series models outperformed behavioural models; and simple time series models were superior.

The data on international tourist arrivals for the past 23 years exhibit an upward trend over time. They indicate that a linear model is appropriate for this data. This is because:

1. It is easier, more accurate and more straightforward to make trend projections than to develop econometric models.
2. No individual projections of independent variables are necessary in projecting them into the future.
3. Taking into consideration the type of data available through secondary sources, time series trend models are adopted for projection in this study even though they are not too satisfactory in terms of explaining behaviour.

Various univariate time series models have been examined in developing the projection model for this study. Choices among the time series models involved a selection of various autoregressive and exponential smoothing methods with linear, trend and quadratic assumptions. The model finally selected for this study is the SAS PROC FORECAST procedure for the application of the Stepar method with a trend assumption.

Trend models tend to be appropriate for capturing long-term behaviour, whereas autoregressive models are more appropriate for capturing short-term fluctuations. In this study, the time trend model and autoregressive model are combined to capture both long-term and short-term behaviour for the projection. Time series models assume that the future value of a variable is a linear function of past values (SAS/ETS, 1990). If the model is a function of past own values for a finite number of periods, it is an autoregressive model that can be written as:

$$x_t = a_0 + a_1 x_{t-1} + a_2 x_{t-2} \cdots \cdots + a_n x_{t-n} + e_t^5$$

The SAS Stepar method is applied in the projection procedure. First, it fits a time trend model[6] to the time series data and takes the difference between each value and the estimated trend. Second, it takes the residuals from the first step and computes the autocovariances to the number of lags[7] and regress the current residual values against the lagged residuals. Third, it removes the autoregressive residuals whose parameters are not significant at the 0.05 level, and only significant parameters remain in the model (SAS/ETS, 1990).

The autoregressive time series model forecasts quite well when there is a reasonable number of years of historical data. It is not perfect, nor are they a substitute for expert opinion and economic behavioural models, but, at the least, time series models provide a useful and relative accurate forecast. The model reflects the past and is able to capture correlations with the past in quite a complex way. One drawback of the model is its inability to show 'unpredictable' noise. The model has some limitations, but it also has real advantages: ease of use, quick generation of forecasts, minor staff power and computational requirements, and finally, accuracy in prediction (Hiemstra, 1991).

The remainder of this chapter will analyse the historical data of international tourist arrivals in 12 destinations in East Asia and the Pacific, and apply the SAS FORECAST autoregressive model to project international tourist flows up to the year 2005. Some of the positive factors of the growth trends will be discussed, and the implication of the growth trends, such as those related to economic, social, cultural, political and environmental issues in the region, will be suggested.

In this study, the projection of international tourist arrivals will be developed at two levels: the total 12 tourist destinations level; and the major individual destinations level.

Overall Projected Trends

The strong growth of international tourism in East Asia and the Pacific started in the 1980s; tourists from all over the world arrived at 12 destinations in the region. Figure 2.1 illustrates the past and projected future growth for international tourist arrivals in the region. During the ten years from 1982 to 1992, the total number of international tourists arriving at the 12 destinations increased from 16.9 million in 1982 to 41.2 million in 1992 with an average annual growth rate of 8.8 per cent, which excluded millions of compatriots travelling from Taiwan, Hong Kong and Macau to China.

Figure 2.1 also indicates that the growth of international tourist arrivals in the region occurred on a constant annual basis during the ten years. The projection for the next ten years, from 1995 to 2005, also shows a constant growth trend. The total tourist arrivals will increase from 56.6 million in 1995 to 155.2 million in 2005, with an average annual growth rate of 10.4 per cent. Experts in international tourism and economics have all foreseen that the region as a whole will be the world's economic dynamo for the next ten years. This dynamic region will within itself provide ample demand for substantial increases in tourist activity, as residents of the region visit each other's countries in ever-rising numbers either on vacation, for business, or both. According to the projected figures (see Table 2.2), Singapore, Hong Kong, Thailand and China will become the top four tourist destinations in the East Asia and the Pacific region in 2005 in terms of actual arrival numbers. The combined share of these four destinations in the region constitute 55.8 per cent of the total tourist arrivals in East Asia and the Pacific. The following

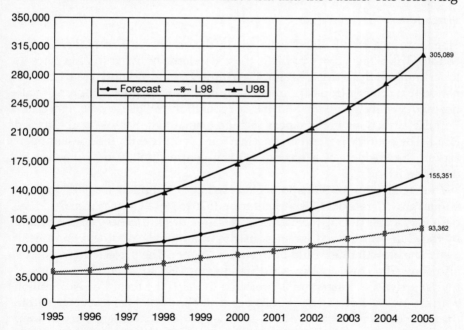

Figure 2.1 Projected international tourist arrivals in 12 East Asian and Pacific tourist destinations, 1995–2005.

Table 2.2   The ranking of international tourist arrivals in 12 tourist destinations in East Asia and the Pacific, 1992 and 2005

Ranking		Tourist	Tourist arrivals ('000)	
1992	2005	destinations	1992	2005
1	2	Hong Kong[8]	6,986	23,354
2	1	Singapore	5,990	25,493
3	3	Thailand	5,136	19,297
4	4	China	4,172	17,781
5	8	Japan	3,582	10,584
6	5	South Korea	3,231	15,655
7	7	Indonesia	3,064	10,717
8	9	Australia	2,603	8,649
9	6	Malaysia	2,346	11,071
10	10	Taiwan	1,873	5,069
11	11	The Philippines	1,153	4,297
12	12	New Zealand	1,056	2,581

Source: PATA Annual Statistical Report (1992)

part will provide detailed discussion of each major destination in the region.

Projected Trends in Top Four Destinations

Singapore

Singapore is a small island situated off the south coast of Malaysia. The country has achieved one of the highest standards of living in Asia since its independence three decades ago. The country is a well-known tourist destination that offers a tropical climate, beautiful scenery, good shopping facilities and variety of goods and has a reputation for being safe and clean. Popular attractions in Singapore include Chinatown, Santosa and Orchard Road. The country is participating in a joint venture with Indonesian interests in the creation of a second tourism centre (Bintan) on a nearby Indonesian Island.

Tourist arrivals in Singapore increased to 5.9 million in 1992 with an annual growth rate of 11.78 per cent from 1970 to 1992. Growth in arrivals has been very stable during the past three decades, despite the disruption caused by the Gulf War to the tourist industries of a number of other countries in 1991. The growth rate would otherwise be higher. The projected growth has also showed a consistent upward trend from 1995 to 2005. The number of tourist arrivals to Singapore is projected to reach the record of 25.5 million with an annual growth rate of 11.34 per cent. The most notable change within the major destinations in East Asia and the Pacific is that Singapore will jump from ranking number 2 in 1992 to the ranking number 1 in 2005 in terms of tourist arrivals figures (see Table 2.2). The constant growth and success of the tourist industry in Singapore has been due to the following factors: promotion, diversification of the tourism product, improving infrastructure, increasing living standards of East Asia, desirable shops and facilities, and the reputation the country has for personal safety and the negligible amount of crime.

Hong Kong

Hong Kong has been one of the most popular tourist destinations in Asia. Due to the success of the tourism industry in Hong Kong, geographic location and many other factors, Hong Kong has become one of the world's busiest transportation hubs. The territory will revert to Chinese ownership in 1997 and the social, cultural, economic, business and financial links with China will further develop Hong Kong as a major transit location for visitors travelling to Asia from all over the world.

Tourist arrivals in Hong Kong have grown steadily. According to the most recent statistics provided by the Hong Kong Tourist Association, the territory welcomed a total of 9.3 million visitors in 1994 (including visitors from China). In 1993, the Hong Kong Tourist Association started counting visitors coming from the People's Republic of China (PRC), following the relaxation of currency restrictions, which had limited their spending in Hong Kong. In 1994, a total of 1.9 million visitors came from PRC, which constitutes 20 per cent of the total tourist arrivals in Hong Kong. The projected growth of tourist arrivals in Hong Kong will reach 23.4 million by 2005 from the current 7.3 million (excluding visitors from China) with an annual growth rate of 9.77 per cent. According to the projection, Hong Kong will drop its number 1 position in 1997 to number 2 (see Table 2.2) in 1998 within the destinations in East Asia and the Pacific. This may be due to certain factors such as a political transition period and the maturity of the tourism industry in Hong Kong.

In order to maintain the future prosperity of the Hong Kong tourism industry, the Hong Kong Tourist Association has been actively marketing Hong Kong as an attractive destination that offers tourists the 'exotic experience', the Chinese cuisine, and a shopping paradise. The most recent marketing campaign undertaken by the Hong Kong Tourist Association carried the theme 'Hong Kong – Wonders Never Cease', which reflects that Hong Kong is indeed a wonder itself, and in fact encompasses an amazing range of wonders, superlatives and achievements.

Thailand

Thailand was one of the first countries within the region to welcome tourism as an industry with a major export potential. According to the Tourism Authority of Thailand, tourism is Thailand's largest source of foreign exchange with receipts from overseas visitors totalling the equivalent of US$3.9

billion in 1991, and the per capita daily average visitor expenditure in 1991 was the equivalent of almost US$109. Tourist attractions in Thailand include the cultural sights of Bangkok, the resorts of Pattaya and Phuket, which can offer tourists tropical forest, dazzling beaches, coral reefs and well-known Thai cuisine.

The number of tourist arrivals in Thailand has been consistently ranked third within East Asia and the Pacific destinations from 1980s to 1990s, and will retain that rank until 2005 (based on the projected figure). Between 1980 and 1990, the tourism industry experienced substantial growth. The number of tourist arrivals tripled from 1.05 million to 3.2 million. The public aware-ness of Thailand as a popular destination has been engendered by the Visit Thailand Year (1987) Campaign, which has played a significant role in the development of tourism. Along with the successful tourism industry in Thailand, there are also some negative impressions among foreign tourists which to some extent affect their perceptions. These include the Aids scare, child prostitution, environmental pollution of natural beaches and land, invasion of the local people's life, traffic congestion in Bangkok and so on. Some of these problems may be due to the mass tourism. The Tourism Authority of Thailand has recognized these negative factors and tried to change them. For example, 1992 was designated as Women Visit Thailand year, to commemorate the sixtieth birthday of Queen Sirikit and to help readdress some of the country's negative external images.

The future for the tourism industry in Thailand looks very promising. Thailand is projected to be the number 3 destination in East Asia and the Pacific in terms of tourist arrivals number. The actual projected number will reach 20.1 million with a constant annual growth rate of 9.91 per cent. In order to accommodate the constant growth of the tourism industry in Thailand, the Seventh National Economic and Social Development Plan 1992–1996 has set tourism as a focus to help the further progress of the country. The Tourism Authority of Thailand has put emphasis on maintain-ing the quality of tourist destinations (ensuring that local people display sufficiently friendly attitudes to tourists to make them feel safe and wel-come), the sustainable development of destinations through wise manage-ment of tourism resources, careful tourism promotion and proper balance of conservation and land use.

China

The People's Republic of China has become one of the leading tourist destinations of East Asia and the Pacific. The country is the biggest in the world in terms of land area and population. China is an old country with more than 5,000 years of history and offers many kinds of attractions for tourists from all over the world. The most popular attractions are numerous, such as the Great Wall, Forbidden City, the Terracotta Army, Yangtze Gorges, and eight different types of Chinese cuisine that are world famous.

The tourist industry has developed since the open-door policy in 1979 and started booming in the past few years even though it slowed down a little due to the political events of 4 June 1989. The total number of arrivals (excluding those made by citizens of Hong Kong, Macau, Taiwan and overseas Chinese in other countries) were more than doubled between 1987 and 1992. The 4 June event in 1989 brought the total arrival in that particular year down 21 per cent. In order to attract tourists and businessmen back to China and reposition China's image, the China National Tourist Administration announced that a series of promotional activities had to be developed to rebuild and reposition the image of China through extensive media coverage. The China Travel Services (CTS) offered 80 per cent discount on tours to attract visitors. When China hosted the Asia Games, foreign visitor arrivals increased more than 55 per cent during 1991, a further 48 per cent during 1992. The quick recovery from the 4 June event is also due to the effective opening up of much of China, not only to tourists, but also to foreign businessmen, as well as closer links with Hong Kong and Taiwan.

The projected growth of tourist arrivals in the year 2005 is even more spectacular. The annual growth rate of tourist arrivals from 1995 to 2005 is projected to be 17.8 million with an annual growth rate of 14.2 per cent. America, Europe and Asia are the three major markets which will constitute 93.2 per cent of the total arrivals in China. To meet this growing demand, the Chinese government has put emphasis on infrastructure development by establishing more tourist resorts. For instance, one of the national tourist resorts of Yalong bay in Sanya on the island of Hainan is to be developed in two stages. The first, from 1993 to 1995, has seen the completion of building infrastructure, including post and telecommunications, transportation, and water and electricity supply. The second phase, from 1996 to 2000, is intended to attract about 2.4 million visitors to Sanya.

Conclusions and Implications

The booming economies in East Asia and the Pacific region are characterized by steadily rising incomes among their populations. Many countries are changing from developing countries into maturing business and manufacturing nations. People in this area have higher disposable incomes than before. They are interested in satisfying not only their basic needs such as food and lodging, but also their socio-cultural needs, and travel has become very popular. Therefore, the demand for both domestic and regional international travel is increasing. Marketing techniques have been used by individual countries or regions to promote their own destinations. Australia, Singapore, Hong Kong and Thailand carried out large international tourism marketing campaigns during the 1980s and 1990s. The Australian Tourist

Commission's advertisements featuring Paul Hogan, Visit China Year 93, Visit Korea, and Malaysia Year 94 are some of the examples. These efforts have helped to create an awareness of each destination and its particular attractions.

The projected growth in international tourist arrivals in East Asia and the Pacific looks quite promising. Tourist arrivals to the region will increase from 41 million in 1992 to 156 million in the year 2005, with an overall growth rate of more than 280 per cent and an average annual growth rate of 10.77 per cent. In terms of projected regional market share, Asia will still keep its dominating position. Singapore, Hong Kong, Thailand, China and South Korea will be the top five tourist destinations in the region.

With the tremendous growth of international tourist arrivals in East Asia and the Pacific, a wide range of issues needs to be addressed. These include economic, social, cultural, political and environmental issues. International tourism has become a very important part of the economy in the region, as tourism grows more rapidly than other sectors of the economy. This means that there will be more jobs and incomes generated by the increasing number of tourist arrivals. But labour shortage may become a concern since jobs in the tourism industry involve long and irregular hours of work such as those in the hotel industry. Quality and committed staff will be crucial in terms of providing good services to tourists. Political stability in the whole region has been and will continue to be a major concern for the growing tourism industry. Many destinations have not been politically stable. Examples are China, and Hong Kong facing transfer of political sovereignty from the UK to China. Impediments to travel such as control of visas, passports and foreign exchange in some of the regions or countries will constrain international travel. Environmentally, countries or regions in East Asia and the Pacific need to create a heightened consciousness of the 'Green Planet'. The over-crowding and degradation of the environment in the region will reduce its attraction to more tourists. The host nations and localities must also be able to provide good hygiene and access to health services if they are to offer quality tourist products. Assuming that these problems do not become more serious, East Asia and the Pacific region can be optimistic for the future and be fully prepared for a promising tourism industry.

Notes

1 As defined by WTO (World Tourism Organization), East Asia and the Pacific region consists of three sub-areas: North-Eastern Asia, South-Eastern Asia, and Oceania.
2 In the study, the number of international tourist arrivals in China excluded compatriots for the comparison purpose.
3 The international tourist arrivals data for China were limited from 1981 to 1992 and for New Zealand were limited from 1972 to 1992.
4 Compatriot includes visitors from Taiwan, Hong Kong and Macau.

5 In this study, the logarithm transformation is used for the international tourist arrivals in the projection model, which is written as:

$$\log x_t = a_0 + a_1 \log x_{t-1} + a_2 \log x_{t-2} \ldots\ldots + a_n \log x_{t-n} + \epsilon_t$$

6 The linear trend is applied in the model.
7 The number of lags applied in the model is determined to be 11, except China is 5 and New Zealand is 10, due to the number of observations.
8 In this study, the projected number of international tourist arrivals in Hong Kong excluded the visitors from China.

Bibliography

Accor Asia Pacific (1993) The outlook for tourism in the Asia-Pacific region. *Tourism – The Growth Industry*. Sydney: Accor Asia Pacific Prospective, 52–3.

Chan, Y.M. (1993) Forecasting tourism: a sine wave time series regression approach. *Journal of Travel Research* Fall, 58–60.

Choy, D.J.L. (1984) Forecasting Tourism Revisited. *Tourism Management* September, 171–6.

CNTA (1986–93) *The Year Book of China Tourism Statistics*. Beijing, China: China National Tourism Administration.

Edgell, D.L. and Smith, G. (1993) Tourism milestones for the millennium: projections and implications of international tourism for the United States through the year 2000. *Journal of Travel Research* Summer, 42–6.

Edwards, A. (1988) *International Tourism Forecasts to 1999*. London: Economist Intelligence Unit Ltd, 172.

Fritz, R.G., Brandon, C. and Xander J. (1984) Combing time-series and econometric forecasts of tourism activity. *Annals of Tourism Research* **11**, 219–30.

Hiemstra, S.J. (1991) Projections of world tourist arrivals to the year 2000. *World Travel and Tourism Review* **1**, 59–65.

Mak, J. and White, K. (1992) Comparative tourism development in Asia and the Pacific. *Journal of Travel Research* (Summer) 14–23.

Martin, C. A. and Witt, S.F. (1989) Accuracy of econometric forecasts of tourism. *Annals of Tourism Research* **16** (3), 407–30.

Payne, M. (1993) Tourism in the Pacific Rim. Growth in a region of Opportunity. *Financial Times Management Report*. London: *Financial Times* Business Information.

PATA (1970–92) *Annual Statistical Report*. San Francisco, CA: Pacific Asia Travel Association.

SAS Institute Inc. (1990) *SAS/ETS® User's Guide, Version 6, First Edition*. Cary, NC: SAS Institute Inc.

Sheldon, P.J. and Turgut, V. (1985) Tourism forecasting: a review of empirical research. *Journal of Forecasting* **4**, 183–95.

Uysal, M. and Crompton, J.L. (1985) An overview of approaches used to forecast tourism demand. *Journal of Travel Research* **23**, 7–15.

Van Doorn, J.W.M. (1984) Tourism forecasting and policymaker-criteria of usefulness. *Tourism Management* **5** (1), 24–39.

WTO (1993) *Commission for East Asia and the Pacific*. Madrid: World Tourism Organization.

3

Impacts of the development of international tourism in the Asian region

CARSON L. JENKINS

Introduction

The purpose of this chapter is to consider three aspects of international tourism. First, to examine the contribution that tourism has made to the development process in Third World countries. Secondly, to consider to what extent this contribution has been real rather than nominal. Thirdly, to examine some of the criticisms of tourism in this process and to ask whether or not the criticisms have substance. These three aspects will then be related to the development of tourism in the Asian and Australasian region.

The global growth of tourism has been a phenomenon since the 1950s. The scale, type and location of tourism has had many impacts, not all favourable. On a global scale, Asian tourism development has taken on an intra-regional character since the 1980s with countries such as Japan, and more recently, Taiwan, Singapore, South Korea and Hong Kong becoming increasingly important generators of intra-regional tourist movements. A region with many levels of development, Asia has become the most dynamic tourism market in the world. This dynamism has not been caused by tourism but rather tourism has benefited from the dynamic economic impetus. As regional per capita incomes rise and cultural perceptions of holidays and travel change, the growth in tourism activity is likely to continue into the future. As Go has noted (Chapter 1) the impetus for regional tourism growth has shifted from long-haul visitor arrivals to more intra-regional demand.

Although the 'Asian Dragons' of Hong Kong, Singapore, Taiwan and South Korea are more accurately described as Newly Industrializing Countries rather than as Developing Countries, the Asian region as a whole is generally characterized as 'developing'. Despite the impressive economic performance of the 'Asian Dragons', other regional countries with above average global growth rates, such as China, India and Indonesia, face formidable difficulties in transferring rapid economic growth into development benefits for their very large populations. Despite the economic dynamism of areas such as the New Economic Zone in China, metropolitan Jakarta in Indonesia, and Bombay in India, for most parts daily life and its challenges in these huge countries seems hardly to change.

There is a fundamental difference in the impact of rapid economic growth on large as opposed to small countries. The larger regional countries such as China, India, Indonesia, Pakistan and the Phillipines will largely remain as tourist receiving countries into the foreseeable future. Within these countries there are affluent middle classes who will continue to generate long-haul and intra-regional tourism, but these small market segments are likely to remain important for the level of per trip spend rather than for the numbers of visitors generated. To consider the impacts of international tourism on the Asian region it is necessary to relate these developments to the wider global context.

Tourism in Development

However, before we can look at tourism in this context, we should have some indication of what constitutes the tourism sector or as it is more usually known, the tourism industry. To describe tourism, which is essentially a multi-sectoral service activity, as an industry would cause most economists some pain. There is no single production function as we would normally understand it. However, the term industry is commonly used because it represents a core of activity that is now well defined and certainly well recognized. One of the complexities of tourism is that it embraces huge developments such as EuroDisney and yet it can also include a very modest scale guest house or a pony trekking centre. It is a difficult sector to delineate but one which requires some analysis to understand its significance.

In 1988, Wharton Econometrics (American Express Co., 1988) undertook a study of the global impact of tourism and travel and described it as the world's largest industry; it is a major contributor to the global economy. The sheer scale of its impact is quite staggering. For example:

1. Travel and tourism generates more than US$2.5 trillion in gross output. This represents 5.5 per cent of world Gross Net Product.
2. Travel and tourism employs more than 1.2 billion people worldwide, which is 1 in 15 employees.
3. Travel and tourism invests more than $350 billion in direct, indirect and personal taxes each year. More than 6 per cent of total global tax payments.

In a second study for the World Travel and Tourism Council (1993) based on detailed research it was claimed that:

By 1994 travel and tourism will generate $2.4 trillion in gross output; create employment for 204 million people or 1 in every 9 workers; produce 10% of

world GDP; invest $693 billion in new facilities and equipment; and contribute
more than $654 billion of tax revenue. (p.4)

These figures are almost too large to comprehend. The World Tourism
Organization estimated that in 1994 international tourist arrivals will total
528 million trips that will generate approximately US$321 billion in inter-
national tourism receipts. These figures need to be put into a perspective.

For example, under the recognized international statistical definition,
international tourism refers to visitors who cross international frontiers and
whose purpose of journey is either business or leisure. There are specific sub-
categories within these definitions that need not concern us at the moment.
However, what is important is that best estimates indicates that international
tourism represents perhaps only 17 per cent of all global tourism movements.
It is the proverbial tip of the iceberg. There is is a huge domestic market that
will substantially enhance these figures. As noted by Steer and Darcy
(Chapter 4), in Australia domestic tourism accounts for 70 per cent of total
tourism expenditure; in Malaysia, Khalifah and Tahir comment (Chapter 10)
that domestic tourist receipts are rising at a rate estimated at around 15 per
cent a year.

In this chapter, reference is made to the Third World. This phrase ema-
nated from attempts by the United Nations to classify levels of development
and relate these levels to types of market structure. The First World referred
to developed market economies, countries which normally were members of
the Organisation of European Cooperation and Development. The so-called
Second World included the countries of Eastern Europe, members of Comecon, and those whose markets were characterized by centralized planning
and guided by socialist principles of development. The residual, the so-called
Third World, were those developing countries mainly in Africa, Asia and
Latin America who have a wide range of levels of development and share, if
anything, centralized planning techniques. Some would argue that within
the Third World there was room for a fourth group comprising those
developing countries that are oil exporters. Since the cataclysmic events in
Eastern Europe, whether the term Third World has any immediacy or any
relevance is a matter now for some debate. However, the title provides the
historical, geographic and developmental reference to the developing countries that, as noted, are mostly to be found in Asia, Africa and Latin America.
These countries tend to have particular characteristics. In identifying some of
these characteristics one would make the usual caveat that not all countries
suffer to the same degree from the difficulties described, but most of them are
fairly representative of the developing world. These characteristics are as
follows (UNDP, 1995).

First, most of the developing countries have narrow resource-based economies. This means that their ability to sustain economic development, and
particularly through exports, is limited. In some countries the potential

resource bases are very wide, countries like Zaire and Namibia obviously have mineral wealth that will be in demand and can be exported; for political, technological and usually financial reasons, this potential has yet to be realized.

Secondly, many of the developing countries are dependent on the export of primary products for the generation of foreign exchange. Primary products, of course, are essentially homogeneous, and most buyers of these products in developed Europe and North America will usually have some type of quota or tariff barrier that limits the import possibilities for developing countries.

Thirdly, over the years the so-called Terms of Trade have moved against the developing countries. Put in non-economic language this means that the quantum of exports required to buy a quantum of imports has moved against Third World countries. An example of this is the need in many developing countries to import oil when oil prices have risen very substantially on the international market. Many of the export prices received by the developing countries have stagnated or declined.

These economic conditions are reinforced by other pressures. In most, but not all, of the developing countries there are very severe population pressures. For example, in Kenya with a rate of population increase now approaching 3 per cent per year, the population will double every 20 years. India has recorded a population of 860 million people, China 1.2 billion. These pressures of population are obviously major constraints on development efforts. It should be noted that most Third World countries have to import many developmental inputs, particularly capital equipment and expertise, at world market prices. Therefore, although their own exports are declining in value and earnings potential, they are forced to pay world prices in order to maintain any development impetus.

Another event that has affected many developing countries has been the freeing of colonial links. Political independence has not brought with it the expected trade freedom, and many countries have found it very difficult to meet rising economic expectations. Against this background of economic, social and political change the developing countries have had to look very carefully at how to maintain their development initiatives. It is against such considerations that we should examine what role tourism might have in the development process.

Robert Erbes (1987) as long ago as 1973 made the following statement: 'Everything seems to suggest that developing countries look upon tourism consumption as manna from heaven that can provide a solution to all their foreign settlement difficulties' (p.1). What has now passed into tourism history is the phrase 'manna from heaven'. To many people this statement is a naive and perhaps simplistic presumption. However, it is also a useful introduction to our understanding of tourism in the development process.

Why would an economic planner, or a politician in a developing country, consider that tourism had the potential to contribute to development? Historically, tourism has been, and largely remains, a by-product of developed and relatively affluent societies. In 1991, approximately 80 per cent of international tourist arrivals were in the developed regions of Western Europe and North America; this percentage has only marginally diminished over the past 40 years (WTO, 1994). Although predominately an activity of developed countries, more tourists from these countries are now travelling to Third World destinations. The new industrialized countries of Hong Kong, Taiwan and South Korea are increasingly contributing to international tourist arrival figures, and above all other examples, Japan has become an important generator of international tourists over the last decade (see Chapter 9).

In these Asian countries, as economic development has improved, it has released more discretionary income to purchase foreign travel and holidays amongst other consumption possibilities. This increasing level of discretionary income is generating a class of leisure travellers in addition to the existing, and important, business travel market.

It is the dramatic impact of tourism in the developed world that has provided the example for developing countries to follow. With tourism now a major international economic activity it has advantages as a contributor to economic development that other industries might not have. What is important is the concept of comparative advantage; does the concentration of investment and resources in tourism generate more economic benefits than if similar amounts of resources had been invested elsewhere, for example in agriculture or industry?

The evaluation is, of course, complex and is outside the scope of this chapter. However, the issues are important because resources are scarce and need to be allocated amongst competing demands. Tourism has no prior claim for advantageous treatment, but should be regarded as one sector of an economy competing for available resources with others. Despite this caution, tourism has, particularly in developing countries, received substantial and continuing support from governments; why should this have happened?

Government Support for Tourism

There are perhaps seven main reasons why governments have supported tourism as part of their development strategies.

First, tourism is historically a growth sector. If you look at the development of modern tourism that can be dated from the 1950s, tourism has had a higher growth rate than world trade in general (WTO, 1994). For the developing world faced with problems of quota and tariff barriers, a growth sector must be a very attractive option to include in a development strategy.

Second, the major consumers of international tourism are the residents of the developed countries of the world, and it is the developed countries that have hard currencies. Hard currencies are needed to buy development goods and expertise. In Asia, the 'Asian Dragons' have also become important generators of hard currency and intra-regional tourists many of whom are leisure rather than business travellers.

Third, unlike manufactured goods and other forms of exports there is a relative absence of tariff barriers relating to international tourism. Very few developed countries now limit either where residents travel overseas or how much money they take with them. So in this sense, international tourism is an industry that faces no quotas or tariff barriers. In Asia, it is interesting to note how, with increasing levels of development, governments in countries such as Taiwan, Republic of Korea and the People's Republic of China have lifted restrictions on outbound leisure travel for their citizens.

Fourth, tourism is a service industry and service depends upon people. Tourism is relatively labour-intensive. This is of particular importance in the developing world where employment-creation needs are paramount. With growing populations heavily skewed towards the young, one of the major political, as well as economic problems, is to absorb people into the work force. Tourism has a relatively low entry-level skills threshold, so it can often employ people who require limited training and have limited skills. This argument does not prevail as you look at higher and more managerial levels of the industry, but the entry threshold in many developing countries is low.

Fifth, in many such countries the attractions for international tourists relates to the natural infrastructure, climate, beach, wildlife and the rest. In this case, we often see tourism developing at fairly low economic costs. It has been argued, for example, in one sense that a beach has a zero marginal opportunity cost but this is a difficult argument to sustain because as people use a beach then related facilities are required. But there is no doubt that the quality of climate, the quality of natural appeal and often the social characteristics of the developing world are major attractions in their own right. As we find more and more of the developed countries becoming highly polluted and more overcrowded, many of the developing countries do have priceless environmental assets that they can sell on the international market.

Sixth, refers to 'intermediate technology'. In many developing countries where labour is in excess supply and cheap to employ, it is socially and politically desirable to create jobs. In tourism and its related service industries it is often advantageous to substitute labour for capital. In developed countries where labour may be scarce and expensive, room service in hotels can be replaced by, for example, tea-making facilities in guests' rooms, also shoe-cleaning services can be offered by machines placed in corridors. In developing countries many of the services are still provided by people. The 'intermediate technology' in these examples, where abundant and cheap labour substitutes for scarce and expensive capital, is often an appropriate type of development policy.

Seventh, if we look at the way in which tourism has and is developing in most of the major generating countries of the world, most observers of the industry are moving away from the old idea of tourism being simply an output of economic wealth. It still is, but evidence suggests that more and more people are seeing the ability to take holidays and to travel internationally as part of a lifestyle. Research indicates that people will protect holiday expenditure even in deteriorating economic climates. This is a very important factor because even after such a major event as the Gulf War, tourism recovered very quickly.

Another factor here, of course, is the available air transport facilities that has shrunk distance in terms of time and comfort and, relatively, has been one of the best buys in international services. Tourism in the developed countries is a social activity with economic consequences, whereas in the developing countries tourism can been regarded as being an economic activity with social consequences.

In looking at the role of tourism in development, there are also disadvantages that should be evaluated. First, for example, although tourism is historically a growth sector, this has not been the situation in every tourist-receiving country. Second, although developing countries earn hard currency, much of it leaks back to the country of origin. Third, although there are no tariff and quota barriers preventing international tourists from travelling, it is a very competitive industry and often prices are determined by tour operators based in the generating countries therefore affecting destination competitiveness. These prices can limit the numbers of tourists travelling, particularly to certain countries.

Tourism does have a low entry-skills threshold. However, this can cause economic and perhaps political problems in the long term unless indigenous people are promoted and developed to the highest levels of the industry. One statement by a Prime Minister of a Caribbean country exemplifies this dissatisfaction: 'tourism has turned us into a nation of barkeepers and waitresses' – this is indicative of the need for human resources development planning. Countries do use their natural infrastructure for tourism but examples of very bad planning, for example Pattaya Beach in Thailand where the type of development, the discharge of effluent and the lack of concern for the environment has created a case-study in how not to develop a resort (Inskeep, 1992).

Within Europe, the tourist-intensive areas of Spain, Turkey and the former Yugoslavia do not enhance the conservation of the many things that attract tourists initially. Intermediate technology does have tremendous importance to change the way in which services and buildings can be provided for tourists. However, to develop intermediate technology requires initiative and determination, and often buildings are products of international design rather than of indigenous materials and traditional styles.

Despite these disadvantages, there is no doubt that tourism has made a substantial contribution to the development process in most tourist receiving countries. This contribution is usually listed under five headings.

First, the contribution of foreign exchange earnings. This is possibly the most critical development factor where, with limited reserves of foreign exchange and limited ability to generate foreign exchange earnings, tourism becomes a very attractive option. In countries like India and Thailand tourism is now the most important net earner of foreign exchange. In Indonesia, despite its oil and timber wealth, tourism is now expected to be the second earner of foreign exchange in 1995. In the highly tourist-developed economies of the Caribbean (Lorde, 1992), tourism is usually the major source of foreign exchange earnings. There are many countries in the Third World where tourism has occupied this particular niche and it is the main reason why tourism is supported by governments in the developing world.

Second, mention has already been made of the capacity of the tourism sector to create employment. This need is, of course, intensified by the fact that most developed countries now have strict immigration policies that allow only limited opportunities for citizens of developing countries to migrate there.

The third aspect of tourism relates to its ability to generate national regional economic development. In some countries, one can cite here parts of Nigeria (TPL Associates, 1991), Indonesia (UNDP/WTO, 1992), Brazil, tourism by using natural resources is able to create employment and economic activity where other alternatives do not exist.

Fourth, economic development will generate both personal and company incomes, and fifth, through direct and indirect taxation, contribute to government revenues.

Modern tourism, characterized by huge movements of people for leisure purposes, can be said to date from the decade of the 1950s. In that decade, recovery from the ravages of World War II provided opportunities for people to enjoy higher levels of income and paid holidays, which, in combination with other factors, boosted international travel. As international tourism grew, it received more attention from governments, specialist organizations and analysts. The analytical studies on tourism can be categorized into three periods. The first period up to about the mid-1970s, saw much concentration on the economic impacts of tourism. Early studies by Bryden (1973), Checci (1989), Zinder (1969), and Archer (1973a, b) were essentially economic analyses of tourism. The second period from about the mid-1970s, saw studies that were more critical of tourism's impact, particularly relating to its effects on people and society. Studies by De Kadt (1979), Smith (1977), Turner and Ash (1975) are examples. In the third period, from the early 1980s onward, much more attention has been given to the question of environmental issues in tourism. The Madrid Conference (WTO/UNEP, 1982a) is an example.

The position in the 1990s is that tourism has achieved recognition as a major economic activity not only on a global basis, but also at regional and at country levels. This recognition is not uncritical; investors in tourism, in both the public and private sectors, realize that risk is inherent in the investment decision, and that short-term economic gains might be submerged by long-term social and environmental problems arising from investment in tourism. Tourism is a 'people industry' and people travel with their preferences, prejudices and behavioural patterns. Cross-cultural conflicts, if not inevitable, are possible. Environmental degradation can arise from poor planning or overcrowding. For these, and many other reasons, the potential benefits and costs of investing in the tourism sector should be considered whenever possible at the planning stage and not after the facility becomes operational. Fortunately, there are well-documented cases of good and poor tourism development from which to learn (Inskeep, 1992).

Many countries in the developing world are slowly but surely recognizing that one of their major attractions is the quality of their natural environment. Planners are attempting to ensure that this is protected (Ata, 1991). However, tourism continues to attract much criticism as a vehicle for development. Many writers, perhaps starting with de Kadt in the 1970s, posed the question 'Tourism – Passport to Development?' The whole emphasis here was on the non-economic impacts of tourism and the way in which society was changed, sometimes radically, by the nature of the tourism phenomena. Critics of tourism raised some very serious objections. Among the most critical of these the following can be noted.

Tourism in Development: Areas of Concern

The first argument is that tourism is a highly dependent activity (Britton, 1989). It is dependent on economic circumstances in the main tourist generating countries, and on the major travel and tour operating companies that greatly influence where people take holidays. It is often felt that this degree of dependency is dangerous as tours operators have it in their power to switch country destinations, according to how they see the international markets. As with most arguments this tends to be overstated.

Most tour operators who send tourists to particular countries often do so over a long period of time and build up a relationship with these countries and sometimes invest in joint marketing. It is not a relationship that is broken easily but it can be changed because of the exogenous circumstances that affect tourism, for example, due to political uncertainties in regions and countries.

Dependency is not a new concept; in international trade it is well recognized. The problem for tourism is that as tourists require particular standards, particular foodstuffs and particular services, they travel in what Cohen (1982) calls 'an ecological bubble'. To provide these Western-style facilities and services is expensive, and normally demands quite a high proportion of imports, which then increases the foreign exchange leakage.

In addition to the dependency argument, there is a second criticism of tourism and that relates to seasonality. Most, but not all, countries have a seasonal flow pattern of tourist arrivals. Seasonality can be caused by institutional factors within the main tourist-generating countries, for example, fixed school holidays and works holidays, which increases the concentration of holiday taking.

Seasonality can also take place because of conditions in the tourist receiving countries. These reasons are usually climatic, for example the coming of the monsoon or the melting of the snow prohibiting winter sports. Seasonality is an important consideration affecting investment in tourism and it tends to have cyclical effects on the economy and income generation. However, the renowned West Indian economist, Sir Arthur Lewis, posed the question almost 25 years ago, whether or not a seasonal job was better than no job at all?

Third, in terms of economic benefits, most countries will have to import capital, expertise and goods and services to support development in the tourism sector. Some economists have questioned whether the leakage factor is greater than any benefit accruing to the country. Most studies would show that there is a benefit, one which sometimes is of substantial importance (ESCAP, 1991). For many countries who do not have alternative export potential, tourism might be the only means of generating foreign exchange to support development.

A fourth argument against tourism relates to the very nature of tourism itself. Tourism is a pleasurable activity. It is a form of relaxation from one's normal life and work style. It is also a form of conspicuous consumption as most tourists save in order to enjoy their holidays. Most people believe, and some sociologists have argued, that international tourism is daily contrasting visitors' affluence with residents' squalor, which is the situation in many developing countries (O'Grady, 1981).

It would appear that many of the critics of tourism have tended to be misled by the emotionalism of this argument. However, it would be wrong to underestimate these views. There is a growing opinion within tourism that, in developing countries, tourism needs to be reappraised. Much of the support for a reappraisal of tourism's role in development is focused on its perceived negative impacts on the social and cultural norms in tourist-receiving developing countries (Harrison, 1992).

There is now a well-developed literature on social and cultural impacts of tourism. Many research studies are highly specific, and may therefore be of more academic interest rather than of relevance to policy-makers. However, experience in many different countries can be said to constitute a general phenomena relating to tourism. In many cases, the regularity with which these phenomena are reported, allows policy-makers to anticipate certain future impacts from current developments in tourism.

It is easy to exaggerate impacts arising from tourism. For example, certain areas of a country may never be visited by tourists; tourist visits to very large countries, such as India, tend to be concentrated in certain areas or circuits. Therefore, to refer to the 'social and cultural impacts of tourism on India' must be an absurdity. Tourism tends to be localized and, therefore, impacts tend to be localized initially. Whether these impacts cause changes, and whether these changes spread through society, will be influenced by a wide range of factors, for example size of country, general spread of tourism activity, basic cultural and religious strengths, etc.

It is unfortunate that many of the writers on social and cultural impacts have tended to react negatively to tourism development. These negative reactions should be viewed in the same way that economic disbenefits are – they are problems that require management solutions. They will not go away and might intensify. As tourism is a great international exchange of people, it is as important to plan for human reaction as it is for economic needs.

Despite these difficulties, governments have ultimately to find means of managing, if not completely eradicating, these problems. This is particularly the case where tourism-related problems impact on the socio-cultural values of the society or on the environment. These wider concerns are the responsibility of government, and it may be that government is the only agent able to introduce required changes (Jenkins 1982, 1991).

De Kadt and O'Grady have both detailed cases where tourism has made very serious changes to the structure, values and traditions of societies. There is continuing debate as to whether these changes are beneficial or not; the interests of society and the individual are not necessary similar. There is little doubt, however, that when international tourism is of any significance in a country, it does become a major 'change-agent'.

The exposure of resident populations to other cultures due to tourism would appear to be an irreversible process. It is often accompanied by an evolution in attitudes of mind, tastes, the judgment of values and may even lead to a certain decline in conservative attitudes – an example of the 'demonstration effect'. On a social level, planned tourism can favour contacts between holidaymakers and the local population, can encourage cultural exchanges and will lead to friendly and responsible enjoyment and, finally, may strengthen links between countries.

In terms of an appraisal, what does seem to be of priority is to identify not just the problems associated with tourism but to implement management solutions. Management solutions in tourism require detailed policy considerations that can then be related to a plan of action. The planning process is now well established in developing countries. Most of these countries have five-year development plans. In countries with significant tourism sectors, specific tourism plans are prepared. Emphasis is being given to the sustainability of resources with phrases such as eco-tourism, green tourism and sensitive tourism prevalent in the literature, as noted by Griffin and Boele (Chapter 18).

Environmental issues are now central to planning; very few projects are developed without an Environmental Impact Analysis being made. More attention is being given at the planning stage to the prevention of bad design rather than having to undertake remedial actions. The quality of the environment is a major issue on a global basis, and for tourism, which depends critically on this input, it is of paramount importance. There is a long catalogue of environmental damage caused by poor design, location or scale of projects; however, tourism developments are not the only offenders.

Environmental damaged caused to, and sometimes by, tourism developments are to be found all over the world:

(i)   Water pollution: discharge of sewerage effluent into beach and bay at Pattaya, Thailand.
(ii) Visual pollution: high-rise hotel developments at Waikiki Beach, Hawaii.
(iii) Congestion: Kutar Beach and town areas, Bali, Indonesia.
(iv) Land use pollution: ribbon development along Spanish coastal areas.
(v)   Ecological disruption: to animal breeding by uncontrolled access to game parks, Africa.

To these common examples can be added the problems of litter, traffic fumes and overcrowding, which afflict many tourist sites both rural and urban. To a large degree these problems have been caused by the too rapid increase in tourist arrivals, which puts pressure on infrastructure and the environment. In most developed countries there is extensive planning legislation and controls to curb the worst excesses of developers, but some projects do proceed. In the developing countries, which often do not have a coherent and comprehensive planning framework, the problems are more acute.

Tourism, however, can make positive contributions to environmental improvement; four examples exemplify this point.

(i)   First, the interest that tourists have in the natural and built environment often allows these areas to be protected and managed. There are many examples in developed countries of areas being designated as 'national parks' or 'areas of outstanding natural beauty'. These areas are so designated to control access and use, and to ensure that they are sustainable in the future. Similar reasoning applies to the conservation of animal species and to the built environment. The designation of sea garden reserves in Western Samoa, and animal sanctuaries in Sumatra are other examples.
(ii) The improvement in environmental quality benefits both visitor and resident. Pedestrianization of many urban attractions has benefited access to visitors and increased the amenity for the residents.

(iii) Improvements in infrastructure for tourists often 'spills-over' to residents. The Adriatic Highway in former Yugoslavia improved tourist access to the South but also improved transport links for residents and industry. Montego Bay Airport in Jamaica is another example.

(iv) Revenue generated by tourism allows funding of conservation and maintenance of facilities and amenities that might otherwise deteriorate, for example Borubudur Temple Complex in Central Java and Dimbulla in Sri Lanka.

In all cases, prevention is cheaper that cure! As part of tourism development planning, environmental considerations must be given a high level of priority. In some environmentally sensitive and fragile areas, development may be prohibited. A central consideration is the carrying-capacity of a destination in relation to visitor use and the development of facilities. Tourism may be an important means to achieve conservation, for without a good quality environment, tourists may choose to visit alternative destinations.

The politics and economics of environmental development and protection are a major subject. Sufficient to note here that in examining the effects of tourism on a destination or project, the aspects of economics, socio-cultural and environmental impacts should be regarded as components of a larger concern. The Manila Declaration of the World Tourism Organization, formulated in 1980, notes the link between national and cultural resources in developing tourism and the need to conserve these resources for the benefit of tourists and residents of the tourism areas. The Joint Declaration of the World Tourism Organization and the United Nations Environment Programme (1982b) stated: .

> The protection, enhancement and improvement of the various components of man's environment are amongst the fundamental considerations for the harmonious development of tourism. Similarly, rational management of tourism may contribute to a large extent to protecting and developing the physical environment and cultural heritage as well as improving the quality of life.

The quotation implies the need for a comprehensive approach to the development and management of tourism at the destination. Without this approach, environmental degradation will occur and sustaining tourism resources in the long term may not be possible.

There has been a major change of view about the role of the market. Traditionally, in the developing countries, planning takes place as part of a centralized decision-making process. We find that government has a central role to play, if only because it often is the only source of funding, the only body available to raise foreign loans and to guarantee repayments. It sometimes has to undertake not just a pioneer role initiating capital development but also in operating facilities. In India, for example, the Indian Tourist Development Corporation runs tour buses, travel agencies, formerly ran airlines and also is a major hotel owner. These pioneering activities were essential, particularly in areas where investors were not prepared to put money into the tourism sector.

There might be an argument now that it could divest itself of at least some of its investments to the private sector. This debate is on-going but the type of activity we see in Eastern Europe, that is the rapid imposition of a market economy, cannot take place in most of the developing countries, certainly not in African countries and probably not in some of the poorer Asian countries. The market simply is not there to provide the investment and development impetus. Much international donor and institutional lender pressure is now being put on governments in developing countries to divest itself of commercial assets, for example hotels, airlines, transport services, etc., and sell them to private sector companies and entrepreneurs. In many countries where Structural Adjustment Programmes are supervised by the International Monetary Fund, the 'privatisation' of state assets is regarded as a fundamental condition to improve asset performance (Edgell, 1990).

Also tourism, unlike many other industries such as manufacturing, is a peoples' industry. Tourists tend not to merge into societies but often unwittingly confront societies. In this sense, government has a role to play in deciding what type, what level and what style of tourism it wishes to encourage. These wishes, of course, will always be constrained by market demand. Tourists can be persuaded to visit a country, they cannot be coerced and this is a reality that is slowly dawning on many tourism planners. Despite this caveat, tourism planners have developed their art. They learn from other countries' strengths and other countries' mistakes. They are sensitive to the market and recognize that the ultimate goal of the development process is the indigenization of jobs, particularly at senior level, and wherever possible, a growing volume of indigenous investment, management and control.

Tourism has made a major economic contribution to Third World countries and this contribution will continue in the future. There are problems; these problems are easy to identify but perhaps more difficult to manage. This is the future challenge. Arguably the problems debated now are the problems that were with us 20 years ago, but with maturity and increasing knowledge we are better able to understand this complex phenomena. It is interesting to note the new Lome IV Convention, which oversees development assistance to the African, Caribbean and Pacific countries associated with the European Union, now concentrates, for the very first time, on policy development in tourism. That is a move away from *ad hoc* requests for assistance, to actually look at tourism as an on-going process and one that requires clear guidelines and clear choices to be made relating to development goals (Ritchter, 1989; ESCAP 1992).

It is encouraging to see that the major lending institutions are regarding tourism as a viable means of aiding development. In this sense, we could conclude that tourism is recognized as having made a substantial contribution to the development process in many Third World countries. Its benefits have been real and are increasingly sought by many such countries (United Nations: Economic and Social Commission for Asia and Pacific, 1992). There are problem and areas of concern, but it would be a fiction to deny the reality of tourism's contribution.

Conclusion

The rapid growth of tourism within the Asian region has been well documented within this volume. A number of comments on these trends might be appropriate. First, as noted by Qu and Zhang (Chapter 2) tourism is expected to continue to grow at a rate of 10.77 per cent per annum leading to an estimate of 156 million visitor arrivals in the region by 2005. In this year 65 per cent of arrivals will be intra-regional travellers. This projected rate of growth will have obvious and immediate impacts on available infrastructure and demands for new investment. Substantial capital investment will be required to fund new infrastructure. In new regional country destinations such as Vietnam, Laos and Cambodia, infrastructural deficiencies may be the main factor inhibiting growth.

Second, major infrastructural projects are likely to have environmental consequences despite required Environmental Impact Audits. If the major tourist destinations in 2005 are going to be Singapore, Hong Kong, Thailand and the Peoples' Republic of China, one wonders about the capacity of the smaller countries to absorb sustained, rapid growth in visitor arrivals. The bigger countries already face major environmental challenges. Perhaps the time has come for governments to ask whether there is an acceptable limit to tourism growth?

Third, as tourism grows there will be a continuing need to develop human resource development policies and related training to stimulate indigenous entrepreneurship. Tourism particularly will have to provide a quality of service that increasingly discriminating tourists demand. Whether it is possible to tailor training to meet cultural modes or whether the sheer pressure to 'do something quickly' will lead to adoption of Western models is an issue raised by Robinson and Yee (Chapter 19). Human resource development, if based on proper analysis and planning, is a long-term commitment and an area where the roles of government and the private sector often converge. It is, however, a major issue for development of tourism in the region and one that will attract a lot of attention in the future.

Fourth, in the Asian region we are seeing a development phenomenon that reflects the European experience – intra-regional dependency. Dependency on the Asian Dragons to generate tourists is becoming acute. Any major slowing of economic growth will have immediate consequences. As noted by Heung (Chapter 7), investor confidence in the tourism sector is a variable factor. As much of intra-regional tourism is now directed to resort/beach tourism it may be difficult to secure the necessary amount of investment funds. Any shortage of funds could trigger expensive competition between countries for available funds through over-generous investment incentive inducements.

It would be prudent for regional countries to maintain their interests in long-haul markets if only to limit their dependency exposure.

Fifth, although it is now generally accepted that tourism is market-driven, given the very rapid growth of tourism in the Asian region, governments must not abandon their regulatory roles. As tourism remains one sector of economic activity – albeit an important one in many regional countries – its progress must be monitored and, where necessary, regulated. In times of continuing rapid economic growth governments will often need to be pro-active rather than reactive to market pressures; unbridled entrepreneurship can bring immediate economic benefits but also generate long-term costs. Tourism is essentially an activity with a long life-cycle, and planning should be similarly focused.

Sixth, in the emerging destinations of the region such as Vietnam, Laos and Cambodia, which now approximate to earlier descriptions of Third World countries, a more careful approach to development is required. Undoubtedly they will all – in time – benefit from intra-regional flows. They may not, however, follow the same path to rapid industrialization. For these countries tourism might be an appropriate catalyst for development implying, initially, a more prominent role for government in this process.

Despite these observations and caveats, the Asian region is likely to remain the most dynamic in world tourism; this will continue to bring with it opportunities, challenges and the need for careful consideration of development options.

Bibliography

American Express Co. (1988) *The Contribution of the World Travel and Tourism Industry to the Global Economy*.

Archer, B.H. (1973a) *The Impact of Domestic Tourism*. Bangor: Economic Research Unit, University of Wales.

Archer, B.H. (1973b) *The Gwynedd Multipliers*. Bangor: Economic Research Unit, University of Wales.

Ata, F. (1991) *Environment and Tourism in Pakistan*. Islamabad: Ministry of Culture and Tourism.

Britton, S. (1989) Tourism dependency and development: a mode of analysis. In Singh, T.J., Theuns, H.L. and Go, F. *Towards Appropriate Tourism: The Case of Developing Countries*. Geneva: Lang.

Bryden, J.M. (1973) *Tourism and Development*. Cambridge: Cambridge University Press.

Checchi and Company (1989) *A Plan for Managing Tourism in the Bahamas Islands.* Washington DC.

Cohen, E. (1982) Towards a sociology of international tourism. *Social Research* **39** (1), 164–82.

De Kadt, E. (ed.) (1979) *Tourism – Passport to Development?* Oxford: Oxford University Press.

Edgell, D.L. (1990) *International Tourism Policy.* New York: Van Nostrand Reinhold.

Erbes, R. (1987) *International Tourism and the Economy of Developing Countries.* Paris: OECD.

ESCAP (Economic and Social Commission for Asia and the Pacific) (1991) *Tourism Development in the Asian Region: Tourism Review,* No. 7. Bangkok: United Nations.

ESCAP (1992) *Economic Impact of International Tourism in Pakistan.* Bangkok: United Nations.

Harrison, D. (ed.) (1992) *Tourism and the Less Developed Countries.* London: Belhaven Press.

Inskeep, E. (1992) *Tourism Planning.* New York: Van Nostrand Reinhold.

Jenkins, C.L. with Henry, B.M. (1982) The case for government involvement in tourism in developing countries. *Annals of Tourism Research* Vol. 9. Oxford: Pergamon Press.

Jenkins, C.L. (1991) Development strategies. In Lickorish, L. (ed.) *Developing Tourism Destinations.* Harlow: Longman.

Lorde, C. (1992) *Development and Impact of Tourism on the Economic and Social Sectors of Island Territories in the Caribbean.* Barbados: Caribbean Tourism Organization.

O'Grady, R. (1981) *Third World Stop-Over.* Geneva: World Council of Churches.

Richter, L.K. (1989) *The Politics of Tourism in Asia.* Honolulu: University of Hawaii Press.

Smith, V.L. (1977) *Hosts and Guests: An Anthropology of Tourism.* Pennsylvania: University of Pennsylvania Press.

TPL Associates (1991) *The Federal Republic of Nigeria – Tourism Development Strategy.* Lagos.

Turner, L. and Ash, J. (1975) *The Golden Hordes.* London: Constable.

WTO (1994) *Yearbook of Tourist Statistics.* Madrid: World Tourism Organization.

WTO/UNEP (World Tourism Organization and United Nations Environment Programme) (1982a) *Workshop on Environmental Aspects of Tourism.* Madrid: World Tourism Organization.

WTO/UNEP (1982b) *Joint Declaration on Tourism in the Environment.* Madrid: World Tourism Organization.

UNDP (United Nations Development Programme) (1995) *Human Development Report* New York: United Nations.

UNDP/WTO (1992) *Indonesia: Tourism Sector Programming and Policy Development* Jakarta: United Nations.

United Nations: Economic and Social Commission for Asia and Pacific (1992) *Economic Impact of International Tourism in Pakistan.* Bangkok: United Nations.

World Travel and Tourism Council (1993) *Annual Report,* p.4.

Zinder, H.S. Associates (1969) *The Future of Tourism in the Eastern Caribbean.* Washington DC.

PART II

Country Profiles

4

Australia: Consequences of the newly adopted pro-Asia orientation

TONY GRIFFIN
SIMON DARCY

Introduction

In the last decade Australia has emerged as a significant international tourism destination. While its share of global arrivals is small, inbound tourism to Australia has grown at a substantially faster rate than the world average and is likely to continue to do so for the foreseeable future. Part of the reason for this has been its geographic proximity to East Asia, the fastest growing region in terms of both world tourism arrivals and departures (Edwards, 1990; Cleverdon, 1993; Payne, 1993). Tourism has been stimulated by the general economic development of the region, which has greatly enhanced the opportunities for Asians to travel. Recent political changes in the region have also served, in some instances, to enable international travel or at least lower barriers to travel.

The overall result has been to substantially increase the significance of tourism to the Australian economy. Tourism is now acknowledged as a major contributor to national income and employment, and the country's major export industry. The main generators of this growth have been Asian nations, initially Japan but more recently countries such as Singapore, Hong Kong, South Korea, Taiwan, Malaysia, Thailand and Indonesia. The growth of arrivals from these countries has significantly outstripped that of such traditional markets as New Zealand, United Kingdom, continental Europe and North America. Moreover this trend is projected to continue.

The effects on Australian tourism from these trends have been manifold. Firstly the political profile of the tourism industry has been enhanced. Greater government support at both state and federal levels has been forthcoming, generating increased funding for the overseas promotional activities of the national tourism organization, the Australian Tourist Commission

(ATC). Much of the additional funding has been directed to the newly emerging markets of Asia. Secondly, the patterns of Australian inbound tourism have changed, with a move away from trips whose main purpose is visiting relatives to more travel purely for holidays. This in turn has broadened the range of destinations visited by overseas visitors. The response has been for the industry to both diversify and develop its range and quality of products. The nature of the industry has consequently changed and a range of new participants have become involved in the provision of tourist facilities and services. Under this scenario of growth the level of investment in tourism has had to expand, and here the Asian connection has also been significant. The supply of capital to fund growth has not been readily forthcoming from Australian sources for a variety of reasons. The subsequent vacuum has been filled initially by Japanese and more recently other Asian investors, especially in major hotel and resort developments.

The general result of the above trends and patterns has been that Australian tourism has been extremely dynamic in recent years. Its fortunes have been closely linked to Asia and, given that this region will continue to provide the bulk of its growth for at least the next decade, this relationship can only strengthen. While superficially this places Australia in a very advantageous position, it also poses some problems. Australia's major growth markets are relatively young as generators of tourism; much change in the preferences of their tourists is likely to accompany the general growth. Thus the Australian tourism industry must cater to the immediate growth but concurrently anticipate how these markets are likely to develop over time. Growth and change must be handled simultaneously. Simply multiplying facilities and services designed to cater for current tourist needs is unlikely to be entirely satisfactory.

The main purpose of this chapter, then, is to review how the growth in tourism from the Asian region is impacting on Australia and the development of its tourism industry. The patterns of growth and the changing composition are examined and their economic implications discussed. It also examines how inbound tourism is projected to grow over the next decade. On the supply-side, the significance of Asian investment in Australian touristic superstructure is examined, along with the response by the ATC in terms of both its market and product development activities. Finally, some implications for the planning, development and marketing of Australian tourism are identified.

The Growth of Tourism

The recognition of tourism as a major industry within the Australian economy is a relatively recent phenomenon. As illustrated in Table 4.1, arrivals of overseas visitors have been increasing since the 1970s, albeit at highly variable annual rates. The most significant period of growth occurred in the latter half of the 1980s when arrivals increased by around 25 per cent for three years in succession, 1986 to 1988, and more than doubled within a four-year period. The subsequent decline in 1989 has been attributed to a plateau effect after the major events of 1988, which included the Bicentennial celebrations and the Brisbane Expo, and the impact of a pilots' strike, which disrupted domestic airline services for nearly six months. Since that time, however, strong growth has resumed although not to the same extent as occurred in 1986–88.

The composition of that growth has also been significant. Generally there has been an increase in the proportion of trips for holidays as opposed to business purposes and visiting relatives (see Table 4.2). The proportion of trips for holidays has increased from 42 per cent to 62 per cent in the last decade, due primarily to the rise in Asian inbound tourism. The Australian industry has had to change in response to this with substantial increases in commercial accommodation and the emergence and growth of pure holiday destinations. The share of arrivals from Asian nations has increased dramatically; in 1976 Japan and other Asian countries accounted for only 15 per cent of total arrivals, but this had grown to 45 per cent by 1993 (see Table 4.3). Japan, in particular, has grown from a relatively minor market to accounting for nearly a quarter of all arrivals, with most of that growth occurring in the last decade. The growth from other Asian countries has not been as rapid or substantial but nonetheless their market share has doubled since 1976 with much of that growth occurring in the last few years, so that visitor numbers from other parts of Asia are now only marginally below Japan. Japan and other parts of Asia have clearly supplanted New Zealand, USA, the United Kingdom and Europe as the major markets for inbound tourism to Australia.

Table 4.1   Short-term visitor arrivals, 1976–93

Year	Arrivals (000s)	Annual growth rate
1976	532	
1977	563	5.9
1978	631	11.9
1979	793	25.8
1980	905	14.0
1981	937	3.5
1982	955	1.9
1983	944	−1.1
1984	1,015	7.6
1985	1,143	12.6
1986	1,429	25.1
1987	1,785	24.9
1988	2,249	26.0
1989	2,080	−7.5
1990	2,215	6.5
1991	2,370	7.0
1992	2,603	9.8
1993	2,996	15.1

Source: Australian Bureau of Statistics (1993)

Table 4.2   Percentage of short-term arrivals by main purpose of trip, 1983, 1988 and 1993

Purpose of trip	1983	1988	1993
Holiday	42	55	62
Visiting relatives	28	20	18
Business	13	10	9
Convention	2	3	2
In transit	7	4	3
Other/not stated	8	8	6

Source: Australian Bureau of Statistics (1993)

When analysed in terms of visitor nights the pattern is slightly different (see Table 4.4). The average length of stay for Japanese visitors is relatively short and consequently it assumes a less dominant position, ranking behind all other major regions of origin in contrast to its position as the major source of visitors. On the other hand the average length of stay for other Asians is not far below that of long-haul visitors from the United Kingdom and Europe, and this group now accounts for the largest proportion of visitor nights. Clearly the bulk of growth in Australian tourism has become highly dependent on the emergent Asian nations.

Economic Significance of Tourism

Tourism is now one of the most valuable sectors of the Australian economy. With its increasing economic significance has come greater political recognition of its potential to address the major problems of sustained high unemployment and a chronic deficit in the nation's current account. The

Table 4.3   Percentage share of short-term arrivals by country/region of origin, 1976–93

Year	USA	NZ	UK & Ireland	Other Europe	Japan	Other Asia	Rest of World
1976	14	28	14	11	5	10	18
1977	14	29	15	12	6	10	16
1978	13	32	15	11	5	10	15
1979	12	35	15	12	5	9	12
1980	12	34	15	12	5	10	11
1981	12	30	16	13	6	12	12
1982	13	24	19	13	6	13	12
1983	15	24	16	12	8	14	11
1984	16	23	15	12	9	15	11
1985	17	21	14	12	9	14	11
1986	17	24	13	12	10	14	10
1987	17	24	12	11	12	14	9
1988	14	24	12	11	16	14	9
1989	13	22	14	12	17	15	8
1990	11	19	13	12	22	16	8
1991	12	20	12	11	22	16	8
1992	10	17	11	11	24	19	6
1993	9	17	11	11	22	22	8

Source: Australian Bureau of Statistics (1993)

Table 4.4 Visitor nights by country/region of origin, 1992

Country/region	Nights (millions)	% of total nights
Japan	5.3	9
Other Asia	3.8	22
UK and Ireland	13.2	21
Other Europe	10.7	17
USA	6.2	10
New Zealand	7.2	12
Rest of World	5.3	9
Total	61.8	100

Source: Bureau of Tourism Research (1993c)

unemployment rate has hovered at around 10 per cent of the work force for a number of years, with the current rate being 8.8 per cent and very little prospect of a reduction in the short to medium term. In 1992 tourism was estimated to account for nearly half a million jobs or 6 per cent of the workforce. Given the expectations about the rapid growth of inbound tourism (see Table 4.5) the industry is projected to generate between 210,000 and 270,000 additional jobs in the 1990s (DoT, 1994a).

In 1991/1992 tourism contributed A$26,200 million to the Australian economy and accounted for 5.5 per cent of Australia's Gross Domestic Product. While the bulk of this amount (70 per cent) was attributable to domestic tourism, the contribution of inbound tourism becomes more significant each year. The inbound component of tourism is growing far more rapidly than the domestic and will exceed it in terms of economic contribution in the early part of the next decade, if current forecasts and targets are achieved. Tourism is already Australia's major export earning industry, accounting for A$10,735 million or 11.8 per cent of total export earnings in 1993/94 (see Table 4.6). That contribution will more than double by the year 2000 if the ATC growth targets are achieved (DoT, 1994a).

Table 4.5 Short-term visitor arrival forecasts and targets, 1994–2001

Year	BTR forecast (000s)	ATC target (000s)
1994	3,124	3,427
1995	3,375	3,907
1996	3,641	4,393
1997	3,919	4,899
1998	4,210	5,480
1999	4,511	6,048
2000	4,824	6,772
2001	4,151	7,276
2002	na	7,643
2003	na	7,977
2004	na	8,394

na: Forecasts not available for these years.
Source: Bureau of Tourism Research (1992a) and Australian Tourist Commission (1994c)

Table 4.6   Tourism's contribution to export earnings, 1985/86 to 1993/94

Year	Total earnings (A$m)	% of export earnings
1985/86	3,019	6.9
1986/87	3,983	8.0
1987/88	5,411	9.2
1988/89	6,343	10.0
1989/90	6,433	9.3
1990/91	7,463	10.1
1991/92	8,262	10.5
1992/93	9,162	10.8
1993/94	10,735	11.8

Source: Department of Tourism (1994a)

Major Asian Inbound Markets

Until recently Japan has been at the forefront of growth in visitor arrivals from Asia. However, as Table 4.7 reveals, other countries are beginning to emerge as significant. Japan's outbound tourism growth can be attributed to its emergence as an economic superpower in the last few decades and in particular to its sustained trade surpluses, which led the government to encourage outbound tourism. Australia has clearly been one of the major beneficiaries of this. The growth of tourism from other Asian countries has similarly been related to economic growth and development. Table 4.8 indicates the rates of economic growth achieved by Australia's major Asian markets other than Japan in 1993. The following section examines the dimensions and some of the consequences of the growth in visitation from each of Australia's major Asian markets in recent years.

Table 4.7   Short-term visitor arrivals from Asian countries, 1982–93 (000s)

Year	Japan	Hong Kong	Malaysia	Singapore	Indonesia	Thailand	Korea	Taiwan	Other Asia
1982	60	21	23	24	16	5	na	na	34 *
1983	72	21	28	30	13	5	na	na	36 *
1984	88	21	29	33	14	5	na	na	44 *
1985	108	24	33	35	15	8	4	6	38
1986	146	34	39	45	18	8	5	12	44
1987	216	43	47	57	22	11	7	16	53
1988	352	49	52	64	30	16	9	19	69
1989	350	54	44	65	29	17	10	22	79
1990	480	55	47	76	34	20	14	25	78
1991	529	63	48	88	37	25	24	35	56
1992	630	75	60	117	46	24	34	64	61
1993	670	75	80	156	72	47	62	108	67

na Not available.
* Separate figures are not available for Korea and Taiwan for 1982–84 as the number of arrivals were considered too low to record. Korea and Taiwan are included in 'Other Asia' for these years.
Source: Australian Bureau of Statistics (1993)

Table 4.8 Economic growth of major Asian markets, 1993

Country	Real GDP growth rate (%)
Korea	6.6
Taiwan	7.5
Hong Kong	5.5
Indonesia	6.7
Singapore	9.8
Thailand	7.5
Malaysia	8.5

Source: Australian Tourist Commission (1994b)

Japan

Japan is by far the largest Asian inbound market for Australia (see Table 4.7). Arrivals expanded at phenomenal rates throughout the 1980s, with Japan overtaking New Zealand as the single greatest source of visitors in 1990. ATC tracking studies have indicated that Australia is the most desired overseas destination for the Japanese, who perceive it as an affordable and safe destination offering a diversity of holiday experiences (ATC 1994b).

The predominant market segments of Japanese tourists are defined as 'Young Office Ladies' and 'Honeymooners', with the latter group ranking Australia as their most preferred destination (ATC 1994b). Fully independent travellers are a growing segment of the market and are made up of repeat and student visitors, who are mainly young and middle-aged males (BTR 1992a). This group is significant for their longer length of stay, greater overall expenditure and more diverse range of destinations visited within Australia. Recently there has been an unprecedented growth in family groups, attributed to the introduction in 1992 of a 50 per cent discount on air fares for children under 12 years of age (ATC 1994b). Like many other developed nations Japan's population is aging, with an expected 25 per cent of the population to be aged 65 and over by 2010. This offers an increasing opportunity to attract the so-called 'Silvers' who already exhibit a greater diversity of visitation patterns than other major segments.

The Japanese have the shortest average length of stay of all international visitors to Australia (see Table 4.9) and a high proportion travel on fully inclusive tours. Both of these factors reduce their overall impact on the Australian economy. The destinations that they visit are heavily concentrated on the eastern seaboard (see Table 4.10): New South Wales and Queensland are the most popular states with Sydney and the Gold Coast the most visited destinations (BTR 1992a). Market segmentation studies have shown that Australia is perceived as a 'wholesome' destination by the Japanese. While other destinations such as Thailand and Hawaii are perceived as having a far stronger image as 'sun' destinations, Australia's position within the Japanese market is enhanced by being able to offer a combination of beaches and the 'great outdoors' (ATC 1993c). Australia ranks highly in terms of its 'software' (service, friendliness, safety, security and professionalism), but its 'hardware' (hotels, convention halls, shopping and entertainment facilities) is ranked last behind all of its competitive destinations (ATC 1994b).

Table 4.9   Visitors by length of stay and country of residence, 1992

Length of stay	Japan	Hong Kong	Indonesia	Malaysia	Singapore	Other Asia	Total
1–7 nights	79	31	36	35	52	39	41
8–14 nights	15	33	29	27	30	27	22
15–21 nights	2	17	9	12	7	10	12
22–8 nights	1	3	3	3	1	3	5
29–42 nights	1	6	4	4	4	6	8
Over 42 nights	2	9	19	19	4	16	12
Average nights in Australia	9	25	34	45	16	32	28
Median nights in Australia	6	12	11	11	7	10	10
Total nights in Australia (millions)	5.3	1.6	1.3	2.4	1.6	13.8	61.8

Source: Bureau of Tourism Research (1993c) *International Visitor Survey 1992*

Table 4.10   Percentage of short-term visitors by region of stay and country of residence

Region of stay	Japan	Hong Kong	Indonesia	Malaysia	Singapore	Other Asia[1]	All countries
NSW	73	69	54	44	36	55	65
ACT	2	17	7	7	3	12	8
Victoria	15	39	25	33	23	32	28
Queensland	77	46	21	18	37	32	51
South Australia	3	5	6	9	5	5	9
Western Australia	5	8	30	36	39	8	13
Tasmania	–	2	2	2	3	2	3
Northern Territory	5	2	6	2	4	3	9
Total[2]	177	170	144	143	147	153	179

1. 'Other Asia' includes all Asian countries other than Japan. Separate figures are not available for Asian countries other than those listed in the Table.
2. This row is the sum of state percentages. It provides a measure of the extent to which visitors visited more than one state; e.g. 200 per cent would mean that on average these visitors visited 2 states.
Source: Bureau of Tourism Research (1993c)

Singapore

Singapore is the largest and most mature Asian inbound market for Australia outside of Japan, although its position is being challenged by Taiwan. It grew steadily but substantially throughout the 1980s and is now the fifth largest single country supplier of visitors behind Japan, New Zealand, United Kingdom and USA. Its rate of growth has accelerated in recent years, due partly to the increasing costs of travel to previously favoured destinations in

Europe and North America (Ping, 1992). It has been identified by the ATC as one of the four developed tourist markets in Asia (ATC, 1993b), as well as one of Australia's priority Asian markets (ATC, 1990b). ATC tracking studies have indicated that Australia is the top destination for Singaporeans both in terms of preferred destination and intention to visit (ATC, 1994b). The potential size of the market for travel to Australia has been estimated at 567,000 (ATC, 1993b), and, with a total of 156,000 arrivals in 1993, that potential has already been substantially tapped to a greater degree than any other Asian market.

Singapore is displaying many of the characteristics of a mature market. There is an increasing proportion of independent travellers, growing repeat visitation, increases in short-break travel to resort destinations, a more even spread of arrivals across the year and a strengthening interest in travel to rural and natural areas (ATC, 1994b). Niche marketing to Singaporeans is becoming more important and there are signs that visitors are becoming more selective and less price sensitive (ATC, 1993b). Traditionally Singaporean travellers have shown a strong preference for shopping and sightseeing but there is an increasing trend towards more independent travel with an emphasis on resort holidays or physical activities and soft adventure (Ping, 1992). Although most trips by Singaporeans are to single destinations within Australia the range of destinations visited by them as a whole is more diverse than for most other national groups, with a particularly strong level of visitation to Western Australia due to its geographic proximity and the frequency of direct flights to Perth (see Table 4.10). Market segmentation studies by the ATC have shown that Australia is perceived by Singaporeans as a wholesome, safe destination, characterized by beaches and unique natural scenery (ATC, 1993c).

Table 4.11 Visitor expenditure by country/region of residence, 1992

Country of residence	Average expenditure per trip (A$)	Average expenditure per night (A$)
Japan	1,241	143
Other Asia	2,315	73
Hong Kong	2,049	84
Indonesia	2,683	79
Malaysia	2,683	60
Singapore	1,563	98

Excludes all money paid in visitor's country of residence for inclusive package tours and international airfares.
Source: Bureau of Tourism Research (1993c)

A factor that reduces the value of the Singaporean market for the Australian economy is the relatively short average length of stay. As illustrated in Table 4.9, Singaporean visitors have the second shortest average and median lengths of stay behind Japan, although they also have the second highest spending per day of all international visitors (see Table 4.11).

South Korea

South Korea is currently Australia's fastest growing international market. In 1993 the number of Korean visitors increased by 83 per cent (ATC, 1994b), a rate that has been sustained through the first half of 1994 (DoT, 1994a). South Korea's emergence as a major travel generator has been due to both economic and political factors. The country has experienced sustained and rapid economic growth for the past decade and there has also been a gradual relaxation of foreign pleasure travel restrictions until their complete removal in 1989 (ATC, 1992). As a result, overseas departures by Korean residents have increased more than threefold since 1989, from 725,000 to 2.4 million (ATC, 1994b). Australia accounts for only a small share of this total market (2.6 per cent), but a considerably larger share of the long-haul market (9 per cent) (ATC, 1994b). Significantly Korean travel to Australia has been increasing more rapidly than the general level of trip departures. Korea is perceived as a priority market by the ATC but one that is still developing (1993b).

Because Koreans have only recently been able to travel internationally for pleasure purposes, the market is regarded as very immature and comprising mainly inexperienced travellers. Most Koreans travel to Australia on group tours that mainly visit the major destinations of Sydney and the Gold Coast. Unlike many other Asian groups, language is a significant constraint to independent travel by Koreans (ATC, 1994b). The ATC believes, however, that the market is changing rapidly and is 'worth monitoring' (1993b: 41) for signs of the emergence of more specialized markets. Despite the rapid growth of inbound tourism from Korea, the Australian industry has been slow to respond for a number of reasons. Korea has been perceived as a relatively price sensitive market (ATC, 1993b) that offers very slim margins to Australian suppliers and inbound tour operators. The ATC has noted that Korean wholesalers have shown little loyalty to Australian ground operators, and have been willing to switch operators for minimal cost differentials. Australian operators have further reported to the authors that Korean wholesalers have developed a reputation for being slow with payments. Cultural differences, and in particular Australian unfamiliarity with Korean ways of conducting business, appear to be part of the problem. In an attempt to overcome these barriers the ATC's most recent marketing manual includes such advice to Australian operators as the significance of 'drinking sessions' in Korean business dealings (1993b).

Taiwan

Like South Korea, Taiwan has only recently emerged as a significant market for Australia, and for similar reasons. Since 1978 the Taiwanese government has been progressively removing travel restrictions, with the only remaining restrictions being on males aged between 16 and 21 years (ATC, 1992). International departures by Taiwanese residents have consequently risen from 485,000 in 1980 to 3.3 million in 1993 (ATC, 1994b). The rise of Taiwan as a tourist generator has been so significant and rapid that by 1990 a higher proportion of the population had travelled overseas than was the case with Japan (ATC, 1992). Over the past few years Taiwan has been Australia's fastest growing market: in 1992 arrivals grew by 83 per cent and by 70 per cent in 1993, when Taiwan was outpaced by South Korea. Australia now has a 15 per cent share of the Taiwanese long-haul market (ATC, 1994b).

The characteristics of the Taiwanese market and its state of maturity are very similar to Korea. Short duration group tours dominate and destinations visited rarely extend beyond Sydney and the Gold Coast. Similar problems are also evident in relation to narrow margins for Australian operators and suppliers, and slow payments by Taiwanese wholesalers (ATC, 1994b). Unlike Korea there is a reasonably strong 'visiting friends and relatives' element, which enhances the potential of this market for longer stays. Within the next ten years arrivals from Taiwan are expected to reach a level that ranks second behind Japan amongst Asian nations, and fifth overall.

Hong Kong

Hong Kong has become the third largest Asian market to Australia after Singapore and Taiwan with a total of 1.6 million visitor nights. Throughout the 1980s the market steadily increased, growing threefold, but relatively slowly compared to most other Asian markets. Analysis of the Hong Kong market is complicated by the political uncertainty in the lead-up to the resumption of Chinese sovereignty in 1997. This has seen two unique groups of travellers emerge: those who travel to assess Australia as a possible migration destination, and the so-called 'astronauts' who conduct their businesses in Hong Kong but have settled their families in Australia (ATC, 1994b). Despite the political outlook the ATC believe that, if no major travel barriers are introduced, the market has a potential to supply 150,000 visitors by the year 2000. While group travel is still pronounced amongst Hong Kong visitors this is largely a function of the price consciousness of a sophisticated and experienced market. However, there is a tendency for more independent travel particularly amongst younger Chinese and expatriates (ATC, 1993c; BTR, 1993c). There has also been an increase in demand for fly/drive and diving holidays.

Like the Japanese market the focus of visitation is to the eastern states of Australia (see Table 4.10), although they are spread more evenly between these three states than other Asian markets. The most popular destinations are Sydney, Melbourne and Brisbane/Gold Coast (BTR, 1993c). While in Australia the average Hong Kong visitor participates in virtually no sporting activity but enjoys sightseeing, shopping, restaurants, botanic gardens and wildlife. Their major areas of dissatisfaction are common to all other Asian areas, that is, limited shopping hours and the price of retail goods (BTR, 1993c).

Hong Kong is a status-orientated market with a strong brand name orientation and preference for the status destinations of USA, Europe and Japan (ATC, 1994b). Australia is seen as an inferior destination offering beaches and natural scenery in a safe and peaceful environment (ATC, 1993c). From an Australian ground operator's perspective the Hong Kong outbound tourism industry is seen as conservative and competitive with respect to both price and destination choice.

Malaysia

Inbound tourism from Malaysia grew steadily throughout the 1980s. It was first identified by the ATC as a priority market in 1990 and is now perceived as one of four 'developed' markets in Asia, along with Japan, Hong Kong and Singapore (ATC, 1993b). Until the last few years its growth rate had closely paralleled that of Hong Kong, but, unlike most Asian markets, visitor arrivals from Malaysia actually declined after 1988 and did not recover to these levels until 1992. Strong growth has now resumed, with arrivals increasing by 33 per cent in 1993 (ATC, 1994b).

In terms of the characteristics of the market and the patterns of tourism within Australia, Malaysia is similar to other South-east Asian markets. Like Singapore and Indonesia there is a high level of visitation to Western Australia, with Perth only slightly behind Sydney as the main gateway city. The non-Japanese Asian market has been characterized as 'Stay-Putters', with few visits to destinations outside a single main city (ATC, 1993b; Faulkner, 1990), and Malaysia displays these patterns more than any other Asian country aside from Singapore (Economist Intelligence Unit, 1990). However, on average, Malaysians stay longer than any other Asian visitors, are involved more frequently in visiting friends and relatives and consequently make less use of commercial accommodation, and are far more likely to be independent travellers (Ping, 1992).

Malaysia is recognized as having the greatest potential of any South-east Asian country in the short to medium term, although there are some constraints to overcome. Australia ranks behind China, Europe and the USA as the most desirable destination and the market is very price sensitive (ATC, 1994b). Therefore the low margins for Australian ground operators and suppliers, which are characteristic of a number of other Asian markets, are also a problem with Malaysia.

Indonesia

Of all the countries reviewed, Indonesia most clearly shows how the growth in tourism to Australia has been due to internal factors in the home country rather than the marketing activities of the ATC or individual operators and suppliers. Arrivals from Indonesia have more than doubled since 1990, increasing by 78 per cent in 1993 alone. The ATC has acknowledged that this strong growth has been 'unaided by large injections of funds or resources' (1994b: 4). In their Business Plan for 1990/91 to 1992/93 the ATC indicated that Indonesia warranted only 'basic marketing' services, and it was alone amongst the Asian countries reviewed in this chapter in not being assigned priority status (ATC, 1990b). It was not until 1993 that the ATC appointed a marketing representative in Indonesia (ATC, 1993b).

Like all other Asian countries, Indonesia's outbound tourism growth has been fuelled by its economic growth. It remains, however, a relatively poor country. Its Gross National Product (GDP) per capita in 1993 was A$940, compared to its nearest neighbours Malaysia with A$4,250 and, even more strikingly, Singapore with A$25,900 (ATC, 1994b). The sheer size of its population (184 million) has meant that a substantial, affluent middle class with rising disposable incomes has emerged in absolute terms (ATC, 1994b) and Australia has benefited from this due to its geographic proximity (Poole, 1993).

In terms of their geographic distribution, Indonesian visitors display similar patterns to other nearby South-east Asian nations: relatively high levels of visitation to Western Australia, although their level of visitation to eastern states, especially New South Wales, is significantly higher than for either Singapore or Malaysia. The average length of stay, 34 nights, is second only to Malaysia, although the majority of trips (65 per cent) are less than two weeks in duration. The ATC believes that short breaks of 3 to 4 days to nearby destinations such as Perth and Darwin represent significant potential for the development of this market (ATC, 1994b). Unlike other South-east Asians, few Indonesians travel to and within Australia independently, apart from those who are visiting friends and relatives (ATC, 1993b). The main constraints to further increases in Indonesian travel to Australia relate to the imbalance in air traffic between the two countries. Substantially more Australians travel to Indonesia than the reverse. The bulk of Australians travel to Denpasar in Bali, whereas the majority of the Indonesian outbound market is located in Jakarta. This imbalance has led to capacity problems ex-Jakarta, particularly in peak periods, a problem which is likely to continue for some time.

Thailand

Thailand has exhibited strong growth over the 1980s with departures to Australia increasing from a small base of 5,400 in 1982 to 46,661 in 1993 (ATC, 1994c). This makes Thailand the seventh largest supplier of short-term visitors from Asia. The ATC envisage an average increase of 21 per cent per annum to the year 2000, bringing total arrivals to 152,000, with the potential size of the market estimated to be over 380,000 (ATC, 1994b). The recent and prospective growth is largely attributed to rising national income and an expanding middle class. However, the market is recognized as immature in terms of experience and product preferences, requiring a sustained marketing effort to develop it gradually (ATC, 1994b).

ATC tracking studies have shown that Australia is regarded as a 'wholesome' destination offering sun and outdoor opportunities. However, Australia is also perceived as offering little culturally and lacking an exotic edge compared to competing destinations and generally its image amongst Thais is not strong, even amongst those destinations with similar images (ATC, 1993c). As with Hong Kong, other Western destinations of Europe, UK and the USA have a greater appeal to Thai tourists (ATC, 1994c). Most tourists are organized through company sponsored group travel and there is limited movement towards independent travel (ATC, 1994c). The immature nature of the Thai outbound travel industry has been recognized as creating problems in the short term for establishing effective distribution channels and promoting Australia within Thailand (ATC, 1994b).

Future Growth

The focus of the Australian tourism industry over the last decade has been on the inbound sector due to the growth in international visitation through the 1980s and early 1990s. At the same time domestic tourism has remained relatively static and has been accounting for a decreasing share of overall tourism. Much of the growth in inbound tourism has come from Asia, which is likely to become even more prominent over the next decade. Even conservative estimates suggest that future inbound arrivals may virtually double by the year 2000, with Asia contributing a disproportionately large share. As Grey et al. have noted, 'The size of the world market will not act as a constraint on Australia's tourism industry, it is, in fact, expanding in directions which favour Australia as a tourist destination' (1991: 8).

A number of organizations have produced a range of projections of Australia's future inbound arrivals (DoT, 1994b). At the lower end of the range are the BTR forecasts, based primarily on econometric modelling. These relatively conservative forecasts, which have not been revised since 1992, suggest that arrivals will exceed 5 million by 2001 with an average annual growth rate of 8 per cent (see Table 4.5). Achieving the longer term forecasts is partially dependent on continued growth from Asia (see Table 4.12). Arrivals from Japan are projected to grow by 110 per cent from 1993 levels, and other parts of Asia by 70 per cent. The resultant shares of total arrivals in 2001 are expected to be 27 per cent and 22 per cent respectively. It is worth noting that actual arrivals exceeded BTR forecasts for 1992 and 1993, and arrivals in 1994 were greater than the forecast levels for 1995 (ATC, 1994d). Some Asian markets are growing well ahead of projected levels and, on this basis, these forecasts could be regarded virtually as a worst case scenario.

Table 4.12 Forecast short-term arrivals, 2001

Country/region	Arrivals (000s)	% of arrivals
Japan	1,407	27
Other Asia	1,127	22
UK and Ireland	543	11
Other Europe	499	10
USA	437	8
New Zealand	732	14
Rest of World	406	8
Total	5,151	100

Source: Bureau of Tourism Research (1992a)

At the upper end of the range are the Australian Tourist Commission's growth targets that project that total arrivals will be 7.3 million by 2001 and 8.4 million by 2004 (see Table 4.13). Compared to the BTR forecasts, these targets consider a wider range of qualitative factors and allow for the marketing input by the Australian tourism industry and the ATC itself. They represent what is 'achievable' rather than what is probable. However, at the time of writing, these targets were being achieved as a whole and exceeded in the case of most Asian markets. The conservative nature of the BTR forecasts is illustrated by comparison with the ATC targets to the year 2004. The targeted arrivals for 2001 exceed the forecast by more than 2 million, with much of that being attributable to arrivals from Asia. By the ATC's reckoning the BTR forecast for 'other Asian' arrivals would bave been reached by 1995, with this region constantly increasing its share of arrivals over the next decade. Each of the current major markets is expected to grow and new markets, notably China, are anticipated to rise to prominence. While Japan's share of arrivals is expected to remain relatively stable, other Asian nations are anticipated to account for a third of arrivals by 2001 and exceed that by 2004.

Re-orientation of Marketing

The growth in inbound tourism, particularly from Asia, has influenced the way Australia is marketed as a destination and the extent of that marketing effort. While domestic tourism still accounts for 70 per cent of tourist expenditure within Australia, its significance has been decreasing over the last decade and will continue to do so as its current and prospective growth rate lags well behind that of inbound. State tourism commissions sought to capitalize on the growth in international arrivals by expanding their activities in overseas markets, the result being both a duplication and a fragmentation of effort. In response to this, a recent initiative in Australian tourism marketing has been the introduction of the 'Partnership Australia' scheme, whereby

Table 4.13   ATC targets for arrivals from major inbound markets, 1995–2004

Country/region	1995 (000s)	1998 (000s)	2001 (000s)	2004 (000s)
Japan	**809**	**1,214**	**1,669**	**1,862**
Other Asia	**1,123**	**1,734**	**2,424**	**2,965**
Singapore	217	284	329	322
Taiwan	221	349	450	502
Hong Kong	126	156	216	276
Malaysia	110	160	215	240
Indonesia	129	218	330	419
South Korea	146	266	382	449
Thailand	83	146	230	311
China	40	87	176	310
Other	51	68	96	136
United Kingdom	**398**	**543**	**714**	**832**
Other Europe	**401**	**542**	**728**	**857**
USA	**339**	**432**	**532**	**581**
New Zealand	**553**	**634**	**712**	**712**
Rest of World	**284**	**381**	**496**	**583**
Total	**3,907**	**5,480**	**7,276**	**8,394**

Source: Australian Tourist Commission (1994c)

the Australian Tourist Commission largely assumed responsibility for overseas marketing and the State commissions were left to concentrate their efforts on domestic markets.

The promotion budget of the ATC has expanded and changed in the pattern of its distribution in recent years, in response to the general growth in inbound tourism and to the changing composition of arrivals. Over the four years from 1988/89 to 1992/93 the ATC's promotion expenditure in overseas markets increased from A$22.5 million to A$55 million, a substantial rise in real terms (ATC, 1989, 1993a). In that same period the pattern of its expenditure shifted towards Japan and other Asian markets as the potential of these markets came to be recognized (see Table 4.14). The most significant shift has been away from expenditure in North America, where the promotional effort has been virtually halved in proportionate terms. It still remains the region of greatest expenditure, however, indicating a certain amount of inertia in the system. In real terms the expenditure in North America has been virtually static since 1988/89. The increased funds available to the ATC since this time have been largely allocated to the newly emerging markets of Japan and other Asian nations, especially the latter where the share of the expenditure has more than doubled.

In addition to the expansion and reallocation of promotional expenditure, there have been other manifestations of the ATC's increasing orientation towards Asia. New overseas offices have been established, most notably in Hong Kong which was intended to create a direct presence in the North-east Asian area. In recognition of the growth of the Indonesian market an ATC representative has been appointed in Jakarta, despite the fact that it has yet to be officially designated as a priority market (ATC, 1994b). The increasing

Table 4.14 Distribution of promotional expenditure by Australian Tourist Commission in overseas markets, 1988/89 to 1992/93

Country/region	1988/89 (%)	1992/93 (%)
Japan	13.0	19.3
Other Asia	10.0	20.4
UK/Ireland[1]	12.8	15.4
Other Europe	14.9	16.1
North America	45.5	25.2
New Zealand	3.8	3.1
Latin America	–	0.5

1. The figures for UK and Ireland in 1992/93 include expenditure in Scandinavia as the ATC's London office had been assigned responsibility for this market since 1988/89.
Source: Australian Tourist Commission (1989, 1993a)

maturity of South-east Asian markets has led to new product development initiatives to cater for anticipated preferences; for example, in 1994 the ATC appointed a Rural Tourism Project Manager whose main task was to develop and promote farmstays and other rural tourism products to Singaporeans and Malaysians (ATC, 1994a). As other Asian markets develop similar initiatives could be expected to emerge.

Asian Investment in Australian Tourism

As could be expected the trends in inbound tourism have dramatically affected the development of tourist facilities and patterns of investment in those facilities within Australia. The surge in inbound tourism in the mid 1980s stimulated a substantial increase in the development of hotels and resorts, particularly at the upper end of the market and in key destinations for international tourists, such as Sydney, Cairns and the Gold Coast. Much of this activity was initiated by Australian developers with a view to selling the properties to overseas investors. Major Australian investors such as insurance companies and superannuation funds, which had long dominated commercial and industrial property markets, displayed a reluctance to invest in tourism. They perceived it as too risky and volatile a proposition and payback periods as too lengthy. Asian investors, especially the Japanese, showed no such reluctance and became the major purchasers of hotels and resorts in the latter half of the decade, with many developers selling their projects to Japanese investors well before completion. Japanese developers also became directly involved in the construction of new facilities, generally retaining ownership on completion of the project (Griffin, 1989).

Table 4.15 shows the growth and extent of foreign investment in tourism over the period 1986/87 to 1992/93. For most of that time Japan has clearly dominated the market, accounting for more than two-thirds of the expected foreign investment up until 1991/92. Its share has fallen dramatically since then. This has been partly the result of the tourism development boom that Japanese investors had fuelled. In most major tourist destinations increases in the supply of new accommodation significantly outstripped demand, the result being that occupancy rates and the operational profitability of hotels and resorts fell. From 1989 onwards a large number of tourism properties became financially distressed, with financiers eventually appointing receivers and in many cases assuming ownership when the original investor went into liquidation. Rarely did the financiers wish to retain ownership and consequently most of these properties were put on the market. The number of tourism properties for sale was swelled by a few Japanese developers and investors seeking to divest themselves of their Australian assets in this climate. The value of hotels and resorts declined significantly due to the large numbers that were on the market simultaneously. New tourism development activity also declined along with foreign investor interest in Australian tourism; expected foreign investment in 1991/92 was only a quarter of what it had been at the height of the boom in 1988/89. Japanese investment had fallen from a peak of A\$3,516 million in 1988/89, representing 70 per cent of total foreign investment, to A\$241 million in 1992/93 (17 per cent), due to both the conditions in the Australian tourism property market and to the onset of an economic recession in Japan. By 1992/93 Japan had fallen behind both the USA and France as the leading foreign investors (see Table 4.16), although the USA's position was largely due to a single project, the development of a new casino in Melbourne. France's position was due to the entry of both Club Mediterranee and the Accor group into the Australian market.

In the light of continuing expansion in inbound tourism, especially from Asia, the depressed conditions described above could not last for long. With few additions to supply in the early 1990s occupancy rates and profitability began to recover. The inflated property values of the late 1980s had been eroded and tourism began to be an attractive investment proposition once more. Asking prices for hotels had fallen below development costs in many cases, as financiers, including some of Australia's major banks, sought to divest themselves of unwanted properties. At this point it appeared that Australian institutional investors may have entered the market, however much the experience of the previous few years had served to reinforce their reluctance to become involved in tourism. A vacuum therefore existed in tourism investment until the entry of new investors from Asian countries other than Japan in 1993. Hong Kong had been a steady investor since 1988/89, although its share of total foreign investment in tourism had never exceeded 8 per cent, while Singapore's share had peaked in 1991/92 at 12 per cent (A\$162 million), which accounted for the majority of the ASEAN nations share of 17 per cent in that year. In 1992 property agents began to report strong interest and enquiry levels from Asian investors, especially from Singapore and Hong Kong. It was a slow process to translate these enquiries into sales, however. One observer noted at the time that:

Table 4.15 Expected foreign investment[1] in Australian tourism, 1986/87 to 1992/93

Country/region of investor	1986/87 $m	%	1987/88 $m	%	1988/89 $m	%	1989/90 $m	%	1990/91 $m	%	1991/92 $m	%	1992/93 $m	%
Japan	1153	74	1385	66	3516	70	2659	68	1242	67	564	42	241	17
ASEAN	12	–	40	2	390	8	162	4	196	11	227	17	11	1
Hong Kong	–	–	0	–	392	8	131	–	139	7	25	2	102	7
EC (including UK)	27	2	81	4	84	2	54	1	18	1	197	15	326	23
New Zealand	69	4	131	6	60	1	265	7	188	10	53	4	4	–
World other	122	8	144	7	286	6	163	5	75	4	183	14	672	47
Australia[2]	166	11	309	15	270	5	458	12	1	–	88	7	71	5
Total	1553		2091		4997		3892		1859		1336		1425	

1. 'Expected foreign investment' relates to amounts contained in foreign investment approval applications to the Foreign Investment Review Board within a given year. No figures are available to indicate whether that investment was subsequently made.
2. The investment identified as originating from Australia represents the contribution by Australian-controlled companies and Australian residents to the total investment associated with foreign investment proposals in which they are in partnership with foreign interests but does not generally include the contribution attributable to minority Australian shareholders in companies with majority or controlling foreign shareholders.
Source: Foreign Investment Review Board, various Annual Reports

At present, the most active enquiry for hotels is coming from the same markets which are expected to be providing the most tourists in the future. The strategic nature of this enquiry is obvious. Buyers are attracted to the market in the hope of securing distressed property at 'bargain basement' prices, secure in the knowledge that the performance of these hotels will improve in the future. (Koloff, 1992: 3)

During 1993 and early 1994 the tourism property market virtually cleared all of its unsold stock. In the 18 months to June 1994, the total value of tourism property sales was A\$1,164 million, of which Singaporean investors' purchases accounted for 57 per cent or A\$664 million (*Sydney Morning Herald*,

Table 4.16 Expected foreign investment in Australian tourism 1991/92 to 1992/93

Country of investor	1991/92 $m	%	1992/93 $m	%
USA	86	6	648	46
UK	24	2	1	–
Germany	–	–	42	3
France	147	11	254	18
Other EC	26	2	29	2
Canada	13	1	24	2
New Zealand	53	4	4	–
Japan	564	42	241	17
Singapore	162	12	–	–
Malaysia	13	1	10	1
Other ASEAN	53	4	1	–
Hong Kong	25	2	102	7
World other	84	6	24	2
Australia	88	7	71	5
Total	1336		1425	

Source: Foreign Investment Review Board (1991/92, 1992/93)

1994). One Singaporean investor, the Thakral Group, purchased the entire hotel portfolio of Westpac, one of Australia's major banks, comprising eight hotels and worth A$260 million (Chong, 1994). In the face of continuing reluctance by Australian institutions to either lend for or invest in tourism property, Asian investors could potentially provide the major stimulus to the development of new tourist facilities in Australia for at least the next decade.

Implications for Development and Marketing

The future of Australia's tourism industry has become very much inter-twined with the economic development and continued growth of outbound travel from Asia. On the surface the prospects look extremely promising, with sustained growth seemingly assured. However, when the trends and patterns are examined more closely this conclusion must be tempered with some reservations.

The fundamental question is whether the current rates of growth can be sustained and therefore the projected growth targets achieved. This will be highly dependent on the economic growth and development of Asia pro-ceeding smoothly. The experience of Japan suggests that periodic cyclical downturns are inevitable, especially as the emergent Asian economies be-come more integrated into the global economy; the subsequent recessionary periods are likely to lead to slower than anticipated growth in outbound travel. This effect has been noticeable in Japan recently, with economic recession slowing its rate of growth of outbound travel (Morris, 1994). This led to Japan being the only Asian market where targeted arrivals to Australia were not achieved in 1994 (ATC, 1994d). The prospect of other Asian nations experiencing economic recession in the future must be acknowledged and the more conservative forecasts of the BTR may be consequently more realistic in the longer term than the currently more accurate ATC targets. Continuing political instability in some Asian nations, such as South Korea, may also restrain the growth in outbound travel in the longer term.

A supplementary question is whether Australia can cope with the antici-pated increase in inbound tourism. Currently this growth is being viewed opportunistically and optimistically, particularly by promotional bodies such as the ATC. However, in determining the economic benefits likely to be generated, little effort has been devoted to examining the costs that may be imposed on the Australian economy, community and environment in the long term. Sustainability needs to be viewed from a supply as well as a demand perspective and must involve an assessment of maintaining the quality of the cultural and environmental assets on which tourism is based. With regard to Asian inbound tourism, Australia's physical environment has been the main attractive feature, but the anticipated growth may impose pressures on that environment which exceed its capacity to cope. This is especially problematic as the pattern of Asian visitation within Australia has been highly concentrated in relatively few destinations that are therefore likely to be subject to the greatest pressure. The planning and development of these destinations needs to be carefully managed and monitored, and more effort may need to be devoted to encouraging Asian visitors to other destinations.

Despite the growth in tourism from Asia, a number of other problems that may diminish its long-term prospects are already evident. The outbound tourism industries in some countries are relatively immature, with high degrees of monopolization evident in some places, such as Taiwan and South Korea (ATC, 1994b). Australian ground operators and suppliers have had to become accustomed to new ways of doing business and new forms of collaborative arrangements with wholesalers or their equivalents in the home markets. Whether Australia can sustain the current rates of growth may therefore be dependent on operators and suppliers learning and adopting these new practices faster than those in competitive destinations. As the examination of the various individual Asian markets has demonstrated, while Australia is a popular destination it is rarely the most preferred destination, and its continued success relies on effective promotion and distribution within these markets. To an extent, this must be achieved through distribution channels and mechanisms with which many Australian operators and suppliers are currently unaccustomed.

Of even more significance is the question as to whether Australian tourism operators will continue to pursue the apparent opportunities in Asia. The problem of price sensitivity and narrow margins has been alluded to in relation to a number of key Asian markets, most notably those with the fastest current growth rates, Taiwan and South Korea. The general growth in visitor arrivals has not been matched by increasing profitability for Australian operators and 'profitless volume' has come to be regarded as one of the most serious problems confronting the industry. Unless profit margins can be successfully negotiated upwards or Australian operators can increase their efficiency and thereby achieve cost reductions, many may choose ultimately not to pursue a number of the Asian markets discussed.

A much broader issue is how Australia will develop as a destination or as a setting for a range of different styles of destination and touristic activities. The diverse Asian markets examined in this chapter are at varying stages of maturity and consequently their requirements differ. Australia must be careful to avoid catering to the short-term demands of the growing, but immature markets in such a way as to diminish its long-term prospects and appeal. Facilities and experiences provided for relatively inexperienced travellers now may be inappropriate for the more specialized needs of repeat visitors of the future. In planning for tourism within Australia some attention must be paid to how the emergent markets may develop and mature.

A possible constraint on the growth of tourism within Australia may be the provision of facilities to cater for that growth. The development of hotels and resorts, for example, has not proceeded along a smooth path in concert with demand. Rather, a pronounced boom-and-bust cycle has been observed in recent years. Throughout that period Australian investors and financiers displayed a reluctance to become involved in tourism, and many that eventually did so suffered severe losses as a result of the excessive development that took place in the late 1980s. Much of the development was driven by overseas investors, but the most significant group, the Japanese, seem to have withdrawn from the market for the time being. Their place has been partially taken by investors from other parts of Asia. However, the future patterns and levels of investment are extremely uncertain for a number of reasons. First, major Australian investors and financiers are likely to be even more wary of tourism in the 1990s than they were in the early to mid-1980s; some major financiers in the aftermath issued directives that effectively bar developers from receiving loans for tourism projects. Secondly, much of the recent Asian investment has been directed at purchasing existing, distressed properties rather than the development of new, additional facilities. It remains to be seen whether this level of investment will be maintained and redirected to new development now that the supply of bargain hotels and resorts has been exhausted. Under these circumstances the supply of new facilities could lag well behind demand and the subsequent increase in prices could reduce inbound arrivals from the most price-sensitive Asian markets to below the anticipated levels.

Conclusion

The economic and touristic growth of Asia has provided tremendous opportunities for the tourism industry and the Australian community in general. Australian tourism's future has become inextricably linked with the expanding outbound travel from the rapidly developing Asian economies and the nation has benefited by virtue of its geographic proximity to Asia and the fact that its unique natural environment has proved attractive to the increasing numbers of Asian travellers. Tourism has consequently become a major generator of jobs, income and foreign exchange earnings within the Australian economy. While on the surface this growth appears to be unambiguously positive, the tourism industry is likely to face some dilemmas in servicing the distinctly different demands of these emerging and dynamic markets. Rather than simply exploiting the opportunities or passively taking advantage of them, a balanced, strategic vision needs to be articulated to guide the future development of tourism in Australia. This will require the industry to not only cater for current growth but also engage in cooperative long-term planning, marketing and development to ensure an appropriate supply of facilities and a quality of service that meets future demands and safeguards the assets upon which the Australian tourism industry is based.

Bibliography

Australian Bureau of Statistics (1993) *Overseas Arrivals and Departures*. Cat. No. 3404.0.

ATC (1989) *Annual Report*. Sydney: Australian Tourist Commission.

ATC (1990) *Three Year Business Plan: Asia Region 1990/91–1992/93*. Sydney: Australian Tourist Commission.

ATC (1992) *North East Asia Market Brief*. Hong Kong: Australian Tourist Commission.

ATC (1993a) *Annual Report*. Sydney: Australian Tourist Commission.

ATC (1993b) *International Marketing Manual*. Sydney: Australian Tourist Commission.

ATC (1993c) *Market Segmentation Studies*. Sydney: Australian Tourist Commission.

ATC (1994a) *Australia*. Winter Newsletter. Sydney: Australian Tourist Commission.

ATC (1994b) *Market Update and Trends for All Markets*. Sydney: Australian Tourist Commission.

ATC (1994c) *Tourism Pulse*. August, No. 28. Sydney: Australian Tourist Commission.

ATC (1994d) *Tourism Pulse*. September, No. 29. Sydney: Australian Tourist Commission.

BTR (1992) *Australian Tourism Forecasts – International Visitor Arrivals 1992–2001*. Canberra: Bureau of Tourism Research.

BTR (1993) *International Visitor Survey 1992*. Canberra: Bureau of Tourism Research.

Chong, F. (1994) The Thakral Group gets an instant hotel chain. *Weekend Australian* (Property) 26–27 March, 8.

Cleverdon, R.G. (1993) *Tourism to the Year 2000: Qualitative Aspects Affecting Global Growth*. Madrid: World Tourism Organization.

DOT (1994a) *IMPACT: Tourism Facts, August*. Canberra: Department of Tourism.

DOT (1994b) Understanding international arrival projections. *Forecast* 1 (1), 7–9.

Economist Intelligence Unit (1990) Australia. *EIU International Tourism Reports* 4, 63–83.

Edwards, A. (1990) *Far East and Pacific Travel in the 1990s*. London: Economist Intelligence Unit.

Faulkner, H.W. (1990) Demand for the Australian tourism product – an overview. In *Australian Tourism Outlook Forum Report 1990*. Canberra: Bureau of Tourism Research, 9–26.

Foreign Investment Review Board (1992) *Report 1990–91*. Canberra: Australian Government Publishing Service.

Foreign Investment Review Board (1993) *Report 1991–92*. Canberra: Australian Government Publishing Service.

Foreign Investment Review Board (1994) *Report 1992–93*. Canberra: Australian Government Publishing Service.

Grey, P., Edelmann, K. and Dwyer, L. (1991) *Tourism in Australia: Challenges and Opportunities*. Melbourne: Longman Cheshire.

Griffin, T. (1989) Hotel development: the case of downtown Sydney. In Blackwell, J. and Stear, L. (eds) *Case Histories of Tourism and Hospitality*. Sydney: Australian-International Magazine Services, 317–33.

Koloff, M.L. (1992) *The Financial Status of Australia's Hotel Industry*. Paper presented at BOMA Forum *Australian Institutions and a Tourism Led Recovery*. Sydney, 17 March.

Morris, S. (1994) Japan outbound. *EIU Travel and Tourism Analyst* 1, 40–64.

Payne, M. (1993) *Tourism in the Pacific Rim: Growth in a Region of Opportunity*. London: Financial Times Business Information.

Ping, O. L. (1992) Malaysia and Singapore outbound. *EIU Travel and Tourism Analyst* 4, 27–46.

Poole, M. (1993) *Tourism and the Economy*. Canberra: Bureau of Tourism Research.

Sydney Morning Herald (1994) Asian Buyers. *Sydney Morning Herald* 10 September, 42.

5

Brunei Darussalam: Sustainable tourism development within an Islamic cultural ethos

TOM BAUM
MICHAEL V. CONLIN

Introduction

The growth of tourism in South-east Asia has been one of the most remarkable features of the social, economic and cultural change in that region over the past 20 years. The impact of this phenomenon on the communities in the countries concerned cannot be underestimated. International tourist arrivals to the member states of the Association of South East Asian Nations (ASEAN), namely Brunei, Indonesia, Malaysia, the Philippines, Singapore, Thailand and Vietnam have grown dramatically over the past 20 years, as reference to other chapters in this book will testify. This growth is accounted for by six countries within ASEAN, which have all actively promoted the development of international tourism as a central feature of economic growth.

The smallest member of ASEAN, Negara Brunei Darussalam or Brunei for short, is the clear exception to this tourism phenomenon. In this chapter, we shall consider the 'minnow' of ASEAN tourism, the economic, social and cultural reasons why tourism development has not, heretofore, been a national priority, and the approach that is likely to be adopted as the country, very gently, releases the brakes on the development of tourism.

For a variety of reasons, Brunei can be classed as a reluctant tourist destination, one that has had few economic reasons to develop this industry and seeks to protect its devout Islamic population from what are seen as the worst excesses of mass international tourism. Brunei is a small country, with limited traditional tourist resources but certainly not devoid of potential in this respect. In addition, it is also a very wealthy country, on a per capita basis the most affluent in ASEAN as a consequence of the exploitation of rich oil reserves. Oil, in fact, dominates the economy to the extent that other resources and activities are of negligible significance. The final factor to be considered in understanding the relationship between Brunei and tourism is the religious ethos of the country, in that Islam is practised by almost 70 per cent of the population and by the ruling Sultan and his senior officials.

This chapter introduces Brunei from geographical, historical and social perspectives. These factors form the backcloth to consideration of the limited developments that have taken place to form the tourism industry in Brunei, the main factors that make the country the regional exception in international tourism terms and the likely future evolution of tourism in the country

In a generic sense, consideration of Brunei in the context of tourism raises a number of interesting points. The country is one of just a small number of nation states to display at best ambivalence and, probably, more of a reluctance to fully embrace the development of modern international tourism. Din identifies a number of other Islamic states where tourism is discouraged (for example, Libya) or where 'prevailing policy is to isolate hedonistic traits from the public life' (1989: 555) (for example, the Maldives and Saudi Arabia). Inskeep, in considering the development of tourism policy in Oman, notes that prior to 1987, 'international tourism was nonexistent in Oman. Foreign visitors were allowed into the country only for business and related purposes' (1994: 87). Tourism was actively discouraged for cultural and religious reasons. Changing circumstances, however, especially the price of oil, had led to a managed change in attitude to tourism so that the character of tourism which resulted was compatible with national ethos, aspirations and ideology. As a result of this new policy, tourism has developed in Oman but on a relatively small and managed basis, concentrating primarily on the country's environmental and cultural attractions. As we shall discuss further in this chapter, Brunei represents a further example where tourism is not a national economic priority, thus permitting parallel defence of the national, cultural and economic environment. The strength of the overall oil economy of Brunei has allowed the country the luxury of isolating itself from the mainstream of tourism development. In this sense, Brunei has much in common with oil-rich states of the Middle East and north Africa. However, this religious and cultural dimension is complemented by a sensitivity to the ecology of the country, especially the tropical rain forests. Environmental sustainability is a national priority that Brunei can afford within its current level of economic well-being. This Brunei case study, therefore, raises wider issues relating to the cost of cultural and ecological sensitivity and sustainability notwithstanding that, arguably, the country's stance is a luxury and privilege which few potential tourism destinations can afford.

Geography of Brunei

Brunei shares the island of Borneo, the world's third largest, with the Indonesian province of Kalimantan and the Malaysian states of Sabah and Sarawak. The total land area of Brunei is some 5,765 square kilometres, consisting of four states, one of which is separated from the rest of the country by part of Sarawak. The country has a coastline on the South China Sea of 161 kilometres.

Brunei consists of coastal plains, rising inland to heights in excess of 1,800 metres. The country has a tropical climate, characterized by a uniform temperature, high humidity and copious rainfall. Daily temperatures range between 22 and 28 degrees centigrade while annual rainfall is highest during the monsoon period from November to March. About 75 per cent of the land area of Brunei is untouched afforestation, with five types of tropical forests identified. About one half of the forested area constitutes State Forest Reserves, which are not open to commercial exploitation.

The 1991 population of Brunei was estimated to be 260,482 (Information Department, undated). This represents a rise from 136,256 in 1971. Close to 100,000 live in the urbanized district around the capital, Bandar Seri Begawan, extending as far as Muara. The other main urban centres are Seria and Kuala Belait while Tutong and Bangar are important district centres. The capital has grown significantly in recent years, reflecting the development of public sector employment, the expansion of public housing, retailing malls and sporting and cultural facilities.

Land communications within Brunei are difficult, especially with the interior. The main road links are coastal with little by way of land links inland. Water transportation constitutes the best option for penetration of the interior. Internationally, Brunei is served by the national airline, Royal Brunei, which has a regional as well as an Australian and European network. A number of other major airlines also serve the country through the international airport at Bandar Seri Begawan.

History of Brunei

In geographical terms, modern Brunei is the small remnant of a once-extensive Sultanate and empire that, in the fifteenth and sixteenth century, extended over the whole of Borneo and as far north as the Philippines. Brunei embraced Islam in the fourteenth century and developed as an important trading centre, exchanging the jungle products of Borneo for the silks, spices and ceramics that arrived via the Indian and Chinese trade routes.

Then as now, Islam was an important factor in the strength of the Sultanate and its rulers and this encouraged trade beyond the ill-defined boundaries of the empire. From its zenith in the mid-sixteenth century, the power of the Sultanate of Brunei declined in the face of the growing power of other regional rulers and the increasing mercantile and, subsequently, colonial aspirations of European countries in the region. According to Cleary and Wong: 'By the early eighteenth century, European travellers depicted the state as a picturesque but faded kingdom, largely bereft of its former power and influence but still proud of its royal traditions, customs and protocol' (1994: 13).

Weakening economic power and specific European interest in Borneo for natural resources such as coal, contributed to a loss of control over outlying parts of the sultanate. Perhaps the most significant intervention in the region was that of the British adventurer, James Brooke, in neighbouring Sarawak. His rule there commenced in 1841 and he pursued an expansionist strategy that led to the general erosion of land holdings within the control of the Sultanate of Brunei. The division of the present country into two is the result of force applied by Brooke's nephew, Charles, in 1890, ostensibly aimed at quelling local unrest in Limbang, then an economically vital part of Brunei. Similar territorial losses were sustained at that time to what, subsequently, became Sabah to the east of Brunei.

Brunei became a British protectorate in 1888, although this did not end erosion of its territories until a full British Residency was established in 1906, with its borders and survival guaranteed by the Crown. By this time, the Sultanate was virtually bankrupt and gravely threatened by incorporation from both Sarawak and North Borneo (Sabah). The nature of the Residency was such that it allowed the British to advise the Sultan on matters of finance, administration, foreign policy and defence, which the ruler was rarely in a position to reject.

The prime focus of the Residency in its early years was to overcome the economic weakness of the country and redress chronic national debt. Commodity development (oil, tobacco and rubber) did not take place at the level of neighbouring states during the early years of the twentieth century. It was not until the discovery of oil and its commercial exploitation in 1929 that the economic fortunes of Brunei really turned round. Bruneian exports remained below or around US$ 1 million for the period 1917 to 1928. By 1932, oil exports of US$ 1 million were recorded and this had risen to over US$ 6 million by 1939, when oil accounted for some 85 per cent of exports. Oil clearly proved the economic salvation of Brunei, without which subsequent autonomy and eventual independence would have been impossible. Following occupation by the Japanese between 1942 and 1945, Brunei recovered very quickly in economic terms. Oil production had outstripped pre-war levels by 1948 and continued to rise to a peak in 1957. This created large surpluses within the national account, a feature of the economy that has been maintained to the present day, despite fluctuations in the price of oil.

Under the rule of Sultan Haji Sir Omar Ali Saiffudin, Brunei moved towards greater autonomy during this period. In 1959, a written constitution was promulgated, giving Brunei internal self-government and replacing the Residency with a High Commissioner who continued to advise the Sultan on all matters other than the Islamic religion and Malay custom. In 1971, the 1959 agreement was revised to give Brunei full, independent self-government with the exception of defence and external affairs. The progress to full independence was measured and, arguably, slow when compared to experience elsewhere but was essentially designed to preserve stability and protect the Islamic ethos of the country. The 1959 constitution contained what Cleary and Wong (1994) call the 'enshrinement of the Malay Islamic Monarchy' and ensured the pre-eminent position of Islam, the Malay language and the Sultan as head of state. These three pillars of the political, religious and cultural order have retained their importance to this day.

Full independence for Brunei came in 1984 under a new Sultan, who came to the throne on his father's abdication. Independence came after considerable debate regarding the most suitable form of severance from Britain. The option of joining the Malaysian Federation in 1963 was widely discussed but opposed by the Sultan on the grounds that this would result in a dilution of oil revenues. Prior to full independence, economic progress based on oil revenues was very substantial in terms of infrastructural development and considerable investment was forthcoming in education, health and social services.

On independence, a ministerial style of government was adopted with the Sultan in Council having ultimate policy responsibility. The Sultan nominates ministers to all positions within the Council and currently retains the posts of Prime Minister and Minister of Defence himself. Other members of the ruling family are also actively involved in government. Government does not operate on the basis of Western-style democracy, although there were attempts to introduce a measure of parliamentary representation during the 1950s. These foundered during the emergency in 1962 although recent moves to create a greater sense of community accountability among ministers is an important recognition of the need to maintain close links with wider society. Representation, ultimately through access to the Sultan and his advisors, is enshrined in a strong hierarchy that places all Bruneians within specific categories, subservient to the tier above. Representation is through the next level above in the hierarchy, from commoners to nobility and, ultimately, to the monarchy. Non-Bruneians are excluded from this hierarchy and thus have no formal route or access to representation.

Melayu Islam Beraja: The National Philosophy of Brunei

Central to an understanding of Brunei and its approach to tourism development is the national philosophy of *Malayu Islam Beraja* (MIB) (Malay Islamic Monarchy). Although the origin of the MIB can be traced back to the embracing of the Islamic faith (Aziz, 1992), it is its modern manifestation that has emerged as a central feature of Brunei life. MIB provides a coherent ideological framework within which to locate the monarchy but, since its formal promulgation within the 1959 constitution, has been increasingly used to protect the country from the perceived problems that material prosperity and openness to the outside world brings. It also ensures the pre-eminence of the Sultan and the Royal family.

> MIB is based, first and foremost, on the centrality of history and tradition. Brunei, it is argued, has a long history as a sovereign state with one of the oldest royal families in the region. It is a Malay, Islamic state adopting Islam at an early stage and committed, not to a multi-ethnic model of political and economic development as in the case of Malaysia but rather to a unique Brunei Malay culture and polity ... Integral to this philosophy is the unquestioning position of the Sultan as ruler of the state, the centrality of Islam to the daily life of Brunei and an inherently cautious attitude to western ideas and values. MIB is seeking to establish a political and social philosophy which remains open to some aspects of the west (in this respect it is not fundamentalist in ethos) whilst continuing to be anchored to a Malay conception of monarch and people (Cleary and Wong, 1994: 130).

The MIB is clearly the source from which part of the concern about exposure to the perceived negative impact of modern mass tourism stems although in essence it has much in common with wider Islamic suspicion about tourism. These concerns match Din's argument that sees mass tourism as

> an industry characterized by hedonism, permissiveness, lavishness, servitude, foreignness, with a lack of cross-cultural understanding and communication ... [and] clearly different from ... what tourism 'should' be within the framework of the Islamic doctrine. (1989: 551)

Din continues

> In Islam, travel is regarded as an instrument for fostering unity among the Ummah (Muslim community). Islam deemphasizes profligate consumption characteristics of modern tourism and enjoins genuine, humane, equitable, and reciprocal cross-cultural communication. The journey in Islam is part of a larger journey in the service of the ways of God. (1989: 554)

In this sense, then, the MIB and wider Islamic doctrinal concerns take a cautious view of tourism on two grounds. First (and foremost) there is the need to protect the community and culture from the excesses of in-coming modern tourism. Secondly, what Din refers to as the perceived nature of international tourism is seen to be incompatible with the notion of travel as exercised by the devout follower of Islam.

Although Brunei is, by its constitution, an Islamic state with the Sultan as head of the faith in the country, the country is by no means mono-cultural. In 1991, the estimated population of 260,482 comprised 68 per cent Malays; other indigenous groups 6 per cent; Chinese 17 per cent; and other races 9 per cent. Thus, the multi-cultural characteristic of the country creates a level of tolerance for other faiths and practices although restrictions on, for example, the sale and consumption of alcohol, reflect the dominant ethos.

The Economy of Brunei

Economically, Brunei is excessively dependent upon the production of crude oil and natural gas. As we have already shown, this dependence is relatively recent, dating from 1929 onwards and continues to run at over 80 per cent of 1991 export revenues of US$ 2.66 billion. However, oil production has not increased in recent years, due to the weakness of world prices and, as a result, there has been a significant impact on Brunei's balance of trade. During the period of the world oil boom up to the mid-1980s, exports outstripped imports by a ratio of almost 10:1. This has declined to a still healthy 3:1, not only as a result of the drop in the international price of oils, but also as increasing demand and expectations at home fuel demand for imported products that the country's fragile agricultural and manufacturing sector cannot meet. In terms of Gross Domestic Product (GDP), the position of oil has declined sharply since the 1970s from 83 per cent of GDP in 1977 to 60 per cent in 1988 (Cleary and Wong, 1994: 78).

Alternative economic activity to oil and gas production are becoming increasingly important to the country in its attempts to maintain economic prosperity through diversification. The Sixth National Development Plan (1991–95) highlighted this focus in allocating 10 per cent of budget to a broad heading of 'industry', covering the manufacturing and agricultural sectors. In 1991, a number of industries were granted 'pioneer' status, identifying them as the focus of the diversification programme. Interestingly, tourism is not included in this list. The impact of this diversification is relatively small and localized in scale. For example, logging in Brunei's extensive forests is confined to production for local needs only.

Brunei suffers from a contradictory labour market situation. Driven by oil revenues, per capita income is among the highest in the region if not the world but its distribution is uneven. Unemployment among Bruneians is surprisingly high and yet, at the same time, there are significant skills and manpower shortages, resulting in the presence of expatriate labour at all levels from teaching and medicine to unskilled areas such as construction and hotel work. Although this source of labour is cheaper than the employment of Bruneians, the need to import labour puts a considerable strain on the potential for extensive diversification in export terms, especially given the competitive success of neighbouring ASEAN countries. It also defeats one of the central planks of diversification, which is to create employment for Bruneians. Ameer Ali (1992) questions the viability of export-driven diversification as a realistic strategy, arguing that unless this is based upon very careful and market-driven criteria it will merely result in surplus production, which may or may not meet external market needs. He argues for import substitution as a more realistic and beneficial approach to economic diversification.

Table 5.1 Material progress, 1970–90

	1970	1978	1988	1990
Motor vehicles	14,156	43,844	110,747	126,588
Airport departures	43,091	157,767	207,200	243,600
Televisions	–	23,123	58,500	67,000
Domestic electricity	43.41mkw	167.75	489.37	533.54

Source: Cleary and Wong (1994)

Employment in Brunei is dominated by the public sector, which has grown substantially since the early 1960s and now accounts for over 50 per cent of the total of approximately 60,000 wage earners, exclusive of members of the security forces, daily-rated employees and domestic servants in private enterprises. The latter two categories include a substantial number of un-skilled expatriates. This public sector dominance reflects the seamless links that exist between the country's public and private wealth, especially in so far as the ruling family are concerned, but also points to the continuing high levels of social, educational and health-related investment made by the state as a means of improving living standards for all Bruneians.

This improved standard of living means that while the material gap between rich and poor remains considerable, overall prosperity, as measured by indices such as education, diet and access to material goods, has risen to a level that is the envy of neighbouring countries. Table 5.1 shows this progress in numerical terms.

Tourism in Brunei

Tourism does not feature as a considered option in any of the public literature on economic diversification in Brunei. In reality, dominance of the economy by oil combined with the suspicion of tourism engendered by cultural and religious considerations, means that tourism has not been encouraged as a means of economic activity up to this point and there is little evidence to suggest significant changes in policy in the future. Therefore, this lack of reference is hardly surprising.

At the same time, the potential for tourism development, in Brunei, is also limited, notwithstanding official hesitation. It is a small country with inter-esting but not outstanding natural and cultural attractions. Bruneian society, up to relatively recently, was largely water-based with communities living in water villages on stilts. Therefore, few old, historic buildings remain. The capital, Bandar Seri Begawan, is a product of the Residency period. However, Kamong Ayer, the water village dating back to the fifteenth century remains as an interesting attraction, threatened by creeping urbanization from across the river. Other resources with unexploited tourism potential include the untouched tropical rain forests and the South China Sea coastline.

Little emphasis has been placed on the development of tourism infrastructure. The country has a total of nine hotels, seven in the capital and two in the oil town of Kuala Belait. Only one is of international standard and size. The number of hotel rooms and hotel beds has remained static since the early 1980s at 587 and 1,174 respectively and these are, primarily, designed for use by business and diplomatic visitors. By contrast, air transportation has developed significantly since independence through the international airport in Bandar Seri Begawan. Royal Brunei Airlines has a rapidly expanding network at a regional and international level. The airline benefits from liberal air regulations in some neighbouring countries so that much of the capacity of the Boeing 767 flying four times per week on the London–Brunei route, for example, is devoted to Singapore-bound or originating traffic or to transit through Bandar Seri Begawan. Other regional airlines also serve the country, although the purpose is primarily Bruneian, business and 'Visiting Friends and Relatives' (VFR).

Because of the lack of interest in tourism, published information on international visitor arrivals is difficult to obtain. World Tourism Organization information provides the most comprehensive source and this shows that there was a steady increase in arrivals from 1978 to 1992, although the early 1990s saw a temporary decline (Table 5.2).

Country of origin data provides a clear indication that the actual international arrivals disguise a significant imbalance in their source, so that in the order of 80 per cent come from neighbouring Malaysia. Table 5.3 presents country and region of origin data for selected years between 1984 and 1992.

This imbalance in arrivals of visitors from ASEAN countries (454,577 in 1992) and, in particular, Malaysia points to the highly localized nature of much of this traffic. This is re-inforced if we consider the means of arrival of visitors to Brunei. Table 5.4 shows that the vast majority of visitors arrive by land or sea from neighbouring East Malaysia.

Consideration of purpose of visit data further points to the non-touristic nature of the majority of Brunei's international arrivals, particularly those

Table 5.2   Visitor arrivals to Brunei Darussalam, 1978–92

Year	Arrivals (000s)	Year	Arrivals (000s)
1978	243	1985	398
1979	258	1986	411
1980	270	1987	411
1981	287	1988	450
1982	347	1989	393
1983	361	1990	377
1984	378	1991	344
		1992	500

Source: World Tourism Organization (1994)

Table 5.3   Origin of visitors, 1984, 1988 and 1992 by region and selected countries

Region/country	1984	1988	1992
North America	4,478	4,461	4,630
Canada	1,200	1,246	2,231
USA	3,278	3,215	2,399
East Asia and Pacific	349,396	433,422	467,414
Australia	3,417	2,140	4,547
Japan	2,017	2,031	4,327
New Zealand	677	453	920
Indonesia	1,756	4,801	6,190
Malaysia	312,323	393,754	406,229
Philippines	4,145	4,839	12,839
Singapore	21,201	18,183	20,624
Thailand	2,470	4,898	8,695
Europe	17,870	14,424	22,343
France	354	813	1,483
Germany	1,194	1,096	1,298
Netherlands	2,281	1,693	3,356
Switzerland	392	436	325
United Kingdom	11,940	9,275	15,516
South Asia	2,570	3,531	5,392
India	1,462	1,601	3,150
Other	4,938	3,144	960
Total	378,010	457,410	500,259

Source: World Tourism Organization (1994)

from neighbouring Malaysia but also from some other ASEAN countries. Table 5.5 presents this information.

The dominant 'other' category includes those arriving for employment purposes and points to the high level of dependence that exists, within the Brunei economy, on unskilled labour from neighbouring countries in the region. Within conventional definitional parameters, it would be reasonable to suggest that tourist arrivals to Brunei remained at or below 50,000 per annum for the period up to 1990. However, 1991 saw a significant increase in

Table 5.4   Arrivals by mode of transport, 1984, 1988 and 1991 (000s)

Mode	1984	1988	1991
Air	77	81	66
Road	135	203	126
Sea	166	173	152

Source: World Tourism Organization (1994)

Table 5.5   Arrivals by purpose of visit, 1984, 1988 and 1991 (000s)

Purpose	1984	1988	1991
Leisure, recreation and holidays	8	9	29
Business and Professional	40	39	64
Other	n.a.	409	251

Source: World Tourism Organization (1994)

this category of arrivals to 93,000 and it is reasonable to assume that this growth has been maintained subsequently. Factors for this growth include the growing route network of Royal Brunei Airlines, providing stopover options for transiting passengers between Europe, Japan and Australia. In addition, the increasing level of expatriates in professional positions in the education and health service means that the VFR category, not identifiable within available data, is also likely to have increased.

Data on tourism expenditure is incomplete but supports the idea that only a small proportion of international arrivals can reasonably be classed as tourists. Total receipts range from US$19 million in 1985 to US$32 million in 1989, representing between $45 and $80 per person per visit. This is clearly not a valid or meaningful calculation. Use of only air arrivals data produces averages ranging from $240 to $430 per visit – rather more realistic figures. What is clear from this data is that 'true' tourism to Brunei is on a very small scale although some indications of growth are evident.

Not surprisingly, the limited level of tourism activity in Brunei is highly dependent on foreign labour. Cabin crew for Royal Brunei Airlines are recruited from all countries of ASEAN, showing determination to reflect a regional status but also the shortage of local labour willing to work in the service sector at realistic salaries by regional standards. Likewise, hotels depend on expatriate labour from the Philippines and elsewhere while management is also, largely, imported. Many restaurants are owned and operated by the Chinese community in Brunei.

This analysis suggests, rightly, that tourism is a marginal activity in Brunei for the reasons addressed earlier in this chapter. However, there is some evidence of gradual if very limited change to this scenario. A major luxury resort project is currently under construction at Jerudong, which will include an artificial ski slope. The ownership is within the royal family and its use will be highly restricted to guests of the family and to a limited number of premium visitors. As such, 'the resort is unlikely to have much impact as a means of attracting tourism to Brunei' (*Far Eastern Economic Review*, 1994). However, even on this restricted level, the development does indicate some change in policy and suggests the direction that Brunei may follow in tourism terms, seeking to attract a very small number of premium-paying visitors in a manner that does not conflict with the country's cultural ethos. (The Sultan's 50th birthday, in 1996, was an atypical event, attracting a short-stay but significant influx of foreign, high-spend visitors.)

The other development strand is represented by the country's tropical rain forest resources, the majority of which have not been commercially exploited. There is some indication that Brunei will seek to use this resource in order to attract a limited number of scientific research visitors or those interested in high cost eco-tourism. The *Universiti Brunei Darussalam*'s tropical rain forest field studies centre at Kuala Belalong already attracts scientific visitors from overseas and could form a model for further, limited development.

There is little doubt that there is a growing but very measured interest in tourism as a possible future development area. During a recent visit to Brunei by one of the authors, the level of interest expressed by Bruneian school leavers in education, training and careers within tourism was very significant and this suggests that the area is perceived to be of potential importance by the younger generation. Whether this perception becomes reality remains to be seen.

Conclusions

This chapter has focused on a case study which represents the antithesis to the mass tourism development that characterises much of ASEAN and other countries in the region. To date, Brunei has not needed tourism for economic reasons and has been reluctant to accept tourists for cultural and religious reasons. The interplay of these two considerations represents one of the most interesting dimensions in the study of tourism in Brunei and has considerable parallels to the environment found in oil-rich, Islamic countries in the Middle East.

Tourism and Brunei merit careful watching in the future as there are indications that the country will, slowly and in a carefully managed way, open its doors to a small and select number of overseas visitors, seeking to visit the country for reasons other than business or family/friends. This development is likely to be achieved through tight carrying capacity management and in a way that retains compatibility with cultural and physical environmental priorities and, as such, could constitute a model for such tourism growth.

Bibliography

Ali, A. (1992) Industrialization or industries? The vision and the viability in Brunei Darussalam. In Apong, A.B. (ed.) *Essays on Brunei Darussalam*. Bandar Seri Begawan: Universiti Brunei Darusssalam.

Aziz, A.A. (1992) Melayu Islam Beraja Sebagai Falsafah Negara Brunei Darussalam. In Apong, A.B. (ed.) *Essays on Brunei Darussalam*. Bandar Seri Begawan: Universiti Brunei Darusssalam.

Cleary, M. and Wong, S.Y. (1994) *Oil, Economic Development and Diversification of Brunei Darussalam*. London: MacMillan.

Din, K. (1989) Islam and tourism: patterns, issues and options. *Annals of Tourism Research* **16**, 542–63.

Far Eastern Economic Review (1994) *Asia 1994 Yearbook*. Hong Kong: FEER.

Information Department, Government of Negara Brunei Darussalam (undated) *Brunei Darussalam in Brief*. Bandar Seri Begawan: Information Department.

World Tourism Organisation/Inskeep, E. (1994) *National and Regional Tourism Planning*. London: Routledge.

6

China: Economic liberalization and tourism development – the case of the People's Republic of China

CARSON L. JENKINS
ZHEN-HUA LIU

Introduction

With a population of 1.2 billion consisting of 56 nationalities, a recorded history of over 5,000 years, and a territory of 9.6 million square kilometres, China is well endowed with cultural and natural tourist resources. However, tourism in China is still a relatively new phenomenon as it did not assume any priority in the government's agenda and had not been developed into a mass industry until the late 1970s.

During the last one and half decades, tourism in China enjoyed a rapid expansion hardly experienced in any other country. Tourist arrivals from abroad increased from 1.8 million in 1978 to 41.5 million in 1993, while its tourism receipts increased from 263 million to 4,683 million US dollars over the same period. Tourism has now become a significant sector in the national economy and China is ranked among the top ten international tourist destinations.

In this chapter, the authors attempt to analyse some of the important aspects of tourism development in China. Beginning with a brief examination of the historical development of the international tourism industry in China, the chapter analyses the broad conditions and impacts of tourism development in China; discusses the major policy issues in tourism development, including foreign investment, government control, domestic tourism, service quality, training and marketing; and finally, explores the future development prospects of tourism in China.

History of Growth

Tourist contacts between China and the West may be traced to the period before the opening up of the 'Silk Road' over 2,000 years ago, but as an integrated business undertaking, tourism in China began only as recently as 1923 when the first travel agency was established in Shanghai.

Travel to China during the first three decades after the founding of the People's Republic of China was strictly controlled. In the 1950s, foreign tourists were mainly 'Visiting Friends and Relatives' (VFR) overseas Chinese and a limited number of holidaymakers from the socialist-block countries, as travel to China was discouraged by the Chinese government by the imposition of strict visa controls, and was forbidden by certain Western governments, for example USA. But following the establishment of diplomatic relations with more countries and the breakdown of Sino-Soviet relations, China began to receive more Western tourists after 1960.

The China International Travel Service (CITS), established in 1954, was the main government body at national level and served as both a government tour operator and the national tourism organization before the establishment of the China Bureau of Travel and Tourism (CBTT), the predecessor of the present China National Tourism Administration (CNTA). In 1965 foreign tourist arrivals numbered 12,877, the highest number received by CITS for ten years. However, the turmoil of the Cultural Revolution began in 1966, and during the following ten years tourism in and to China was virtually suspended.

Prior to 1978, tourism in China was not thought of as an industry but considered as 'a part of foreign affairs', as the government's main objectives on international tourism were political rather than commercial. It was essentially a public relations exchange with representatives of a few friendly countries. Because of this the CBTT was the responsibility of the Foreign Ministry, and local tourist issues were handled by the local foreign affairs offices. With the introduction of reform and the open-door policy since 1978, tourism has become a vital economic force to earn foreign exchange for China's Modernization. The government has attached great importance to tourism and has taken a series of measures to actively develop the industry.

In 1978, the CBTT was upgraded to ministerial level and renamed the State General Administration for Travel and Tourism (SGATT). Since then, local tourist bureaus have been set up in the various provinces, autonomous areas and municipalities directly under the central government and many tourist cities and counties. In 1981, the SGATT began to establish its overseas offices in major tourist markets. In 1983, the current name, China National Tourism Administration (CNTA), was adopted. The Tourism Coordination Group was established in 1986 within the State Council taking charge of coordination at ministry level, which was replaced by the National Tourism Committee (NTC) two years later.

In 1986, for the first time ever, tourism as an industry was included in the national plan for social and economic development – the Seventh Five-Year Plan 1986–90. The government prioritized seven key tourist cities and provinces in tourist investment: Beijing, Shanghai, Xi'an, Guilin, Hangzhou, Jiangsu and Guangdong Province (including Hainan Island until 1988 when the latter was upgraded to province level). The targets set were to enable the country to receive 3 million foreign tourists in 1990 and 7–8 million in the year 2000, making China one of the top tourist destinations of the world.

The development of international tourism from 1978 to 1988 was impressive as it recorded a 16.5 times increase in tourist arrivals and 7.5 times increase in tourism receipts, representing an annual growth rate of 33.15 per cent and 23.93 per cent respectively. There was little doubt that the planned targets could be easily reached. However, this growth momentum was suddenly broken down by the well-publicized event which happened on 4 June 1989 on the Tiananmen Square. It was anticipated by some Western experts that China's tourism receipts in that year would fall by 75 per cent (Lavery, 1989: 96) and it was even questioned 'will anyone want to go to China?' (Wei *et al.*, 1989: 322). Nevertheless, China's tourism industry responded to this event exceptionally well as it only experienced a decline of 17 per cent in receipts in 1989 and fully recovered two years later. This success can be attributed mainly to the continued commitment of the government to reform and open-door policies; the rapid growth of the Chinese economy; and the industry's successful responding strategies in terms of product development, market positioning and overseas promotion.

In an effort to transform China's traditional sightseeing tourism to a combination of sightseeing and holidaymaking and to realize the goals of achieving 10 billion US dollars in tourism receipts by the year 2000, in 1992 the State Council decided to construct national holiday resorts and gave a series of favourable policies for resort areas in development and encouraged foreign investment. The 11 approved national holiday resorts started infrastructure construction in 1993. Table 6.1 below lists the key events of tourism development in China.

Statistical Analysis

Tourist statistics pre-1978 are almost non-existent, and no arrivals and receipts figures are available. Since 1978 there have been dramatic increases in arrivals and in tourism receipts. As Table 6.2 shows, total tourist arrivals increased from 1.8 million in 1978 to 41.5 million in 1993, of which foreign tourists increased from 0.2 to 4.7 million, representing an average annual growth rate of 23.23 per cent and 23.06 per cent respectively. Tourism receipts also enjoyed a 17-fold increase, from 263 million to 4,683 million dollars over the same period, representing an average annual growth rate of 21.17 per cent.

The growth trend of China's international tourism industry has been quite consistent during the past 16 years, it only experienced one decline – in 1989, tourist arrivals decreased by 22.7 per cent and tourism receipts reduced by 17.2 per cent. In all the other years, it enjoyed rapid expansion in both arrivals and receipts with annual growth rates well over 10 per cent with the exception of two years – 1982 and 1993 (see Figure 6.1).

There are, loosely, three categories of overseas visitors to China. Foreign travellers of non-Chinese origin are grouped into the 'foreigners' category. Chinese travellers from abroad are classified into two categories, 'overseas Chinese' and 'Compatriots' from Hong Kong, Macau and Taiwan; separate statistics were kept for visitors from Taiwan since 1988. Compatriots are by far the largest group which accounted for 88 per cent of the total visitor arrivals in China in 1993; while foreigners accounted for 11 per cent of arrivals. In terms of the contribution to tourism receipts, the Compatriots' role tends to be much less significant as most of them are VFRs, excursionists or simply cross-border day-trippers who spend much less. On the contrary,

Table 6.1   Main events in China's tourism development

Year	Event
1949	Establishment of the People's Republic of China
1953	Establishment of Beijing Overseas Chinese Travel Service
1954	Establishment of China International Travel Service (CITS)
1963	Establishment of Overseas Chinese Travel Service
1964	Establishment of China Bureau of Travel and Tourism under Foreign Affairs Office within the State Council
1966	Beginning of the Cultural Revolution
1974	Establishment of China Travel Service (CTS) to replace Overseas Chinese Travel Service
1976	Death of Chairman Mao. End of the Cultural Revolution
1978	Reform and Open-door policy adopted
	Upgrading of CBTT to ministerial level renamed SGATT
	Provincial Travel and Tourism Bureaus established
1980	Establishment of China Youth Travel Service (CYTS)
1981	Limited decentralization of tour operation
	China Tourist Offices began to be established abroad
1982	First joint-venture hotel, Jianguo Hotel, opened in Beijing
1983	SGATT changed into China National Tourism Administration (CNTA)
1984	Decentralization of authority for visas, tour sales and operations
1985	Tourism was incorporated into the Seventh Five-Year Plan (1986–90)
	Travel agencies allowed to be established by collectives or private citizens
1986	Tourism Coordination Group established, which was replaced by the National Tourism Committee in 1988
1988	Tourist hotel star-rating began
1989	First major set-back since 1978 after the 4 June Tiananmen Square event
1992	The State Council emphasized domestic tourism
	The State Council approved the construction of national holiday resorts

Source: Gao and Zhang (1983), Choy and Can (1988), China National Administration

Table 6.2 Annual tourist arrivals in People's Republic of China, 1978–93

Year	Total arrivals	Foreigners	Overseas Chinese	Compatriots* Total	Of which Taiwan	Tourism receipts (US$ mil.)
1978	1,809,221	229,646	18,092	1,561,483	–	262.90
1979	4,203,901	362,389	20,910	3,820,602	–	449.27
1980	5,702,536	529,124	34,413	5,138,999	–	616.65
1981	7,767,096	675,153	38,856	7,053,087	–	784.91
1982	7,924,261	762,497	42,745	7,117,019	–	843.17
1983	9,477,005	872,511	40,352	8,564,142	–	941.20
1984	12,852,185	1,134,267	47,498	11,670,420	–	1,131.34
1985	17,833,097	1,370,462	84,827	16,377,808	–	1,250.00
1986	22,819,450	1,482,276	68,133	21,269,041	–	1,530.85
1987	26,902,267	1,727,821	87,031	25,087,415	–	1,861.51
1988	31,694,804	1,842,206	79,348	29,773,250	437,700	2,246.83
1989	24,501,394	1,460,970	68,556	22,971,868	541,000	1,860.48
1990	27,461,821	1,747,315	91,090	25,623,416	948,000	2,217.58
1991	33,349,757	2,710,103	133,427	30,506,227	946,632	2,844.97
1992	38,114,945	4,006,427	165,077	33,943,441	1,317,770	3,946.87
1993	41,526,945	4,655,857	166,182	36,704,906	1,526,969	4,683.17

Source: China National Administration
* Compatriots from Hong Kong, Macau and Taiwan.

foreign tourists stay longer and spend more per capita touring throughout the country. Consequently, they are the ones targeted by the industry for bringing in foreign exchange and most of the tourism infrastructure development is directed at this group.

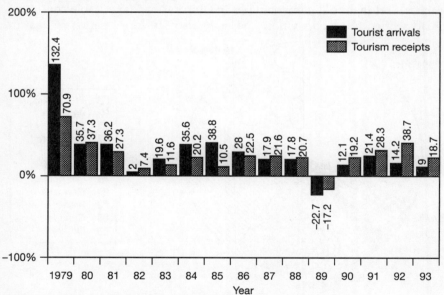

Figure 6.1 Annual growth rates of tourist arrivals and receipts, 1979–93.
Source: Data from China National Administration.

Half of China's foreign tourists are from Asian countries and 34 per cent are from Europe. Figure 6.2 indicates the composition of foreign tourists in 1993. The former USSR and Japan rank as the largest foreign markets in terms of arrivals, followed by the United States. These three countries altogether account for 48 per cent of all foreign arrivals. Clearly, in terms of tourism receipts, the former USSR is less important than Japan and USA as most of its visitors to China are cross-border day-trippers. The former USSR is also the fastest growing market of tourist arrivals in China, which during the last ten years increased over 100 times; Singapore, Thailand and Germany increased more than 5 times; while Japan and USA increased by 244 per cent and 138 per cent respectively.

Current Conditions

The current conditions of tourism development in China will be presented in this section according to the five components of tourism supply, the 5As – attractions, amenities, access, agencies and administration.

Attractions

The tourist resources of China are notable in its numerous and fascinating natural and cultural attractions. China's natural conditions are complex and diversified, with beautiful landscapes and scenic spots spread all over the country. Mountains, rivers, lakes, hot springs, waterfalls, caves and grottoes, beaches, and manifold climatic types in China afford favourable conditions for diversified tourist activities. There are also 510 forest parks, 760 nature

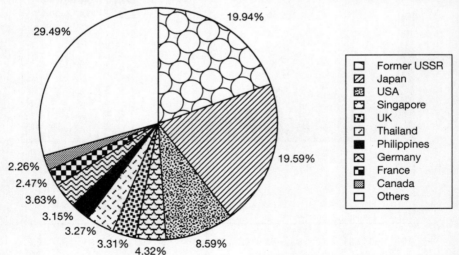

Figure 6.2 The composition of international tourist market of China 1993.
Source: Data from China National Administration.

reserves, 480 scenic areas, and 110 botanic gardens, which receive millions of visitors every year.

With a recorded history of over 5,000 years, China has carried within itself the heritage of a resplendent culture that goes back to ancient times. In particular, the Great Wall, the Grand Canal, the Forbidden City and the Terracotta Warriors are known as some of the wonders of the world. China also has 99 national historic cultural cities and 500 national heritage sites. Chinese cuisine, herbal medicine and traditional treatment, arts and handicrafts, the Chinese language and daily life, are all things overseas tourists like to see, to know and to have. As a united multinational country of 56 nationalities, China has rich and colourful national traditions, festivals, lifestyles and local habits.

Since the early 1980s the Chinese government, both central and local, has invested billions of yuan in the development, renovation and protection of the historical sites and scenic tourist spots in the more than 1000 cities and towns now open to foreign visitors. In recent years, many purpose-built tourist attractions have opened to the public, such as the Magnificent China and China Folk Customs Village in Shenzhen and the Europe Garden in Wuxi. Events for attracting overseas tourists like traditional festival celebrations (e.g. lantern festival, boat-racing, kite festival, etc.) and art festivals of various kinds (e.g. acrobatics, operas, movies, etc) have been arranged.

Accommodation

The undercapacity and poor standard of the hotel industry was the bottleneck to tourism development when China opened its door to the world. In order to rapidly increase the hotel capacity, an investment policy for tourist hotels was set up focusing on the renovation and construction of tourist hotels in joint ventures with foreign investors, and using the collective capital of central and local government.

As a result, the rate of construction of tourist hotels in China has been very fast. While in 1980 there were only 203 tourist hotels in the whole country offering 31,788 rooms, by 1993, the number of hotels and rooms had risen to 2,552 and 386,000 respectively. This means an average annual increase in room numbers of 21.17 per cent, far surpassing the annual growth of 16.50 per cent in tourist arrivals during the same period. At present, there are 88 new luxury tourist hotels in construction, with 25,600 rooms and total investment of 1.88 billion dollars. Tourist accommodation is the area of the industry that has improved most over the past 16 years, largely as a result of foreign participation, which has brought both world-class facilities and international management practices to China.

The rapid growth of hotel accommodation has given rise to low occupancy rates since the mid-1980s. It has also been argued that the imbalance of hotel supply in terms of spatial and especially grade structure has made the situation worse because the oversupply of luxury hotels coexisted with an underprovision of medium-price and budget hotels that are of a quality acceptable to overseas tourists. Nevertheless, the CNTA officials believe that the 1:3:6 ratio between high, medium and low grades of the 1,223 star-rated hotels is in accordance with China's tourism development needs and its national conditions; it is also compatible with the demand of various domestic and international tourists. The claim of overprovision of tourist accommodation in China (e.g. Mings, 1989; Zhang, 1989; Zhao 1989) could also be questioned as the increase in foreign tourist arrivals has surpassed the growth of hotel rooms by a large margin since 1990. During the first quarter of 1994 in particular, hotel room rates in Beijing and Shanghai increased by 95 per cent and 75 per cent respectively over the same period last year, caused by the shortage of rooms currently and expected in the near future.

Access

China's much criticized aviation industry has been viewed as a major constraint to its tourism development. However, attempts to restructure the industry and to decentralize air operations have been made and there is substantial investment in new aircraft and airports.

Over the past 45 years, the number of air routes has increased dramatically. The country had only 12 routes in 1949 and 167 routes in 1978. By the end of 1993, China had 647 routes, including 71 international, the majority of which had satisfied the demand of passengers. There are also some 30 foreign airlines that have opened routes to China. Civil aviation passenger turnover in China increased from 2.8 in 1978 to 51.5 billion/person/kilometres in 1993, which means a average annual growth rate of 21.43 per cent.

The civil aviation fleet has finished the transition from one primarily consisting of small and medium-sized aircraft to one with advanced medium and large-sized aircraft as the backbone. China's 17 airlines now have a fleet of 754 modern aircraft, including 164 Boeings and 340 airplanes with over 100 seats; total civil aviation seats available exceed 60,000. It is estimated by Boeing that China is currently receiving one sixth of the new Boeing aircrafts and it will become the third largest aviation market in the world, just after the USA and Japan (*People's Daily*, 8 August 1994). At present there are 110 civil airports in operation (over half of which were built or expanded since 1978), over 60 of which are capable of accommodating passenger planes to the size of a Boeing 737.

Given the sheer size of China and the low levels of car ownership and air capacity, rail travel is by far the most common form of domestic travel. Railway open to traffic has reached more than 57,000 kilometres, which is used for 70 per cent of the freight and 60 per cent of passenger transportation of China. All major tourist cities and scenic spots of the country are linked by railways. The railway department has been meeting the challenge of the increased flow of tourists by adding soft berth, air-conditioned carriages, more runs, arranging special train services for tourists and additional passenger trains during peak times. Currently, 46 special tourist trains run to tourist attractions seasonally or all year round. There are more than 20,000 luxury coaches, mostly imported, in use by tourist companies. Taxicabs in the major cities have increased even faster.

Despite the rapid development of transport in China since 1978, due to the large size and population of the country, the booming economy and the rapid increase in overseas tourists, transport now seems to remain the bottleneck in China's tourism development since the hotel undercapacity has largely been tackled. In particular, transport facilities have become seriously lacking in the major tourist cities and routes during peak seasons when congestion, overcrowding and overbooking occur.

Travel agencies

Travel to China has been affected by the early development of two separate government-operated travel agencies based upon the type of traveller to be served. CITS was established in 1954 to handle foreign (i.e., non-Chinese) travellers and CTS was established in 1953 to handle primarily Chinese travellers from abroad.

CITS, the biggest nationwide international travel enterprise, is under the direct control of CNTA. Its volume of business has increased each year, from 124,000 visitors in 1978 to 647,000 in 1992. The China Travel Service (CTS), as well as its predecessors, is under the direct control of the Overseas Chinese Affairs Office (OCAO). CTS received 562,000 overseas visitors in 1978 and 962,000 in 1992. The China Youth Travel Service (CYTS), set up in 1980, belongs to the tourist department of the Chinese All-Nation Youth Union. Its chief objectives are to develop friendly relations between Chinese youth and the youth of the world. The number of tourists from abroad organized by CYTS increased from 11,000 in 1980 to 150,000 in 1992.

Local tourist corporations have been formed since 1980 to build tourist facilities and provide travel services at local and provincial levels. Up to 1983, however, only CITS, CTS and CYTS as class I agencies were allowed to handle foreign arrivals. In 1985, central government regulations were issued allowing collectives and private citizens to operate travel agencies. Privately owned travel agencies typically were allowed to handle only domestic tourists as class III agencies. Collectively owned agencies could register either as class I agencies, which were permitted to receive all types of tourists, or as class II agencies, which were restricted to handling only Chinese tourists, that is, overseas Chinese, Compatriots and domestic tourists. Now, a nationwide network of more than 3,000 travel services has been set up to handle international and domestic tourist businesses. Among the 3,086 travel agencies, 285 were class I agencies, 721 were class II agencies and 2,080 were class III agencies. Clearly, competition with the previous three key national agencies to handle foreign tourists has intensified from provincial bureaus, local tourist corporations, and new class I travel agencies.

As China is becoming more open, visa and border formalities more simplified and easier, and tourists more experienced, the proportion of independent travellers is increasing and the dominance of travel agencies in receiving tourists appears to be declining. This statement could be supported by two facts. The first is that the number of organized tourists has been increasing more slowly than that of tourist arrivals since 1978, the former had an average annual growth rate of 15.91 per cent compared with 23.23 per cent of the latter. Consequently, the share of organized tourists in total tourist arrivals declined during the last 16 years, from 42.34 per cent in 1978 to 16.59 per cent in 1992 (see Table 6.3).

The second fact is that the share of tourists organized by non-tourist organizations has increased rapidly, from 10.44 per cent in 1978 to 50.34 per cent in 1992. As Table 6.3 shows, government departments handled more arrivals in 1992 than the combined totals for all travel agencies, especially the foreigners category of which 68 per cent was received by government departments. Another change is that the relative importance of the three key travel agencies – CITS, CTS and CYTS – has also been reduced substantially as the share of other tourist agencies increased rapidly.

Administration

The CNTA is the government body responsible, under the State Council, for national tourism development including formulation of policies, plans and overseas promotion. The main function of CNTA is to develop short-term and long-term policies for the development of tourism in China. It acts as the primary tourism planning, coordinating, regulatory and administrative body at the national level. CNTA also represents China in international organizations and at international gatherings relating to tourism. However, the introduction of complete decentralization in 1984 gives CNTA only

Table 6.3   Tourists received by travel agencies and other organizations (000s)

	All tourists			Foreign tourists		
	1978	*1985*	*1992*	*1978*	*1985*	*1992*
Tourist arrivals	1,809	17,833	38,115	230	1,370	4,006
Organized tourists	766	3,009	6,326	230	1,370	3,827
By travel companies	686	2,360	3,141	152	936	1,225
CITS	124	469	647	124	469	576
CTS	562	773	962	28	169	255
CYTS	–	52	150	–	25	100
Other tourist corporations	–	1,066	1,382	–	273	294
By other organizations	80	649	3,185	78	434	2,603

Source: Data from the China National Administration

limited control, and often no control at all, over travel agencies, other than the CITS Head Office which is under its direct control, tourism facilities, branch offices and provincial or city tourism bureaux.

Although CNTA is the national body for tourism administration, the air, rail, road and water transportation is controlled by the CAAC, the Ministry of Railways and the Ministry of Transportation respectively. This is said by CNTA officials to be one of the major obstacles to the coordination of the travel industry. All governments of provinces, autonomous regions, and cities under direct jurisdiction have set up their own tourist bureaux of government agencies. This also leads to difficulties in coordinating tourism development between regions and sectors across the country and the industry.

The National Tourism Committee (NTC) is the tourism coordination organization at the ministry level. Headed by one of the vice premiers and including officials representing all tourism-related industries and areas, the responsibilities of the NTC are 'to formulate principles, policies and legislation concerning tourism' and 'to approve large tourist construction projects'.

Sectoral Contribution

As a sector providing employment, generating foreign exchange, and support for heritage renovation and conservation, tourism has had many positive effects on China's economic and social development.

First, it has generated significant amounts of badly needed foreign exchange. From 1978 to 1993, China's international tourism industry generated a total of US$ 27.5 billion in foreign exchange. In 1993 its tourism receipts were 4.68 billion, the largest invisible trade earnings, which accounted for 5.1 per cent of China's total exports and about 1 per cent of its GDP (*People's Daily*, 2 March 1994).

Secondly, it has provided more employment opportunities. The number of people directly involved in the industry has exceeded one and half a million. At present, the international tourism industry alone employs 880,000 people directly. If the domestic travel and hotel sectors are included, this figure reaches 2.4 million.

Thirdly, it has helped to diversify the national economy and promote regional economic development. As a service industry, its interaction with other sectors has stimulated development far beyond the industry itself. It has also made a significant contribution to the development of transportation, communication, urban construction, commerce, public utilities, and industries manufacturing tourist goods. The rapid development of international and domestic tourism in China has also opened up an important channel to invigorate the local economies of many tourist cities and areas, expand regional economic ties and exchange of information.

Fourthly, it has served to preserve and revitalize traditional crafts and cultural relics. International tourism development in particular provides a much needed boost to the restoration and renovation of the cultural heritage after years of depredation by the Red Guards during the Cultural Revolution. Tourism's stimulus to arts and cultural preservation may also be seen as supporting a source of national pride.

Finally, it has expanded international cooperation, promoting friendship and understanding between the Chinese people and the people of the world. Tourism is also a way of wooing overseas Chinese, especially those from Taiwan; the large tourist flow across the Taiwan Straits since 1988 is a significant force in the possible reunification of the mainland and Taiwan. Since 1978, 314 million people visited China.

As experienced in many other developing countries, tourism development in China has also brought about negative impacts on Chinese society. Foreign influences, of which face-to-face encounters with foreign tourists are an important source, are causing dramatic changes to family ties, work ethics, social relations, to social value and belief systems. It has caused rising materialism, a decay in traditional values and doubt about the system as many, especially the young, perceive that the institutions and values of Western societies are superior. In particular, the subtle form of enclave tourism in which 'Chinese and tourists are kept apart under a system of portable apartheid' (Richter 1989: 47) has led to a strong feeling of loss of national pride. The 'demonstration effect' of tourism has caused changes not only in social values but more importantly in lifestyles, which has significant adverse effects on the Chinese economy because of the strong demand for imported consumer goods.

Tourism growth has particularly been blamed for increases in venereal disease, prostitution, pornography, drug addiction and drug trafficking. Prostitution and drug addiction were wiped out in China in the early 1950s and did not reappear in the 1980s, while now prostitution is becoming a major social problem. In 1993 alone there were 26,191 drug trafficking cases, involving people numbered at 40,834 (*People's Daily*, 23 June 1994).

Major Policy Issues

The tourism policy of China was largely cautious and often negative during its first 30 years of existence. However, great importance has been attached to the industry by the government since 1978 and a series of measures have been taken to develop tourist facilities and attract overseas visitors. Some of the important policy issues are discussed below.

Foreign involvement

In building the infrastructure for tourism, the central government has put a great deal of stress on encouraging the initiatives of local governments, collectives, individuals, and in particular using foreign capital and management expertise.

In introducing foreign capital and management to develop tourism, the hotel sector took the lead. This is because hotel undercapacity appeared to be the critical issue in tourism development when China began to expand its tourism industry in the late 1970s. Meanwhile, hotels in China proved to be extremely lucrative investments for foreign capital since they combined high demand, low building costs and cheap labour, with the ease of repatriating profits.

Encouraged by the success of the Jianguo Hotel, which was the first joint-venture hotel opened in Beijing in 1982, many foreign hotel chains started their involvement in the construction and management of hotels in China. As a result, of the 2,354 hotels and 351,044 rooms available for tourists at the end of 1992, 476 hotels with 100,209 rooms were with some form of foreign involvement. This means that 28.5 per cent of all hotel rooms in China have an element of overseas investment (see Table 6.4).

According to CNTA, tourism has become the industry with the highest proportion of foreign investment. By the end of April 1994, foreign companies had invested over 10 billion dollars (while the total foreign investment in China was 76.6 billion) in China's hotels, tourist transportation, tourist commodity development, scenic spot construction, tourist amusement and entertainment, restaurants and food services. At present, 53.3 per cent of the total investment in tourism comes directly from foreign capital, if one includes the planned foreign capital usage target, this figure will be as high as 72.9 per cent, the highest among all the industries in China.

Table 6.4   Breakdown of tourist hotels by ownership 1992

Hotel ownership	Hotels	Rooms	Beds	Occupancy (%)	Total revenue (yuan mil.)	Fixed capital (yuan mil.)
Total	2,354	351,044	737,674	66.22	26,480.5	45,022.8
Domestic-owned	**1,878**	**250,835**	**551,592**	**67.09**	**13,605.4**	**22,126.2**
State-owned	1,683	230,660	506,954	66.99	12,519.2	20,331.9
Domestic joint venture	7	1,207	2,506	71.50	93.6	235.1
Collective	184	18,886	41,950	68.05	987.4	1,555.5
Private	4	82	182	63.41	5.3	3.7
Foreign-invested	**476**	**100,209**	**186,082**	**64.05**	**12,875.1**	**22,896.6**
Foreign owned	8	1,686	2,773	55.75	147.1	624.4
Sino-foreign joint venture	246	54,496	99,253	63.04	6,517.2	13,875.1
Sino-foreign cooperative	222	44,027	84,056	65.62	6,210.8	8,397.1

Source: Data from China National Administration

To date, overseas involvement in China's hotel sector has undergone a transformation from the initial provision of special purpose government loans to a range of more diversified types of international participation. There is a large variety of overseas involvement now permitted: international commercial loans, joint ventures, cooperative operations, sole foreign invested business, and foreign management agreements (Economist Intelligence Unit, 1989; Yu, 1992).

Many well-known hotel chains, such as Sheraton, Hilton, Holiday Inn and Shangri-La, have joined the management of hotels in China. At present 80 per cent of the five-star hotels are run by foreign hotel management companies. China is also in cooperation with a French hotel management company in an attempt to establish a standardized below three-stars hotel management chain. Without any doubt, the introduction of foreign investment and management in the hotel sector has not only speeded up the increase in hotel capacity, but, more importantly, has also brought with it worldwide operational experience, scientific management skills and modern high technology. Therefore, using foreign management corporations is necessary and beneficial in the development process of the hotel sector.

However, in order to reduce the foreign dominance and high management costs in hotel operations, domestic hotel management companies are encouraged by the CNTA. The 16 domestic hotel management companies that have emerged since 1984, such as Jinjiang in Shanghai, Jinlin in Nanjing and the White Swan in Guangzhou, have already developed Chinese-style international hotel management systems and offered management services to other hotels, hoping to develop Chinese hotel chains. In hotels managed by foreign companies and along with the maturing of Chinese personnel, the number of foreign employees has been decreasing in an effort to reduce costs and foreign exchange leakages. For instance, the Sheraton-managed Great Wall Hotel in Beijing reduced its foreign employees from over 80 in the beginning to 14 now, and Huatin Hotel in Shanghai from 69 to 9.

Competition and decentralization

For a long time, the official travel services (CITS and CTS) were the only tour operators and travel agencies. All contacts and sales to foreign tour operators were monopolized and centralized in the head offices of CITS and CTS in Beijing. In an effort to increase competition and efficiency and as part of a more general effort to diffuse decision making to lower levels, the limited decentralization of travel operation began in 1980. Provincial administrations were given authority to establish contact directly with tour operators and branch offices were given control over the distribution of visas. From 1984, complete decentralization of authority was granted to local travel bureaux to process visas, develop tour packages, determine prices and independently finance their operations. Collectives and private individuals were allowed to operate travel agencies beginning in 1985, though privately owned travel agencies were only allowed to handle domestic tourists. By the end of the 1980s, an open, multi-channelled tourist operating system came into being with a dozen national key tour operators and some 1,000 travel agencies in three different categories.

There are now 3,086 travel agencies in China, nearly double the number of 1991: 285 of which are of the category I type that liaise with foreign tour operators directly and notify visa-issuing authorities as well as receiving all kinds of overseas visitors to China; 721 are of the category II type that do not deal directly with overseas tour operators but receive visitors from abroad who are either organized by the category I agencies or come to China independently; and the remaining 2,080 are in the third category of the travel agencies that may be owned by both public and private sectors and are solely in the business of domestic tourism. It is also worthwhile to note that in recent years, the first two types of agencies are also engaged in organizing domestic travel.

Similar reforms have been conducted in the air transport sector since 1984. The structural change since 1980 splits the policy making function of the China Civil Aviation Administration (CAAC) from the civil aviation operation, and from airport management. To introduce an element of competition and encourage greater productivity and better service, CAAC was divided into six regional carriers and a dozen other new airlines were allowed to operate.

Obviously, decentralization has helped enliven the trade, but it has also brought about negative impacts. Travel agencies seem to be competing against each other by cutting prices rather than promoting the destination as a whole. The proliferation of travel organizations created confusion as prices and service quality vary greatly among different agencies and no national standards were implemented. Decentralization has allowed each province, city and area not only to package its own tours, but also to seek foreign investment for developing tourist facilities on a joint venture basis. Both government and private investment throughout the country were not well coordinated and with very little integration of infrastructure, transportation, trained manpower and other required resources.

Decentralization has also made the coordination of tourism operation and development for the country more important and more difficult. The CNTA and NTC need to exercise more authority to coordinate between government departments, administrative areas and industrial sectors so that tourist operations, planning and development, utilization and protection of tourist resources and construction of infrastructure can be well integrated and balanced. The industry needs to develop official categories that communicate the quality of attractions, accommodation services and tour packages ranging from deluxe to budget based on international standards. Necessary regulations should be established and implemented in order to provide a fair and attractive macro-environment for the operation of tourist business.

Domestic tourism

Domestic tourism is usually the predecessor of international tourism. In China, however, it received little attention, if any, until the mid-1980s. This is because for a long time, most Chinese people had little discretionary income and no long holidays. For a long time leisure travel was considered the lifestyle of the bourgeoisie, which was not socially sanctioned but criticized by the government (Zhang, 1989). Even after 1978, domestic tourism was initially restricted mainly due to the conviction that, especially in peak periods, domestic tourists compete with international tourists for the under-supplied transport, space at tourist attractions and supplies.

Consequently, China did not devote any of its scarce resources to domestic tourism and the CNTA was virtually not involved in domestic tourism prior to 1983. With increasing disposable income, the introduction of paid vacations, the relaxation in political control, and the impact of the growth of international tourism, leisure travel became fashionable among the newly emerged wealthier people and in the prosperous coastal area. Domestic tourism became a widespread billion yuan business with millions of participants since the mid-1980s. To coordinate the growth of both international and domestic tourism, a special Domestic Travel and Tourism Department was set up within CNTA.

In 1992, the Party Central Committee and the State Council made the decision to speed up the development of the tertiary industry, which resulted in the fast growth of the third category travel services that mainly handle domestic tourists. Most of the first and second-category travel services also set up departments for domestic tourism. There are now more than 3,000 travel services handling domestic tourist business, whereas hardly any full-time domestic tourism organizations existed before 1980. This helped bring about a breakthrough in domestic tourism development, especially in cities and coastal areas. One survey in the economically booming Guangdong province in 1993 reported that 100 per cent of the respondents considered travel as their favourite leisure activity. Of the workers in that province, 60 per cent took at least one domestic holiday in 1993 (*People's Daily*, 4 February 1994).

Nevertheless, domestic tourism in China is still at an early stage with only a small proportion of the population involved and with low spending levels. Although there are no reliable data available yet on domestic tourism, it is officially estimated that in 1986, 270 million people participated in domestic tourism, which generated an income of 10 billion yuan; by 1993, the figures were 350 million and 32 billion respectively, which represents an annual growth rate of 3.78 per cent in tourists and 18.08 per cent in income.

Although the majority of domestic tourists are independent travellers, more and more are joining inclusive tours for the convenience and guaranteed accommodation and transport facilities. According to data collected from the 2,456 travel services in China that were handling domestic travel in 1992, the number of organized travellers was 105.6 million, 7.24 times over the previous year. Domestic tourism is now being transformed from simply spontaneous travel to one marketed and organized by travel services.

Besides domestic travel, outbound international travel has also been developed rapidly since the late 1980s. The Chinese government approved its citizens' VFR travel to Hong Kong and Macau in 1983 and opened VFR travel to Singapore, Malaysia and Thailand and border tourism 'day trips' to neighbouring countries in 1988. Along with the development of the economy, the improvement in living standards, the booming of border trade, and the relaxing of outbound travel formalities, travelling abroad is becoming a new fashion and outbound tourism is developing rapidly. In 1993, 3.5 million people from China went abroad for business and holiday travel, of which 1.45 million were self-supported holidaymakers. Among the 960,000 organized tourists in 1993, 484,000 joined Hong Kong and Macao tours, 476,000 joined tours to other countries, including 330,000 to Russia, Vietnam and Myanmar and 140,000 to Thailand, Malaysia and Singapore. With the rapid expansion of domestic and outbound travel flows, tourism in China is being transformed from only receiving inbound tourists to combining inbound tourist reception and domestic and outbound travel operation.

Concentration and diffusion

Like many other countries, China looks upon tourism as an effective means of regional development, particularly the economy of backward and remote regions with substantial tourism potential. The most obvious attempt of the government to diffuse overseas visitor flows and allow areas throughout the country to benefit from tourism has been the striking increase in the number of cities open to foreign tourists. In 1979, only 60 cities were open to foreigners, by 1987 this had increased to 496, and in mid-1994, the number reached 1147, including many cities and towns in minority regions like Xinjiang and Tibet (*People's Daily*, 14 June 1994).

However, in view of limited investment capital to build the necessary tourist infrastructure, the laudable desire to defuse tourism gains around the country by opening up more and more cities simply over-stretched an already inadequate tourist infrastructure. This rapid diffusion process has also encouraged false hopes in many backward regions where luxury hotels have been built at the expense of other more productive investments, such as transportation, agriculture and manufacturing industries, and with low occupancy rates. An analysis of the spatial distribution of tourism receipts indicates that the benefits of tourism development are still concentrated in a few key regions as the top eight cities and provinces received four-fifths of the tourist dollars earned from international tourism in 1993, while the remaining 22 provinces and regions, with 40 per cent of the national hotel capacity, accounted for only 20 per cent of the total tourism receipts.

Clearly, greater efforts should be devoted to creating a master national plan for tourism development and a realistic timetable for staging and diffusing the development process. Investment should be concentrated on the main tourist centres so that tourism development is kept in the key tourism areas and spread out step by step in a planned way in line with market demand and local conditions (Zhang, 1989: 60).

Conclusion

There is little doubt that tourism in China will have a promising future. Overall, the trend of rapid expansion is expected to continue well into the next century while the growth rate may not be as high as it was in the 1980s. This claim could be justified by a brief analysis of the key elements from both the demand and supply sides of China's tourism industry.

With regard to the market demand, three key trends will help China to maintain its development momentum well beyond the 1990s. First, the rapid growth of the East Asian and Pacific region in terms of both per capita income and outbound travel flow, together with the shift in popularity of destinations for the world mass tourist market from America–Europe to Asia and the Pacific will certainly improve China's locational advantage as a tourist destination and bring new visitors to China. Second, the fast growing Chinese economy (which has enjoyed an annual growth rate of over 9 per cent since 1978) will continue to stimulate business travel flows to China and enhance China's image as an attractive business and holiday destination. An increasingly prosperous population and especially the emerging of a middle class in coastal areas will soon produce a substantial domestic travel market more closely integrated with the international tourist market. Third, the return of Hong Kong in 1997 and Macau in 1999 to China and the possible re-unification of the mainland and Taiwan in the future may greatly boost the travel flows between the four regions of greater China.

There are, however, a variety of important variables upon which the full realization of the tourism development potential of China depends. The key factors constraining the industry's growth are, among others: inadequate tourist transport capacity and other facilities; an imperfect management and coordination system; poor service quality; limited capital for investment; and an inadequate supply of skilled labour and professionals. China also has to face increasing competition from other destinations in the Asia and Pacific region, many of which are well established, for example Singapore and Thailand, with similar products, but better service or cheaper prices.

It is also worthwhile emphasizing the importance of political factors in China's tourism development. China's travel industry has shown itself to be highly sensitive to political events as demonstrated by the 4 June 1989 incidence and any further upheavals could spark off an even more extreme reaction. More frequent changes are those in government policy and regulation. Historically, tourism in China has suffered from politics. There appear to be three main potential sources of instability in China in the future. First, from within the ruling Communist Party as a result of the conflicts between the liberal and conservative forces; second, from possible civil riots caused by increasing expectation of democracy and freedom, the widening gap between the rich and the poor, increasing corruption and crime, and economic difficulties caused by high inflation or natural disasters; and third, from internal ethnic minority regions, such as Inner Mongolia, Xinjiang, Tibet, and possible conflict between the mainland and Taiwan. In order to maintain political stability, social order and national unity, the government might adopt extreme measures to suppress troubled regions and people that may damage its image abroad and harm its international relations with the major tourist-generating countries in the West.

Despite these cautions, China has demonstrably increased its tourism activity as a consequence of the open-door and economic liberalization policies. It is steadily developing its own tourism management and expertise. It may yet have to set limits to tourism growth in certain areas and probably prioritize its regional development initiatives. However, it has enviable tourist resources and as yet, vast untapped potential.

Bibliography

China National Administration *Yearbook of China Tourism Statistics* (annual). Beijing.

Choy, D.J.L. and Can, Y.Y. (1988) The development and organization of travel services in China. *Journal of Travel Research* 27 (1), 28–34.

Economist Intelligence Unit (1989) Foreign investment in China's hotel sector. *Travel and Tourism Analyst* 3, 17–32.

Gao, D.C. and Zhang, G.R. (1983) China's tourism: policy and practice. *Tourism Management* 4 (2), 75–84.

Lavery, P. (1989) Tourism in China: the costs of collapse. *Travel and Tourism Analyst* 4, 77–97.

Mings, R.C. (1989) Emerging tourism in China: the case of Xian. *Tourism Management* 10 (4), 333–6.

Richter, L.K. (1989) *The Politics of Tourism in Asia*. Honolulu: University of Hawaii Press.

Wei, L., Crompton, J.L. and Reid, L.M. (1989) Cultural conflicts: experiences of US visitors to China. *Tourism Management* 10 (4), 322–32.

Yu, L. (1992) Hotel development and structures in China. *International Journal of Hospitality Management* **11** (2), 99–110.

Zhang, G.R. (1989) Ten years of Chinese tourism: profile and assessment. *Tourism Management* **10** (1), 51–62.

Zhao, J. (1989) Overprovision in Chinese hotels. *Tourism Management* **10** (1), 63–6.

7

Hong Kong: Political impact on tourism

VINCENT C.S. HEUNG

Introduction

The Hong Kong hotel and tourism industry has been growing very rapidly in terms of visitor arrivals in the past decade. It is now the territory's second largest earner of foreign exchange. With the transfer of sovereignty in 1997, Hong Kong is entering the final phase of the transition period. The tourism industry is inevitably affected by this and is facing some uncertainties brought about by social and economic changes. Some of these changes may be considered favourable to the development of the hotel and tourism industry, while others are thought to be unfavourable. The future of the Hong Kong hotel and tourism industry will be significantly influenced by the 1997 issue and other changes in the region. In this chapter, we will briefly describe the Hong Kong hotel and tourism industry since 1985, discuss the current issues affecting the industry, highlighting the positive and negative effects of the handover to tourism planning and development, and conclude with a summary overview of prospects.

Tourism Growth

Hong Kong's hotel and tourism industry has been enjoying a substantial growth since the 1980s. The territory is Asia's leading visitor destination. In 1992, there were 6.9 million visitors, a 103 per cent growth over 1985 (see Table 7.1). Total tourism receipts were HK$ 48.4 billion, representing about 6.5 per cent of Hong Kong's Gross Domestic Product (GDP) and making it the second largest generator of foreign currency (Barrow, 1994).

In 1994, there were 9.3 million visitors and total visitor spending amounted to 64.3 billion; the largest contribution was from Taiwan, representing 22 per

Table 7.1   Visitor arrivals and tourism receipts 1985–94

Year	Visitor arrivals (millions)	Arrival growth (%)	Tourism receipts (HK$ billion)	Receipts growth (%)
1985	3.4	9.7	14.4	4.7
1986	3.7	8.8	17.9	23.4
1987	4.5	21.6	25.4	42.4
1988	5.6	24.4	33.3	31.0
1989	5.4	−3.6	36.9	10.7
1990	5.9	9.3	39.3	6.4
1991	6.0	1.7	39.6	0.9
1992	6.9	15.0	48.4	22.2
1993*	8.9	22	60.0	24
1994*	9.3	4.4	64.3	7.1

* Includes visitors from Mainland China.
Source: Hong Kong Tourist Association. 1985–1994

cent of the total, followed by Japan and China (see Figure 7.1). An analysis of the spending pattern reveals that visitors spend most money in shopping, which represents more than half of the total tourist expenditure and a growth of 9.6 per cent over 1993. There is a sharp growth in the number of visitors embarking on a tour, which shows an increase of 13.9 per cent over 1993 (see Table 7.2).

In terms of room supply, according to the Hong Kong Tourist Association, there were 18,180 rooms in 1985. The number of hotel rooms in 1994 was 35,230 and it is projected to increase to 37,193 by 1998 (see Figure 7.2). With

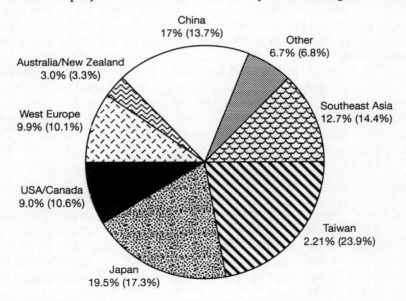

Figure 7.1 Receipts from visitors by major market areas 1994 (1993).
Source: Hong Kong Tourist Association (1995a).

Table 7.2 Total visitor spending by expenditure category in 1994

Expenditure category	HK$Mil.	% of total 1993	Growth % over
Shopping	32,451.89	51.9	+9.6
Hotel bills	17,619.77	28.2	+10.4
Meals out	7549.67	12.1	+2.3
Entertainment	992.65	1.6	−15.5
Tours	1805.07	2.9	+13.9
Other	2092.82	3.3	−19.2
Total	62,511.87	100.0	+7.2

Source: Hong Kong Tourist Association (1994b)

booming tourism in the 1980s, the average occupancy rate was as high as 84.2 per cent, which is substantially above the world's average of 66 per cent (see Figure 7.3).

There are several major reasons for the rapid growth of the tourism industry in Hong Kong. First, Hong Kong is strategically located on the main trading route between East and West. Its proximity to China makes it a gateway for tourists as well as investors. Second, Hong Kong has been one of the world's growing economies over the past 25 years and is one of the best places to do business (Hawksley *et al.*, 1989). Third, Hong Kong offers a unique blend of East and West: an exciting destination with independent tourist attractions that go beyond shopping and dining (Guernier, 1992). Fourth, Hong Kong has a sophisticated and efficient infrastructure. Like most large cities in the world, Hong Kong has developed and maintain advanced systems ranging from telecommunication and transport to electricity and water supply. Fifth, the legal system in Hong Kong (which is based on the British system) is comparable to many Western industrialized countries.

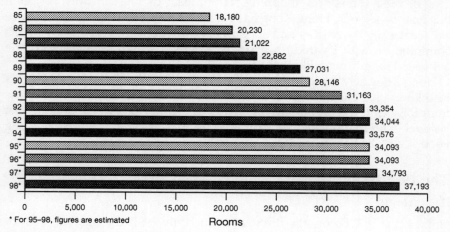

* For 95–98, figures are estimated

Figure 7.2 Hotel supply situation 1985–98.
Source: Hong Kong Tourist Association (1994a).

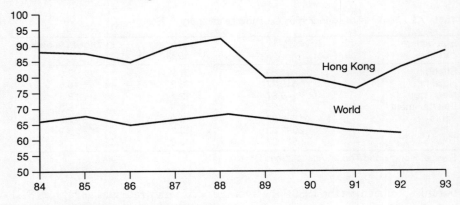

Figure 7.3 Hotel room occupancy rate 1984–93.
Source: Hong Kong Tourist Association (1985–1994).

Hong Kong has one of the best police forces in the world and its crime rate is relatively lower than many other major cities. Last, but not least, is the dexterity, docility, adaptability and industriousness of workers in Hong Kong and the territory has an outstanding reputation for efficient service and value for money.

Tourism in the Hong Kong Economy

Tourism plays a significant role in the Hong Kong economy. It is the second largest earner of foreign exchange and creates some 187,000 jobs (*Ming Pao Daily*, 1994). It has consistently contributed an average of 6.5 per cent to the GDP (see Table 7.3). As mentioned earlier, visitors spent more than 50 per cent of their money on shopping. The impact of tourism on local retail business is obvious. Hong Kong has become a major commercial and financial centre in the world and its success will depend very much on its continual tie with its trading partners. Tourism would strengthen the tie between Hong Kong and other countries.

Hong Kong is referred to as 'Asia's most popular travel destination'. It has its own unique culture: a culture that combines Western style with Chinese traditions. Cultural events such as 'Heritage Tour', 'Hong Kong Dragon Boat Festival – International Races', 'Hong Kong Arts Festivals' and 'Hong Kong Food Festivals' help to project a favourable image overseas.

The 1997 Issue

Background

Hong Kong will become part of China on 1 July 1997, the date marked for change in sovereignty from Britain to China. It was a historical issue which originated in 1841 when the island of Hong Kong was seized by the British

Table 7.3 Contribution of tourism to GDP 1984–93

Year	Tourism receipts*	Annual Growth %	GDP*	Annual growth %	% contribution to GDP
1984	13,820.62	22.5	247,933	20.2	5.6
1985	14,470.80	4.7	261,070	5.3	5.5
1986	17,863.21	23.4	298,515	14.3	6.0
1987	25,437.16	42.4	367,603	23.1	6.9
1988	33,328.30	31.0	433,657	18.0	7.7
1989	36,905.24	10.7	499,157	15.1	7.4
1990	39,251.31	6.4	558,859	12.0	7.0
1991	39,606.78	0.9	642,930	15.0	6.2
1992	48,389.99	22.2	745,407	15.9	6.5
1993	60,025.28	na.	847,813	13.7	7.1

* HK$ million
Source: Hong Kong Tourist Association (1995a)

Royal Navy. Following the defeat of the Chinese by the Japanese, Britain sought to consolidate its position in the region by successfully negotiating a 99-year lease for the northern part of Kowloon and the New Territories in 1898 (Hobson and Ko, 1994). The area of Hong Kong was then enlarged to include Hong Kong Island, Kowloon Peninsula and the New Territories. Under the colonial rule of Britain, Hong Kong has turned poverty to prosperity and has become one of the major financial centres in the world.

With the expiration date of the lease approaching, the British and Chinese governments tried to resolve the issue and to reach a politically and mutually acceptable solution. In 1982, the economic reforms in China under Deng Xiaoping's leadership began to take shape and the idea of 'One country, two systems' was raised and finally agreed by the British Government. In 1984, the Sino-British Joint Declaration was signed between Britain and China. Through this treaty, the Chinese government guaranteed to preserve Hong Kong's way of life for 50 years after 1997 (Deng Xiaoping, 1993). Hong Kong will become a Special Administrative Region (SAR) within the People's Republic of China (PRC) with a high degree of autonomy. In handing over a successful capitalist and *laissez faire* economy to a communist government, it is likely that there will be changes in the social, political and economic conditions in Hong Kong. The hotel and tourism industry, being one of the major sectors in the local economy, is inevitably affected before and after 1997. The major changes and their impacts, both positive and negative, will be examined in the following sections.

Positive impacts

The airport and infrastructure projects

The development of the new airport and transportation links with China will greatly improve accessibility and remove the capacity constraint of the present airport, which will be unable to cope with the increasing number of visitors. The Chep Lap Kok airport is planned to replace the Kai Tak airport after 1997. This plan includes 100 hectares of land for commercial, retailing, hotel and freight-forwarding activities. The government and the Mass Transit Railway Corporation proposed that nine new hotels be built along the Chep Lap Kok airport railways (Wong, 1994). The new airport is no doubt a boost to the growth of tourism in Hong Kong and strengthens Hong Kong's position as a regional hub. The Provisional Airport Authority projections anticipate 28.5 million air passengers will arrive in Hong Kong in 1997 and this number will increase to 87.3 million in 2040. In addition, Chek Lap Kok, Lantau Island and the area along the railways, such as Tsuen Wan and Cheung Sha Wan, connecting the airport with Kowloon Peninsula may become a new tourist and business district.

Besides the airport project, there are other planned transport infrastructure developments. The major road developments include a six-lane road linking Guangzhou–Shenzhen–Zuhai and form a network from Hong Kong via China to Macau. A bridge to Zuhai from Hong Kong across the Pearl River Delta is also planned. Therefore, new tourist destinations are likely to emerge in the Pearl River Delta.

Changing market mix

Hong Kong has six major tourist markets: Taiwan, Japan, South-east Asia, Western Europe, North America and Australasia (Australia and New Zealand). In the past ten years, there has been a shift in the market mix for Hong Kong tourism. The South-east Asian markets (like Taiwan, China and Japan) have taken over from the Western markets (USA and Canada, Australia and New Zealand) as major market segments (see Table 7.4). In 1994, over 70 per cent of the visitors came from Asia and China compared with 22 per cent from USA/Canada and Western Europe.

The rise of China's economy and living standards, plus a closer link with China has created significant new opportunities for the Hong Kong tourism

Table 7.4 Percentage change in market share of major markets

	1985	1986	1987	1988	1989	1990	1991	1992	1993	1994
SE Asia	21	20	18	14	13	14	17	15	14	13
Taiwan	5	6	8	20	21	23	22	21	20	18
Japan	19	20	22	22	22	22	21	16	14	16
USA/Canada	22	22	21	16	15	14	13	11	11	10
Western Europe	15	15	15	14	13	12	13	12	12	12
Australia	9	8	7	5	6	5	4	4	3	3
Other	9	9	9	9	10	10	10	7	7	7
China	–	–	–	–	–	–	–	14	19	21
Total	100	100	100	100	100	100	100	100	100	100

1. Figures are rounded up.
2. Statistics for China visitors from 1985–91 were not included in the total visitor arrivals.
Source: Hong Kong Tourist Association 1985–1994

industry. In particular, China has allowed mainlanders to visit Hong Kong and, consequently, the number of Chinese visitors has increased dramatically over the past few years. According to the official Visitors Arrival Statistics in 1994, China led Taiwan as the largest single market for Hong Kong tourism with 1.9 million visitors, which represented 21 per cent of total arrivals. The Hong Kong Tourist Association sees China as one of its biggest growth markets, with ever-increasing visitor arrivals from the mainland as the key to the long-term health of the local tourism industry.

Both the Immigration Department of Hong Kong and China's Bureau of Public Security are looking for ways to lift the restrictions on the present 800 two-way permits a day and, importantly, the Minister of Public Security called for the relaxation of travel restrictions (Forsell, 1993). The number of mainland Chinese visitors to Hong Kong in 1994 was 1,943,678, up 12.2 per cent over 1993, and a growth rate of 69 per cent over 1992. Chinese visitors spend an average of HK$5,469 per capita compared with an average of HK$6,699 per capita by all visitors. China allowed travellers to bring out RMB 6,000 or HK$ 6,240. They would normally spend all this money in Hong Kong. Tourism experts estimated that mainlanders from southern China filled nearly 1,500 rooms per day in Hong Kong, which is almost 5 per cent of all rooms available (Forsell, 1993).

Another travel relaxation announced recently is on foreign visitors to the Economic Zones: Shenzhen, Zhuhai and Xiamen. China allows foreigners to stay in the Economic Zones for 72 hours or less without a visa if they enter through Hong Kong on a tour. This recent border crossing facilitation will spur even more tourists to use Hong Kong as a gateway to China and help to boost international tourism in southern China.

Negative impacts

The hotel and tourism industry is facing a totally unique set of political circumstances due to the change of sovereignty in 1997. It is necessary to view the development of tourism not only as an economic development issue, but also as a political one. During 1993, five hotel companies announced that they would be demolishing their properties, as some of them believe that they could maximize the profits from the sites by redeveloping them into office space, which would yield twice the profits of hotels. By mid-1995, at least six hotels – one just seven years old – are expected to be torn down to give way to office buildings (*Asia week*, 1994). This would reduce the total number of hotel rooms in Hong Kong by 3,000. The demolished hotels include Lee Gardens, Ambassador, China Harbour View, China Merchants, Fortuna and the Hilton (see Table 7.5). Moreover, there are rumours circulating about the potential future closures, which include the Hyatt, Omni Prince, Sheraton and the Ritz-Carlton hotels. Even without that loss, analysts

Table 7.5   Changes in number of hotel rooms in Hong Kong during 1993–95

Year	Hotel opened	No. of rooms	Hotel demolished	No. of rooms
1993	Silvermine Beach	135	Lee Gardens	(660)
	Regal Hong Kong	423	China Harbor View	(310)
	Ritz-Carlton	216		
	Gold Coast	443		
	BP International House	536		
1994	Peninsula Extension	150	China Merchants	(285)
	Pearl Seaview	253	Ambassador	(313)
			Harbor	(156)
			Fortuna	(187)
			Emerald	(315)
			Miramar	(500)
1995	YMCA Extension	145	Hilton	(739)
	San Diego	99	Victoria	(536)
	The Harbor Plaza	418		
Total		+2818	Total	−4001

Source: Hong Kong Tourist Association (1994a)

reckon that Hong Kong will need 5,000 more rooms over the next four years to keep up with surging demand (*Asia week*, 1994).

The glut of rooms coming onto the Hong Kong market during 1989 and 1990, combined with uncertainties in the tourism industry, have prompted many local developers to scuttle plans for new hotels. For example, Henderson Land and the Yau Tai Hing Group scrapped plans to develop a business class hotel in Yaumatei in favour of a residential/commercial project (*Building Journal*, 1990). As 1997 is coming closer, the level of investment tension may well rise if the British and Chinese governments cannot agree on a range of political issues. This might cause further uncertainty and more hotel closures. The net effect of the decline in hotels could be a sharp decrease in the number of overseas visitors, who would be unable to find accommodation and the reputation of the industry would be ruined in the longer term.

Tourism Marketing and Planning

Cooperation

Selling Hong Kong beyond 1997 has been a major issue for the Hong Kong Tourist Association (HKTA). A small market, Hong Kong has to explore opportunities on a macro-economic level (Ocampo, 1992), which implies a further regional integration with China. In 1993, a Pearl River Delta Marketing Organization was formed between the HKTA, Guangdong Provincial Tourism Bureau (GPTB) and the Macau Government Tourist Association to promote the three destinations, Hong Kong, Macau and southern China as a single package. The organization has already put together promotional brochures and a video, which is aimed primarily at long-haul visitors from Europe, USA and Australia. Amy Chan, Executive Director of the HKTA and convenor of the marketing organization's working group, commented: 'This initiative has special significance for each of the destinations because the whole product would offer much more than the sum of the three areas each working on its own' (Tsang, 1994). The organization had identified some tourist attractions in Guangdong, which require upgrading of the tourist facilities and is looking into other aspects of tourists' services such as accommodation and transport in the three areas. This cooperative marketing approach, if implemented effectively, can maximize the tourism potential of the entire area and bring greater benefit to all parties involved in the long run. Hong Kong will be the 'hub' of the emerging megalopolis (Go *et al.*, 1994) and is expected to benefit from the synergy of the joint promotion effort.

Taiwan issue

Taiwan's policy towards China is based on three negative government policy factors: 'no contact, no negotiation and no compromise'. In 1987, Taiwan dropped the travel restrictions on its citizens and Taiwan's outbound tourism grew quickly. Since there are no direct routes between Taiwan and China, Hong Kong became the stopover for many Taiwanese visiting China. Taiwan is now the second biggest single market for Hong Kong tourism and half of the Taiwanese travel to China is via Hong Kong. With the political changes that are taking place, there is a great chance that direct flights between Taiwan and China will be established. This would have a disastrous effect on Hong Kong's visitor arrivals and tourism receipts. Recently, the effect of the drop in Taiwanese travel to Hong Kong was illustrated by the Qiandao Lake tragedy in 1994. The Taiwan Government banned tour groups from travelling to China following the pleasure boat fire on Qiandao Lake, which took the lives of 24 Taiwanese visitors. It was estimated that 30,000 passengers cancelled trips to Hong Kong during the month that Taiwan prohibited its citizens from travelling to the mainland. The ban had a particularly serious impact on Cathay Pacific and China Airlines and both airlines were forced to cancel several flights between Hong Kong and Taiwan (Tsang, 1994).

China issue

The growth of tourism in China certainly helps to boost the occupancy levels for Hong Kong hotels. As 1997 approaches, the interdependence between Hong Kong and the Pearl River Delta is growing stronger. The idea of a Greater South China economic circle, which would enable free economic exchanges between the four provinces of coastal southern China (Guangdong, Fujian, Guangxi and Hainan, and eventually Hong Kong and Macau when these two territories return to China in 1997 and 1999), is likely to establish an institutional base or formal status that is bidding to become a significant player in the global economy of the twenty-first century (Stewart *et al.*, 1992). More businessmen will look for opportunities in this region and Hong Kong will share the booming economy of this economic circle. The five-day work policy announced recently by the Chinese government will foster the growth of domestic travel and would bring more Chinese mainlanders to Hong Kong after 1997. The China tourism industry has been expanding. China had approximately 2,500 hotels that catered specifically for overseas visitors in 1994, the average occupancy of which was 65 per cent and is increasing each year. In 1993, official figures revealed that there were 40 million arrivals in China and the total tourism receipts were US$4.5 million (Davie, 1994). As China has reduced its travel restrictions, both on its people and foreigners, Hong Kong is expected to reap the benefits of tourist traffic to and from China.

China will also use the transfer of Hong Kong's sovereignty to gain a foothold in the international tourist market and plan to hold a major tourist promotion festival on the mainland in 1997. China expects to use the handover of Hong Kong in 1997 and Macau in 1999 to double its tourism revenue from 50 billion yuan (HK$44.7 billion) in 1995 to 100 billion yuan by the year 2000. Many of Hong Kong's hotels are already fully booked on 30 June 1997, the date of the handover (Chan, 1994).

Convention business

Hong Kong's convention industry has been expanding rapidly since the 1970s. As the European and US markets are stagnating and business travel in Asia is growing, convention and incentive planners have shifted their sights on Asia and the Pacific Region.

In 1986, the Hong Kong Convention and Incentive Travel Bureau (HKCITB) was set up under the Hong Kong Tourist Association (HKTA) to promote and attract more convention travellers to Hong Kong. Since then, the convention business has been increasing. With the opening of the Hong Kong Convention and Exhibition Centre in 1988, Hong Kong's potential for convention business was greatly improved. Presently it is a popular venue for conferences, meetings and conventions among organizers and has become a major convention centre in the region. The volume of convention delegates increased from 93,795 in 1985 to 299,407 in 1994, almost 300 per cent (see Figure 7.4). Hong Kong has earned a reputation as the 'Events Capital of Asia' and offers first-class facilities for convention activities (Chan 1995). Although Hong Kong is facing competition from all the neighbouring areas, it is envisaged that the convention sector will continue to grow. As Ellen Kwan, General Manager of the Hong Kong Convention and Incentive Travel Bureau commented: 'No matter which destination in Asia wins the actual convention event, all neighbouring destinations stand to benefit, especially from long-haul delegates who are eager to make pre and post convention tours' (*Hong Kong Travel Bulletin*, 1994). The Hong Kong Government has long recognized the importance of maintaining the competitiveness of Hong Kong as a convention city and, in 1994, proposed to build an extension to the Hong Kong Convention and Exhibition Centre in order to further develop this contribution. According to the government, the small size of Hong Kong's existing centre meant organizers were holding events at other venues in Asia. The Centre was making use of the restaurant and other areas to accommodate exhibitions. The project was planned for completion in mid-1997 and it was estimated that the additional facilities would bring at least HK\$9 billion into the territory in its first year of operation (Colclough, 1994).

New cruising hub of Asia

Cruising is becoming more and more popular in Asia. Experts have predicted that there will be 500,000 cruise passengers originating from the Far East to take up a cruise in the Caribbean by the year 2000. According to a study on cruising (Gebhart, 1994), 92 per cent of Hong Kong holiday-travellers were interested in taking a 'fly–cruise', where Hong Kong holiday-makers would fly to other places in the world and take a cruise. Among these holidaymakers, 40 per cent showed an interest in a cruise in Hong Kong. The growth of the cruise market has already been realized by many cruise liners and travel agencies. Hong Kong is surrounded by water and the sea is a vital part of Hong Kong's life. Hong Kong has a beautiful harbour that can accommodate large and small vessels making it an ideal destination for cruising. Located at the heart of the Asia's cruising map, Hong Kong offers various attractive fly–cruise options and exciting cruise itineraries to various

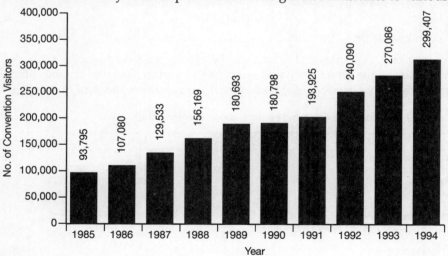

Figure 7.4 Convention visitors 1985–94.
Source: Hong Kong Convention and Incentive Travel Bureau (1995).

other Asian destinations. As Amy Chan, Executive Director of the Hong Kong Tourist Association pointed out: 'The commencement of a cruise service to Hong Kong is a very important development for the territory and for the Asian market as a whole. Traditionally, the Caribbean was the world's primary cruise destination, but this trend is changing and Asia has huge potential as a cruise destination' (PATA, 1995). In 1993, the International Cruise Council was formed in Hong Kong. The Council has nine founding members that consists of Carnival Cruise Lines, Club Med, Cunard Lines, Orient Lines, Princess Cruises, Royal Caribbean Cruise Line, Royal Cruise Line, Royal Viking Line and Star Cruise. One of the objectives of the Council is to promote holiday cruising to all travel agencies as they are important intermediaries in the tourism industry.

Challenges: Capacity Constraints

Airport

According to *Hang Seng Economic Monthly* (1994), the Hong Kong tourism industry is running up against capacity constraints both with the airport and hotel room supply. The Kai Tai Airport handled 24.5 million passengers in 1993, which has exceeded its design capacity of 24 million. The Civil Aviation Department reported that 6,700 extra flights were turned down in 1993, losing an estimated 1.4 million passengers and by 1997, the projected lost flights would be 59,000 and some 12 million passengers would be turned away (see Table 7.6). If the new airport at Chap Lap Kwok were not in place by early 1998, the loss might be even greater. The growth of the tourism industry would undoubtedly be restricted as a result.

Accommodation

As property investors reckoned that the return on a commercial property would be higher than an hotel operation in certain locations, some hotel properties have been redeveloped into office buildings and other uses, thus

Table 7.6　Projected losses arising from the airport operating at capacity

	1993	1994	1997
No. of flights (per week)	128	336	1,130
(per year)	6,700	17,500	59,000
Passengers (000s)	1,400	3,500	12,000
	1993–97		
	HK$Mil.		
Associated Financial Losses			
Landing and parking charges	380		
Departure tax	700		
Tourism receipts	22,280		
Total	23,360		

Source: Hang Seng Bank Ltd 1994

the total number of hotel rooms has already been reduced by almost 5,000 in the past two years. In 1994, the total number of rooms was 33,795 and was forecast by the Hong Kong Tourist Association to grow to 37,780 by 1998, less than 3 per cent per year. It is expected, however, that tourist arrivals will maintain a steady growth of 6 per cent per annum and demand for hotel rooms will remain strong. Hong Kong will receive 14 million visitors by the year 2000 according to the Hong Kong Tourist Association's forecast. 'Hong Kong's 35,000 rooms will not be able to cope with demand if Chek Lap Kok airport is built, we will need about 15,000 more hotel rooms and 25,000 more staff' claimed Manuel Woo, the Executive Director of the Hong Kong Hotel Association (Pasieczny, 1993). With few hotels opening for business for the next few years and, as earlier mentioned, existing properties being converted into more lucrative office space, it is envisaged that Hong Kong will face an increasing shortage of hotel rooms in the coming few years (see Table 7.7). The lack of accommodation could push up hotel room rates and threaten tourists coming to Hong Kong. Though there are a number of hotels being planned with the Chap Lap Kok airport project, such properties will not come on-stream until at least 1998.

Competition

Due to rising costs, political uncertainty and the emergence of rival centres throughout the region, Hong Kong may lose its competitiveness as a tourist and business centre to other Asian capitals (Go *et al.*, 1994). Over the past decade, Hong Kong has had a relatively high inflation rate, averaging 9 to 10 per cent a year. Rising land and labour costs have been the main causes for high inflation rates in recent years due to scarcity of land and labour shortage (Heung, 1993). Inflation has been pushing prices up at a much faster rate than any other country. As a result, goods and services in Hong Kong have become more expensive than many other destinations, and it is no longer the unique shopping paradise it was renowned to be. Shopping in Hong Kong has been the main attraction for foreign visitors. Over 50 per cent of tourist expenditure is allocated to shopping. As the price of tourist products moves up at a speed faster than other destinations, Hong Kong may lose this

Table 7.7 Balance of hotel room supply and demand

Visitor arrivals (annual growth)	Surplus (Shortage)				
	1994	1995	1996	1997	1998
2%	1,988	2,118	3,167	3,711	3,341
4%	1,369	844	1,199	1,008	(140)
6%	751	(455)	(846)	(1,856)	(3,899)
8%	132	(1,788)	(2,971)	(4,887)	(7,953)
10%	(468)	(3,126)	(5,175)	(8,090)	(12,318)

Room demand forecast based on an average hotel accupancy rate of 92 per cent.
Source: Hang Seng Bank (1994)

attraction. The impacts of high inflation on the hotel industry are obvious. Hotel room rates have been increasing in line with inflation. By having an inflation rate of about 10 per cent Hong Kong is totally at odds with the economic situation in other industrialized countries, where inflation is running at 3 to 4 per cent or even less. In an address to the Hong Kong Pacific Asia Travel Association, Governor Chris Patten has warned that inflation is becoming a threat to the territory's general competitiveness (Chew, 1994). As the construction of the Chep Lap Kok airport is underway and the supply of building materials and labour becomes tight, it is forecasted that inflation will remain high in the next few years.

Conclusion

Despite the uncertainties Hong Kong is facing, mainly brought about by the 1997 issue, its tourism industry still continues to grow. On balance, there are more positive than negative signs, and more opportunities than threats for Hong Kong. As Hong Kong is linking up more closely with China, its bargaining power will be strengthened. Hong Kong will most likely continue its dynamism into the twenty-first century, further improving its well-being and also contributing to China's economic development (Woo, 1991). Business leaders in Hong Kong see a prosperous future for the territory after 1997 and beyond. 'Becoming part of China is an opportunity, not a threat. In the 21st Century, we see Hong Kong as the leading commercial city of China and the services capital of Asia' claimed Vincent Lo, Chairman of the Business and Professionals Federation of Hong Kong (Hui, 1993).

In the short to medium term, however, Hong Kong has to find ways of overcoming the problems of capacity limits, rising costs and investment tensions. However, much depends on the cooperation between Britain, China and Hong Kong in resolving the many political issues before 1997.

Bibliography

Asia week (1994) Next year, no room at the Inn? *Asia Week* 20 April, 42.

Barrow, M.G. (1994) The second-largest foreign exchange earner, Tourism, *Hong Kong Business Annual*, **13**, 138–143.

Building Journal Hong Kong China (1990) Hotel survey 90–91: Construction takes a holiday. December, 64–5.

Chan, A. (1995) Message from the Executive Director, HKTA. *Hotel and Tourism. The Year Book*. Hong Kong Polytechnic University, 14–15.

Chan, L. (1994) China's 1997 tourism cash-in. *Hong Kong Standard*, 12 July.

Chew, A. (1994) Patten warns on inflation threat. *South China Morning Post* 10 May.

Colclough, N. (1994) Convention project will bring in $9b in first year. *Hongkong Standard* 25 February.

Davie, E. (1994) On the threshold of the Asia-Pacific century. *Asian Hotel and Catering Times*, September, 16–17.

Deng Xiaoping (1993) Our basic position on the Hong Kong question, *Beijing Review* 4–10 October, 7–8.

Forsell, J. (1993) Southern Exposure. *Journal of the American Chamber of Commerce in Hong Kong*, May, 12–14.

Gebhart, F. (1994), The big guys get bigger. *Travel News Asia: Cruise News* 21 February–6 March, 18.

Go, F., Pine, R. and Yu, R. (1994) Hong Kong: sustaining competitive advantage in Asia's hotel industry. *The Cornell HRA Quarterly* **35** (5), 50–61.

Guernier, A. (1992) Hong Kong hotels – 1997 and beyond. *Asia Travel Trade* December, 42.

Hang Seng Bank Ltd (1994) Tourist industry running up against capacity constraints. *Hang Seng Economic Monthly* February.

Hawsley F., Fisher E. and Grey, S. (1989) The best place to do business. *Accountancy* November, 65–71.

Heung, V. (1993) Hong Kong Tourism Industry. In Baum, Tom (ed.) *Human Resource Issues in International Tourism*. Oxford: Butterworth-Heinemann, 161–76.

Hobson, P. and Ko, G. (1994) Tourism and politics: The implications of change in sovereignty on the future development of Hong Kong's tourism industry. *Journal of Travel Research* (Spring) 2–8.

Hong Kong Convention and Incentive Travel Bureau (HKCITB). *1990–95 Statistical Data*.

HKTA (Hong Kong Tourist Association) *1985–1994 Statistical Review of Tourism* (annual publication).

HKTA (1994a) *Hotel Supply Situation*, No. 4.

HKTA (1994b), *Tourism Receipts*.

HKTA (1995a) *Annual Report 93/94*.

HKTA (1995b) *Visitor Arrival Statistics* (January).

Hong Kong Travel Bulletin (1994) MICE 1994 and Beyond. *Hong Kong Travel Bulletin* June, 6–8.

Hui, N. (1993) Gazing into the crystal ball. *Hong Kong Business* July, 18–19.

Ming Pao Daily (1994) Tourism industry: impacts on Hong Kong economy. *Ming Pao Daily* 14 June.

Ocampo, R. (1992) HK should promote big neighbour. *Hong Kong Standard* 10 December.

Pasieczny, L. (1993) New airport will aid tourism. *South China Morning Post* 6 July.

PATA (Pacific Asia Travel Association) (1995), Hong Kong. *Pacific Asia Travel News* March/April, 14–16.

Stewart, S., Cheung, M. and Yeung, D. (1992) The latest Asian newly industrialized economy emerges: the South China economic community. *The Columbia Journal of World Business* (Summer) 30–6.

Tsang, S.W. (1994) Tour plan cash boost. *Eastern Express* 28 May.

Tsang, S.W. (1994) Tourist boom to gain pace near 1997. *Eastern Express* 27 May.

Wong, L. (1994) New hotels on airport rail route will meet demand, says HKTA. *South China Morning Post* 19 November.

Woo, H. (1991) The Challenge of 1997 and the Hong Kong Response. *Intellectus* **19**, 11–12.

8

Indonesia: The impact of regionalization

GEOFFREY WALL

Introduction

Indonesia is characterized by its great size and diversity (Indonesia Tourist Promotion Board, undated). It consists of a vast equatorial archipelago stretching between 6 degrees north and 11 degrees south latitude, and 95 degrees west and 141 degrees east longitude. Indonesia has a greater east – west spread than North America. The national territory is 84 per cent sea and the 5,193,166 square kilometres of land are comprised of more than 13,500 islands. The five largest land areas are Kalimantan, Sumatra, Irian Jaya, Sulawesi and Java. With a population approaching 200 million people, Indonesia is the third largest country in Asia in terms of both population and area after China and India, and the fifth most populous country in the world.

Straddling the equator, Indonesia has a tropical climate. However, there is great variation in precipitation from place to place, and most areas are characterized by wet and dry seasons rather than by major seasonal differences in temperature. Indonesia is part of one of the most highly active volcanic regions in the world and has more than 400 volcanoes, many of which continue to erupt on occasion. At the time of writing, Gunung Batur in Bali is smoking, adding to the attraction, but Gunung Tangkubanperahu near Bandung is releasing poisonous gases and preventing visitors from using the overlooks and trails. The archipelago is also home to an exceedingly rich flora and fauna. The Wallace line, which passes between Bali and Lombok, separates the Asian and Australian continental plates and has contributed to the major differences that exist, particularly in fauna, between the eastern and western parts of the archipelago. Thus, the physical characteristics of Indonesia constitute a rich and varied resource for tourism with beaches, reefs, volcanic uplands and a diversity of flora and fauna to attract tourists, including eco tourists.

The population of Indonesia is both unevenly distributed and very varied culturally. About 62 per cent of the population live in Java, which constitutes only 7 per cent of the country's land area. Conversely, there are large areas of the outer islands with low population densities. Although the capital, Jakarta, is congested and polluted, it offers sophisticated shopping and entertainment facilities as befits a city with approximately 7 million people. On the other hand, there are tribes in Irian Jaya whose lifestyles have changed little over centuries. With approximately 90 per cent of the population adhering to the Islamic faith, Indonesia has numerically the largest Moslem population in the world, yet ethnic and cultural diversity is considerable as suggested in the national motto, *Bhinneka Tunggal Ika*, or unity in diversity. Indonesia has more than 300 ethnic groups who speak 250 different languages. The expressions of their cultures in landscapes, structures, music, dance, ceremonies, arts and crafts contribute greatly to Indonesia's attraction as a tourism destination. History, too, as in the UNESCO World Heritage sites of Borobudur and Prambanan on the outskirts of Yogyakarta, Java, has left a legacy that can be harnessed for tourism. Thus, the resources, both natural and cultural, on which tourism could be based are immense. However, their full potential has yet to be realized.

The Status and Importance of Tourism

Tourism is of great importance to the economy of Indonesia and has been accorded progressively higher priority in the Repelitas (five-year plans). Uncertainty over oil revenues has encouraged the government of Indonesia to look for alternative sources of foreign exchange and it has increasingly turned to tourism over the past decade. Tourism (US$2,518.1 million in 1991) is now the fourth highest as a generator of foreign exchange earnings after oil and gas (US$10,706 million), textiles (US$4,075.4 million) and timber (US$3,659.8 million). Rapid increases in international tourism have been achieved through deregulation of airlines, simplification of entrance requirements, and the expansion of tourism plant, especially hotels, associated with the provision of investment incentives and increased opportunities for private sector involvement. There has also been considerable planning activity in an attempt to direct the form and locations of tourism development. Some of these activities will be described in subsequent sections.

The growth in numbers of visitors

International tourism has grown rapidly in Indonesia in recent years, the number of visitors more than doubling between 1987 and 1991 with annual growth rates averaging in excess of 27 per cent in this period. In 1987, there were 1,060,347 international visitors; the 2 million mark was breached in 1990; 2,569,870 visitors came in 1991; and 3,064,161 arrived in 1992. In spite of the Gulf War, an 18 per cent growth rate was achieved between 1990 and 1991, reflecting the success of Visit Indonesia Year, rising to 23 per cent between 1991 and 1992.

An unknown but substantial number of domestic tourists must be added to the international visitors to get a complete picture of the magnitude of tourism. Unfortunately, systems are not currently in place to monitor domestic tourism so, of necessity, this chapter will focus upon international visitors. However, domestic travel is regarded as important by the government of Indonesia, and is viewed as a means of contributing to national identity and cohesion.

The characteristics of visitors

The origins of visitors in 1987 and 1992 is presented in Table 8.1. More than half (57 per cent) of arrivals are now from Singapore, Japan, Malaysia and Taiwan combined, with Asia contributing 75.9 per cent of all arrivals. Absolute growth is occurring in most markets but the relative importance of Asia as a generator of visitors is expanding at the expense of Australia and Europe that, nevertheless, continue to be important sources of visitors. The number of visitors from North America continues to be small, largely because of distance, associated travel costs, and the many intervening opportunities.

Table 8.1   Country of residence of visitor arrivals in Indonesia 1987 and 1992

Country of residence	1987		1992	
	Total	Share (%)	Total	Share (%)
Singapore	243,240	22.9	809,144	26.4
Japan	134,445	12.7	394,693	12.8
Malaysia	89,826	8.5	338,049	11.0
Australia	133,151	12.6	234,723	7.6
Taiwan	23,891	2.3	220,326	7.1
USA	64,497	6.1	125,337	4.0
Germany	49,364	4.7	118,244	3.8
United Kingdom	49,020	4.6	117,826	3.8
Netherlands	47,814	4.5	86,034	2.8
South Korea	13,471	1.2	82,526	2.6
France	33,972	3.2	62,388	2.3
Italy	27,827	2.6	56,947	1.9
Switzerland	17,061	1.6	33,450	1.1
Hong Kong	31,471	3.0	29,054	2.6
Philippines	9,684	0.8	41,852	1.4
Others	91,640	8.9	313,568	8.9
Total	1,060,347	100	3,064,161	100

Source: Calculated from Directorate General of Tourism (1994: 35)

Reflecting its status as an archipelago, most (64 per cent) visitors in 1992 arrived by plane. The exception is those entering through Batam, whose traffic is dominated by visitors from nearby Singapore arriving by boat. Many of the visitors entering through Batam are on brief visits to Indonesia so their characteristics tend not to be typical of Indonesia as a whole. The great majority of visitors arrive in one of three major entry points, namely Jakarta (31.6 per cent), Batam (22.3 per cent) and Denpasar (24.3 per cent), with Medan as the next most important point of entry with only 5.5 per cent of arrivals in 1992. Thus, visitor arrivals are highly concentrated spatially. Of all international visitors, 81.1 per cent were on holiday and 13.0 per cent on business in 1991. More than half (58.4 per cent) of all 1991 visitors indicated that it was their first visit to Indonesia.

Partially reflecting the large size of the country, the average length of stay in 1991 was in excess of 13 days if Batam is excluded and almost 12 days incorporating Batam arrivals. Not surprisingly, visitors from farther away tend to stay longer, those from Europe and America staying longer on average than travellers from ASEAN and Asia–Pacific countries. They also tended to have the highest overall expenditures, although Japanese visitors had the highest spending per day. The average expenditure of tourists per visit was US$967 in 1991 and $1,100 if those entering through Batam are excluded; business travellers spent approximately 31 per cent more than those travelling for pleasure. Similar to most destination countries, accommodation accounted for 30.8 per cent of expenditures, souvenirs and shopping 20.0 per cent, food and beverages 17.4 per cent, local transport 10.8 per cent and other purchases 21.0 per cent.

As a tropical country that spans the equator and draws visitors from both hemispheres, although there are peaks of visit in August and December, Indonesia experiences less seasonal variations in visits than most other countries.

Tourism plant

In 1992 there were 515 classified and 4,855 non-classified hotels registered in Indonesia, with a total of 45,245 and 87,247 rooms respectively. Comparative figures for 1989 were 403 classified and 3,787 non-classified hotels, with 32,842 and 87,325 rooms respectively. Again, very high rates of growth are evident. Occupancy rates and proportion of domestic guests declined progressively with the status of the accommodation (Table 8.2). Occupancy rates were highest in Jakarta in 1992 reflecting the importance of business traffic. However, no other province exceeded a 62 per cent occupancy rate and half were less than 50 per cent suggesting over-supply in many locations at a time when hotel construction continues apace. Length of stay tends to be greater for foreigners and for higher standard hotels.

Table 8.2   Hotel occupancy rates and guest origins 1989

Class	Occupancy %	Number of guests International	Domestic	Ratio
5-star	77.5	576,390	142,601	80:20
4-star	67.8	457,955	394,595	54:46
3-star	56.6	463,662	771,007	37:63
2-star	47.0	364,217	992,449	27:73
1-star	42.3	174,018	1,050,971	14:86
Non-Star	31.2	484,313	9,041,645	5:95

Source: Engineering Consulting Firms Association, Japan (1992: 8)

Uneven distribution

It should not be surprising given the size, uneven levels of development and great differences in both external and internal accessibility from place to place, that tourism within Indonesia is highly concentrated. For example, 1992 statistics indicate that 23.8 and 20.9 per cent of all classified hotel rooms in Indonesia were in Bali and Jakarta. Tourism is even more concentrated than the accommodation statistics indicate when one considers that occupancy rates in these two areas, at 62.0 per cent and 69.9 per cent, are the highest in Indonesia. The third most visited destination in Indonesia, after Jakarta and Bali, is Yogyakarta with 3.5 per cent of classified hotel rooms and an average length of stay of only 1.7 days.

At another scale, concentration is even more marked than is evident in the provincial statistics. Not surprisingly, in Jakarta, hotel accommodation is concentrated in the centre of the city. In Bali, tourism activity is highly concentrated in the south of the island in three resorts (Nusa Dua, Kuta and Sanur) reflecting the initial tourism plan dating from 1971 (Wall and Dibnah, 1992). Hassall and Associates (1992) showed that 50.6 per cent of the 25,546 starred hotel rooms in operation were in Bandung Regency, that 33.8 per cent of 5,198 starred hotel rooms under construction were in Bandung, that 80.3 per cent of the 17,914 starred hotel rooms approved for construction were in Bandung, and that all the 3,230 starred hotel rooms awaiting approval were in Bandung.

Given the extreme levels of concentration, it is not surprising that a strong goal of tourism development policy is to disperse tourism activities more widely. In Bali, the recent Spatial Arrangement Plan has identified 16 areas (now increased to 21 including the existing major resorts) throughout the island for tourism development. Thus a long-standing policy of concentration to protect the integrity of Balinese culture is being reversed in the search for more balanced regional development (Wall and Dibnah, 1992). Some of the initiatives which are being taken at the national level will be discussed below.

The National Tourism Strategy

In May 1992, the Government of Indonesia released a National Tourism Strategy, consisting of a national report and 27 provincial reports: one for each province. The aim of the strategy is to 'assist the Government in its policy of obtaining, maximum benefit from tourism ... more income and employment and increasing the amount of foreign exchange earned' (Directorate General of Tourism/UNDP, 1992, p.1) Thus, the strategy has a predominantly economic focus. At the same time, it is designed to assist in the establishment of an administrative framework to enable the Government to meet the targets that have been set for the tourism sector.

There were 19 specific recommendations identified in the strategy as follows:

1. The government should select tourism as a national development component with higher economic priority.
2. Improvement and development of the product be undertaken in line with market demands and trends.
3. An international image for Indonesia be created.
4. Tourism development in Indonesia should concentrate on the 'plus beach' concept targeted at high-expenditure visitors.
5. The ASEAN/Asia–Pacific region becomes the primary area on which to focus market development.
6. Special interest tourism activities (e.g. cultural, marine, adventure) be developed according to market demand and with selective government support.
7. The development of tourism in Indonesia be supported on a regional rather than a provincial basis.
8. The established market importance of Bali be used as a 'hub' to encourage 'spoke' developments in regional locations, with priority being given to eastern Indonesia.
9. The upgrading of accommodation at all levels be the main thrust of product development in the short and medium term.
10. Studies be undertaken in specified locations to determine tourism development opportunities.
11. The initiatives for development be provided by the tourism development corporations working with the private sector.
12. Air access policies both nationally and internationally be more market sensitive.
13. The management of the development of tourism be restructured to coordinate sectoral activity.
14. An appropriate budget be allocated to ensure that Indonesia is able to maintain and increase its share of international tourist arrivals.
15. Domestic tourism be promoted as a component of the overall development of the tourism sector.

16. All tourism development must conform to the highest standards of environmental care and be developed with consideration given to the social and cultural norms of the host community.
17. A system of fiscal incentives be introduced to stimulate the creation and development of tourism-related small businesses.
18. The provision of training and training facilities be increased to improve managerial capability in the tourism sector.
19. The Director General of Tourism be given an improved capacity to undertake tourism research.

Space does not permit the detailed examination of each recommendation individually. Rather, selected topics will be discussed and illustrated through exemplification of specific tourism initiatives that have been or are currently being implemented or explored. In particular, the following four themes will receive attention: image, product, spatial structures and administrative arrangements.

Image

Unfortunately, Indonesia does not have a clear image in most potential international markets. In fact, the image of Bali is probably stronger than that of the country as a whole. This may be a reflection of the great size and diversity of Indonesia. The size means that it is not practical for most visitors to see all the country in one visit and this may auger well for future repeat visits provided first-time visitors have positive experiences and feel that they received value for money, which is currently the case. However, as a relatively new destination (with the exception of Bali), the proportion of repeat visitors is currently small.

The challenge of diversity is illustrated in the discussion over a slogan in the national tourism strategy. Should it be 'plus beach' or 'beach plus'? The former puts emphasis on the unspecified 'plus' which, presumably, implies the rich diversity of cultures and their expressions and, possibly, emerging eco tourism opportunities. The latter stresses traditional sea, sun, sand vacations. It is important that there is congruence between the image or images and the products that are available, otherwise visitors may be disappointed. It is appropriate, then, to make some comments concerning the products.

Product

The tourism strategy makes a clear statement in support for the upgrading of accommodation as a major thrust to be taken in product development. This may be appropriate for many peripheral locations but, in the current major destinations, there are many fine hotels with low occupancy rates and, with continued construction, the number of competitors is increasing rapidly.

Adopting the model of the Nusa Dua resort enclave in Bali, which was developed by government and private investors under the leadership of the Bali Tourism Development Corporation and is in line with the desire to stimulate development throughout the country, eleven new destination areas have been designated for development. These are: Lombok, Manado, Biak Irian, Krakatau, Padang, Belitung, Baturaden, Bintan, Pangandaran, Goa Makassar and Nias (Figure 8.1). In each of these locations, a tourism development corporation will lease hotel lots to investors and manage the estate. According to consultants (Engineering Consulting Firms Association, Japan, 1992), the participation of provincial governments will facilitate the acquisition of licenses and permits, make land acquisition or consolidation easier, and support the development of necessary infrastructure, including airports, roads, water, electricity and sewerage systems. However, they also point out that there are various obstacles beyond the capacity of tourism development corporations to solve. These are mainly the shortage of funds and a lack of integration among relevant agencies and executing organizations.

Also, it is unclear how these destinations will be differentiated in the marketplace so that they become complementary rather than competitive. In addition, if a major goal is to promote regional development, then additional attention should be given to the establishment of economic linkages between the resorts and their surrounding communities. The above strategy suggests that Indonesia, like many other destinations, is attempting to attract 'quality' tourists, which is usually a euphemism for rich tourists. However, there are not many rich people to go around and they are likely to be all part of the existing market. The growth market appears to be the middle class of Asia.

While the lion's share of investment, public and private, domestic and foreign, has gone to major tourism complexes, other tourism development strategies are being considered. For example, over the past decade, initiatives have been taken to designate specific villages for tourism development. For example, the World Tourism Organization and United Nations Development Programme (1986) sponsored an investigation of the potential for village-based tourism in Nusa Tenggara, one of the poorer areas in eastern Indonesia. Villages were selected for appraisal and a subset of these villages were selected for tourism development, which was to include small-scale physical developments, including infrastructure improvements and training programmes for local people. Similar programmes have since been initiated in Bali and Java. There is growing interest in facilitating such small-scale tourism initiatives. However, there is also an opportunity to evaluate the achievements of the early projects so that the lessons of their experiences can be incorporated into more recent ventures.

Spatial structures

Although the National Tourism Strategy produced provincial reports, it acknowledges that provinces may not constitute the best units for tourism planning and marketing. There is a growing interest in the development of tourism clusters, as is seen in the activities of tourism development corporations at the sub-provincial scale, and tourism circuits that cover more than one province (Engineering Consulting Firms Association, Japan, 1992). For example, the Strategy identifies the opportunity to encourage visitors to Bali to explore other areas in Indonesia before returning home. Clearly, these strategies reflect a desire to spread tourism more widely and reduce regional imbalances. Their success will depend to a considerable extent on the willingness of visitors to make multi-destination trips to places that are viewed as complementary. This is likely to vary substantially with the market segment. For example, casual field experiences suggest that most international visitors in Yogyakarta visit Bali but that the flows are not reciprocal although both destinations offer forms of cultural tourism, albeit of very different type. One wonders if tourists who have elected to go to Nusa Dua for rest and relaxation can be persuaded to go elsewhere for similar or

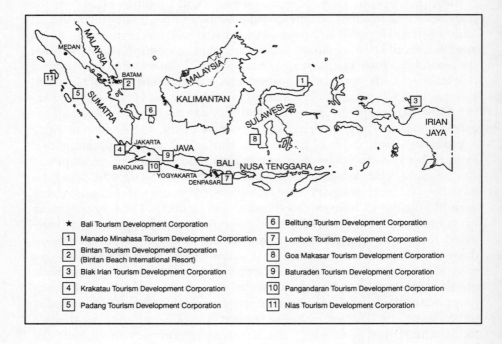

Figure 8.1 Tourism Development Corporations in Indonesia.

different experiences. Unfortunately, the market research required to answer such questions appears not to have been undertaken. It seems that many decisions are being made both at the strategic and destination levels in the absence of a strong information base and there appears to be an urgent need to strengthen the research underpinnings of policy decisions.

Administrative arrangements

Coordination of activities is always a challenge for tourism that tends to intersect most other economic sectors and Robert Cleverdon Associates (1993) have suggested the need for a study to clarify responsibilities. There are numerous tourism development studies in progress but they are not always integrated well with other plans and activities.

Part of the reason for the lack of awareness of Indonesia as a tourism destination is the limited resources accorded to promotion and marketing in the principal markets. There are signs that this may be changing. The recent establishment of the Indonesia Tourism Promotion Board, with a network of offices in major markets and an enhanced budget over that which was previously available for marketing, suggests that this issue is being addressed. On 1 April 1994, Indonesia launched a five-year campaign to promote areas outside of Java and Bali. In the initial phase of the campaign, the top priority markets are Japan, Taiwan, Singapore, Germany and Australia. The first year's budget is projected at US$14.4 million and the total budget is expected to exceed US$100 million (Anon, 1994).

Human resources development will continue to be a challenge, particularly given the likely rapid growth rate of tourism in Indonesia. Again, steps are being taken to address these needs through the development of new programmes and centres of excellence at colleges and universities (Guerrier, 1993).

Conclusion: The Future

Indonesia is growing rapidly in a fast expanding region. It is located in the East Asia and Pacific Region which has experienced, and is likely to continue experiencing, the most rapid rates of tourism growth among world regions. Within the Asia Pacific Region, Indonesia's growth rate is expected to be among the fastest. According to Robert Cleverdon Associates (1993), using 1990 as a base, between 1990 and 2000, Indonesia is expected to experience more than double the global average growth rates. Whereas Indonesia's share of global international tourist arrivals in 1990 was 0.5 per cent, it is expected to grow to 1.1 per cent by 2000. The share of arrivals in the East Asia and Pacific Region will grow from 4 to 7 per cent in the same period. By 2000 Indonesia is expected to receive 7.113 million annual visitors, a growth rate of 12.6 per cent per annum over the 1990s. The Asian countries will dominate the market but Indonesia is expected to become increasingly competitive in the smaller European market, with its share of arrivals in the East Asia and Pacific Region from European OECD member countries rising from 8 per cent in 1990 to 12 per cent in 2000. In the year 2000, one out of every eight European tourist arrivals in the countries of East Asia and the Pacific is likely to be in Indonesia.

The prospects for tourism in Indonesia are very good. The rich resource base for attracting tourists has been described. Also, it is clear that decisive steps are being taken to improve accessibility, to enhance the tourism products especially through the development of new destinations, to expand the supply of qualified labour, to increase the marketing budget and to enhance capabilities to undertake relevant research. At the same time, tourism is a competitive industry and competition is likely to increase as other countries adopt similar strategies and new countries, such as Laos, Cambodia and Vietnam, enter the market. Nevertheless, both external and internal forces are likely to be positive for tourism to Indonesia. The regional economies are strengthening, the regional market is growing, and Indonesia is taking decisive steps to ensure that it enhances its competitive position and increases its market share.

Acknowledgements

This chapter has benefited from collaboration with colleagues at Gadjah Mada University (especially Ms Wiendu Nuryanti), Udayana University and the University of Waterloo through participation in the Bali Sustainable Development Project that was funded by the Canadian International Development Agency.

Almost all of the statistical information reported above has been compiled by the Directorate General of Tourism and the Department of Tourism (1994), Post and Telecommunications, Jakarta. In some cases figures have been obtained from unpublished reports, in some cases calculations have been made by the author, and in some cases numbers have been taken from secondary sources, including those listed in the references.

Bibliography

Anon (1994) *News and views. Indonesia* April, 7.

Directorate General of Tourism (1994) *Tourism Data and Statistics 1993*. Jakarta: Directorate of Marketing, DGT.

Directorate General of Tourism and Department of Tourism, Post and Telecommunications (1993) *Tourism in Indonesia 1992*. Jakarta: DGT and DPPT.

Directorate General of Tourism and United Nations Development Program (1992) Tourism sector programming and policy development output 1. *National Tourism Strategy*. Jakarta: Government of Indonesia.

Engineering Consulting Firms Association, Japan (1992) *Preliminary Study for Tourism Clusters Development Project in Indonesia.* Tokyo: Pacific Consultants International.

Guerrier, Y. (1993) Bali. In Baum, T. (ed.) *Human Resources in International Tourism.* Oxford: Butterworth-Heinemann, 108–15.

Hassall and Associates (1992) *Comprehensive Tourism Development Plan for Bali Annex. 3 The Tourism Sector.* Denpasar: UNDP and Government of Indonesia.

Indonesia Tourist Promotion Board (Undated) *Discover Indonesia: A Travel Guide to the Indonesian Archipelago.* Jakarta: ITPB.

Robert Cleverdon Associates (1993) *Tourism Forecast – Indonesia.* Jakarta: Directorate General of Tourism.

Wall, G. and Dibnah, S. (1992) The changing status of tourism in Bali, Indonesia. *Progress in Tourism, Recreation and Hospitality Management* 4, 120–30.

World Tourism Organization and United Nations Development Programme (1986) *Village Tourism Development Programme for Nusa Tenggara.* Madrid: WTO.

9

Japan: The characteristics of the inbound and outbound markets

STEPHEN MORRIS

Introduction

Since assuming the mantle of a major tourist generating country in the 1980s, Japan has played a leading role in stimulating tourism growth in the Asia Pacific region. For most destinations in this region the Japanese market is a major source of visitors and tourism revenue. Data from national and international sources attest to the importance of the Japanese market. According to figures compiled by the Pacific Asia Travel Association (PATA), approximately 20 per cent of visitor arrivals to Asia Pacific destinations in 1992 originated from Japan. Measured in economic terms the global impact of the surge in the number of Japanese overseas travellers has been immense. In 1992 Japan ranked third behind the USA and Germany in terms of overall tourism payments, according to data for the member countries of the Organisation for Economic Cooperation and Development (OECD, 1995).

There is good reason to be optimistic about the future growth of the outbound market despite Japan's present economic and political problems. In 1993 the number of outbound Japanese travellers reached 11.9 million. Impressive as this total appears it represents only 9.6 per cent of the total population, one of the lowest foreign travel participation rates among the world's leading industrialized countries. Although the market may grow at a slower pace than in the 1980s, an annual average growth rate between 4 and 6 per cent through to the year 2000 is still deemed possible. Certainly the gap between actual and desired participation levels suggests that the latent demand for overseas travel is immense. Undoubtedly the benefits to flow from realizing this potential could be enormous, especially for destinations in the Asia Pacific region, which is where the bulk of Japanese visitation is concentrated. On the negative side, however, the expansion of the market could pose problems for some destinations similar to those created during the boom period of the late 1980s. Potential problem areas could involve capacity and service-related issues, and possibly relations between Japanese visitors and their hosts, particularly if an increase in Japanese visitation is accompanied by another surge in overseas investment in real estate ventures.

In stark contrast to its importance as a tourist-generating country, Japan's development as a tourist receiving country has not progressed at anything like the same rate. During the last ten years the growth in outbound travel has greatly outpaced that of inbound travel. In fact Japan's standing could slip even further behind over the next few years as competition from other destinations in the Asia Pacific region increases. Ironically it is the strength of the Japanese yen, which has done so much to power outbound demand, that is partly to blame for the slow growth in inbound travel. In 1993 Japan suffered a 4.8 per cent decline in visitor arrivals; an occurrence that is mostly attributed to the rise in the value of the yen.

The problems facing Japan's inbound tourist industry are further complicated by the external pressures being applied to the Japanese government to cut the nation's trade surplus. Despite the efforts of the Japan National Tourist Organization (JNTO), the Japanese government only pays lip-service to encouraging inbound travel. Since inbound tourism constitutes an indirect form of export activity, the government's ambivalence towards stimulating inbound travel looks likely to continue while Japan's trade surplus is a source of international friction.

This chapter examines the contrasting roles of Japan as a tourist-generating and tourist-receiving country within the context of the Asia Pacific region. The main demand characteristics of outbound travel from and inbound travel trends to Japan are analysed.

Travel From Japan

General background

The early years
The Japanese have a long tradition of domestic travel dating back hundreds of years involving pilgrimages and visits to temples and hot springs (Tokuhisa, 1980). Overseas travel, however, is a relatively new phenomenon for the Japanese. Compared with other major industrialized nations, the Japanese have been slow to participate in overseas travel. The slow uptake of foreign travel stems from the whole gamut of socio-economic factors, and deeply ingrained cultural and institutional barriers that coloured the development of Japan in the period after the end of World War II.

For most of the post-war era the pursuit of growth has been the paramount goal of Japanese economic policy. Over the same period Japan has witnessed profound changes to the structure of its society due to ever increasing industrialization and urbanization. Yet despite these developments, social attitudes have changed rather more slowly causing a gap to emerge between the nation's social and economic development. Even when the economy began to improve in the late 1950s and early 1960s, and the economic constraints became less of a problem, the social and institutional barriers to expanding leisure activities beyond a few days, or to taking vacations at times other than those dictated by convention and corporate convenience, remained largely unchanged for the average worker.

For many Japanese the turning point came in the 1980s. On the economic front the appreciation of the yen suddenly created a wealth of overseas purchasing power that spurred the demand for overseas travel. On the social front recognition of the need to modify lifestyles and to improve social and welfare conditions in Japan began to gain wider acceptance. In the latter case the underlying social and demographic changes affecting the fabric of Japanese society have played, and are continuing to play, an important part in reshaping Japanese values and attitudes. Thus, it has only been in the last two decades or so, as the economic, social and institutional barriers have gradually lessened, that the average Japanese has felt able to explore new leisure horizons, including overseas travel.

The opening up of outbound travel

Until the mid 1960s opportunities for overseas travel were severely limited due largely to the government's tight controls on the use of foreign currency. A strengthening economy, however, enabled the government to relax travel restrictions in 1964, opening the way for well-to-do Japanese to travel overseas for tourism purposes. The travel industry's response was the introduction of the organized brand package tour; a product admirably suited to the needs of the inexperienced Japanese traveller of the day. Along with the advent of the package tour, transportation developments – symbolized by the introduction of the Boeing 747 jet in 1970, and the consequent reduction in group air fares and package tour costs – paved the way for the early travel booms of the late 1960s and early 1970s.

Despite some setbacks along the way the overall trend for outbound travel during the last 30 years has been one of market growth. Between 1965 and 1973 the average annual increase in overseas travel was 40 per cent, reaching a peak of 64 per cent in 1973. During this period two significant developments happened. First, a turnaround occurred in 1969 when pleasure-related travel replaced business-related travel as the dominant component of the outbound market. Second, in 1971 the number of outbound travellers overtook the number of inbound travellers for the first time – the gap widening ever since. Currently, the ratio of outbound to inbound travel stands at more than three to one (Figure 9.1).

The 1970s and 1980s: from oil crises to Endaka

The first oil crisis in 1973 brought an abrupt halt to the travel boom, but after two sluggish years double-digit growth resumed and continued until 1980 when the lingering effects of the second oil crisis prompted a 3.2 per cent decline in outbound travel. Travel demand was slow to recover taking two years to surpass the level reached in 1979. The slow growth of the early 1980s contrasts vividly with the boom of the post-1985 period when the market surged from 4.9 million in 1985 to 10.9 million in 1990 recording an annual average growth rate of 17.4 per cent. The main impetus behind the travel boom was *endaka* – the rapid appreciation of the yen. Following the decision by the Group of Five industrial nations to drive the level of the US dollar down, the value of the yen soared from 238 yen to the US dollar in 1985 to 128 yen in 1988 before easing to 144 yen in 1990. Figure 9.2 indicates the correlation between the level of the yen and the flow of travel to and from Japan. It should be noted that the demand for overseas travel was also fed by

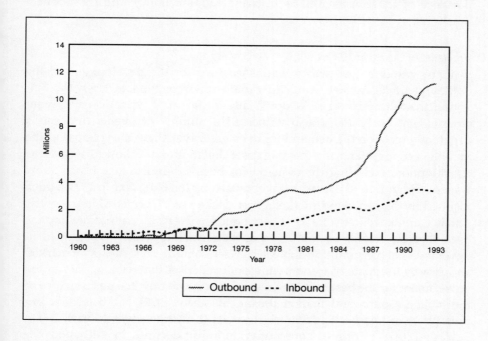

Figure 9.1 International travel to and from Japan.
Source: Ministry of Justice (compiled by Japan National Tourist Organization, 1994).

the air of affluence created by the 'bubble' economy and the rising stock market during the latter half of the 1980s.

The introduction of the Ten Million Programme

It was against this bullish economic climate in 1987 that Japan's Ministry of Transport (MOT, 1987) launched the Ten Million Programme (10MP) to double the number of outbound travellers in five years to expand Japan's tourism deficit. The announcement of this programme was a new departure for the government since tourism policy had not previously figured highly among its priorities. In reality the timing of the announcement of the 10MP had more to do with the level of international criticism directed at Japan's huge trade surplus than regard for the development of international tourism. The 10MP was among the proposals introduced to help dampen down the issue of trade friction. Consequently, although the 10MP was well received overseas, it did not go down particularly well with the Japanese travel industry, which perceived the programme to be merely a public relations exercise that skirted the issues and problems affecting the travel industry. At best, the 10MP can be credited with creating more awareness of the importance of tourism as well as bringing tourism policy into the political limelight.

Problems in the early 1990s

In many respects 1990 was a watershed year for the development of the outbound travel market. After the rapid growth of the late 1980s the outbound market began to slow down due in part to physical capacity constraints. The early 1990s also witnessed a number of events that had a negative impact on the demand for overseas travel. First, the collapse of the 'bubble' economy and the massive asset deflation that followed weakened consumption, including the demand for business and luxury travel. Next was the disruption to overseas travel caused by the Gulf War in 1991, which resulted in the outbound market's first decline in 11 years. More recently, public confidence in the nation's economic and institutional framework has been severely shaken by the depth of the recession, which has resulted in lower levels of consumption and cut-backs in some areas of the travel market, and also by the spate of scandals and political crises that have paralysed the government for the best part of two years. Consequently, the performance of the Japanese outbound market during the early 1990s has been less impressive than had been previously forecast (Edwards, 1988; Morris, 1990). Still, despite a record 10 consecutive monthly declines in outbound departures from September 1992 through to June 1993, the number of overseas travellers edged up to a record 11.9 million in 1993.

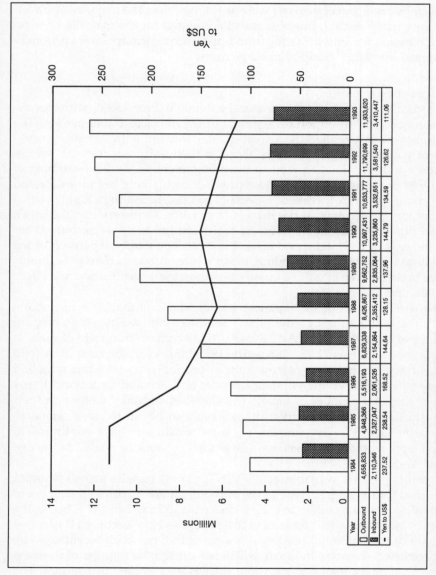

Year	1984	1985	1986	1987	1988	1989	1990	1991	1992	1993
Outbound	4,658,833	4,948,366	5,516,193	6,829,338	8,426,867	9,662,752	10,997,431	10,633,777	11,790,699	11,933,620
Inbound	2,110,346	2,327,047	2,061,526	2,154,864	2,355,412	2,835,064	3,235,860	3,532,651	3,581,540	3,410,447
Yen to US$	237.52	238.54	168.52	144.64	128.15	137.96	144.79	134.59	126.62	111.06

Figure 9.2 International travel and currency trends.
Source: Ministry of Justice, Management and Coordination Agency (compiled by Japan National Tourist Organization, 1994).

Market characteristics

Changing profile of the Japanese market
Over the years the pattern of overseas travel has undergone considerable change reflecting not only the market's overall expansion, but also the changing style and composition of the travel market. In the 1960s, when overseas travel was a novelty enjoyed by very few Japanese, the three main characteristics of travel demand were as follows: first, the majority of travellers were male; second, business travel accounted for the majority of trips; third, pleasure travellers (mainly from upper income groups) were generally organized into large group or package tours.

The start of mass tourism
Towards the end of the 1970s market demand broadened with honeymooners became an important segment of the overseas travel market. The 1980s, however, signalled the arrival of mass tourism with increasing numbers of young women, especially those in their early twenties, as well as students and middle-aged women travelling overseas. By the beginning of the 1990s the image of the Japanese traveller had largely been transformed with young, pleasure travellers, especially females, becoming a highly visible and important segment of the market. According to research by the Japan Travel Bureau (1993), single women in the age group 18–44 accounted for 18.4 per cent of the total travel market in 1992. The steady expansion of the outbound market notwithstanding, Japan's core outbound market segments can be broken down into three broad categories: the under 35s, the mid 30s to late 40s, and the over 50s.

The early growth of the Japanese outbound travel market – essentially from the late 1960s through the 1970s – was characterized by a high preponderance of male travellers. As late as 1979 the composition ratio of male to female travellers was 72:28. During the 1980s, however, the ratio of male to female travellers began to narrow quite appreciably. By 1993 this ratio had narrowed to 57:43. Women in their twenties now account for around 40 per cent of the total number of female travellers. In addition, women in their early thirties and those in their fifties have also begun to travel more, as shown in Table 9.1. By contrast, vacation constraints have continued to inhibit opportunities for overseas travel among working males in the age group 30–50.

According to data available for 1993 (JNTO, 1994), females in their twenties accounted for the largest share of the outbound market with 17.3 per cent of the total, followed by males in their forties with 13.7 per cent. This marks the second year in a row that females in their twenties have occupied the largest segment of the outbound market. It is a trend that has been accentuated by the protracted recession in Japan, which has caused the number of business travellers (largely males in their late thirties and forties) to contract. The

Table 9.1 The number of Japanese leaving Japan classified by age and sex 1989 and 1993

Age	Total	Male	Female	Share of total (%) Total	Share of total (%) Male	Share of total (%) Female	Share by sex Male	Share by sex Female	Ratio (%) Male	Ratio (%) Female	% change 1993/89 Total	% change 1993/89 Male	% change 1993/89 Female
1989													
0–14	324,677	163,590	161,087	3.4	1.7	1.7	2.7	4.4	50.4	49.6			
15–19	319,900	132,138	187,762	3.3	1.4	1.9	2.2	5.1	41.3	58.7			
20–24	1,214,873	432,125	782,748	12.6	4.5	8.1	7.2	21.2	36.6	64.4			
25–29	1,477,297	732,931	744,366	15.3	7.6	7.7	12.3	20.2	49.6	50.4			
30–34	981,639	685,744	295,895	10.2	7.1	3.1	11.5	8.0	69.9	30.1			
35–39	934,420	715,154	219,266	9.7	7.4	2.3	12.0	5.9	76.5	23.5			
40–49	2,055,827	1,577,127	478,700	21.3	16.3	5.0	26.4	13.0	76.7	23.3			
50–59	1,403,645	952,241	451,404	14.5	9.9	4.7	15.9	12.2	67.8	32.2			
Over 60	950,396	583,889	366,507	9.8	6.0	3.8	9.8	9.9	61.4	38.6			
Unknown	78	43	35	0.0	0.0	0.0	0.0	0.0	55.1	44.9			
Total	9,662,752	5,974,982	3,687,770	100.0	61.8	38.2	100.0	100.0	61.8	38.2			
1993													
0–14	465,334	232,675	232,659	3.9	1.9	1.9	3.4	4.5	50.0	50.0	43.3	42.2	44.4
15–19	429,856	177,606	252,250	3.6	1.5	2.1	2.6	4.9	41.3	58.7	34.4	34.4	34.3
20–24	1,566,629	519,763	1,046,866	13.1	4.4	8.8	7.7	20.2	33.2	66.8	29.0	20.3	33.7
25–29	1,828,979	811,387	1,017,592	15.3	6.8	8.5	12.0	19.6	44.4	55.6	23.8	10.7	36.7
30–34	1,238,458	766,213	472,245	10.4	6.4	4.0	11.3	9.1	61.9	38.1	26.2	11.7	59.6
35–39	958,382	672,468	285,914	8.0	5.6	2.4	10.0	5.5	70.2	29.8	2.6	−6.0	30.4
40–49	2,302,467	1,638,530	663,937	19.3	13.7	5.6	24.3	12.8	71.2	28.8	12.0	3.9	38.7
50–59	1,830,886	1,156,799	674,087	15.3	9.7	5.6	17.1	13.0	63.2	36.8	30.4	21.5	49.3
Over 60	1,312,568	779,010	533,558	11.0	6.5	4.5	11.5	10.3	59.4	40.6	38.1	33.4	45.6
Unknown	61	30	31	0.0	0.0	0.0	0.0	0.0	49.2	50.8	−21.8	−30.2	−11.4
Total	11,933,620	6,754,481	5,179,139	100.0	56.6	43.4	100.0	100.0	56.6	43.4	23.5	13.0	40.4

Source: Japan Immigration Association (1990, 1994) (based on data from Ministry of Justice)

increase in the number of children under the age of 14 showing up in the immigration statistics (Japan Immigration Association, 1994) suggests that there is growing interest in overseas travel among young families. This is a segment of the market that the Japanese travel industry has been slow to recognize; consequently, it has only been in the last two years that travel products geared to the needs of young families have appeared in the marketplace. At the top end of the age spectrum the steady growth in the number of overseas travellers in their fifties and above reflects the degree of leisure time available to this group as well as the demographic factors of an ageing population.

Package tour developments
The growth of the Japanese outbound market is closely associated with the development of the all-inclusive package tour. Since their introduction in the late 1960s package tours have been, and continue to be, a very popular form of travel for the Japanese. According to a *Mainichi Shimbun* (1993) survey report, the overall utilization rate of package tours was 58.3 per cent in 1993. In recent years, however, the increase in the number of repeat, women and younger travellers has caused a number of changes to occur in the structure, operation and development of package tour travel. While conventional package tours are still popular among first-time and older travellers, the needs of the more experienced or adventurous travellers tend to be quite different. Not only do these segments show a marked preference for less structured or organized tours compared with first-time travellers, they are more inclined to travel with friends or in small groups rather than in large groups. As a result, tour wholesalers are having to produce a much wider range of products to accommodate the increasingly diverse needs of an expanding market. Though the travel agent and the tour wholesaler continue to exert an important influence on the direction of the travel market and on consumer buying decisions, their control has clearly waned. Market maturity has fostered a degree of confidence and independence among the Japanese, encouraging a growing number to look at travel alternatives to the conventional, fully organized package tour such as the so-called skeletal or minimum-organized tour product, and, of course, independently organized travel.

Another feature of Japan's expanding travel market is the shift towards cheaper forms of travel. Although older age groups and honeymooners retain a preference for the top brand products, independently minded travellers, repeaters and young travellers are moving towards products at the lower end of the price spectrum. While the current surge towards cheaper forms of travel has certainly been exacerbated by the recession, the trend predates the onset of the recession. Initially, the sale of discounted airfares and budget tours began as an industry tactic to alleviate the seasonal travel constraints that had quickly built up in the wake of the travel boom. Latterly, the demand for cheaper travel products reflects the outbound market's growing diversity and gradual progress away from relying on highly organized package tour travel to more independently organized forms of travel.

The shift in travel attitudes and requirements stemming from the changing composition and needs of the market is also reshaping the pattern of outbound travel. In recent years there has been a movement away from city-based tourism featuring multi destination tours towards mono-destination trips featuring beach/resort tourism. Industry surveys (Japan Air Lines, 1990; Japan Travel Bureau, 1993) indicate that this trend reflects the increase in the number of younger Japanese, and families travelling overseas as well as a growing desire among the Japanese to relax and enjoy vacations rather than pursue the rushed itineraries of past years. This trend is beginning to have a discernible impact on destination flows as evidenced by the increased popularity of destinations such as Indonesia, Australia and Micronesia. On the other hand, city-based tourist destinations such as Hong Kong, Taipei, and Seoul have witnessed slower, or in some cases negative, growth.

Seasonality becomes less evident

The upsurge in travel in the second half of the 1980s quickly exposed not only the rigidity of Japanese vacation patterns but also the inadequacies of Japan's airport infrastructure, particularly at Narita and Itami, the gateways to Tokyo and Osaka respectively. With the peak travel periods subject to capacity constraints, the travel industry began to resort to discounting to encourage people to travel during the off season. Discounting has proved to be very successful in opening up new areas of demand particularly among students and budget-minded travellers. As a result the peaks and troughs that once characterized overseas travel demand have become less acute.

Purpose of travel

In terms of trip motivation the overseas leisure market makes up the largest component of travel demand. For the past decade the share of the leisure market has hovered around the 82–84 per cent level while the business market has fluctuated between 12–16 per cent (Prime Minister's Office, 1993, 1994). Over the six-year period 1988–93 there has been greater growth in leisure travel than in business travel – the average annual growth rates being 10.3 per cent and 8.6 per cent respectively. Classified by sex, the ratio of male to female leisure travellers closed to 55:45 in 1993; however, the ratio of male to female business travellers remained far apart at 69:31.

Destinations Visited by The Japanese

Data problems
A common problem in tracking Japanese visitor flows is the lack of uniform data. Official Japanese data compiled by the Ministry of Justice (MOJ) on the destinations visited by the Japanese are not wholly accurate as the data record only the first destinations mentioned on immigration cards. This accounts for the discrepancies often found between Japan-sourced and destination-sourced data.

Regional breakdown
On a regional basis, however, the MOJ statistics are held to be a fairly accurate guide to Japanese visitor flows. Although the trend in recent years has seen Asia's share of the Japanese market drop, it is still the most popular region for Japanese visitors. In 1993 Asia (including the Middle East) attracted 45.4 per cent of the total market, North America 32 per cent, Europe 12 per cent, and Oceania 9.8 per cent (Japan Immigration Association, 1994). Strong growth towards Oceania has been a noticeable feature of the outbound market for several years.

Despite the huge increase in outbound travel from Japan, there have been relatively few major changes in the top destination preferences for the Japanese over the last decade. This is partly because first-time travellers tend to choose tried and tested destinations and also the main tour wholesalers concentrate their sales activities on high-volume destinations. In addition, besides the obvious considerations of proximity and time, the concentration of travel to destinations in East Asia (Hong Kong, South Korea, Taiwan and China) is also influenced to some extent by ethnic and family ties. That said, the increase in young travellers going overseas especially those aged in their twenties and early thirties has certainly enhanced the popularity of beach resort destinations. Furthermore, there is a growing demand for new destinations to be found among the more adventurous and experienced travellers. On the other hand, older market segments retain a preference for destinations and tours featuring traditional sightseeing activities and cultural attractions.

Hawaii the main destination
The main destinations jostling for the status of being Japan's premier destination are Hawaii, South Korea, Continental USA and Hong Kong (Table 9.2). In 1993 Hawaii was the market's top choice, attracting approximately 13.3 per cent of the total outbound Japanese market. The island continues to hold a unique appeal for the Japanese. It is undoubtedly the most mature and developed destination for the Japanese market.

Of late there has been a very strong upsurge in travel to China, which seems to indicate that the market's confidence in that destination has been

Table 9.2   Japanese visitor arrivals to selected Asia–Pacific destinations

Destination	1990	1991	1992	1993	Share %	% Change 1993/90
China (n)	463,265	640,859	791,531	912,000	7.6	96.9
Hong Kong	1,331,677	1,259,837	1,324,399	1,280,905	10.7	−3.8
Indonesia (n)	267,970	294,679	400,615	440,265	3.7	64.3
South Korea (n)	1,460,291	1,455,090	1,398,604	1,492,069	12.5	2.2
Malaysia	500,094	394,437	247,671	243,038	2.0	−51.4
Philippines	201,982	197,540	221,578	243,412	2.0	20.5
Singapore	971,637	871,313	1,000,775	1,000,973	8.4	3.0
Taiwan (n)	914,484	825,985	795,018	697,916	5.8	−23.7
Thailand (n)	635,555	543,097	568,049	579,470	4.9	−8.8
Hawaii	1,439,710	1,385,340	1,637,030	1,591,920	13.3	10.6
Guam	637,569	582,270	676,659	549,343	4.6	−13.8
Marianas	329,581	310,274	354,941	378,719	3.2	14.9
Australia	479,900	528,500	629,900	671,100	5.6	39.8
New Zealand	107,840	114,718	128,962	135,934	1.1	26.1
Fiji	21,619	27,802	35,960	38,203	0.3	76.7
Total outbound travel from Japan	10,997,431	10,633,777	11,790,699	11,933,620	100.0	8.5

Sources: Ministry of Justice, National Tourist Offices and PATA (compiled by Japan National Tourist Organization (1994)

restored following the slump in demand after the Tiananmen incident in 1989. Within South-east Asia, Indonesia has assumed a larger share of the market due to the growing popularity of Bali among younger Japanese. Elsewhere, one destination that has witnessed a huge surge in popularity both in terms of actual and desired levels of visitation is Australia having recorded an annual average increase of 18.3 per cent between 1989 and 1993.

Length of stay

The short-haul leisure market – composed mostly of mono-destination tours to East Asia/Micronesia – is also generally a short-stay market with most travel completed within five days. Trips to popular destinations such as Hawaii and those in South-east Asia tend to average five to seven days while long-haul trips, for example to Europe and North America, average between 8 to 14 days. According to official MOJ data (Prime Minister's Office, 1994), the average length of stay for overseas trips was 8.0 days in 1993; however, 53–56 per cent of Japanese travellers regularly complete their overseas trips within five days. In general the short-stay characteristics of the Japanese market reflect the traditional limitations on taking extended vacations, that is more than one week. Until more fundamental changes in work and leisure attitudes occur, this short-stay pattern is likely to continue since the Japanese use on average only 56 per cent of their annual paid vacation entitlement.

The origin of Japanese travellers

The highest concentrations of outbound travellers are to be found in the Tokyo and Kansai metropolitan areas. In 1993 the Tokyo metropolitan region, which covers the prefectures of Tokyo, Chiba, Saitama and Kanagawa, generated 42.1 per cent of total outbound traffic and the Kansai region (covering Osaka, Hyogo, Kyoto and three other prefectures) 16.7 per cent. In total, seven out of Japan's 47 prefectures generated more than 500,000 departures each in 1993. One trend evident in recent years is that travel from Japan's regions has grown at a faster rate than travel from the two main metropolitan areas. Over the period 1990–93 travel from Hokkaido has increased 14 per cent, from Tohoku 22 per cent, from Shikoku 22 per cent, and from Kyushu 17 per cent. In contrast, travel from the Tokyo region has increased 5.3 per cent, and from the Kansai region just 0.2 per cent. This trend can be explained by the increase in scheduled and non-scheduled air services from local airports, and also by the recession, the impact of which has been greater on the metropolitan areas. As to the future, the opening of the Kansai International Airport in September 1994 is expected to boost the demand for outbound travel particularly from the western regions of Japan.

Expenditure trends

Influence of outbound travel
Over the last decade Japan's international tourism balance sheet has registered a tremendous increase in travel expenditure resulting from the huge growth in outbound travel and the stronger purchasing power of the yen. As a result the gap between tourism expenditure and tourism receipts has widened dramatically. In 1993 total expenditure was estimated by the Bank of Japan to be $26,860 million, while receipts brought in $3,557 million resulting in a record deficit of $23,303 million – an amount equal to 16.5 per cent of Japan's trade surplus (Table 9.3). The political significance of Japan's travel deficit has not been lost on the government, which explains why tourism policy has tended to favour the promotion of outbound rather than inbound travel.

Trip expenditure varies according to market segment and the destination chosen. According to JTB's 1993 survey report (figures based on package

Table 9.3 Japan's balance of travel account and balance of payments, 1991–93 (US$mn)

	1991	1992	
Travel account			
Expenditure	23,983	26,837	26,860
Receipts	3,435	3,588	3,557
Travel Balance	−20,548	−23,249	−23,303
Balance of payments			
Trade Balance	103,044	132,348	141,429
Current Balance	72,901	117,551	131,350

Sources: Bank of Japan, in JNTO (1994); Ministry of Finance, in JETRO (1993, 1994)

tours), honeymooners continue to outspend all other market segments. Their average total expenditure was Y625,000 in 1992, well above the market average of Y458,000. By destination, expenditures tend to be greater relative to the increase in distance from Japan. The least costly trips, and generally those of shortest duration, are to Micronesia, East Asia and South-east Asia. On trips to Micronesia average expenditure was estimated at Y245,000; to South-east Asia Y312,000; and to Oceania Y543,000.

Expenditure impact on destination economies
National statistics in a number of Asia Pacific countries testify to the economic importance of tourism and, in particular, Japanese tourism. The impact of the concentration of Japanese visitor flows in the Asia Pacific region can be gauged more readily when visitor numbers are juxtaposed with expenditure levels (Table 9.4). For tourism dependent destinations such as Hawaii, the Japanese market is of major importance. In 1993 the Japanese accounted for 58.3 per cent of foreign visitors to Hawaii, and contributed 63.5 per cent of foreign visitor revenue, an amount equal to 9.7 per cent of the gross state product. *En masse*, the Japanese will continue to be the region's most prolific market. That said, the past performance of the Japanese market in terms of per capita expenditure should not be taken for granted.

Problems and issues facing the outbound sector

The need for change
During the late 1980s the rapid expansion of the Japanese outbound market led to problems developing in both Japan and in several destinations in the Asia Pacific region. As the market expands further the possibility of similar or new problems occurring in the future cannot be ruled out. At the very least the changing character of the market will warrant some new approaches on the part of the travel industry and receiving countries. The following are among the more important areas of concern.

Table 9.4 Share of Japanese arrivals and expenditure in selected Asia–Pacific destinations

	Japanese share of total		
Destination	Visitor Arrivals	Visitor Expenditure	Year
	%	%	
Hawaii*	58.3	63.5	1993
Hong Kong	14.3	17.3	1993
Taiwan	42.4	44.4	1992
Singapore	16.7	10.9	1992
Indonesia	11.1	11.6	1993
Australia	24.2	17.1	1992

* Excludes domestic visitors.
Sources: Hong Kong Tourist Association (1994); Hawaii Visitors Bureau (1994); Bureau of Tourism Research (1993); Department of Tourism (1994); Singapore Tourist Promotion Board (1993a and b); Tourism Bureau (1993)

Growth potential v capacity

Japan's Ministry of Transport forecasts that the number of outbound travellers could reach 14–18 million people by the end of the decade (industry forecasts are a little more bullish at 17–20 million), assuming moderate growth in the economy and a stable yen. Undoubtedly the growth potential of the Japanese market remains considerable. However, the expansion of the market will add to existing capacity problems in Japan, which could yet hamper future growth. The major concern in Japan is the state of airport infrastructure. The expansion of Japan's airport infrastructure to alleviate capacity constraints and facilitate market access is vital. However, airport construction in Japan remains a highly charged and contentious issue, which means any serious delay in improving airport infrastructure could inhibit the market's growth potential. From the standpoint of receiving countries, an increase in the Japanese market could also open up the possibility of aggravating capacity issues and social tensions in some destinations in the Asia Pacific region.

Market composition

Recent trends indicate that the character and composition of the market is changing. The emphasis is gradually moving from group to individual travel, and from package to independent travel. As a result destination services and marketing strategies will have to be geared accordingly in the future to accommodate the more individualistic needs and demands of the Japanese. In the short term this could create some problems for destinations if such facilities and services are not readily forthcoming.

Expenditure

One trend that has become more noticeable in the 1990s is that while more Japanese are travelling, they are spending less. Since reaching a peak in 1990 average per capita expenditure measured in yen terms has decreased year on year. The greater purchasing power of the yen and the impact of the recession notwithstanding, Japanese spending habits are changing. The Japanese have always been a value-conscious market, but now they are becoming more price conscious and more discerning in their buying decisions. The impact on destinations will depend on how readily they can adapt to the changing expenditure profile of the Japanese. In the long term the expectation is that as their vacation time increases, the Japanese will become less time conscious but more price conscious in their attitude towards overseas travel.

Japanese overseas investment in tourism
While Japanese visitation has been eagerly sought after because of its high economic potential, Japanese investment in the region has drawn a mixed reaction. During the 1980s the huge appreciation of the yen and its impact on the currency's overseas purchasing power triggered not only a massive increase in outbound travellers but also a substantial movement of Japanese capital overseas, a significant proportion of which was channelled into tourism-related and real estate ventures within the Asia Pacific region. Japanese investment has clearly played an important role in facilitating and encouraging the development of tourism in the region; however, it has not been entirely welcome in some quarters. In Australia, for example, the sheer scale and pace of these capital movements coupled with the contentious issue of the foreign ownership of land sparked off some resentment towards the Japanese.

At present the Japanese are following a much more cautious and selective approach to their overseas ventures in the wake of the collapse of Japan's 'bubble' economy and the domestic recession. However, given the long-term potential for growth in overseas travel, Japanese investment can be expected to pick up once the economy improves. As tourist numbers grow and the pressures to reconcile local interests and environmental concerns with the demands for increased tourism development mount, the task then will be to ensure that the excesses of the 1980s are not repeated.

Travel to Japan

General background

The early years
The emergence of an economically vibrant Japan in the 1960s brought not only the post-war period of austerity to a close but also laid the foundations for inbound travel to develop. Against a backdrop of a booming economy and events such as the 1964 Tokyo Olympics, the number of foreign visitors rose from 352,832 in 1964 to 609,000 in 1969, an average annual increase of 11.7 per cent.

During the 1970s the growth rate slowed to an average 7.2 per cent due mainly to the disruptive effects of the two oil crises subduing demand for international travel, and the sharp increase in the value of the yen in 1978. The slowdown in arrivals from North America and Europe proved to be highly significant as it opened the way for Asia to become Japan's main generating region.

Developments in the 1980s and early 1990s
Partly as a result of improved economic conditions and because of the partial liberalization of overseas travel from Taiwan, the first half of the 1980s saw quite a strong increase in foreign visitors with the number rising to 2.3 million by 1985. In 1986, however, inbound travel fell 11.4 per cent largely as a result of the increase in the value of the yen following the signing of the Plaza Accord in September 1985.

The gradual recovery of the inbound travel market was due initially to the resilience of the business travel sector, which continued to grow, albeit at a reduced pace. However, it was the opening up of the Korean outbound travel market in 1989 that provided the major stimulus to Japan's inbound industry. In the period 1988–92 the number of foreign visitors to Japan increased by 1.2 million, of whom Koreans accounted for 43 per cent. In 1990 the inbound market surpassed the three million mark for the first time, and reached a total of 3.5 million visitors by the end of 1992.

Market characteristics

Data sources
As with the outbound sector the primary source of data on visitor arrivals to Japan is the Ministry of Justice (MOJ). Since the MOJ's remit is concerned more with immigration rather than tourism matters, the amount and type of data collected is limited and not wholly compatible with international standards. The JNTO (1994) recalculates basic visitor figures to bring them into line with international standards, but revised statistics on visitor characteristics are not available.

Current trends
Although the overall inbound total for 1992 showed an increase of 1.4 per cent, demand over the last half of the year was down 3.1 per cent. The fall off in demand continued through 1993 resulting in an overall drop in inbound arrivals to 3,410,447, a decrease of 4.8 per cent over 1992. According to the JNTO, the main reasons for the 'temporary' decline in inbound visitors were the combined effects of the rise in the value of the yen and the protracted business recession in Japan's main generating markets, coupled with a

weakening in demand from South-east Asian countries because of a tightening up in travel procedures by Japanese immigration authorities.

Japan's main origin regions

In 1993 arrivals from Asia accounted for 65.2 per cent of the total inbound market (Table 9.5). In fact, just four Asian markets (South Korea, Taiwan, China and Hong Kong) accounted for 55 per cent of the total inbound market. Besides geographical considerations, the importance of Asia as a generating region, and in particular these four markets, has been magnified by the following factors:

- The rapid economic growth achieved in neighbouring Asian countries.
- The lifting of travel restrictions in South Korea and Taiwan.
- A wide variety of motivational factors including strong ethnic and cultural ties with China, Taiwan and Korea.
- The expansion of regional air services especially between East Asia and Japan.

By contrast, although the overall number of visitors originating from North America has increased, North America's share of the market has contracted dramatically from 31.3 per cent in 1979 to 18.2 per cent in 1993. Over the last decade growth out of North America has been mostly limited to the business travel market. In terms of tourist travel, the US tourist market, which makes up the largest component of travel out of North America, has remained largely stagnant because of the weakness of the dollar and the US economy.

Long-haul travel from Europe, Japan's other main regional market, has followed a similar growth pattern to North America but in a less volatile fashion. The slightly better stability in the traffic flow from Europe can be ascribed to the fact that business travel forms the largest component of the market. In 1993 visitors from Europe accounted for 15.1 per cent of the total inbound market, though if Hong Kong holders of UK nationality are excluded Europe's share drops to 11.7 per cent.

Elsewhere, arrivals from Oceania continue to grow at a moderate pace accounting for 2.7 per cent of the market total; however, the recent surge in arrivals from South America, which was prompted mainly by revised immigration laws allowing South Americans of Japanese ancestry easier entry into Japan for the purposes of working, has come to a halt in the wake of the domestic recession in Japan.

Arrivals to Japan by destination

Up to 1988 Japan's largest visitor-generating country was the USA, but that changed the following year with the lifting of travel restrictions in South Korea. In 1989 the Korean market increased by the huge margin of 78.7 per cent to 610,000 visitors, and since then it has been Japan's leading source market (Table 9.6). Although the rapid growth of the Korean market has

Table 9.5 Visitor arrivals classified by region and purpose 1992–93

1992	Tourist	Share %	Business	Share %	Others	Total	Share %	% Share of Total		% Change 1992/91		
								Tourist	Business	Tourist	Business	Total
Asia (a)	1,374,994	65.4	481,323	51.5	376,450	2,232,767	62.3	61.6	21.6	-0.3	3.4	1.7
(b)	1,482,415	70.5	501,980	53.7	385,870	2,370,265	66.2	62.5	21.2	1.0	3.4	2.5
Europe	271,942	12.9	200,517	21.5	61,022	533,481	14.9	51	37.6	7.2	-4.4	2.4
(c)	164,521	7.8	179,860	19.2	51,602	395,983	11.1	41.5	45.4	-0.8	-5.1	-2.0
North America	351,298	16.7	217,887	23.3	76,179	645,364	18.0	54.4	33.8	4.4	3.4	4.2
South America	60,027	2.9	5,525	0.6	6,846	72,398	2.0	82.9	7.6	-36.6	-3.5	-32.7
Oceania	40,081	1.9	24,220	2.6	18,721	83,022	2.3	48.3	29.2	15.2	2.9	10.9
Others	4,704	0.2	5,036	0.5	4,768	14,508	0.4	32.4	34.7	-9.6	-9.9	-3.5
Total	2,103,046	100.0	934,508	100.0	543,986	3,581,540	100.0	58.7	26.1	-0.0	1.5	1.4

1993	Tourist	Share %	Business	Share %	Others	Total	Share %	Tourist	Business	% Change 1993/92		
										Tourist	Business	Total
Asia (a)	1,245,293	64.7	489,497	52.3	371,659	2,106,449	61.8	59.1	23.2	-9.4	1.7	-5.7
(b)	1,334,976	69.4	508,575	54.4	381,147	2,224,698	65.2	50.1	22.9	-9.9	1.3	-6.1
Europe	258,517	13.4	193,140	20.7	64,380	516,037	15.1	42.4	37.4	-4.9	-3.7	-3.3
(c)	168,834	8.8	174,062	18.6	54,892	397,788	11.7	42.4	43.8	2.6	-3.2	0.5
North America	327,258	17.0	215,686	23.1	77,448	620,392	18.2	52.8	34.8	-6.8	-1.0	-3.9
South America	47,161	2.5	5,986	0.6	6,890	60,037	1.8	78.6	10.0	-21.4	8.3	-17.1
Oceania	41,558	2.2	25,805	2.8	25,121	92,484	2.7	44.9	27.9	3.7	6.5	11.4
Others	5,048	0.3	5,163	0.6	4,837	15,048	0.4	33.5	34.3	7.3	2.5	3.7
Total	1,924,835	100.0	935,277	100.00	550,335	3,410,447	100.00	56.4	27.4	-8.5	0.1	-4.8

a: includes Middle East
b: Includes UK Hong Kong holders of British passports.
c: excludes UK Hong Kong holders of British passports.
Source: Ministry of Justice (compiled by JNTO, 1994)

tapered off, South Korea accounted for 24.8 per cent of the total inbound market in 1993, followed by Taiwan with 19.6 per cent, the USA with 15.6 per cent and China 6.1 per cent.

Classifying arrivals by purpose

One of the distinctive characteristics of the inbound market to Japan is that the composite ratio of tourist to business travellers is much narrower than is the case for the outbound market. Arrival statistics for 1993 show that tourists accounted for 56.4 per cent of the total inbound market; business travellers 27.4 per cent; 'others' (a group that includes study, training, educational visits as well as trips by so-called entertainers) 13.2 per cent; and shore excursionists, that is temporary visitors in transit or on ships staying less than 72 hours, 2.9 per cent. However, official statistics hide the fact that business travel is the bedrock on which the development of the inbound market largely rests. Business travel is not only crucial in sustaining long-haul visitor flows, but also forms a growing segment of the market originating from Asia. It is widely thought in the travel industry that the tourist/business ratio is even closer than official statistics suggest. The travel industry alleges that the tourist share is overstated because it includes business travellers who find it

Table 9.6 Visitor arrivals to Japan classified by nationality 1991–93

	1991	1992	Change (%)	1993	Change (%)	Share(%)
Total	3,532,651	3,581,540	1.4	3,410,447	−4.8	100.0
China	130,487	183,220	40.4	206,743	12.8	6.1
Taiwan	658,106	715,487	8.7	668,581	−6.6	19.6
Hong Kong[a]	38,526	40,174	4.3	34,203	−14.9	1.0
Indonesia	43,263	40,647	−6.0	37,552	−7.6	1.1
South Korea	861,820	864,052	0.3	845,423	−2.2	24.8
Malaysia	77,423	60,894	−21.3	46,165	−24.2	1.4
Philippines	114,383	105,195	−8.0	91,199	−13.3	2.7
Singapore	42,882	40,956	−4.5	38,446	−6.1	1.1
Thailand	107,770	97,234	−9.8	70,946	−27.0	2.1
France	50,119	48,605	−3.0	49,178	1.2	1.4
Germany	61,227	63,930	4.4	62,795	−1.8	1.8
Italy	30,199	26,866	−11.0	25,283	−5.9	0.7
Russian Fed.	31,828	26,386	−17.1	31,897	20.9	0.9
UK[b]	219,425	241,893	10.2	225,737	−6.7	6.6
Canada	62,306	69,620	11.7	72,395	4.0	2.1
USA	543,075	560,940	3.3	533,401	−4.9	15.6
Brazil	69,503	41,487	−40.3	33,444	−19.4	1.0
Australia	54,520	59,844	9.8	69,439	16.0	2.0
New Zealand	18,120	21,014	16.0	21,014	0.0	0.6
UK[c]	102,859	104,395	1.5	107,488	3.0	3.2
UK/HK[d]	116,566	137,498	18.0	118,249	−14.0	3.5

a. Figures denote Hong Kong Certificate of Identity holders only.
b. Figures include Hong Kong holders of British passports.
c. Figures exclude Hong Kong holders of British passports.
d. Figures refer to Hong Kong holders of British passports.
Source: Ministry of Justice (compiled by JNTO, 1994)

simpler to gain entry as tourists and *pseudo* tourists, that is those whose sole intent is to work in Japan.

Visitor age and sex characteristics

Of the 3,747,157 foreigners who entered Japan in 1993, 2,159,355 were males and 1,587,802 were females (Japan Immigration Association, 1994). (It should be noted, however, that the MOJ's inclusion of re-entrants, that is foreigners residing in Japan, in the figure for total arrivals compromises the data to some extent.) Differentiated by age group, visitors in their thirties made up the largest age segment with 27.2 per cent of the total, followed by those in their twenties and forties. While the number of males was greater than that of females in most age groups, females in the 20–24 age group exceeded males by almost 2:1. Writing in the 1980s, Iyori (1987) noted that a large number of young women, particularly from the Philippines, South Korea and Taiwan were lured to Japan to work as hostesses and prostitutes in Japan's seedy entertainment industry. Immigration statistics suggest that this trend, concerning the so-called *Japayuki-san* (those who go to Japan), is continuing.

Inbound sector problems

In 1992 Japan was the fifth most popular destination for visitor arrivals to PATA member destinations. This ranking, however, appears to be in danger of slipping. Leaving aside the fact that other destinations in the region have obviously benefited enormously from the huge growth of the Japanese outbound market, Japan's position is being undermined by external as well as internal forces as described below.

The level of the yen

There is no doubt that the strength of the yen particularly against the US dollar has been one of the main stumbling blocks to expanding Japan's inbound market. Since the mid 1980s Japan's image as an expensive destination has hardened in line with the appreciation of the yen and this certainly had an adverse effect on long-haul leisure travel to Japan especially from North America, and more recently on the short-haul market too. The situation has been exacerbated by the economic recession of the early 1990s among the major industrialized countries of the world, which has caused some softening in business travel demand especially from Europe and North America. Needless to say the sudden surge in the yen's value in 1994, which saw the currency break the psychological Y100 to $1 mark, could have a further dampening effect on inbound travel.

Market appeal

Besides the perennial problems with the yen, Japan's market appeal seems to be more narrowly based than many of its Asian rivals. From within Asia, Japan attracts a wide range of market segments for leisure, study and business purposes. On the other hand, trip motivations for long-haul leisure travellers tend to be more narrowly focused. For example, citing the growth in popularity of package tours to South-east Asia and Hong Kong, Cockerell (1994) asserts that Europe's long-haul leisure travellers to Asia generally prefer one or two-centre trips featuring a beach resort location combined with some city sightseeing/shopping activities. The implications for Japan are clear. With its main attractions based largely around cultural and traditional sightseeing activities, Japan is at a disadvantage in trying to secure a larger share of the long-haul leisure market. Furthermore, the re-emergence of China as a tourist destination means that Japan has to vie with a strong competitor for the smaller, cultural and special interest tourist markets.

The role of government
Arguably one factor that has contributed to Japan's relatively low profile as a tourist destination is the government's tardiness in drawing up and pursuing a coherent tourism policy. Compared with the competitive policies pursued by many other Asian countries, Japan has traditionally employed a passive approach to developing inbound tourism. Apart from establishing a framework of regulations for the industry and overseeing the activities of the JNTO, the Ministry of Transport, which is the government body responsible for setting tourism policy in Japan, has largely been content to allow the private sector to take the lead in encouraging inbound tourism.

Government neglect of tourism stems in part from the hidebound attitude that tourism is not a sector in which government should take an active role. This conservative thinking, widely held in the portals of the all-important Ministry of Finance (MOF), derives from the fact that the economic benefits generated by the flow of inbound tourism have been relatively limited. Given the nature of Japan's export-driven economy, it is hardly surprising that tourism's contribution to the Japanese economy is much less significant than in other countries. The OECD (1995) notes that in 1993 Japan's ratio of travel account receipts to Gross Domestic Product was 0.1 per cent, and its share of travel account receipts in exports of goods and services was 0.6 per cent, the lowest percentages recorded among the member countries. In 1993 the Bank of Japan (JNTO, 1994) reported that visitors to Japan spent $3,557 million, down from $3,588 million in 1992 (Table 9.7). Over the last three years visitor receipts have remained largely stagnant due mainly to the recurring strength of the yen.

This detached attitude held sway until 1987 when the international repercussions of Japan's escalating trade surplus pushed the MOT into creating the very one-sided 10 Million Programme. For the next four years official tourism policy remained slanted towards the promotion of outbound travel with little support or encouragement given to the inbound sector. By 1991, however, significant pressure had built up in Japan for a more balanced tourism policy that catered to inbound as well as outbound needs. In

Table 9.7   Japan's international tourism receipts

	Total arrivals ('000)	Total US$mil.	Tourist receipts* Ratio to GDP %	Share of receipts in exports of goods & services %
Year				
1990	3,236	3,578	0.1	0.8
1991	3,533	3,435	0.1	0.7
1992	3,582	3,588	0.1	0.7
1993	3,410	3,557	0.1	0.6

Source: Ministry of Justice, Bank of Japan, in JNTO (1994)
* OECD 1994, 1995

particular, several of Japan's less developed regions and those burdened with declining smokestack industries were keen to develop tourism (both domestic and foreign) as a new source of economic activity. In 1991, therefore, the MOT came out with a follow-up programme called Two Way Tourism 21 (TWT21). According to the MOT, the programme aims 'at facilitating tourist flow to and from Japan to enhance mutual understanding and goodwill between Japan and the rest of the world' (MOT, 1991: 2).

This programme marks the first time that the central government has laid out a tourism policy that purports to encourage inbound tourism. It is an important step forward; however, in practical terms, three factors continue to undermine the efficacy of the programme. First, like its predecessor the 10 Million Programme, TWT21 lacks the wherewithal to make a notable impact on the growth of tourism itself. Secondly, the political problems associated with Japan's ongoing trade surplus weaken the MOT's position in relation to the stand taken by the MOF, which remains wary of policies that could blunt the political and economic value of the balance of travel account. Thirdly, the importance of external factors in shaping demand decisions, economic considerations such as exchange rate movements and relative travel costs coupled with increased regional competition remain the key variables in influencing visitor flows.

The role of the travel industry v the government
Japan's inbound travel industry is generally of the opinion that it is the government's responsibility through the activities of the JNTO to promote inbound travel to Japan not that of the travel industry. At issue here is the role of the JNTO. Undoubtedly, the effectiveness of the JNTO is hindered by the financial limitations placed on the organization. In 1994 the JNTO's annual budget was $33.3 million, of which $15.5 million was allocated to overseas tourism promotion (including personnel expenses). Since the JNTO's resources have to be spread quite thinly, and the travel industry is content to concentrate its sales activities on securing high-yield markets such as convention and trade fair delegates, and company and special interest

group tours, it is inevitable that gaps in the market emerge. In particular, the needs of independent travellers and the (reputedly) low-yield Asian visitor markets are not sufficiently catered for.

Two other areas of concern for the state of inbound travel to Japan relate to the average length of stay of foreign visitors and the concentration of visitor stays in and around the main metropolitan regions. As far as the average length of stay is concerned, the number of days has been declining since 1988. The downward trend is consistent with the market's overall tendency to cut down on the costs of a stay in Japan. In 1994 the average stay was 9.6 days, down from 10.2 days in 1993 and 11.2 days in 1992 (Prime Minister's Office, 1995), but perhaps more significantly, 51.2 per cent of visitors left within five days.

The concentration of visitor arrivals in the main metropolitan regions is a trend that is more evident among Western visitors than Asian visitors. Whereas Western visitors have a tendency to take in a trip to Japan as part of a multi-destination itinerary leaving little time for anything but the main tourist sights, Asian visitors, especially those from countries such as Taiwan, South Korea and Hong Kong, are more inclined to view Japan as a mono-destination, and thus have more opportunity and time to travel to other areas of Japan.

To encourage visitors to travel more widely in Japan, that is to places other than the well-worn tourist route between Tokyo and Osaka and its environs, the MOT has designated a number of areas worthy of tourism interest under the slogan *New Sites of Discovery*. The scheme, however, is plagued by two related problems: access and cost. In terms of access most air travellers to Japan use either Tokyo or Osaka as their entry and exit points and this tends to set the parameters for a trip to Japan. This is particularly true of Western visitors. A further barrier to travelling around Japan is the high cost of domestic transportation. On the positive side the expansion of intra-regional air services using Japan's local airports should help to reduce this problem and facilitate the spread of Asian visitors to more places around Japan. For Western visitors, however, the continued concentration of long-haul air services on Tokyo and Osaka, not to mention time and money constraints, will probably mean that their itineraries will not be affected that much.

Conclusion

As the decade progresses towards the year 2000 the prospects for travel to and from Japan will depend to a considerable extent on the future performance of the yen. For the immediate future Japan's appeal as a tourist destination is likely to remain vulnerable to shifts in market demand brought on by changing economic circumstances and, in particular, the value of the yen. In the longer term, the key to Japan's growth as an inbound destination would seem to lie in the development of intra-regional visitor flows from

Asia's burgeoning outbound markets. In this respect the portents are reasonable since economic and travel forecasts for many of the countries in the region are generally quite favourable. Rising levels of disposable income, and increased social and economic development should create greater opportunities for both tourist and business travel to Japan assuming that the value of the yen does not appreciate sharply and that the Japanese travel industry repositions itself to cater to the needs of these developing markets.

In contrast to the rather moderate expectations for travel to Japan, more dynamic growth can be anticipated in the area of outbound travel subject to certain criteria being met. Long-term forecasts put the number of Japanese overseas travellers between 14 million to 18 million by the turn of the century, which could mean an additional two to six million visitor-trips over the 1993 level provided the domestic economy picks up and the yen remains relatively stable. (One caveat here relates to the level of Japan's trade surplus, a lowering of which could bring the value of the yen down causing some fluctuations in travel demand.) Besides these economic considerations, the actual level of growth achieved will also be influenced by the interaction of changing social and demographic trends in Japan, by the pace with which increased leisure time becomes available to the bulk of the Japanese workforce, and by the continued development of infrastructure both overseas and in Japan. In short, given that for reasons of economy, convenience and familiarity the majority of Japanese choose to visit Asia Pacific destinations – a trend that is unlikely to change in the future – the rising demand for overseas travel should ensure that the Japanese continue to play a major role in accelerating tourism growth in the Asia Pacific region.

Bibliography

Bureau of Tourism Research (1994) *International Visitor Survey 1992*. Canberra: BTR.

Cockerell, N. (1994) Europe to the Asia Pacific Region. *Travel & Tourism Analyst* 1, 65–82.

Department of Tourism (1994) *Statistical Report on Visitor Arrivals to Indonesia*. Jakarta: Department of Tourism.

Edwards, A. (1988) *International Tourism Forecasts to 1999*. London: Economist Intelligence Unit, 172.

Hawaii Visitors Bureau (1994) *Visitor Expenditures 1993*. Honolulu. HVB.

Hong Kong Tourist Association (1994) *A Statistical Review of Tourism 1993*. Hong Kong: HKTA.

Iyori, N. (1987) The traffic in Japayuki-san. *Japan Quarterly* 34 (1), 84–8.

JETRO (1993, 1994) *Nippon Business Facts and Figures*. Tokyo: JETRO.

Japan Air Lines (1990) *Overseas Travel To and From Japan*. Tokyo: JAL.

Japan Immigration Association (1990, 1994) *Statistics on Immigration Control, 1992*. Tokyo: Japan Immigration Association.

Japan National Tourist Organization (1994) *Statistics on Tourism*. Tokyo: JNTO. Japan National Tourist Organization (1995) *Tourism in Japan 1995/96*. Tokyo: JNTO/ MOT.

Japan Travel Bureau (1993) *JTB Report '93* Tokyo: JTB.

MOT (Ministry of Transport (1987) *Ten Million Program*. Tokyo: Printing Bureau, Ministry of Finance.

MOT (1991) *Two Way Tourism 21*. Tokyo: Printing Bureau, Ministry of Finance.

Morris, S. (1990) *The Japanese Overseas Travel Market in the 1990s*. London: Economist Intelligence Unit.

Organisation of Economic Co-operation & Development (1994) *Tourism Policy and International Tourism in Member Countries*. Paris: OECD.

Pacific Asia Travel Association (1993) *Annual Statistical Report 1992*. San Francisco, CA: PATA.

Prime Minister's Office (1993, 1994, 1995) *White Paper on Tourism*. Tokyo: Printing Bureau, Ministry of Finance.

Singapore Tourist Promotion Board (1993a) *Survey of Overseas Visitors to Singapore*. Singapore: STPB.

Singapore Tourist Promotion Board (1993b) *Singapore Monthly Report on Tourism Statistics*. Singapore: STPB.

The Mainichi Shimbun (1993) *On Japanese Overseas Air Travellers*. Tokyo: The Mainichi Shimbun.

Tokuhisa, T. (1980) Tourism within, from and to Japan. *International Social Science Journal* **32** (1), 128–49.

Tourism Bureau (1993) *Annual Report on Tourism Statistics*. Taipei: R.O.C. Tourism Bureau.

10

Malaysia: Tourism in perspective

ZAINAB KHALIFAH
SHAHARUDDIN TAHIR

Introduction

Tourism is a newly emerging industry in Malaysia and is a relatively new phenomenon compared with neighbouring Singapore or Thailand. The earlier lack of emphasis on tourism development and the relatively passive role of the Tourist Development Corporation of Malaysia (TDCM) in the early years of its formation are largely attributed to Malaysia's rich natural resource endowments and its dependence on the traditional export earnings of rubber, tin and palm oil. The poor performance of traditional exports in the recession period of the mid-1980s prompted the Malaysian government to promote its tourist industry on a more vigorous scale in an attempt to find alternative exports to reduce the country's negative balance of payments. With aggressive promotion and marketing by the Malaysian Tourism Promotion Board (MTPB) or Tourism Malaysia, great success has been achieved in creating substantial awareness and recognition of Malaysia as an attractive tourist destination. Malaysia is, today, one of the world's emerging destinations (Tahir and Khalifah, 1994).

This chapter aims to provide an introduction to the Malaysian tourist industry and is divided into five main parts. The first examines briefly the development of tourism, followed by an analysis of the tourism resources available. The third part looks into the demand of the various markets and is followed by the contribution of tourism to the economy. The chapter concludes by looking at the growing importance of domestic tourism and the future prospects and challenges facing the tourism industry.

The Development of Tourism

Malaysia is a large country covering 328,562 sq. km, situated in the central part of South-east Asia and lying entirely in the equatorial zone. It had an estimated population of around 19.5 million in 1994 (Bank Negara, 1995: 6) within its federation of 13 states. Peninsular Malaysia has 11 states, and separated by 530 km of the South China Sea are the two east Malaysian states of Sabah and Sarawak on the island of Borneo. Being in the tropics, the climate is hot and humid throughout the year with no distinct seasons.

The government's involvement in tourism development was initiated in the early 1970s. Although it was not a substantial sector of the economy during that period, it was seen to have huge potential in meeting the objectives of development, such as foreign exchange earnings, to increase employment and income levels, to foster regional development, to diversify the economic base and to increase government revenue. The government also had high aspirations that through tourism, a better understanding of the various cultures and lifestyles of the multi-ethnic population would be created, and thus contribute to socio-cultural integration and a national sense of unity.

Initially in the 1970s, the emphasis was on the development of basic infrastructure such as highways and airports and to foster the development of tourist sites and facilities in each state. Similar to other developing countries, during the initial stages of development, the government played a central role, providing the necessary tourism infrastructure, and at times engaged as entrepreneur and guarantor for overseas investment (Jenkins, 1994).

In the 1980s, more incentives were given for the development of new accommodation, visitor centre facilities, manpower development and encouraging the participation of native Malays in the tourism industry (GOM, 1981, 1986). Various incentives were given to encourage the involvement of the private sector, while the government continued to develop certain facilities and locations where the private sector was reluctant to venture.

In the nation's five-year development plan, continuous attention was given to the tourism sector, with generous allocation of funds in recent years for the development of tourism. During the Second Malaysia Plan (1971–75), the amount allocated was RM17.2 million (GOM, 1971). In the Sixth Malaysia Plan (1991–95), the allocation was increased substantially to RM533.9 million (GOM, 1991), which was later, during its mid-term review, revised to RM719.1 million (GOM, 1993). This additional allocation is mainly for the improvement and expansion of facilities and infrastructures (Table 10.1).

The elevation of the tourism industry to cabinet status in 1987, with the establishment of a separate Ministry of Culture and Tourism that later expanded to become the Ministry of Culture, Arts and Tourism in 1990, was the beginning of a new era in Malaysia's tourism industry. Tourism was then

Table 10.1   Tourism development allocation (RM million) during the Fifth and Sixth Malaysia Plans

Programme	5MP (1986–90)		6MP (1991–95)		
	Allocation	Expenditure	Allocation	Revision	Expenditure 1991–93
Preservation of national/ historical heritage	1.5	0.7	41.1	41.1	6.0
Tourist accommodation	2.0	0	171.7	169.8	27.5
Beautification/cleanliness programmes and environmental protection	2.5	2.5	43.6	43.6	10.1
Cultural product development	2.5	2.5	112.9	150.1	54.6
Facilities and infrastructure	79.2	76.7	157.4	307.3	116.1
Others	52.8	49.7	7.2	7.2	4.8
TOTAL	140.5	132.1	533.9	719.1	219.1

Source: GOM (1991: 247), GOM (1993: 16)

recognized as an important economic activity and there was full support from the government in terms of funding, planning, coordination, regulation and enforcement.

Much constructive criticism had been given to the first tourism master plan (TDCM, 1975), which was prepared mainly under the advice of foreign consultants due to the lack of local tourism expertise at that time. Therefore, the formulation of a national tourism plan was proposed in the Sixth Malaysia Plan (1991–95) report. This plan is much needed and will provide new guidelines for the future expansion of the industry, emphasizing a greater collaboration between the government and the private sector and increasing the participation of the private sector in tourism development (GOM, 1991).

Tourism Resources

Malaysia is a relatively large country with a wide range of attractions. The primary natural ones include the long stretches of sandy golden beaches on the west and east coasts of Peninsular Malaysia. These beach resorts promote the sun, sea and sand attractions and are principally found in Penang, Langkawi, Pangkor, Tioman, Redang and Cherating-Kuantan coastal stretch. Hill resorts such as Genting Highlands, Cameron Highlands and Fraser's Hill with its cooler climate are popular among those seeking relief from the heat and humidity of the lowlands.

Malaysia's population of a highly diversified ethnic mix makes it one of the prime examples of a multi-racial society in the world. According to the 1980 Statistical Census, the *bumiputera*, or 'the sons of the soil', make up over half of the population (59.0 per cent). The *bumiputera* consist of: the aborigines (*orang asli*); the Malays; and the ethnic groups of Iban, Bidayuh, Melanau,

Kenyah, Kayan and Bisayah (in Sarawak) and Kadazan, Murut, Kelabit, Bajau and Kedayan (in Sabah). While the Chinese make up 32.8 per cent of the population, Indians (8.2 per cent) and other races make up the remainder. The different ethnic groups create diverse cultures reflected in festivals, religious events, languages, the variety of architecture, the choices of cuisine and lifestyles. The people and their cultural heritage are the cultural resources that are often promoted by Tourism Malaysia in marketing Malaysia abroad.

Although the tourism authority in both states of Sabah and Sarawak are keen to promote the nomadic traditions and festivals of their native population, their efforts are made difficult by the limitations in accessibility and accommodation. In Sarawak, entry into many interior regions is still restricted. However, a planned development approach, spreading over the medium and long-term periods is needed to retain the cultural integrity and preserve the heritage of the people.

The tropical rain forest of Malaysia is one of the oldest, most complex and richest ecosystems in the world. Various types of flora and fauna, which are exotic and endemic to this part of the world, are found here. The more established national parks are Taman Negara and Endau-Rompin in Peninsular Malaysia, Kinabalu Park in Sabah, Niah Caves, Gunung Mulu and Bako National Park in Sarawak. Visitor numbers to protected areas are still low but steadily increasing. The distribution, quantity and quality of accommodation and the limited access to parks are some of the factors restricting their growth. The potential of this special interest tourism is great, especially when it is combined with a high-quality beach resort product and is likely to be saleable in the markets of Europe and North America (Peat Marwick, 1993). Although currently there is no urgency to restrict the number of visitors to these parks, the management agency must recognize the limits of the ecosystems and this must be the first priority, ahead of the economic return.

Although not a major player in the more up-market worldwide incentive and convention market, Malaysia is able to attract the smaller groups. At present, only the Putra World Trade Centre (PWTC) in Kuala Lumpur has the capability to offer premier state-of-the-art facilities for large conventions and exhibitions. In 1994, there were 90,258 foreigners participating in meetings and conventions, a decrease of 12.1 per cent compared with the previous year (MTPB, 1995). Besides Kuala Lumpur, Penang is also establishing itself as an attractive MICE (Meetings, Incentives, Conventions and Exhibitions) centre. In the international perspective, most basic facilities of MICE business are relatively homogenous. For Malaysia to compete with other international MICE destinations and venues, ancillary product ingredients such as river cruises, jungle trekking, golfing or other unusual product attributes will prove crucial, and marketing MICE facilities alone will not be sufficient to compete favourably in the long term (Peat Marwick, 1993).

The city of Kuala Lumpur is fast becoming a shopper's paradise with many of the world's leading fashion houses being represented. Duty-free shopping is available and this combined with a city-based tour can be an attractive alternative for certain markets. In terms of a shopping destination, Malaysia currently ranks third after Singapore and Hong Kong in the East Asia region (Khoo, 1993).

Many of the country's attractions mentioned above are very similar to those of the neighbouring destinations. Other factors such as safety, political stability, language and the more favourable currency exchange, compared with certain neighbouring countries, are some of the advantages to be emphasized when marketing Malaysia abroad. Although Malaysia appears to be in competition with its neighbours, they also complement each other when these destinations are offered as multi-destination ASEAN (Association of South East Asian Nations whose members comprise Malaysia, Thailand, Singapore, Indonesia, the Philippines, Brunei and recently Vietnam) packages.

Accommodation

International hotel companies have increasingly explored their opportunities for expansion in Asia Pacific, not only due to the lower cost of labour and land but also the astounding tourist arrivals (Choy, 1988). In Malaysia, the hotel room supply has been increasing steadily, at an average of around 10 per cent since 1991 (MTPB, 1994) (Table 10.2). There were 38 new hotels in 1994, bringing the total number of hotels to 1,128 with 65,907 rooms (MTPB, 1995). Due to the rapidly growing economy and the huge potential of the tourism industry, many major international hotel consortiums see Malaysia as having a good environment for investment and are keen to extend their operation in the country. Mariott, Hyatt, Westin, Sheraton, New World, Nikko and Mandarin Oriental are among those who intend to penetrate the Malaysian hotel industry in the next few years (Schlentrich and Ng, 1994).

The dispersion of hotels reflects the geographical distribution of tourists in the country. Kuala Lumpur, the major gateway city, has around 12,400 rooms while Penang has close to 8,500 rooms. The hotel industry in Malaysia is dominated by four- and five-star hotels. Realizing the potential of the

Table 10.2   Supply of accommodation 1989–94

Year	Hotel supply	Growth (%)	Rooms supply	Growth (%)
1989	958	–	43,149	–
1990	989	3.2	45,032	4.4
1991	1,049	6.1	49,874	10.8
1992	1,085	3.4	55,866	12.0
1993	1,090	0.4	61,005	9.2
1994	1,128	3.5	65,907	8.0

Source: MTPB (Annual Statistical Tourism Report, various years)

domestic market and the demand of certain foreign markets notably China, Singapore and Thailand, the government is pushing the private sector to invest in more budget-class hotels. The increasing price of land and cost of construction has made the development of this range of accommodation less attractive for investors, especially in Kuala Lumpur. Instead the mid-price hotels are expanding into secondary cities such as Penang, Kota Kinabalu and Kuching, offering a wider selection in terms of price (Schlentrich and Ng, 1994).

The average occupancy rate of hotels in 1994 is estimated to be around 65.3 per cent (MTPB, 1995). Most hotel occupancies have increased in 1994, due to the aggressive promotions by the various state governments and the private sector in the Visit Malaysia Year 1994 campaign. Hotels in Kuala Lumpur and Penang both enjoyed a higher occupancy rate at 76.7 per cent and 63.6 per cent respectively. However, many of the island resorts such as Langkawi, Tioman, Pangkor and the hill resorts of Fraser's Hill and Genting Highlands recorded a decline in the occupancy rate compared with the previous year (MTPB, 1995). Softening of rates is common due to the excess capacity and increased competition. However, many believe this is only a temporary phenomena, due to the cyclical nature of the hotel business and demand will soon catch up with the supply.

Arrivals Trend

Tourist arrivals into Malaysia is on an upward trend, increasing continuously from 3,109,106 in 1985 to 7,197,229 during the second Visit Malaysia Year in 1994. Table 10.3 highlights the fluctuation in the arrivals, exceptionally higher than average growth rates were recorded in 1989 and 1990, which were mainly due to the generous government grants and aggressive promotion and marketing abroad, in conjunction with the first Visit Malaysia Year 1990. A negative growth rate was subsequently seen in 1991, partly due to the Gulf war and recession in some of the tourist-generating countries.

According to the Economist Intelligence Unit (EIU) report (1994: 44), Malaysia is the third most important destination, after China and Hong

Table 10.3 Tourist arrivals and receipts 1989–94

Year	Arrivals	% Growth rate	Revenue RM (million)	% Growth rate
1989	4,846,320	–	2,803	–
1990	7,476,772	54.3	4,473	59.6
1991	5,847,213	– 21.5	4,283	– 4.8
1992	6,016,209	2.9	4,595	7.3
1993	6,503,860	8.1	5,066	10.2
1994	7,197,229	10.7	8,298	63.8

Source: MTPB (Annual Statistical Tourism Report, various years)

Kong, in the East Asia Pacific region, based on the figures of the number of arrivals compiled by the World Tourism Organization (WTO). However, the Pacific Asia Travel Association (PATA) ranked Malaysia in tenth position because it excludes all tourists from Singapore arriving by land from the overall count. Tourists arriving by air to Malaysia is only about 20 per cent, in comparison with an average 80–90 per cent for the region as a whole, placing Malaysia only in tenth position in the WTO regional ranking in terms of tourism receipts.

In contrast to other ASEAN destinations (e.g. Singapore, Thailand and Indonesia), Malaysia's main market had traditionally been from within the ASEAN region (Table 10.4). In 1994, almost 7.20 million arrivals was recorded, an increase of 10.7 per cent over the 1993 figure. Singapore remained the dominant feature in terms of demand, with a 62.1 per cent share of arrivals in 1994 (62.3 per cent in 1993). This is followed by Thailand, with a 7.5 per cent share of the total arrivals (7.2 per cent in 1993). Together, these two markets account for almost 70 per cent of international arrivals to Malaysia. This high number of Singaporean tourist arrivals is due to its close proximity and the strong purchasing power of its dollar. The important markets in 1994, after the neighbouring ASEAN countries are: Japan (4.0 per cent), Taiwan (3.5 per cent), United Kingdom (2.2 per cent), Hong Kong (1.9 per cent) and Australia (1.8 per cent) (MTPB 1995: 20–5).

Most Singaporeans cross into Malaysia by road, to take a short break, visiting friends and relatives (VFR), shopping, eating out or filling their car tank with Malaysian fuel. The high growth of the Singaporean market is unlikely to be sustainable in the long-run due to its limited size and small population. Increasing the length of stay, repeat visitation and expanding the tourism product, which will encourage more spending, are some of the ways to develop this market.

ASEAN over the past years 'have recognised that its greatest market is itself' (Peat Marwick, 1993) due to its rapidly growing economy and the increasing demand for outbound travel in this region. Attracting visitors from the member countries will be an easier task due to the higher level of awareness among the people of neighbouring destinations. The ASEAN countries could be viewed as partners rather than competitors, this is especially true of Singapore. Due to its close proximity to Malaysia and the position of Singapore as a gateway city with a short average length of stay, there is a great opportunity for Malaysia to offer add-on travel that would benefit both countries in sustaining the tourist flows.

Apart from ASEAN, priority should also be on the Japanese and the East Asian markets due to their impressive economic growth, the higher disposable income available and the increasing trend of travelling. All key markets in this region registered growth. The Japanese share, however, has declined from 6.9 per cent in 1990 to 4.0 per cent in 1994. Much of the Japanese travel to Malaysia is associated with business and this segment has decreased due-

Region	1990 Arrivals	%share	1991 Arrivals	%share	1992 Arrivals	%share	1993 Arrivals	%share	1994 Arrivals	%share
ASEAN	5,495.1	73.8	4,155.3	71.1	4,515.9	75.1	4,883.0	75.1	5,427.1	75.4
Brunei	215.0		145.1		145.7		142.8		150.0	
Indonesia	140.1		178.4		153.7		181.0		225.9	
Philippines	56.5		55.8		39.6		38.3		42.2	
Singapore	4,569.1		3,261.0		3,744.7		4,051.6		4,469.8	
Thailand	514.7		514.9		432.1		469.3		538.5	
Asia and Pacific	1,188.5	16.0	1,012.0	17.3	916.6	15.5	988.9	15.2	1,103.7	15.3
Hong Kong	103.1		92.0		96.5		119.2		136.0	
India	108.4		71.4		94.5		42.2		52.3	
Japan	507.8		405.2		259.5		255.6		286.3	
Taiwan	193.6		156.8		201.8		250.1		250.6	
China	6.9		12.8		46.8		81.9		95.8	
South Korea	59.7		80.2		38.0		40.1		55.0	
West Asia	33.9		47.8		24.2		24.4		26.9	
Australia	149.1		121.9		120.9		121.7		128.4	
New Zealand	26.1		24.0		15.0		15.4		24.9	
Others	–		–		13.4		38.3		47.5	
Europe	455.1	6.1	420.8	7.2	343.9	5.7	373.2	5.7	401.2	5.6
UK	196.3		166.8		142.1		154.5		157.9	
Germany	71.8		63.8		47.3		58.4		70.2	
France	35.6		32.0		24.3		26.1		29.0	
Scandinavia	56.3		51.3		29.5		29.8		35.9	
Benelux	32.1		36.3		25.1		25.7		28.5	
Others	63.0		70.8		75.6		78.7		79.7	
Americas	192.6	2.6	140.4	2.4	112.2	1.8	120.2	1.9	132.5	1.8
United States	146.1		105.2		78.8		85.9		94.4	
Canada	28.9		30.2		24.1		24.7		28.1	
Latin America	17.6		5.1		9.3		9.6		10.0	
Others	114.6	1.5	188.7	2.0	127.6	1.9	138.6	2.1	132.7	1.8
Grand Total	7,445.9	100.0	5,846.2	100.0	6,016.2	100.0	6,503.9	100.0	7,197.2	100.0

1. Asia and Pacific arrivals excludes tourists from other ASEAN countries, but includes those from the Middle East and Africa.
2. UK figures in 1990 and 1991 include arrivals from Ireland.
3. Data for India since 1992 refers to arrivals from the South Asia sub-continent.
Source: MTPB (Annual Statistical Tourism Report, various years)

to the current recession in Japan. However, China performed well, registering the highest growth of 17.0 per cent, although it only accounted for 1.3 per cent of the total arrivals in 1994. This is followed by Taiwan and Hong Kong (MTPB, 1994). The growth of the Chinese market over the past few years has been rapid, a similar trend is observed in other Asian destinations too. The Chinese are generous in their spending, mainly on shopping, and items bought are not only gifts to friends and relatives but are also for sale to third parties, 'a characteristic for which the Chinese are fast becoming renowned' (EIU, 1994).

Foreign tourists visiting Malaysia exhibit considerable differences in terms of their travel characteristics and their activities while in the country. An inbound survey conducted by MTPB in 1992 shows that the purpose of visits varies, with 59 per cent for holiday, followed by 24 per cent VFR, 13 per cent for business and 2–3 per cent for the conferences and conventions market (EIU, 1994: 52). The overall average length of stay to Peninsular Malaysia in 1994 was 4.8 nights (MTPB, 1995). This shorter average length of stay compared with other ASEAN destinations is again influenced by the 'Singapore-factor'. According to the preliminary findings of a survey conducted by Tahir (1994), travel motivations differ between tourists from different regions. The field survey was carried out over a three-month period from July to September 1994. A total of 315 useable responses were obtained from the interviews conducted at the international airports, main railway stations, and major tourist attraction areas in Peninsular Malaysia.

Some of the major characteristics derived from the study are summarized in Tables 10.5 and 10.6. Table 10.5 indicates that 63 per cent of the sample were mainly on their first visit (63 per cent), single (44 per cent), travelling from either Singapore or Thailand (50 per cent) before visiting Malaysia and half of them stayed at least 9 days. Majority travelled with a friend, spouse or family members and only 20 per cent travelled alone. The main reason cited for visiting Malaysia was for vacation/holiday (75 per cent). Of the total interviewed, 42 per cent had visited at least three destinations. The most frequently named destinations in the survey, apart from Penang and Kuala Lumpur, were Taman Negara (National Park), Malacca, Kota Bharu, Cameron Highlands and Tioman.

In comparing the travel motivations between tourists from Asia and Europe/North America (listed as 'Other' region), both differences and similarities emerged. Table 10.6 ranked the travel motivations based on mean scores and standard deviations for the two groups. Both groups ranked 'natural beauty and scenic attractions' as the most important reason and 'to play golf' as the least important reason for visiting the country. There are a few differences in ranking the variables, but generally the first five variables are similar, only changing positions. The Asian tourists appear to assign more importance to 'reasonable prices', 'rest and relaxation', 'shopping', 'interesting night life', and familiarity with the place ('visiting places friends had visited before' and 'people speaking the same language'). However, tourists from Europe and North America preferred educational purposes ('to understand new culture', 'to taste the local food', 'to see monuments and historical buildings'), and are more active ('beaches', 'sea-sports', 'sunbathing' and 'camping and jungle adventure') tourists.

Tourism in the Economy

Tourism contribution to the Gross National Product (GNP) fluctuates from 3.02 per cent in 1988 to 5.64 per cent in 1990 and 4.7 per cent in 1994 (MTPB, 1991 and 1995), while foreign exchange earnings from tourism rose from RM4.6 billion in 1992 to RM8.29 billion in 1994 (MTPB, 1993, 1995). Tourism has grown considerably, exceeding some of the country's traditional exports, improving from seventh position in 1985 to fifth position in 1993. Table 10.7 highlights the contribution of tourism in terms of foreign earnings compared with the other main exports. In 1990, during the first Visit Malaysia Year, its performance was overwhelming, it became the country's fourth highest

Table 10.5 Characteristics of tourists to Malaysia
  a. Where do tourists came from?
- Country of residence: Europe – 48.2%, Middle East and Africa – 4.8%, Asia – 42.9%, North America – 4.1%
- Point of entry: Kuala Lumpur – 49%, Penang–22%
- Entry to the country: 50% of visitors came via Singapore and Thailand
- Exit from the country: to Singapore – 37%, to Thailand – 16%
  b. What type of tourists visit Malaysia?
- Type of visitors: Male – 62%,
                      Single – 44%,
                      under 31 years old – 50%,
                      University educated – 44%
- Time spent away from home: more than 18 days – 49%
  c. Reasons for visiting Malaysia
- Purpose of visit: Vacation/holiday – 75%
                      Business – 12%
                      Seminar – 5%
- First visit – 63%
- Had visited Malaysia twice in the last five years – 30%
  d. While in Malaysia
- 42% visited at least 3 destinations
- 72% visited Penang, 58% Kuala Lumpur, 18% Taman Negara, 18% Malacca, 14% Kota Bharu, 14% Cameron Highlands, 13% Tioman Island
- Method of travelling: package tour – 44%
- Mode of travelling: public buses – 40%, rented autos – 18%
- Souvenirs – 48% spent at least US$100
- Length of stay – 50% stayed at least 9 days
  e. Overall
- Visit Malaysia Year 1994 – 57% had not heard before arrival
- 73% who had heard about it were not at all influenced by it
- 85% intend to visit Malaysia again
  Source: Tahir (1994)

foreign income earner and for the first time the country became a net foreign

Table 10.6   Travel motivation between 'Asia' and 'Other' region tourists[a]

Variables	'Asia' Tourists[b] (n=150)			'Other' Tourists[c] (n=165)		
	Rank[d]	Mean	s.d.	Rank	Mean	s.d.
• Availability of natural beauty/ scenic attractions	1	5.63	1.29	1	6.01	1.04
• Reasonable prices of food and accommodation	2	5.44	1.38	4	5.45	1.45
• To understand new cultures	3	5.41	1.58	2	5.98	1.12
• Mostly to rest and relax	4	5.38	1.48	6	4.71	1.59
• To taste the local food	5	5.34	1.63	3	5.68	1.34
• There is a wide variety of products	6	4.93	1.61	9	4.41	1.70
• The quality of products is good	7	4.72	1.52	8	4.04	1.66
• Shopping is convenient	8	4.50	1.80	13	3.72	1.68
• To see monuments and historical buildings	9	4.23	1.69	5	4.98	1.42
• Many recreational and sport activities	10	4.11	1.61	15	3.32	1.58
• To meet new friends with same interest	11	3.95	1.83	14	3.66	1.91
• There is interesting nightlife	12	3.88	1.74	20	2.90	1.69
• Experience many cultural shows/events	13	3.84	1.78	10	4.04	1.58
• Buy local souvenirs	14	3.77	1.72	17	3.22	1.77
• Visit places I/my friends had visited before	15	3.65	1.76	19	2.99	1.78
• To learn some local words/ language	16	3.63	1.83	16	3.27	1.68
• Visit places where people speak same language	17	3.60	1.76	23	2.30	1.62
• To visit friends and relatives	18	3.53	2.14	21	2.65	1.99
• There are lot of attractive beaches	19	3.51	1.79	7	4.53	1.56
• Camping and jungle adventure	20	3.51	1.80	12	3.81	2.03
• Scuba diving, water skiing/ sailing	21	3.37	1.77	18	3.02	1.85
• To sunbathe	22	3.35	1.94	11	4.00	1.79
• Prefer to be on guided tour	23	3.15	1.87	22	2.35	1.65
• To play golf	24	2.47	1.78	24	1.54	1.28

a. Using a seven-point Likert type scale, respondents were asked to indicate whether they agree or disagree to the 24 statements on the reasons for taking holidays and the activities they had done/plan to do while in Malaysia (scale ranging from: 1 = strongly disagree to 7 = strongly agree).
b. Included also in this group of Asia region tourists were those from Middle East and Turkey (9) and Africa (6). Residents of Australia (43), Singapore (28), Hong Kong (18), Taiwan (14), Japan (11) were the main respondents in this group.
c. Europeans and North Americans were listed under this group. The main respondents were from the UK (63), Germany (36), Switzerland (12), France (11), USA (11) and Holland (10).
d. Ranking was based on the mean score. For variables with the same mean score, ranking was based on their standard deviations (variables with smaller std. dev. were given higher priorities).
Source: Tahir (1994)

Table 10.7 Malaysia's top foreign exchange earners by item (RM million)

Descriptions	1989	1990	1991	1992	1993
Manufactures	36,592[1]	46,654[1]	61,394[1]	71,124[1]	85,349[1]
Crude petroleum	7,883[2]	10,109[2]	10,200[2]	9,147[2]	7,848[2]
Palm oil	4,681[4]	4,312[5]	5,527[4]	5,412[4]	5,841[4]
Tourism	2,803[6]	4,473[4]	4,283[5]	4,595[5]	5,066[5]
Sawn logs	7,262[3]	7,106[3]	7,107[3]	7,330[3]	7,622[3]
Rubber	3,949[5]	3,128[6]	2,690[7]	na	na
LNG	2,063[7]	2,634[7]	3,448[6]	2,540[6]	2,765[6]

1. The figures in brackets are the rankings.
2. From 1992, the export commodity sawn logs had been revised to sawn logs and sawn timber.
Source: Ministry of Finance (1991, 1993) Economic Reports

exchange earner in terms of a travel account surplus of RM508 million in the balance of payments (Bank Negara, 1992). The net contribution of tourism to the services account of the balance of payment has remained positive since 1990 (GOM, 1993: 157).

The Committee on Invisible Trade (COMIT) has identified tourism as having great potential to alleviate the deficit in the services account of external trade (ESCAP, 1991). An Input–output Analysis on Tourism conducted by ESCAP in 1990 indicates that in Malaysia, the three sectors that benefit most from tourism are the hotels and restaurants, air transportation and business services. The three collectively account for half of the Gross Domestic Product (GDP) generated in the economy through tourism. Agriculture and livestock, and fishing are the two other sectors that benefit indirectly through tourism. A substantial amount of its GDP is being generated through food purchased in hotels, restaurants and 'stalls' or eateries outside the hotels. Much of the production activity in these two sectors is also significantly directed towards tourism, thus creating additional income and employment.

The potential for income generation in the tourism sector is great. The direct, indirect and induced income multipliers are respectively greater than the economy average (ESCAP, 1991). The Economic Report 1989/90, however, declare that about 50 per cent of foreign exchange earned in tourism is lost from the economy. Goh (cited in Tan, 1991: 169) estimated that 65.8 per cent of gross tourism earnings in 1985 were lost through leakages. More efforts in developing a strategy of minimizing revenue leakages would be beneficial.

Leakages mainly occur through the purchases of imported goods; overseas payments of profits and capital remittances of foreign tourist companies; wage remittances of expatriate workers; interest payments on foreign loans; management, royalties and other fees to foreign companies; and promotion and publicity abroad (Tan, 1991). To reduce some of the leakages, an approach creating more backward linkages between tourism and other domestic productive sectors, particularly the wage-intensive sectors should be encouraged. A greater integration with labour-intensive rural and small scale supplying industries should be fostered.

The total expenditure incurred by international tourism in 1994 was RM8.3 billion, with an average per capita expenditure of RM1,153 and per diem expenditure of RM240 (MTPB, 1995: 36). Major components of tourist expenditure are accommodation, then shopping followed by food and beverages. Shopping represented 24 per cent of the total expenditure, recently overtaking the traditional food and beverage sector. This trend is further enhanced by the 1995 budget, which included the abolishment and reduction of duties on many categories of goods, such as clothing, electrical and electronic goods.

The non-ASEAN market, although lower in terms of arrivals, contributes significantly in terms of revenue. This is mainly due to the longer distance travelled, which encourages more spending and a longer average length of stay. Domestic and Singaporean tourists have a similar expenditure pattern on major items with spending on shopping and souvenirs representing the highest component. On average, other foreign tourists spent more on all major items compared with a Singaporean tourist. A domestic tourist expenditure on all items is least when compared with the other two (ESCAP, 1991).

Table 10.8 highlights the contribution of the main markets to tourism receipts. Singapore dominates the ranking in terms of total receipts, but its per diem expenditure is much lower compared to other markets such as Japan, Taiwan, China and most Western markets.

Regional Development

The 1975 Tourism Development Plan (TDP) had made specific reference to the New Economic Policy (NEP), that is 'to provide a basis upon which Malaysia may develop her tourist potential in an orderly and balanced manner within the framework of the national development plan and the New Economic Policy' (TDCM, 1975). National unity was the main objective of the NEP and this would be achieved through the eradication of poverty irrespective of race and the restructuring of the Malaysian society to reduce and eventually eliminate the existence of race with economic function and geographical location (GOM, 1976, 1981). The Tourism Development Plan proposed the development of eight tourist regions with tourist corridors in the rural areas linking each other. The development of tourist facilities away from the urban areas would help to diversify the resource base of the tourism industry and the redistribution of wealth, narrowing the economic imbalance in the urban–rural regions as proposed in the NEP (GOM, 1976; Din, 1982).

Table 10.8   Breakdown of selected international tourism receipts by market 1993–94

Country of residence	1993 Receipts (RM mil.)	1993 % share of total	1993 Average per diem expenditure (RM)	1994 Receipts (RM mil.)	1994 % share of total	1994 Average per diem expenditure (RM)
Singapore	1,729.0	34.1	135.2	4,200.6	50.6	288.0
Japan	528.2	10.4	433.3	621.1	7.5	414.0
Taiwan	429.3	8.5	337.6	478.3	5.8	352.0
UK	269.5	5.3	213.3	288.4	3.5	203.0
Thailand	204.4	4.0	40.3	532.6	6.4	92.0
Australia	179.8	3.5	197.7	221.7	2.7	200.0
Brunei	178.5	3.5	248.9	174.8	2.1	249.0
China	170.9	3.4	321.5	180.7	2.2	262.0
Indonesia	161.3	3.2	132.5	218.9	2.6	140.0
Hong Kong	155.9	3.1	276.0	181.6	2.2	271.0
USA	129.3	2.6	241.6	143.5	1.7	241.0
Germany	83.8	1.6	157.6	101.9	1.2	147.0
South Korea	75.8	1.5	356.2	87.5	1.1	332.0
India	12.0	0.2	84.4	16.8	0.2	87.0

Source: MTPB (1995)

The distribution of hotels and that of hotel guests are spatially concentrated on the western stretch of Peninsular Malaysia. In 1994, hotels on the west coast received an estimated total of 8.6 million hotel guests, with Kuala Lumpur receiving the majority, almost 42 per cent of the share, followed by Penang with 21 per cent. The east coast towns of Peninsular Malaysia, namely Kuantan, Dungun, Kuala Terengganu and Kota Bharu receiving an estimated total of 1 million guests (MTPB, 1995). Since tourists are dependent on accommodation, which often takes a significant share of their expenditure, 'it has been accepted that spatial variation of accommodation depicts the spatial differences in the economic impact of tourism' (quoted in Oppermann, 1992: 228).

If tourism is to stimulate regional development as proposed in the Tourism Development Plan (TDCM, 1975), little success has been achieved. Several hotels on the east coast were built in the 1980s solely by the private sector or jointly with TDCM and various State Economic Development Corporations (SEDC) such as Club Mediterranean and Hyatt in Pahang, and Tanjung Jara Beach Hotel and Pantai Primula in Terengganu. With little response from the private sector, not many projects have taken place after this initial development (Oppermann, 1992). Tourism as a development strategy to promote redistribution through the expansion of new tourist facilities in the peripheral regions as stated in the NEP is limited in reality.

From the preliminary findings on travel motivations of foreign tourists (Table 10.6), it can be seen that the non-Asian tourists are 'active' tourists and are looking for experience rather than a rest. While Oppermann (1992), in his study of the intra-national travel behaviour patterns of foreign tourists in

Malaysia, listed the 'active' tourist as: on average younger, smaller male sex-bias, travelling in small groups and having a longer average length of stay. In looking for experience, their travel patterns are more evenly distributed all over Malaysia. These travel patterns have contributed towards redistribution and regional development meanwhile those of the 'less active' were reinforcing the existing spatial disparities. Perhaps identifying and promoting this segment of the tourist market (cultural–interest tourists) may help to alleviate the current disparities, moving closer to achieving the objectives of the NEP.

Employment and Manpower Development

Estimating the direct and indirect employment provided by the tourism sector is a difficult task. Nevertheless, there is no doubt about the importance of tourism as a source of employment. A World Travel and Tourism Council (WTTC) report estimated that the industry employs one out of every ten of the Asia and Pacific region's working population (WTTC, 1993: 8). In Malaysia, with an estimated total labour force of 8.074 million in 1995 (GOM, 1993: 38), this would translate into 0.8 million workers employed within the industry. Estimates from the Economic Planning Unit (EPU) of The Prime Minister's Department, indicates that in 1994 the wholesale and retail trade, hotels and restaurants subsector had created jobs for 1.316 million persons or 17.3 per cent of the total employment (Bank Negara, 1995: 252).

Abdul Razak and Shaharuddin (1993), using the UNDP and WTO formula in its 1986 report on 'Tourism Manpower Planning and Training' for the Malaysian government and the number of new and existing hotels, estimated that 91,731 jobs will be created in 1993 in the hotel (including its restaurants, bars and duty-free shops) and the travel agencies sector. While, MTPB (1995: 44), based on its manpower survey, had estimated that 104,989 people were employed in this industry in 1994. Table 10.9 displays the breakdown of the employment provided by the various sectors of the industry.

Projections of increase in foreign tourists, higher domestic tourism and the development of more tourism projects will increase the demand for manpower in the tourism industry. Overall labour shortages in the tourism sector is likely, due to the lower unemployment rates and the rapid economic growth the country is currently experiencing. This situation is becoming more serious in places such as Penang where factories producing high-tech products are competing for skilled and semi-skilled employees with the hospitality sector (*The Economist*, 1993).

Skilled manpower shortages in the tourism industry have long been expected by both the private sector and the government, and this issue was specifically addressed in the Fifth Malaysia Plan. Formal education and training for tourism is not sufficient to meet the needs of the growing tourism industry. Institute Technology MARA (ITM), responsible to the Ministry of

Table 10.9 Tourism employment in various sectors, 1993–94

Descriptions	Hotel		Tour & Travel Agencies		Airlines		Others[1]	
	1993	1994	1993	1994	1993	1994	1993	1994
1.Total employed	56,977	61,174	20,405	21,416	20,378	19,982	22,579	3,488
2.Gender ratio (%)								
Male	63.2	60.0	55.4	51.5	52.9	73.8	n/a	n/a
Female	36.8	40.0	44.6	48.5	47.1	26.2	n/a	n/a
3.Employment levels (%)								
Managerial	8.5	8.6	19.3	n/a	13.0	15.4	n/a	n/a
Supervising	12.7	12.0	17.2	n/a	15.5	17.7	n/a	n/a
Skilled	34.9	37.4	42.9	n/a	68.6	42.6	n/a	n/a
Semi-skilled	29.4	29.1	16.9	n/a	2.7	16.6	n/a	n/a
Unskilled	14.4	12.7	3.6	n/a	0.2	7.7	n/a	n/a

Note: [1]The 1994 Manpower Survey did not include those working in restaurants, retail outlets and shopping complexes. Hence the 1993 and 1994 total employed figures under 'Others' are not comparable.
Sources: MTPB (1994) and (1995)

Education, and the National Productivity Centre (NPC), responsible to the Ministry of Trade and Industry, are two main public agencies responsible for tourism education and training. Lately, there has been an increase in private institutions offering a wide range of tourism programmes, which are often linked to overseas colleges and universities. This is mainly due to the insufficient capacity of the public institutions to cope with the increasing demand and the growing acceptance among the younger generation to choose tourism as a viable career option.

Importation of foreign labour, especially from the Philippines and Sri Lanka could help to ease the short-term difficulties faced by the industry, while the expansion of education and training opportunities by both the public and private sector would diminish this need in the future. But many are against the recruitment of foreign labour, because they believe the urgency of training local personnel may decrease due to easy access of foreign labour and this may be counter productive in developing and upgrading the skills of the current and future tourism workforce.

Domestic Tourism

Domestic tourism receipts are currently rising at an estimated 15 per cent a year, which is mainly due to the buoyant economy, a more equal distribution of national income and a higher living standard experienced by Malaysians. It was estimated that the number of person trips made by domestic travellers increased from about 20.3 million in 1990 to 25 million in 1993 and the average expenditure per person per trip increased from RM130 to RM230 (GOM, 1993). Hotels in Malaysia received around 6 million domestic guests in 1993, representing 51 per cent of the total number of hotel guests, exceeding the number of foreign guests.

Using 1978 prices, Malaysia's GNP in 1995 was estimated to be around RM113 billion and GNP per capita at RM9,947, which puts Malaysia among the more successful developing countries (GOM, 1993: 23). Besides the higher income, favourable circumstances such as reduced working hours and major improvements in the transportation system, especially in the north–south highways network, have contributed significantly to this growth. The purpose for domestic trips was mainly for business, followed by VFR and vacations (GOM, 1993).

The holiday-taking culture is still new among Malaysians. Television and radio are likely to play a vital role in the transmission of tourism information to the population. Domestic travellers tend to create an awareness of the different attractions in the various states and help in the redistribution of income between the regions. The government is currently encouraging the private sector to increase the supply of affordable accommodation, which will make tour prices more acceptable for the locals. Resident expatriates and Malaysian youth are some of the potentially profitable market segments of domestic tourism that are yet to be taken advantage of.

The outbound travel in Malaysia is high, around 18.3 million trips in 1994 (MTPB, 1995). Deeply concerned with the amount of money leaving the country, the government is paying more attention to the demands of the local market and also educating the price-conscious local tourist regarding the value for money in taking a holiday within the country. Among the emphasis put forward by MTPB in its 'Marketing Plan 1994' to promote domestic tourism are: encouraging Malaysians to 'buy Malaysia', creating awareness of the products available, attractively priced tour packages, tourism as a subject in the school syllabus, and encouraging the local private and public sectors to utilize local destinations and venues for their MICE-oriented activities.

Conclusion

The Malaysian Prime Minister, Datuk Seri Dr Mahathir Mohamad, recently said 'Malaysia hopes the tourism industry will grow faster to achieve the target of one tourist per head of population by the year 2020' (*New Straits Times*, 1995).

The government had also hoped that 20 million tourists will be visiting the country by the year 2000, but this is unlikely because the current influx of tourists is only about 7 million a year. The Prime Minister has urged the people to smile and play the role of unofficial hosts to ensure the tourists will have a pleasant experience while in Malaysia (*New Straits Times*, 1995).

Looking at the Prime Minister's statement, it is beyond doubt that the government has accorded high priority to tourism and is eager to promote it on a larger scale. Moreover, since tourism is one of the fastest growing industries, there is firm belief that tourism will bring substantial economic benefits to the country. As mentioned earlier, Malaysia's entry into the tourism industry is relatively late and at a disadvantage compared to the neighbouring countries who have already established themselves in the international market. But it is also a blessing in disguise since it is in a position to foresee the trend of tourism development and gain insight from the mistakes of others. Too much emphasis on tourist numbers can be misleading, as they unveil nothing on the type of tourists, their duration of stay or their spending habits. Tourists who are generous with their expenditures and stay longer are certainly more profitable than an equal number of tourists with low expenditures and a short length of stay. At present, most of the indicators used to assess the progress of the tourism industry are purely economic, other indicators are needed to review the socio-cultural and ecological consequences of tourism.

More resources should be invested in understanding the impacts of tourism since tourism, just like any other industry, will have impacts on the environment. To minimize conflict, tourism should be integrated with the environment since tourism development can only be sustained by realizing that economic and environmental issues are complementary. During the planning stages, all tourism developments should be subjected to environmental and social impact assessments. Mitigating these adverse impacts is vital and are dependent upon an understanding of the types of tourism and their compatibility with other activities. It should be realized that as tourism evolves, so do these impacts. The establishment of systems on monitoring and evaluating the progress of achieving the objectives and goals of tourism planning and adapting to the current changes will ensure the long term effectiveness and survival of the industry.

Since April 1988, Environmental Impact Assessment (EIA) has become a mandatory requirement for tourism projects in Malaysia through the 1985 amendment of the Environmental Quality Act of 1974. Developers of tourism projects should submit an EIA to the Department of Environment (DOE) to be passed prior to their approval by the relevant federal, state or local authorities. This requirement is only for 'the building of resorts and hotels at the seaside which exceeds the capacity of 80 rooms and the development of tourism attractions and recreational areas at National Parks' (Zainuddin, 1995: 11).

However, many tourism projects are exempted from this requirement, but are advised to incorporate the environmental dimension in their development proposals. Another weakness is at the implementation stage, where many of the measures recommended in the EIA are not being strictly adhered to and enforcement is being restricted by the lack of manpower in the controlling agencies. The penalties imposed might also not be sufficient enough to deter the profit motivated developers, since it is a very small amount compared to the total cost of the project.

It has been realized that advertising and promotional activities are fundamental catalysts in stimulating the overseas market. Overall, Malaysia's budget allocation for marketing is relatively high compared to neighbouring countries. In 1990, this amount was RM86 million (Peat Marwick, 1993: 56) while the tourism development allocation for the whole of the Fifth Malaysia Plan (1986–90) was only RM140.5 million (GOM, 1986). Although this illustrates the commitment of the government in promoting the destination, nevertheless, too much concentration of the available resources on advertising may create a situation where the overall product impression presented in campaigns is largely superior to reality.

Tourism Malaysia has the tendency to promote an image and product that the country is largely unable to deliver once tourists arrive (Peat Marwick, 1993). Maintaining and upgrading of the existing facilities and developing new products in response to the changing demands will sustain the tourists flow, reducing the possibility of 'oversell' and consumer dissatisfaction in the long run. With more neighbouring countries such as Vietnam, Burma and Laos opening their doors to tourism, a more competitive environment is expected and collaboration and integration of all the 'stakeholders' is very much needed to meet the challenges of the future.

International consultants are often engaged in the preparation of the national tourism development plan. Strategies and policies proposed are impressive, but they often lack the implementation side and occasionally are insensitive or ignorant of the country's sociocultural and political constraints (see also Jenkins, 1994). Since local experts in tourism is now available, it is suggested that they are included as part of the team in preparing the plan.

Further research is also necessary to assess the demands and preferences of tourists. Often, 'visitation is assumed to indicate fulfilment of needs and preferences of visitors, and repeat visitation is seen as a reinforcement of this success' but this 'may also be a reflection of a lack of alternative opportunity, of economic or access considerations, of ignorance by visitors, or good marketing' (Butler, 1993: 38). Understanding the changing taste of tourists and identifying their preferences would be beneficial, especially in developing specialized products to cater for their needs.

The recent awareness of conservation and the demand for 'environmentally friendly' products gives Malaysia the competitive advantage in developing many of its natural attractions. Eco-tourism has the potential to be a major market segment to be targeted for the expansion and the promotion of the nature-based tourism resources, especially in the states of Sabah and Sarawak. Proper planning and management allows the opportunities for sustainable tourism through the 'marriage of economy and environment' as recommended in the Brundtland Report (WCED, 1987). Moreover, since many of these natural attractions are located away from urban areas, eco-tourism has great potential for regional revitalization. Sustainability also requires the social dimension, that is the environment and the economy, should be integrated with the society, therefore the involvement of local communities and their participation in the decision-making process is essential.

Bibliography

Abdul Razak, C. and Shaharuddin, T. (1993) Sumbangan Industri Pelancongan Dalam Mempelbagaikan Peluang-peluang Gunatenaga Negara (Tourism contribution towards diversifying the employment opportunities in Malaysia). *Sumber* **7**, 77–98.

Bank Negara (1992) *Annual Report 1991*. Kuala Lumpur: Bank Negara Malaysia.

Bank Negara (1995) *Annual Report 1994*. Kuala Lumpur: Bank Negara Malaysia.

Butler, R.W. (1993) Tourism – an evolutionary perspective. In Nelson, J.G., Butler, R. and Wall, G. (eds) *Tourism and Sustainable Development: Monitoring, Planning, Managing*. University of Waterloo: Department of Geography, Publication Series no. 37, pp. 27–43.

Choy, D.J.L. (1988) Pacific Asia: The Mass Market in travel *Cornell Hotel and Administration Quarterly* **28** (4), 83–8.

Din, K.H. (1982) Tourism in Malaysia: competing needs in a plural society. *Annals of Tourism Research*, **9** (3), 453–80.

Din, K.H. (1989) Towards an integrated approach to tourism development: observations from Malaysia. In Singh, T.V., Theuns, H.L. and Go, F.M. (eds) *Towards Appropriate Tourism: The Case of Developing Countries*. Frankfurt am Main: Verlag Peter Lang GmbH, 181–204.

EIU (Economist Intelligence Unit) (1994) Malaysia. *EIU International Tourism Reports*, **2**, 41–61.

ESCAP (Economic and Social Commission for Asia and the Pacific) (1991) *The Economic Impact of Tourism in Malaysia*. New York: United Nations.

GOM (Government of Malaysia) (1971) *Second Malaysia Plan 1971–1975*. Kuala Lumpur: Government Printer.

GOM (1976) *Third Malaysia Plan 1976–1980*. Kuala Lumpur: Government Printer.

GOM (1981) *Fourth Malaysia Plan 1981–1985*. Kuala Lumpur: Government Printer.

GOM (1986) *Fifth Malaysia Plan 1986–1990*. Kuala Lumpur: Government Printer.

GOM (1991) *Sixth Malaysia Plan 1991–1995*. Kuala Lumpur: Government Printer.

GOM (1993) *Mid-term Review: Sixth Malaysia Plan 1991–1995*. Kuala Lumpur: Percetakan Nasional Malaysia Berhad.

Jenkins, C.L. (1994) Tourism in developing countries: the privatisation issue. In Seaton, A.V. *et al.* (eds) *Tourism: The State of the Art*. Chichester: John Wiley & Sons, 3–9.

Khoo, H.A. (1993) Tourism and travel – inbound revenue for corporate growth. *Business Trends: The Annual 1993*. Kuala Lumpur: National Broadcasters' Association of Malaysia, 68–77.

Ministry of Finance (GOM) (1989) *Economic Report 1989/90*. Kuala Lumpur: National Printing Department.

Ministry of Finance (GOM) (1991) *Economic Report 1991/92*. Kuala Lumpur: National Printing Department.

Ministry of Finance (GOM) (1993) *Economic Report 1993/94*. Kuala Lumpur: National Printing Department.

MTPB (Malaysian Tourism Promotion Board) (1991) *Annual Tourism Statistical Report 1990*. Kuala Lumpur: Pempena Consultants Sdn. Bhd.

MTPB (1992) *Annual Tourism Statistical Report 1991*. Kuala Lumpur: Pempena Consultants Sdn. Bhd.

MTPB (1993) *Annual Tourism Statistical Report 1992*. Kuala Lumpur: Pempena Consultants Sdn. Bhd.

MTPB (1994) *Annual Tourism Statistical Report 1993*. Kuala Lumpur: Pempena Consultants Sdn. Bhd.

MTPB (1995) *Annual Tourism Statistical Report 1994*. Kuala Lumpur: IMN Green Sdn Bhd.

New Straits Times (1995) *New Straits Times* 25 January.

Oppermann, M. (1992) International tourism and regional development in Malaysia. *Tijdschrift voor Econ. en Soc. Geografie* **83** (3), 226–33.

Peat Marwick (1993) *Tourism Policy Study: Marketing Sectoral Report*. Prepared for the Ministry of Culture, Arts and Tourism, Government of Malaysia. Kuala Lumpur: Peat Marwick Consultants Sdn. Bhd.

Schlentrich, U.A. and Ng, D. (1994) Hotel development strategies in South-east Asia: the battle for market dominance. In Seaton, A.V. *et al.* (eds) *Tourism: The State of the Art*. Chichester: John Wiley & Sons, 402–14.

Tahir, S. (1994) Visit Malaysia Year 1994: A benefit based study of inbound tourists. Preliminary findings of PhD thesis, The Scottish Hotel School, University of Strathclyde.

Tahir, S. and Khalifah, Z. (1994) Malaysia: an emerging destination in the ASEAN region. Paper presented at conference on Tourism: The State of the Art. University of Strathclyde, 10–14 July.

Tan, W.H. (1991) International tourism in Malaysia: development, achievement and problems. *Malaysian Journal of Tropical Geography* **22** (2), 163–173.

The Economist (1993) Powerhouse Penang, **327** (7812). *The Economist* 22 May, 29.

TDCM (Tourist Development Corporation, Malaysia) (1975) *Malaysia: Tourist Development Plan*. Kuala Lumpur: TDCM.

WCED (World Commission on Environment and Development) (1987) *Our Common Future*. New York: Oxford University Press.

World Travel Organization (WTO) and United Nations Development Programmes (UNDP) (1986) *Malaysia: Tourism Manpower Planning and Training*. Madrid: WTO.

World Tourism Organization (1995) *WTO News* No. 2 (March). Madrid: WTO.

World Travel and Tourism Council (WTTC) (1993) *The 1993 WTTC Report: Travel & Tourism – The World's Largest Industry*. Brussels: WTTC.

Zainuddin, M.Z. (1995) Eco Tourism. Paper presented at The Third East Asia–Pacific Hubert H. Humphrey Conference on Development and Environment. Kuala Lumpur, 16–17 January.

11

New Zealand: Tourism – the challenges of growth

DOUGLAS G. PEARCE
DAVID G. SIMMONS

Introduction

International tourist arrivals in New Zealand doubled in the 1980s and are projected to maintain or exceed this rate of growth during the present decade. Despite this growth, the international tourist traffic to New Zealand remains relatively modest on a global scale, with 1 million annual arrivals first being recorded in 1992. The development of tourism in the country has been influenced by its relative remoteness in the South Pacific and distance from the major world markets. Europe and North America are long-haul markets for New Zealand; Australia, the country's only significant short-haul market, is three hours flying time away. Much recent growth has occurred from Asia due to more general developments in outbound travel from this region. As the number of arrivals has increased, so tourism has become a more important and visible sector of the national economy and attracted more attention from policy-makers. The expansion of international arrivals has also often obscured the social and economic significance of domestic tourism and the growth in travel by New Zealanders abroad. The purpose of this chapter is to provide an overview of tourism in New Zealand, by giving attention to all three sectors – domestic, international outbound and international inbound – and by concentrating on recent changes that have occurred. In particular, emphasis is given to those challenges that the growth of tourism presents to New Zealand as the country approaches the year 2000.

Attempting such an overview in itself presents many challenges. With regard to research interest, resource allocation and policy-makers' priorities, domestic tourism has been very much the poor cousin of international tourism (Pearce, 1993). International tourism has essentially been perceived to consist of overseas visitors and the foreign exchange earnings that they bring and as a result much market research has been undertaken to establish the composition and characteristics of this sector. In contrast, the outbound sector is all but neglected: details on departing New Zealanders are still routinely collected but are no longer regularly published. Any attempt to analyse all three sectors comprehensively is thus hampered by the coverage and consistency of the data available. Nevertheless, it is still possible to draw on information from a range of sources and build up a reasonably broad picture of overall demand, the structure of the industry and the economic impacts that tourism generates before addressing the various development issues confronting the country.

Patterns of Demand

Domestic Tourism

Holiday-taking is a well established part of the New Zealand lifestyle with summer holidays at the beach and visits to friends and relatives being complemented by trips to sporting events, skiing holidays or long weekends spent at the bach (holiday home). Early regional surveys of such activities (e.g. Johnston *et al.*, 1976) indicated that about two-thirds of the population took an annual holiday away from home. More comprehensive national data became available in the mid-1980s with the establishment of the Domestic Travel Study (DTS). Although the DTS does not enable net or gross travel propensities to be calculated, it did provide other measures of domestic demand. Data from the last four surveys (the DTS was discontinued after 1990) indicate domestic travel in New Zealand was declining during the latter part of the decade as the total number of person nights fell from 46.8 million in 1986/87 to 41.4 million in 1989/90 (New Zealand Tourism Department, 1991). While part of this decline may be due to tighter economic conditions, the following section shows outbound travel was actually increasing over this period, suggesting some substitution of international for domestic travel. Nevertheless, domestic tourism remained a significant economic and social activity as New Zealanders are estimated to have spent an average of 18 nights away from home each year over the period 1987/88–1989/90 (Pearce, 1993).

Other data from the DTS highlight the often informal and unstructured character of domestic tourism in New Zealand. Around three-quarters of all domestic trips, for example, are made by private car and over half of all trips involve staying in the homes of friends and family (Table 11.1). Commercial accommodation is nevertheless important, with stays in hotels and motels accounting for 15 per cent of all person nights. In 1989/90 purpose of travel was fairly evenly split between visits to friends and relatives (VFR)(35 per cent), holiday trips (31 per cent) and business and other trips (34 per cent).

Table 11.1 Distribution of domestic tourism in New Zealand by accommodation and mode of transport 1989/90 (000s of trips)

	Licensed hotel/motel	Unlicensed motel	Camping, hut	Holiday home	Friends/ relatives	Other	No main accommodation	Total	percent
Air	216	43	15	2	233	41	7	558	5
Rail	5	2	0	2	12	0	0	21	< 1
Bus or coach	63	33	29	10	224	37	0	397	4
Campervan, car	6	5	26	5	21	35	8	106	1
Rental car	18	15	5	3	19	3	3	65	1
Private car	704	616	597	701	4142	602	262	7624	74
Other	24	13	34	15	82	74	4	248	2
No main transport	274	69	47	34	705	106	86	1321	13
Total	1310	794	754	774	5439	897	370	10339	100
Per cent	13	8	7	7	53	9	4	100	

Source: New Zealand Tourism Department (1991)

A detailed geographic analysis of domestic travel patterns revealed the influence of the three main metropolitan centres – Auckland, Wellington and Christchurch – on patterns of demand and the regionalized nature of much domestic travel (Pearce, 1993). Comparison of the distribution of net demand and nights spent in each region by purpose of visit underlined the significant role that attracting holiday visitors can have on determining net flows. It was the more discretionary holidaymaker who was shown to produce positive flows (i.e. the number of nights spent in a region exceeded those generated by that region's residents elsewhere) compared to the VFR and 'other' travellers whose travel patterns appear to be influenced more by population distribution. This emphasizes the value that the promotion of domestic tourism may have in regional development as holidaymakers redistribute income generated in the metropolitan centres to other parts of the country.

Outbound Tourism

Despite the constraints of distance that have limited their opportunities for travel abroad, New Zealanders have been keen international tourists who have increasingly taken advantage of improved air access since the introduction of jet services in the 1960s. The number of short-term (less than one year) departures almost quadrupled during the 1970s, passing from 112,082 in 1970 to 426,805 in 1980. Since then growth in outbound tourism has been much more erratic as indicated by departure trends in Table 11.2. Recessionary conditions in the early 1980s saw the number of New Zealanders going abroad decline significantly before picking up again in the latter part of the decade. After little change in 1990, departures increased by over 8 per cent in 1991, only to fall back again in 1992. Almost 800,000 departures were recorded in 1993. Estimates for expenditure on overseas travel, however, show a steady increase throughout the period, the sole decline in 1985/86 being related to an unduly large increase the previous year occasioned by a major devaluation in 1984 as well as perhaps to some discontinuity arising out of revisions in the balance of payments travel estimates (made in 1993 and taken back to 1985).

Data from the national household expenditure survey also reflect this growth in overseas travel. This item accounted for around 2 per cent of net household expenditure in the early 1980s and a decade later was fluctuating around 4 per cent. In 1993 New Zealand households spent on average about NZ $1,100 a year on overseas travel (down from a peak of NZ $1,325 in 1990). The average amount spent, in relative and absolute terms, is a function both of the number of households who incur expenditure on overseas travel and the amount those travelling actually spend. Although not published every year, available figures indicate an overseas trip has become more accessible to New Zealand households. In 1989, 25 per cent of households reported expenditure on overseas travel compared to 16 per cent in 1984. As the survey data refer to households rather than individuals, this does not necessarily mean that one in four New Zealanders was travelling overseas each year. The number doing so is not directly recorded in the migration statistics, which include multiple departures as well as business travel. However, the gross travel propensity (i.e. the total number of departures relative to the population of New Zealand) in 1992 was 21.5 per cent, 8 per cent over 1980. The household expenditure trends suggest at least part of this

Table 11.2   Evolution of outbound tourism from New Zealand 1979/80–93

| | Departures[a] | Per cent change[b] | Current account travel debit | | Household expenditure on travel overseas | | | Gross travel propensity |
			NZ $mil.	per cent change[b]	per cent households reporting	average annual expenditure	per cent households expenditure	(per cent)[c]
1979/80*	426805	–	500	–	–	$221.00	2.1	13.4
1980/81*	451300	5.74	529	5.80	–	$277.16	2.3	14.1
1981/82*	419458	–7.06	622	17.58		$279.76	2.0	13.0
1982/83*	373193	–11.03	647	4.02	–	$285.48	1.9	11.4
1983/84*	361662	–3.09	669	3.40	15.8	$591.24	3.3	11.0
1984/85*	382316	5.71	1016	51.87	16.3	$640.12	3.3	11.6
1985/86*	389937	1.99	920	–9.45	15.0	$733.72	3.4	11.8
1986/87*	514978	32.07	1115	21.20	16.3	$700.96	2.9	15.4
1987/88*	658265	27.82	1216	9.06	20.0	$1011.92	3.8	19.7
1989	716329	8.82	1560	28.29	25.0	$1247.48	4.3	21.3
1990	717278	0.13	1577	1.09	–	$1325.48	4.2	21.0
1991	778956	8.60	1639	3.93	–	$1248.00	3.9	22.6
1992	750883	–3.60	1745	6.47	–	$1279.20	4.3	21.5
1993	799659	6.50	–	–	–	$1097.20	3.6	–

* Year ended 31 March.
a. Short – term departures by New Zealand residents.
b. Over previous year.
c. Gross travel propensity represents the total number of departures as a percentage of the total population.
Sources: New Zealand Tourism Board, New Zealand Yearbook, Consumer Expenditure Statistics

increase is due to more people travelling abroad rather than just greater travel frequency.

Income, age and family structure are major determinants of expenditure on overseas travel (Table 11.3). Section a) shows a reasonably steady increase in such expenditure with rising income levels, the biggest jump in the trend, in both absolute and relative terms, affecting the largest earners (NZ $78,000 plus). There is also a constant rise with age until the early 60s age group when earning power and discretionary income appear to peak. Those aged 65 and over spend less in absolute terms than most younger age groups but proportionately their spending on overseas travel is greater than all groups under 50 years old. The presence of children in a household depresses expenditure on overseas travel – section c) of Table 11.3 shows older couples with no children spent 6.2 per cent of their weekly expenditure on this item compared with 1.9 per cent for a couple with three children.

Australia continues to be by far the single largest destination for New Zealand tourists, a function of distance, size, variety and close social, cultural and economic ties. Australia accounts for approximately half of all departures, its share remaining largely unchanged throughout the 1980s and early 1990s. Asian destinations such as Singapore, Indonesia (Bali) and Hong Kong have increased in popularity over the past decade (13.1 per cent of departures in 1993) and have come to rival the small islands of the Pacific (13 per cent) in terms of market share. This increase has in part been at the expense of travel to longer-haul destinations in Europe (8.8 per cent), especially the United Kingdom, and North America (8.7 per cent) though in absolute terms the number of New Zealand visitors to these places has continued to grow.

Inbound

New Zealand has experienced significant growth in the inbound sector in recent years, with 1 million international arrivals per year first being recorded in 1992 (Figure 11.1). The number of arrivals doubled over the decade 1984–93, passing from 567,611 in 1984 to 1,156,978 ten years later. Patterns of growth have been far from uniform throughout this period, both in terms of total arrivals and the performance of individual markets. The high rates of growth in the mid-1980s (18 per cent in 1985, 15 per cent in 1987) were followed by a levelling off in demand (2 per cent in 1988, 4 per cent in 1989), and a decrease in 1991 of − 1.3 per cent (slightly greater than the worldwide decrease that year). The decade ended with a marked upswing in total arrivals as annual growth rates reached almost 10 per cent. Growth out of Australia, New Zealand's largest source of visitors and the country's only significant short-haul market, has been sluggish, with four annual decreases being recorded throughout the period. The American market declined sharply from its 1987 peak and is now being challenged for second place by

Japan. The Japanese market showed sustained annual increases of more than 20 per cent in the first half of the decade, since when it has settled back to more modest rates as absolute numbers have expanded. From a small base other Asian markets have grown rapidly in the early 1990s, particularly Taiwan and South Korea. Consistently high rates of growth have been experienced throughout from Germany, which ranked fifth in 1993.

As a consequence of these differing rates of growth, significant changes have occurred during the decade in the overall market mix that has become increasingly diverse and less dominated by English-speaking tourists from the traditional markets of Australia, the USA and the United Kingdom. The British share has remained reasonably constant at 7–9 per cent, but that of Australia has dropped from 44 per cent in 1983 to 31 per cent in 1993, while

Table 11.3 Average weekly New Zealand household expenditure on overseas travel (year ended 31 March 1993)

	Total net expenditure $ c	Expenditure on overseas travel	
		$ c	%
a) **Annual household income**			
< 12,100	292.40	6.90	2.4
12,100–17,399	287.80	5.70	2.0
17,400–20,299	358.80	7.20	2.0
20,300–25,599	391.30	11.70	3.0
25,600–32,399	497.70	13.10	2.6
32,400–40,099	566.50	20.10	3.6
40,100–49,099	645.00	22.40	3.5
49,100–60,099	778.70	23.60	3.0
60,100–77,999	833.40	30.40	3.7
78,000+	1,220.20	70.30	5.8
all	586.80	21.10	3.6
b) **Age group of head of household**			
15–24	597.30	9.0	1.6
25–29	583.70	11.4	2.0
30–39	665.40	18.5	2.8
40–49	723.70	24.7	3.4
50–59	670.20	33.5	5.0
60–64	511.90	37.2	7.3
65+	322.70	14.9	4.6
all	586.80	21.1	3.6
c) **Family Type**			
Young 1 person household	390.20	13.10	3.3
Older 1 person household	267.90	10.70	4.0
Young couple with no children	787.70	27.80	3.5
Older couple with no children	540.20	33.20	6.2
Couple with 1 child	743.40	27.10	3.7
Couple with 2 children	705.80	24.20	3.4
Couple with 3 or more children	802.10	15.50	1.9
1 parent with children	382.50	9.00	2.3
Family with others	736.60	25.30	3.4
Non-family households	730.50	17.80	2.4
All family types	586.80	21.10	3.6

Source: Consumer Expenditure Statistics 1993

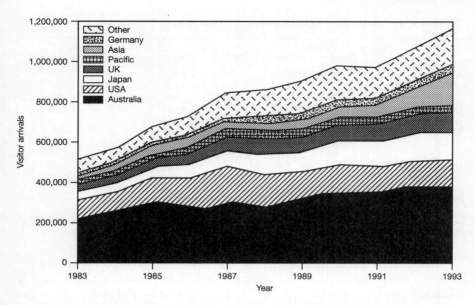

Figure 11.1 Evolution of international visitor arrivals in New Zealand 1983–93.
Source: New Zealand Tourist Department; New Zealand Tourism Board.

the Americans' share has fallen from a peak of 21 per cent in 1987 to 12 per cent in 1993. Over the decade the proportion of Japanese visitors has grown from 6 to 12 per cent, Asians from 3 to 11 per cent and Germans from 2 to 5 per cent. The percentage of arrivals from the Pacific (4–5 per cent) and 'Other' countries (14–18 per cent) has remained largely unchanged.

Arrivals, however, are just one measure of inbound demand and the shares of the different markets vary by nights and total expenditure (Table 11.4). Both Australia and the USA, for example, see their shares reduced on these measures; Japan accounts for a relatively greater share of expenditure and a lesser proportion of total nights, and both Britain and Germany generate a larger amount of nights. These differences reflect variations in length of stay, spending patterns and style of travel. Figure 11.2, for instance, shows the majority of Asian and American holidaymakers and a large share of Australians take a package in New Zealand, while the British, Other Europeans and Other visitors are predominantly free independent travellers (FIT) and the Germans constitute an intermediate group of free and semi-independent travellers. In total, half of the international holidaymakers (i.e. VFR, business and other travellers excluded) in New Zealand were package travellers, a third were FITs and the remainder semi-independent travellers.

Much international tourism in New Zealand is characterized by circuit tourism, consisting of entry through either Auckland or Christchurch international airports followed by a sightseeing tour, at first by coach and

Table 11.4   Distribution of international arrivals in New Zealand 1992/93

	Arrivals		Nights		Total Expenditure	
	(000s)	per cent	(000s)	per cent	($m)	per cent
Australia	322	31.85	4440	23.86	425	20.59
USA	130	12.86	1803	9.69	244	11.82
Japan	125	12.36	1657	8.90	392	18.99
UK	91	9.00	2779	14.93	194	9.40
Germany	48	4.75	1515	8.14	159	7.70
Taiwan	34	3.36	483	2.60	84	4.07
Canada	25	2.47	674	3.62	49	2.37
Singapore	19	1.88	188	1.01	36	1.74
Hong Kong	19	1.88	262	1.41	43	2.08
Other Europe	52	5.14	1633	8.77	128	6.20
Other Asia	54	5.34	824	4.43	106	5.14
Other Countries	93	9.20	2354	12.65	205	9.93
All Arrivals	1011	100.00	18611	100.00	2064	100.00

Source: NZTB (1993a) *New Zealand International Visitors Survey 1992–93*

increasingly by air or independently (e.g. rental car or campervan), of the country's major natural and scenic attractions such as the geothermal area of Rotorua, Mount Cook, the Southern Lakes, Milford Sound and perhaps the glaciers of the West Coast (Forer and Pearce, 1984). As the inbound traffic has

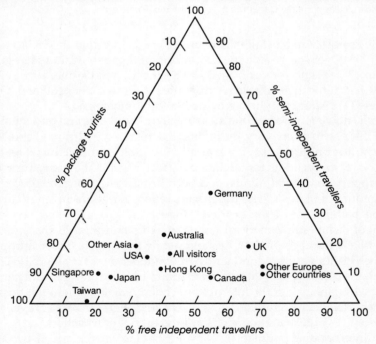

Figure 11.2 Travel styles of international holiday visitors in New Zealand 1992/93.
Source: Data from NZTB (1993a).

grown and its composition changed, so have travel patterns evolved throughout the country (Figure 11.3). During the 1980s the relative increase in shorter stay American and Japanese visitors has seen growth progressively concentrated in the international gateway cities and major resorts of Rotorua and Queenstown (Pearce, 1990). This might largely be attributed to declining lengths of stay associated with the changing market mix but Oppermann (1994) also suggests there has been some shift in visitor preferences, largely to the benefit of Auckland. More dispersed travel patterns are exhibited by the Germans and British, with the growth of the former market in particular resulting in some peripheral spread of demand into such regions as the West Coast, Nelson and the Coromandel. In 1992/93 the three leading regions accounted for over half of all the country's bednights: Auckland (27.9 per cent), Canterbury (14.6 per cent) and Otago (10 per cent). The share held by these three regions of each market's bednights provides a useful summary measure of spatial variations in demand: Taiwan (82 per cent, of which 60 per cent in Auckland alone), Japan (80 per cent, including 33 per cent in Canterbury), the USA (52 per cent), Australia (46.6 per cent), the United Kingdom (42 per cent) and Germany (41 per cent). At the same time as there has been a strengthening of urban-centred tourism, there has also been significant growth in recent years in more active pursuits and adventure tourism, as typified by the increasing popularity of bungy jumping and whale watching (Wilson, 1993). Such developments further testify to the changing nature and growing diversity of New Zealand's growing inbound international tourist industry.

Structure of the Tourist Industry

Major changes have also occurred in the structure of New Zealand's tourist industry in recent years but the details of this are difficult to document. Adequate supply-side statistics are even more limited than those relating to demand. As elsewhere, comprehensive measurement of the industry is bedevilled by problems of definition, lack of separate tourism categories and the multidimensional aspects of many functions such as transport, entertainment and retailing. Tourism in New Zealand, as in many other countries, is characterized by a mix of a large number of small businesses and a handful of medium to large operators. Table 11.5 provides an overview of those enterprises that might be identified at the five digit SIC (standard industrial classification) level as being primarily tourist-oriented businesses. In other instances the 'tourism' dimension cannot be readily disaggregated or identified, such as the proportion of the more than 6,000 jobs in licensed and BYO ('Bring Your Own' Liquour) restaurants, which might be attributed to tourists, or many of the diverse businesses that make up the attractions sector. In total, the enterprises listed in Table 11.5 amounted to more than 5,000 activity units in 1992, employing nearly 40,000 full-time employee equivalents, each

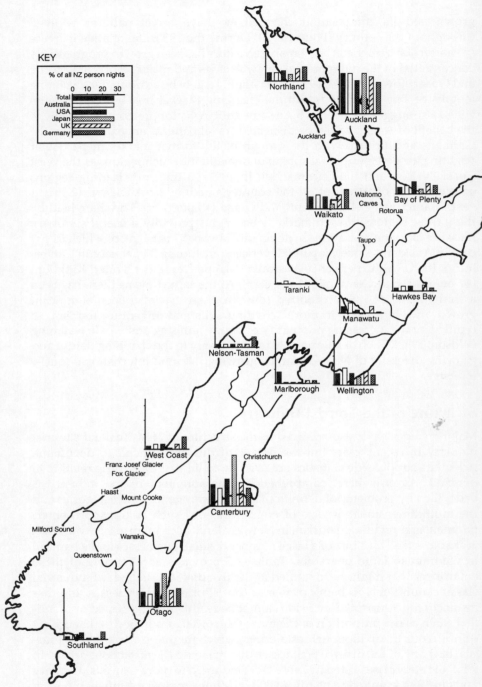

Figure 11.3 Regional distribution of international person nights in new Zealand 1992/93. *Source*: NZTB (1993a).

unit accounting on average for just over seven employees. Several forms of accommodation and tourist retail activities generate on average only two to five jobs, many of these being small owner-operated businesses. Only in the hotel, air transport and tour wholesaler categories does the average number of employees per activity unit exceed ten. These averages conceal the size of some of the major companies. Air New Zealand employed more than 7,000 staff in its core airline related operations in 1993, making it by far the sector's largest enterprise.

Also included in the latter group are several comparatively large businesses that have grown through processes of integration (Collins, 1977), as tourism in New Zealand has developed and expanded. The Helicopter Line, a New Zealand public listed company, has now emerged as the largest of the general tourist operators, having a gross turnover in excess of NZ $100 million in 1993. The company operates throughout New Zealand and increasingly overseas. It portrays itself as being engaged in three activities: 'people gathering' (inbound operators and market wholesalers), 'people moving' (sightseeing, tourist transport and rental cars and campervans) and 'people doing' (activities and attractions). This third sector includes a range of ventures that typify tourism in New Zealand, particularly the expansion of adventure tourism: helicopter sightseeing and heli-skiing, rafting, jet boating, guided walks, scenic boat trips, Kelly Tarlton's Underwater World. Following its recent acquisition of the Quality Hotel chain and five Kingsgate

Table 11.5 Structural characteristics of the tourist industry in New Zealand 1992

NZSIC	Category	Activity units	FTEs	FTEs/unit
6321	unlicensed motels	1176	3599	3.06
63213	private hotels, boarding houses	469	2370	5.05
63220	motor camps, etc	369	909	2.30
63231	tourist hotels	101	2715	26.88
63239	other licensed hotels and motels	786	12237	15.57
63290	other accommodation (not elsewhere considered)	95	310	3.26
	accommodation sub-total	3023	22140	7.32
71133	bus charter operators	137	1155	8.43
71310	air transport carriers	282	7890	27.98
71911	travel agents	807	3563	4.42
71913	inbound tour operators	48	471	9.81
71914	other tour operators (not elsewhere considered)	162	434	2.68
71915	tour wholesalers	17	276	16.24
	transport sub-total	453	13789	9.49
39093	New Zealand souvenirs	52	232	4.46
62952	gift, handcrafts	851	2701	3.17
94501	ski fields	36	120	3.33
	other sub-total	939	3053	3.25
	total	5415	38982	7.20

FTE=full-time job equivalents.
Source: Business Activity Statistics 1992–93

hotels, CDL Hotels New Zealand Ltd has become the largest hotel owner-operator in the country (19 hotels, 2,447 rooms, 1,700 employees). Reflecting the growing trend towards greater foreign investment in New Zealand, this company is a subsidiary of CDL Hotels International, the hotel arm of the largest public listed property developer in Singapore, City Developments Ltd. All but one of the major hotels in Queenstown have now been sold to offshore interests, mainly in Asia (Freeman, 1994). To date most foreign investment has been in existing plant rather than new products.

The recent increase in foreign investment results from several factors including: a general opening up in the New Zealand economy as part of the economic restructuring initiated by the Labour Government in 1984, a slump in the New Zealand property market following the share market crash of 1987 and the increase in visitor arrivals, particularly from Asia. Restructuring has also seen a marked reduction in direct government intervention in tourism (Pearce, 1990, 1992). The country lays claim to having one of the oldest, if not the first, national tourist organizations in the world, the Department of Tourist and Health Resorts having been established as early as 1901. At its peak in the 1960s and 1970s, the department not only undertook more common activities, such as marketing, but also operated tours and travel agencies while the government Tourist Hotel Corporation (THC) managed a chain of hotels. Restructuring saw the government pull back from many of these activities. The Tourist Department withdrew from its commercial operations, was reorganized and then replaced in 1991 by the New Zealand Tourism Board whose role has been tightly focused on international marketing. The THC hotels were sold off and hotel investment incentives for the private sector were discontinued. Air New Zealand was privatized in 1989 (New Zealand shareholders retain a majority but, in line with airline trends elsewhere, significant holdings have been obtained by QANTAS and Japan Airlines). Today the government is most directly involved on the supply-side through the Department of Conservation (DOC), which is responsible for managing national parks and other protected areas of the conservation estate (covering 30 per cent of New Zealand's land area). This is a very significant role given the importance of the DOC estate for both domestic and international tourists – half of all overseas visitors, for example, visit a national park (Pearce and Booth, 1987; NZTB, 1993a).

Restructuring also saw significant deregulation of the transport sector and policy changes favouring a more open skies policy in civil aviation. As a result of these opportunities a second major domestic carrier, Ansett New Zealand, introduced main trunk services in 1987 as a joint New Zealand – Australian owned venture, becoming wholly owned by the Australian partner, Ansett Transport Industries, the following year. The competition Ansett brought has resulted in improved domestic services but the new carrier has yet to record a profit. In the spirit of the Closer Economic Relations agreement between Australia and New Zealand, moves to initiate a trans-Tasman single aviation market were undertaken in the early 1990s (Pearce, 1995). While the scope of the aviation agreement is far-reaching, subsequent progress in its implementation has been slower than originally anticipated and major impacts on international tourism have yet to be felt. Air New Zealand has been the most active of the Australasian carriers, seeing opportunities in the widened beyond rights now granted to tap the growing Asian markets using Brisbane as a hub.

Economic Impacts

In the popular press much has been made of the growth in international tourism and its contribution to New Zealand's economy. While there is no doubt that tourism is a net contributor to the New Zealand economy, there exists considerable confusion over its exact size. However, while much confusion arises from problems in trying to define tourism as an economic activity, such confusion also allows ample opportunity to overstate the benefits of tourism and 'engrandise government funding' (Leiper, 1990).

At the national level tourism is often measured by the gross expenditure of various visitor groupings, although there is increasing recognition of the limitations of input–output models and of Gross National Product as a full measure of economic benefit (NZIER, 1992). In 1991/92 expenditure on international inbound tourism was estimated at NZ $2.73 billion while domestic private travellers were estimated to have spent NZ $2.75 billion and domestic business travellers NZ $1.7 billion. In 1992 tourism was estimated to contribute 5.5 per cent of Gross Domestic Product (GDP), about 5 per cent of national expenditure and generate about 5.7 per cent of the full-time equivalent (FTE) employment units. International tourism accounted for about 38 per cent of expenditure (2.1 per cent GDP) and domestic tourism the other 62 per cent (3.5 per cent GDP).

Two aspects of the analysis of domestic tourism are of concern. First, expenditure data from the last domestic travel study (1989/90) have been presented in two forms, as NZ $2.6 billion in the study itself (New Zealand Tourism Department, 1991) and as NZ $2.2 billion domestic private travel and NZ $1.56 domestic business travel by Lim (1991). The derivation of this latter set of figures is not clear and appears to incorporate some elements of double counting of domestic travellers as 'part of production or as inputs into the production process' (Lim, 1991: 129). Second, this derivation has been brought forward into subsequent analyses and therefore raises doubts about the exact outputs (income, employment and household) that might flow from domestic tourism.

International inbound visitors' gross contributions to foreign exchange earnings continue to be emphasized, particularly by industry sources, and are often reported alongside earnings from agricultural sub-sectors. Provisional estimates for 1992 put earnings from inbound tourism at NZ $2.73

billion, just behind meat (NZ $2.7 billion), but ahead of dairy products (NZ $2.2 billion), wool *(NZ $1.1 billion) and horticulture (NZ $0.9 billion) (NZIER, 1992). The inbound tourism figure consists of NZ $1.8 billion expenditure within New Zealand and NZ $0.9 billion of airfare receipts, approximately half of which could be attributed to the national carrier, Air New Zealand. Given their markedly different downstream effects these two items might more appropriately be listed as separate items. In relative terms, international inbound tourism generates 12.9 per cent of foreign exchange earnings (airfares included).

In 1982 'foreign tourism' was found to be a high net foreign exchange earner at 87.7 per cent 'first round' retention, compared with agricultural exports (86.7 per cent) and manufacturing exports (71.7 per cent) (BERL 1982; NZTC 1984). However, a further analysis of the net flow-on effects placed tourism in the mid-range of other foreign exchange earning sectors. The basis of multiplier calculations has changed since these early attempts at modelling the New Zealand economy. The NZIER (1992) are quick to point out that calculations for their study are based on a 1986/87 national input–output model – since when there has been considerable change in the New Zealand economy (Pearce, 1992) and significant changes in overseas investment and growth, both in numbers and market mix (Figure 11.1), within the tourism sector. These factors remain as 'important caveats which should be listed in any application of the data' (NZIER, 1992: 6). Clearly the analysis of tourism has not kept pace with its growth and structural changes. In particular, there has been no attempt to assess the net contribution of the different markets outlined in Figure 11.1 and Table 11.4 as no details are readily available on leakages associated with individual market segments or forms of tourism.

Mention has already been made of New Zealanders' propensity to travel abroad with the amount spent on such travel steadily increasing (Table 11.2). In total, expenditure by New Zealanders travelling overseas has been estimated to generate NZ $1.8 billion or 9.2 per cent of foreign exchange costs (NZIER, 1992: 15). No analysis of this expenditure has been undertaken but much of it could be expected to leave the national economy, aside from such items as commissions to travel agents, some profits and the proportion of airfares remunerated to Air New Zealand. A small but undetermined share of the employment shown in Table 11.5 is nevertheless generated by the outbound sector.

Tourism is also seen to contribute well to government revenue. Total state revenue from tourism was estimated at NZ $950 million in 1989, comprising NZ $435 million (46 per cent) as taxes on salaries and wages and NZ $409 million (43 per cent) from indirect taxes (Lim, 1991). This latter category includes an estimated NZ $196 million 'Goods and Service' tax (GST) (NZTB, 1994), a tax from which other 'export' sectors are excluded. Government companies operating international airports were excluded from the 1989 figure, with departure fees paid by tourists in 1993 estimated at NZ $23.1

million (NZTB, 1994). (The same departure fees would also have been paid by the 800,000 New Zealand tourists going abroad, yielding a further NZ $16 million). These 'extraordinary' taxes applicable to tourism have generated considerable discussion, especially with respect to funding public resource inputs into tourism, such as the conservation estate.

With the increase in visitor arrivals has come concomitant growth in employment. In 1982 tourism was estimated to generate directly 5 per cent of the full-time job equivalents (FTEs) in the labour force (65,000 FTEs), rising to 7 per cent when flow-on effects were included (90,000 FTEs) (NZTC, 1984). More recent estimates for 1993 place tourism-related employment at 82,000 direct, 34,400 indirect and 73,000 induced FTEs, comprising 7.9 per cent of the workforce (Table 11.6). Indirect and induced jobs occur primarily in the service, manufacturing and construction sectors. Data in Table 11.6 also indicate that more than half of the employment generated arises from domestic tourism. As unemployment remains one of the intractable conditions within the New Zealand economy, lack of attention by policy-makers to domestic tourism remains puzzling.

Considerable caution is again required in interpreting these data. The 1993 data are simple extrapolations of the 1989 figures (reported in 1991), which in turn are based on the 1986/87 input–output model of the economy. Comparison of the data in Tables 11.4, 11.5 and 11.6 indicate there are wide variations in the size and effects of tourism in the New Zealand economy. In the absence of a separate tourism model, a more comprehensive and updated database and standard definitions of the tourist industry, there remains a tendency to overstate the benefits of tourism, and in the absence of appropriate analysis, considerable opportunities for confusion in policy development exist.

Development Issues

There seems little doubt that the 1990s will be a decade of growth for tourism in New Zealand. Reflecting its new marketing focus, ambitious targets for growth in international tourism were outlined by the New Zealand Tourism

Table 11.6 Employment effects of tourism in New Zealand

Category	FTEs		%	%
International	Direct	33,000	42.1	
	indirect	14,286	18.1	
	induced	31,502	39.8	
	Total	79,088	100.0	41.7
Domestic	Directi	48,698	44.1	
	indirect	20,118	18.2	
	induced	41,511	37.6	
	Total	110,327	100.0	58.3
Total		189,414		100.0

Sources: Lim (1991); NZTB (1994)

Board in its first policy documents, namely 3 million international arrivals by the year 2000, generating NZ $9 billion in foreign exchange and creating 185,000 jobs (NZTB, 1991, 1993b). The 3 million target, it was acknowledged, was a million or so greater than past trends would suggest (Figure 11.1), yet one that could be achieved 'if we all work together'. This cooperative approach is perhaps best seen in the additional budget allocations the Board has received to foster international marketing through a series of joint ventures with private sector partners. The 55 new joint ventures established are credited by the Board with generating 'the equivalent of more than 83 per cent of the growth in visitor arrivals during 1992' (NZTB, 1993b). Despite such performances the 3 million target remains rather ambitious given the 1993 figure of 1.15 million arrivals recorded. Other analysts give greater credence to the 2 million forecast (Ernst and Young, 1993; Duncan *et al.*, 1994). Further reflecting its international focus, the NZTB has not set targets for growth in domestic demand. However, Ernst and Young (cited by Duncan *et al.*, 1994) see much more modest rates of increase in the home market, projecting domestic bednights will grow by 28 per cent in the period 1992 to 2005, from 41.8 million to 53.7 million.

While growth targets expressed in visitor arrivals are relatively easy to measure, it is debatable whether they are the most appropriate indicator of tourist development and whether greater emphasis might not be given to the economic measures such as employment, foreign exchange earnings and contribution to GDP. In this regard the differences in the contributions of the various markets shown in Table 11.4 might be recalled. Another example of variations in arrivals and impact is provided by recent analysis of the different contributions of mono- and dual-destination visitors to New Zealand (Pearce, 1995). Mono-destination visitors, that is those visiting just New Zealand, were found to spend on average twice as much as those combining a visit to this country with one to Australia and to travel more widely throughout New Zealand, thereby dispersing their expenditure further. As the development of dual-destination traffic is one strategy being employed to take advantage of the new beyond rights through Australia, the broader implications of these patterns need to be noted. Attention also needs to be directed at assessing the net contribution of the various market segments – is the impact of the higher spending Japanese, for example, reduced by relatively higher levels of leakages associated with the styles of tourism in which this market engages? In the absence of detailed studies of this nature, the real value of each market and each type of tourism remains speculative.

Whatever the exact number and composition of international visitors is by the year 2000 and whatever changes occur in domestic demand, three major interrelated development issues resulting from the growth of tourism in New Zealand during the 1990s might be identified: investment, environmental management, planning and research.

Investment

In the immediate future it will be possible to accommodate a proportion of the new demand by existing over-capacity in some areas and better seasonal and regional distribution of demand, though the market potential to broaden the shoulder season, reduce the winter trough and increase regional spread should not be overestimated. In the early 1990s average hotel occupancies were around 55 per cent, Air New Zealand's domestic passenger load factors had fallen below 60 per cent while the airline's international passenger load factor was 69 per cent in 1993 (Duncan *et al.*, 1994). Already hotel occupancies appear to be improving and excess capacity thereby diminished – an Ernst and Young report projected room occupancies in the country's top hotels increasing from 68.5 per cent in 1994 to 79.8 per cent in 1996 (Compton, 1994). Withdrawal of Continental from the South Pacific has reduced airline capacity out of North America and growing pressure is being felt on other routes.

Whether the number of international arrivals is projected to double or treble by the end of the century, substantial investment will clearly be needed in all sectors of the industry to cater for the increases envisioned for the tourist traffic. Indeed without it growth will be severely constrained. The NZTB (1993b) has emphasized investment requirements in its growth strategies, indicating that investment of more than NZ $6 billion (in 1992 dollars) would be required 'to accommodate the target rate of tourism growth between now and the year 2000'. This would consist of:

- NZ $2.4 billion for accommodation
- NZ $2.1 billion for upgrading and expanding the transport fleet
- NZ $1 billion for upgrading airports
- NZ $0.5 billion for the development of tourism attractions.

Conscious of the large sums required, the NZTB has been actively promoting investment in the sector, for example by sponsoring seminars within New Zealand and abroad. The need to do this reflects both the magnitude of the funding required and the relatively low levels of profitability in many areas over recent years. Certainly there have been significant local developments in some places recently. Christchurch, for example, has seen the city council-financed Worcester Street Boulevard project (first stage opened in 1991), the Mount Cavendish gondola (opened in 1992) and the new Antarctic Centre (completed in 1992). More striking has been the growth of foreign investment in New Zealand tourism noted earlier, particularly in the accommodation sector. Further offshore financing would seem to be the only way of obtaining the large amounts of investment capital for commercial activities identified by the Board.

As yet in New Zealand there has been little analytical evaluation of, or public debate on, the merits of increasing foreign investment as a development strategy for tourism. Duncan *et al.* note, for example, that government agencies are actively fostering foreign investment in general and they review some of the arguments in Australia resulting from work by Dwyer and Forsyth (1992) before concluding that some of the results 'serve as a reminder that while foreign investment has the potential to generate significant net economic effects, distributional effects, some negative for current investors, may be involved.' (1994: 56). From time to time public reaction to foreign investment has been expressed, for instance in the proposal to sell the Wairakei golf course to Japanese investors and the rejection of a Japanese resort development in Hopai Bay (Marlborough Sounds). What appears to be a critical factor here is the nature of the projects involved, there perhaps being greater public acceptance (or lack of awareness) of foreign investment in urban hotels than in recreational resources or natural areas that New Zealanders may use themselves or view as part of their heritage. It is also interesting to observe in this context that the Ministry of Tourism saw the need to produce a multi-lingual booklet on suggestions for 'addressing environmental, cultural and community concerns that might arise in the process of tourism development'(1993).

Although sufficient private sector investment may be stimulated in these ways to meet many of the projected requirements in commercial facilities, significant new demands are also being generated in other areas, notably infrastructure and the conservation estate. These have traditionally been funded by local and central government whose ability or willingness to meet these growing pressures is being increasingly tested. Roading is a particular infrastructural concern given the touring nature of much tourism in New Zealand and the relatively remote location of many major attractions. Closure of the Milford Road through flooding early in 1994, for example, severely taxed the affected agencies as well as disrupting the travel plans of many tourists. The Ministry of Tourism was active in working with Transit New Zealand to increase the profile of the tourist traffic (Institute of Transport Studies *et al.*, 1992) and to incorporate the views of tourism operators in the identification of roading priorities. Some success has been achieved in this area, for example the 1993 budget included an extra NZ $7 million for extending the seal on three important tourism routes, but ensuring roading continues to meet the needs of tourists and other users will provide ongoing challenges throughout the country. Private developers have recently proposed the construction of a NZ $100 million road linking Milford Sound to Haast, the cost to be recovered by road-user tolls in what would be, with the exception of some skifield access roads, the first toll road in the country (Conway, 1994). Taxpayer funding is being sought to undertake a more in-depth study. Finance is not the only issue involved here as the proposed road would run through a World Heritage designated area, raising many environmental concerns and being assured of strong opposition from conservation groups. Such innovations in funding new, or in maintaining existing, infrastructure are likely to become more apparent as visitor demand and financial pressures increase. Indicative of these changes is the Milford Development Authority in Fiordland National Park, which has brought together key operators and the local council to rebuild the boat terminal and redevelop other facilities at Milford Sound, with a loan being raised on the open market and paid for by a levy on sightseeing passengers.

The provision of services and facilities on the conservation estate is coming under increasing pressure as expansion of the Department of Conservation's budget has not matched the growth in visitor numbers. As a result long established practices, by which freedom of access to national parks has essentially been equated by most New Zealanders with free entry, are coming under closer scrutiny and a range of economic instruments for providing visitor services on the conservation estate are under active review (Clough, 1993). This is likely to see more co-funding of facilities and services and some widening of user charges beyond the current operator concessions (net income from concessionaires was less than NZ $1 million in 1993) and relatively modest hut fees. However, a range of issues first have to be resolved including the desirability and practicability of differentiating being domestic and international users and of implementing charging in what are often quite remote, open or dispersed locations.

Environmental management

Funding is but one critical aspect of the management of visitors on the conservation estate and in other environmentally sensitive areas. New Zealand has a well-established network of national parks and other protected areas, together with much experience in interpretation, handling visitors and preparing management strategies. However, distance from the major markets coupled with a small domestic population base have meant that up until recently only relatively localized pressure has been felt and neither management practices nor facilities have been really put to the test. This is now beginning to change, stresses and strains are starting to appear in the system and questions of carrying capacities or limits of acceptable change are emerging.

Indicative of these pressures and the importance attached to the country's 'clean green' image and natural resources is the recent joint NZTB/ Department of Conservation (1993) report on the conservation estate and international visitors. This attempts to quantify current and projected demand from international visitors at major natural attractions and on major tracks. Recommendations for capacity enhancement, for example by improved access at Milford Sound, opening an additional cave at Waitomo, upgrading parking and tracks at the Fox and Franz Josef glaciers and doubling hut accommodation on tracks elsewhere, have been suggested. While such measures may increase capacities they will not necessarily enhance visitor experience. Already there is growing anecdotal evidence of social carrying capacities being reached on some tracks and the increase in helicopter and ski-plane flights is raising issues about acceptable noise levels in glacier valleys and intrusion on other users. The neglect of domestic users in the NZTB/DOC study is particularly disturbing, not only because sound management practices cannot be effectively developed when overall demand is not taken into account but also because of the messages that such an approach may send to New Zealanders who value such environments highly for their intrinsic worth and for the recreational opportunities they provide. Equally unfortunate is the report's failure to consider other areas that are being heavily promoted and where signs of pressure are also emerging. Wilson concludes her examination of nature-based tourism in the South Island, for example whale-watching and trips to observe other marine mammals and rare or endangered bird species, by noting:

> The present system, where management and planning are site specific and monitoring is ad hoc, is for the moment adequate. If, however, operations are sold to (or set up by) unscrupulous operators, or the number of tourists participating in wildlife viewing increases further, the system is unlikely to be able to cope. If this occurs, tourists may become dissatisfied and wild life will probably be harmed. (1993)

In addition, the importance of environmental matters in and around urban areas and the major resorts should not be overlooked given the number of bed nights already spent there and their potential for future growth. Christchurch, for example, has already seen prolonged and extensive debate in recent years over proposals to extend the city's attractions and accommodation (Hart 1992). Some projects have ultimately not gone ahead (e.g. the 167 m Tourist Tower for Victoria Square) while others have proceeded only after very protracted planning procedures (e.g. the Mount Cavendish Gondola). In Queenstown some disquiet is now being expressed that projected increases in visitor numbers and hotel construction would result in too many changes occurring too rapidly and at too large a scale (*The Press*, 12 July 1994).

In the social area, the Ministry of Tourism commissioned a survey of residents in 15 locations that revealed most New Zealanders hold generally favourable views towards tourism and support its expansion (Forsyte Research, 1992). However, spatial and temporal variations in the findings also indicate localized pressure is emerging and greater caution may be needed in forthcoming years. Derivation of a Tourism Acceptance Index based on a series of attitudinal statements indicated acceptance remains relatively high – the 1992 average value was 72 (cf 73.5 in 1988 and 71.2 in 1989), 'on a scale in which scores below 50 denote lack of acceptance, and between 50 and 100 increasing acceptance'. It is noticeable, however, that the lowest values were recorded in some of the smaller communities that are already significant tourist destinations: Queenstown (64.2), Whitianga (65.9), Wanaka (67.3),

Pahia/Russell (67.7) and Taupo (67.9). More than half of the respondents (57 per cent) in 1992 thought New Zealand should have a lot more tourists, but this figure was down on the 66 per cent recorded in 1989 and the 68 per cent of 1983. Support for growth in individual national markets revealed greater preference for more Canadians, Britons and Australians. Least support was expressed for the Japanese but even so three-quarters of those surveyed approved of a doubling of visitors from Japan. These findings need to be seen in terms of the trends towards a greater share of non-English speaking visitors shown in Figure 11.1.

Planning and research

The recent growth in international tourism in New Zealand has largely been market driven, reflecting the international marketing focus of the NZTB, initiatives of the national carrier and favourable trends in key emerging markets, especially in Asia. As just outlined, the scale and rate of growth envisaged has brought into question the country's ability to continue to keep pace with the projected increases in demand. The time is now overdue for this demand-led approach to be complemented by more emphasis on issues of development and impact, of matching demand and supply more carefully and of formulating and articulating in a more reasoned and informed manner the development goals for tourism. In short, a comprehensive strategic planning framework for tourism in New Zealand is needed, one which would take account of all aspects and forms of tourism, not just a set of international marketing targets.

It is doubtful, however, whether such a plan will eventuate. The country does not have a history of sectoral planning and previous attempts to produce a national tourism plan in the early 1980s resulted in a much watered-down issues and policies document (Pearce, 1992). Current government policies favour a free market approach rather than public sector intervention. It is noticeable that the small Ministry of Tourism, which had commissioned many of the policy documents referred to earlier, was downgraded in June 1994 to a Tourism Policy Group within the Ministry of Commerce. At the same time the NZTB, conscious of many of the issues raised above, has begun reviewing the infrastructural needs of tourism in New Zealand but it remains to be seen whether this will constitute part of any broader planning framework.

A research gap has also emerged with many of the issues outlined above not being supported by a sound and comprehensive data base and in-depth understanding of all the factors and processes involved. This gap is evident in many areas including: comprehensive up-to-date information on domestic demand and outbound travel, analysis of the net benefits of different forms of tourism, evaluation of the implications of foreign investment, development needs and processes, social impacts and community change, understanding of the limits of acceptable change in wilderness and other areas and an adequate scientific basis for developing appropriate management techniques for wildlife viewing. A national review of tourism research was initiated by the then Ministry of Tourism in mid-1994 – it is hoped that this will identify priorities more closely, increase the sector's profile and needs before research funding agencies and in general enhance the capacity for more effective research on tourism.

Conclusion

The 1990s may prove to be a very decisive decade for the development of tourism in New Zealand. The growth in international arrivals promoted for many years is now starting to assume significant dimensions in absolute terms, for the country if not on a global scale. This growth is now beginning to generate many challenges and the country's continuing ability to cope must be seriously questioned. For the country's clean green image and that of the friendly, hospitable Kiwi to be maintained, and for economic benefits to keep on expanding, the current narrow international marketing focus must be abandoned and a broader perspective on tourist development adopted. Tourism policies need to consider all sectors not just the inbound traffic, more than lip service must be paid to such concepts as sustainable development, impacts must be seen in other than purely economic terms, greater attention should be given to supply-side considerations and the place of tourism within New Zealand society and economy debated more fully. If the overview provided by this chapter contributes to stimulating this debate then its aims will have been achieved.

Bibliography

BERL (1982) *Tourism in the New Zealand Economy*. Wellington: Business and Economic Research Limited.

Clough, P. (1993) *Economic Instruments and Visitor Services on the Public Estate: Summary Report*. Wellington: Ministry of Tourism.

Collins, N.J. (1977) Integration in New Zealand's Tourist Industry. MA thesis (unpublished), University of Canterbury, Christchurch.

Compton, M. (1994) Improving hotel profitability. In *Winning the Game*. Christchurch, New Zealand Tourism Industry Association, 20–1.

Conway, M. (1994) $100m toll road plan for scenic tourist area. *Sunday Star-Times* 10 July, A2.

Department of Statistics/Statistics New Zealand (various years) *Consumer Expenditure Statistics*. Wellington: Department of Statistics/Statistics New Zealand.

Department of Statistics/Statistics New Zealand (various years) *New Zealand Official Yearbook*. Wellington: Department of Statistics/Statistics New Zealand.

Duncan, I., James, D., Ngan, T. and Hamilton, S. (1994), *Tourism Investment in New Zealand: Opportunities and Constraints*. Wellington: New Zealand Institute of Economic Research.

Dwyer, P. and Forsyth, L. (1992) *The Benefits and Costs of Foreign Investment in Australian Tourism.* Sydney: Faculty of Business and Technology, University of Western Sydney.

Ernst and Young (1993) *Tourism Sector Review.* Wellington: Ernst and Young.

Forer, P.C. and Pearce, D.G. (1984) Spatial patterns of package tourism in New Zealand. *New Zealand Geographer* **40** (1), 34–42.

Forsyte Research (1992) *Residents' Perceptions and Acceptance of Tourism in Selected New Zealand Communities.* Wellington: Ministry of Tourism.

Freeman, S. (1994) Hotel Building Boom in Southern Alps Resort Centre. *Asian Hotelier* June.

Hart, A.J. (1992) Planning for tourism in Christchurch: a comparative study. MA thesis (unpublished), University of Canterbury, Christchurch.

Institute of Transport Studies and Beca Carter Hollings and Ferner (1992) *Quantifying Tourism Economic Benefits and Evaluation of Road Projects.* Wellington: Ministry of Tourism.

Johnston, D.C., Pearce, D.G. and Cant, R.G. (1976) Canterbury holiday makers: a preliminary study of internal tourism. In Cant, R.G. (ed.) *Canterbury at Leisure.* Christchurch: Canterbury Branch New Zealand Geographical Society, 129–138.

Leiper, N. (1990) *Tourism Systems: An Interdisciplinary Perspective.* Palmerston North: Department of Management Systems, Massey University.

Lim, E.E.S. (1991) *The Economic Impact of Tourism in New Zealand.* Auckland: Deloitte, Ross, Tohmatsu.

Ministry of Tourism (1993) *Environmental and Social Factors in Tourism Investment.* Wellington: Ministry of Tourism.

New Zealand Tourism Department (1991) *New Zealand Domestic Travel Study 1989/90.* Wellington: New Zealand Tourism Department.

NZTB (1991) *Tourism In New Zealand: A Strategy for Growth.* Wellington: New Zealand Tourism Board.

NZTB (1993a) *New Zealand International Visitors Survey 1992/93.* Wellington: New Zealand Tourism Board.

NZTB (1993b) *Tourism in New Zealand: Strategy & Progress.* Wellington: New Zealand Tourism Board.

NZTB (1994) *New Zealand Tourism Industry Backgrounder.* Wellington: New Zealand Tourism Board (unpublished report).

NZTB and Department of Conservation (1993) *New Zealand Conservation Estate and International Visitors.* Wellington: New Zealand Tourism Board and Department of Conservation.

NZIER (1992) *Tourism In New Zealand – A Regional and National Multipier Analysis.* Wellington: BERL.

NZTC (New Zealand Tourism Council) (1984) *New Zealand Tourism: Issues and policies.* Wellington: NZ Tourist and Publicity Department.

Oppermann, M. (1994) Regional aspects of tourism in New Zealand. *Regional Studies* **28** (2), 155–167.

Pearce, D.G. (1990) Tourism, the regions and restructuring in New Zealand. *Journal of Tourism Studies* **1** (2), 33–42.

Pearce, D.G. (1992) *Tourist Organizations.* Harlow: Longman.

Pearce, D.G. (1993)Domestic tourist travel patterns in New Zealand. *GeoJournal* **29** (3), 225–232.

Pearce, D.G. (1995) CER, Trans-Tasman tourism and a single aviation market. *Tourism Management* **16** (2), 111–20.

Pearce, D.G. and Booth, K.L. (1987) New Zealand's National Parks: use and users. *New Zealand Geographer* **43** (2), 66–72.

Wilson, P.M. (1993) Commercial wildlife viewing tourism in the South Island: a comparative analysis. MA thesis (unpublished), University of Canterbury, Christchurch.

12

Philippines: The development of Philippine tourism in the post-Marcos era

LUDWIG G. RIEDER

Introduction

When the Aquino administration took office in February 1986, it inherited a tourism industry marked by the absence of a coherent development plan; a very negative image of the Philippines as a destination caused by years of public protest against the Marcos regime; a total disregard for domestic tourism; a plethora of 'white elephants' including hotels, resorts, and lodges sponsored by individuals who failed to draw a distinction between public, personal and commercial interest; total public cynicism towards the industry; and where the value of professionalism in tourism at a public or private sector level had been virtually extinguished. The net effect of these factors for the country's inbound tourism is best illustrated in the steady decline in foreign tourism arrivals to the Philippines between 1980 and 1985, just before Ferdinand Marcos fled the Philippines (Table 12.1).

The Ministry of Tourism (MOT) and its attached agencies, the most prominent of which was the Philippine Tourism Authority (PTA), had become mere tools of special interests connected with the Marcos regime.

Table 12.1   History of arrivals to the Philippines 1980–85

Year	Foreign arrivals	Change (%)
1980	1,008,200	Base
1981	939,000	6.9
1982	890,800	5.1
1983	860,600	3.4
1984	816,700	5.1
1985	773,100	5.3

Source: Department of Tourism (1994)

Thus, at the end of the Marcos era, the tourism industry of the Philippines, like so many other industries, lay in ruins, plundered by personal greed and interest over the previous 20 years.

This chapter traces the faltering steps, the successes and the failures of the Philippine tourism industry since the ousting of the Marcos regime in February 1986, the period referred to as the post-Marcos era in the title of this chapter. The effort to re-focus the thrust of tourism development and promotion policy away from personal interest and towards national socio-economic goals, with particular reference to the development and implementation of a long-term blueprint or master plan for the industry, is reviewed and evaluated. Finally, the chapter considers the prospects for the future, given the circumstances the country finds itself in, and its aspirations as expressed in its tourism master plan.

The Revival Programme

The immediate task of the new administration was to take stock and begin to plan and implement the revival of the tourism industry.

Taking stock

Without a transition period and without a formal turnover from the Minister of Tourism who had exiled himself to the province, the new leadership began to look for documents that would guide them in their formidable task of rebuilding from the ruins of the Marcos regime (Lim, 1994). The first thing they looked for was a framework plan for tourism development. What guided the previous administration in its thrust for infrastructure development? Why were luxury hotels built in Ilocos Norte and Leyte, home provinces of Ferdinand and Imelda Marcos, respectively? What was the rationale for building lodges in remote places that were not accessible to tourists? Could it be true that all these were built on the couple's whims and to satisfy personal needs?

Instead of a framework plan, several disparate plans were found throughout the MOT building, which also housed the PTA, the infrastructure arm of the MOT. The PTA was popularly perceived to be the milking cow of the Marcoses. It collected the travel tax, imposed during the first year of martial law, purportedly to limit the number of people travelling abroad and to conserve precious dollars. A portion of the travel tax (38 per cent) went directly to the PTA for tourism infrastructure projects and this became the source of funds for the Marcoses' pet infrastructure and image-building projects. It was general knowledge that the PTA embarked on several infrastructure projects at the behest of the First Couple and because money was to be made on them.

One of the most difficult challenges that faced the new leadership was to prepare an inventory of PTA's properties all over the Philippines. It owned real estate, hotels, resorts, restaurants, travel lodges, museums and commercial buildings. However, record keeping was not a strong point of the previous administration. In fact, there was very poor documentation of assets. It was believed that this was done deliberately to hide the anomalies prevalent during that period. In the end, the inventory of assets and the untangling of their complicated acquisition and ownership schemes took five years.

It was also widely believed that Ferdinand Marcos formed the MOT in 1973 to camouflage the human rights abuses and the graft and corruption that was happening in his regime – to show to the world that, in spite of martial law, 'the Philippines was where Asia wore a smile' (Richter, 1989). It was also thought that the MOT was founded to reward Jose Aspiras, a journalist who saved Imelda Marcos from an attempted assassination. Aspiras was named the first Minister of Tourism and remained in that post until February 1986 when the Marcoses and their faithful followers fled the country in ignominy and the Cory Aquino government came to power. The motives for creating the new Ministry were thus, suspect, and such suspicions were substantiated by events that followed. Rather than making tourism an activity for the Filipino people first and foremost, the Marcoses, through Aspiras, started to sponsor lavish activities such as the Miss Universe Pageant in 1974, for which a new building, the Folk Arts Theater, was especially built in 70 days, supervised by no less than Imelda Marcos herself. Another major international event, the International Film Festival, was hosted in the early 1980s. Again, a new building, the International Film Center, was built for that purpose. Several international conferences were hosted by the Philippines from 1973 to 1980: the World Tourism Conference, the Pacific Asia Travel Association Annual Meeting, and the American Society of Travel Agents, among others. The last one failed, creating a very negative image of the country and negating all the propaganda that the MOT churned out about the Marcos regime.

Tourism was thus seen as a propaganda gimmick, an elitist activity meant only for foreigners and worse, as a prostituting activity. In the late 1970s, sex tourism in the Philippines was rampant (Lim, 1992). Organized sex tours were condoned by the Ministry of Tourism. Tourist arrivals increased and hit 1 million for the first time in 1980. Whilst this was a source of pride for the administration, the people, especially the women, were furious. They took to the streets to protest at the policies of the MOT, which they saw as degrading the image of the Filipino woman and of the country in general. This was the stigma of the MOT that the new leadership had to overcome when it took over in 1986.

Given these circumstances, it was clear that any tourism restoration programme for the Philippines would have to address a number of factors, the most important of which were to:

- Move immediately to restore the image of tourism in the minds of Filipinos and to make domestic tourism a key element of any future tourism programme.
- Reposition the image and product of the Philippines as a destination in international markets.
- Reorganize and streamline the MOT and its attached agencies, especially the PTA, including the privatization of its many non-performing assets.
- Secure the financing base required to implement its programmes.
- Prepare a long-term framework plan for the development and promotion of tourism in the country.

Some of the principal features of the programmes adopted to address these issues are reviewed below.

Long-term Framework
Because there was no framework plan, the new leadership commissioned the preparation of one. The assistance of the National Economic Development Agency (NEDA), the central planning body of government, was sought to obtain technical and financial assistance for the Ministry from multilateral aid institutions. Tourism did not seem to be a priority of the NEDA. It took two years and much perseverance from the Ministry to obtain technical assistance from the United Nations Development Programme (UNDP) and the World Tourism Organization (WTO) in order to commission the design study for the tourism master plan that was very much needed to guide the development of Philippine tourism. Another two years would pass before this plan could be completed.

In the meantime, a one-year rolling National Tourism Plan (NTP) was prepared by the Department of Tourism (DOT). (In 1987, the Philippine government returned to the Presidential form of government from the semi-parliamentary form that Marcos had instituted. Hence, all government Ministries were converted into Departments and Ministers and Deputy Ministers were called Secretaries and Undersecretaries) (DOT, 1987b). This was done with the cooperation of, and with inputs from, the tourism private sector. It should be noted that under the new administration, the private sector became very active in government affairs. In the spirit of 'people power', people participation in affairs of state was strongly encouraged by President Aquino. The DOT was no exception. The existing sectoral organizations – namely, the Philippine Travel Agencies Association (PTAA); the Philippine Tour Operators Association (PHILTOA); the Hotel and Restaurant Association of the Philippines (HRAP); and many other sectoral organizations that were practically moribund towards the end of the Marcos regime – were revived and became active participants in the shaping of tourism policies and programmes. The NTP was one document produced by both the DOT and the private sector working closely together.

An examination of the NTP document reveals that it was very much a product of the early days of the new government. It is a statement of policy rather than a plan. It had four main goals: economic, socio-cultural, environmental and governmental. The tourism industry's aims were to maximize and distribute the economic benefits of tourism to a wide base of the Filipino population and to make tourism a vehicle by which Filipinos would get to know, love and appreciate their country.

Tourism was seen to be the vehicle to build a sense of national identity and unity. It was also the aim of the DOT to change the negative public image of tourism in general and of the Department and the PTA in particular. Thus, the National Tourism Plan is heavy on domestic tourism programmes for various sectors of society: youth, government workers, the disabled, Filipinos living in the far north and the far south of the country, and the economically disadvantaged. Tourism was meant for Filipinos first; this was the message the new Department was imparting.

Domestic Tourism Programme

The domestic tourism programme involved launching an awareness campaign called '*Huwag maging dayuhan sa sariling bayan*' ('Don't be a stranger in your own country') (DOT, 1987a). This programme provided: opportunities for students, the disabled, government workers, and the general public to visit other parts of the Philippines through a subsidy scheme; a north–south exchange programme to foster better understanding between the indigenous peoples of the northern and southern regions of the Philippines; and re-focused the programmes of the PTA to the development of domestic resorts and excursion sites that were accessible and affordable to the ordinary Filipino. These programmes were commenced in 1987 and continued into the first year of the Ramos administration, which also introduced the '*Mang Pandoy*' programme, which is designed to help ordinary people to benefit from tourism by running tourist facilities such as pensions, lodges, home-stay programmes, etc. Up to 1992, the main visible achievements of this programme were to facilitate the travel of about 80,000 Filipinos within their own country and the development by the PTA of US $51.7 million of new tourism facilities for the domestic market (DOT, 1992).

Foreign tourism programme

The foreign tourism programme focused on moving away from the old slogan 'Where Asia Wears a Smile' to 'Come and see our new Philippines'. This was to be achieved principally by repositioning the image of the Philippines as a newly restored democracy where a brave people resisted the guns of a dictator in a non-violent 'revolution' that millions of television viewers all over the world witnessed and admired. The first-year campaign of the tourism industry was therefore built on the newly recovered pride, self-respect and dignity of the Filipino people. In mid-1987, a new marketing campaign was formulated and implemented in late 1988, which focused on the Philippines as 'Fiesta Islands' – a land full of festivals, music, dance, exotic cuisine, colour, history and folklore. The new image being projected was that of a country with a culture and history it can be proud of. The 'Fiesta Islands' marketing theme was carried from 1988 to 1991 when it was replaced by 'Islands Philippines'. In addition to the marketing campaign, the programme also called for the strengthening of DOT's foreign field offices and focusing the promotions programme to very specific markets that DOT knew would generate the number of tourists needed to boost its visitor arrivals. These markets were the short-haul markets of Japan, Hong-Kong, Taiwan and the new market of Korea, which had just liberalized restrictions on foreign travel by their nationals.

Reorganizing and streamlining the MOT and its attached agencies
Based on criteria provided by the Aquino administration – namely to make the MOT cost effective, more efficient in the delivery of front-line services, more accountable to the public, more decentralized, and responsive to private initiative – the MOT was reorganized in January 1987 through Executive Order No 20, signed by President Aquino. The streamlining of the MOT and its attached agencies, required that its total staff complement be reduced from 1,600 to 700 (DOT, 1992a). The MOT was one of the first line agencies under the new administration to reorganize and reduce its personnel complement. However, in 1992, after a prolonged court battle, the Supreme Court ruled on the side of those who were declared redundant, and ordered the DOT to reinstate them, and for those who refused to receive their redundancy pay in 1987, to be paid their back wages. As a result, the DOT was required to pay Peso 26.5 million in back wages and reinstate 111 personnel. Thus at the end of the Aquino administration, the DOT's total staff complement was 767.

The Aquino government had embarked on a privatization programme wherein government assets were to be privatized to raise funds for the economically crippled country. The new Minister of Tourism wanted to rid the PTA of its many assets that it was managing very poorly and that were proving to be a financial drain. However, only two hotels were sold between 1986 and 1992, the period of the Aquino administration. These were the Cebu Plaza, sold in 1988 and the Fort Ilocandia Hotel, sold in 1991.

Securing the financing of its programmes
Traditionally, the MOT received an appropriation from Congress but this was very inadequate. To survive, the leadership of the MOT under the previous administration had collected a travel tax from every Filipino resident travelling abroad, 38 per cent of which went directly into PTA's coffers

to finance its tourism infrastructure projects. The balance went to the Treasury. The other attached agency of the MOT, the Philippine Convention Bureau (later renamed the Philippine Convention & Visitors Corporation when MOT was reorganized), had a share of the hotel room tax to be used for marketing the Philippines as a destination for the meetings, incentives, conventions and exhibitions market. However, under the new administration, these independent sources of funds were threatened as the economic managers of the Aquino government frowned upon earmarking of funds and automatic appropriation. The new Minister for Tourism, foreseeing that the DOT and its attached agencies would be ineffective without the funds required to implement its programmes, worked for the awarding of the franchise of the Duty Free Shops to the DOT/PTA. This ensured that a steady stream of finance from profits was available to finance its programmes. Until the time of this writing, the DOT still enjoys the benefits of this source of finance.

The United Nations Development Programme (UNDP)/World Tourism Organization (WTO) Tourism Master Plan

The centrepiece initiative of the Aquino administration was the preparation of a long-term master plan for the development of tourism in the Philippines. Even though the original request for this master plan had been made in early 1987, it took another three years before the development of this plan was commenced and another year before it was completed and adopted.

The Tourism Master Plan for the Philippines provides a long-term policy framework for the development of tourism to the year 2010, and a medium-term (5 year) action programme related to achieving the medium- and long-term objectives of the plan. The plan was prepared using a combination of 'expert technical advice' to frame the scope and options available, in-depth interviews, analysis and search workshop techniques involving 'key players' to arrive at consensus on strategy, policy, priorities and activity programming.

At the time of the preparation of the plan (1990 and 1991), the economy was highly dependent on foreign support and struggling under an enormous external debt problem. Inflation and interest rates were running at unacceptably high levels. The tourism sector was almost exclusively centred in the northern Philippines (Luzon), the vulnerability of which was well demonstrated when the whole sector was shut down for two weeks in 1991, as a result of the Mount Pinatubo eruption. The social fabric of the Philippines was under enormous strain from overpopulation, extensive poverty, large regional income imbalances, rising unemployment, all exacerbated by the bloody coup attempt in late 1989. Even the tourism sector was 98 per cent concentrated into the Metro Manila area. The environment was in a critical state, with 80 per cent of the country's forest cover gone, massive erosion, loss of critically needed ground water, and the destruction of up to 90 per cent of its coral reef ecology through illegal fishing methods and siltation. Finally, much of the country, comprising over 7,000 islands, was subject to the destructive impact of typhoon, earthquake and volcanic activity. Whilst these issues were already being addressed by the national government, it was evident that the precarious socio-economic, political and environmental situation would place significant limits on the future carrying capacity for tourism development, and that any development would need to be highly sensitive to these factors.

To achieve the broad economic, social and environmental goals that the country had set for itself, and to which the tourism sector was harnessed, a long-term policy framework was evolved that called for:

1)   The development of three complementary destination clusters based on the grouping of the Philippine Islands into the northern (Luzon and Palawan), central (Visayas) and southern Philippines (Mindanao), and within these, the development of five priority destinations. (See Figure 12.1)
2)   The pursuit of a mixed niche and mass-market development strategy based on the development of special interest, natural and cultural attractions, small and large-scale resorts, and facilities for the meetings, incentive, convention and exhibition markets.
3)   A balance of development between foreign and domestic tourism.

The cluster development strategy was based on the principle of redundancy of destinations and dispersal of benefits. Each cluster would have at least one international gateway centre (Manila in Luzon, Cebu City in the Visayas, and Davao City in Mindanao), near which would be located at least one or two mass-market beach resort destinations. Satellite destinations within the cluster were to concentrate on niche or mass-market development, consistent with their capacity to sustain development in environmental, socio-economic and accessibility terms. The satellite destinations were grouped into established, emerging and potential destinations to facilitate further planning and development at a local level.

Within the context of the cluster strategy, five priority areas were identified based on criteria that included diversity, quality and complementarity of tourism resources, accessibility, availability of human resources and other supporting infrastructure. The five priority areas selected and planned at a structure plan or conceptual level were: an integrated resort estate for 3,000 resort units located on Samal Island, in the Gulf of Davao, near Davao City; a second integrated resort estate for 6,000 resort units on Panglao Island near Cebu; an eco-tourism destination based on the main land and smaller islands of the environmentally pristine Northern Palawan area; a day and overnight touring and resort destination based on the scenic and historic Tagaytay/ Taal/Batangas coast near Manila; and an area for a mix of mass and niche-market tourism development in North Luzon including the 100 Islands of Pangasinan, the mountain resort area of Baguio and the beach resort areas of the La Union Coast. The preparation of these plans involved the use of a sustainable development planning process to ensure that the pace of development did not exceed the capacities of the wounded environment, the community and infrastructure. Development standards and guidelines were then prepared as a basis for controlling development to ensure sustainability. Detailed documentation of these plans are provided in the Technical Papers to the main report (UNDP/WTO, 1991).

The concept of a mixed-market development strategy reflected the reality that the Philippines was the closest ASEAN destination to a large and growing short-haul market that was seeking vacation, meetings, incentive, convention and exhibition opportunities in large-scale resort centres and cities in the ASEAN region. Whilst the country could not expect to develop the resort capacities possible in the larger land masses of ASEAN, it could nevertheless attract a small yet significant share of this market. At the same time, the long-haul market for special interest travel was seen to be growing strongly, providing opportunities for niche-based resort and touring activities centred on the natural and cultural attractions of the country.

The need for balance between foreign and domestic tourism was imperative, not only because of the perception of foreign tourism as an elite activity, but also as the only way to ensure that the infrastructure and commercial development needed, as well as the viability of these facilities, was assured over the long term. This meant that ideally, the development and marketing of infrastructure and tourism products should meet the needs of both foreign and domestic tourism markets.

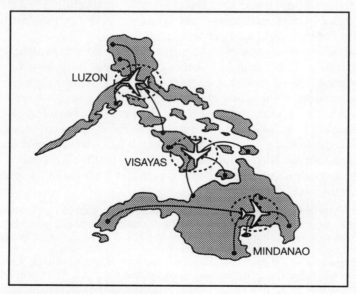

Fig 12.1 Complementary destination clusters.

Based on these broad strategic considerations, and in the context of the environmental, social and economic capacity constraints, modest domestic and foreign visitor targets were set. Basically, it was envisaged that by the year 2010, the Philippines would aim to attract about 5.4 million foreign visitor arrivals, balanced by a target of about 12 million domestic visitors staying in commercial accommodation facilities. In terms of average annual growth rates, the achievement of these targets required a 7.8 per cent annual growth in the foreign market, and a 4.2 per cent annual growth in the domestic market. These growth rates are broadly consistent with the average projected growth of foreign tourism arrivals in the ASEAN region up to the year 2010 and in the projected growth of the domestic economy over this period. The target visitor volumes were further broken up into a short (2 years) and medium term (5 years) to frame specific action programmes for the target dispersal of tourism by cluster, and ultimately into the emerging and potential destinations over the longer term.

From a timing point of view, in the short to medium term, the main aims of the plan's programmes were to:

- Improve the quality of existing destinations such as Manila, Cebu and Baguio City and to increase the utilization levels of the tourist facilities in these.
- Lay the groundwork for the development of the policy, infrastructure, planning and investment framework needed to bring about the development of the emerging and potential destinations.

Specific policies to frame action in the medium term were recommended for the development of tourist accommodation facilities, transportation – including airport development and civil aviation policy, marketing, product development, training and manpower development, and for the institutional organization of the public and private sector.

The draft plan was finalized in August of 1991 and then presented to the President and the Cabinet in November of that year. A short video on the plan was prepared to facilitate presentations to a wide range of sectors including legislators, business, local communities, local governments, the travel trade and potential investors. After the peaceful transition of government from President Cory Aquino to President Fidel Ramos in June of 1992, the plan was presented to him and his Cabinet, which subsequently endorsed it for implementation through Presidential Proclamation No 1 88.

To date, the following elements of the plan have, or are in the process of being implemented:

- The gradual liberalization of a civil aviation policy to increase capacity within and between the Philippines and its key international tourism markets in East Asia, and to allow foreign airlines access to Cebu, Davao City and Laoag, whose airports are already able to accept international services.
- The upgrading and expansion of international passenger terminals, runways, apron areas, freight and instrument landing facilities at Manila, Cebu and Davao, with plans for the upgrading of San Fernando Airport in La Union to international airport status.

- Launching of a major international marketing programme to reposition the Philippines as a destination in the region.
- Continuation of the domestic tourism programmes, including investment by the PTA in infrastructure for domestic tourists.
- Creation of a new centre for meeting the human resource training requirements under the plan at a management level, with plans for the provision of skills training in the process of being implemented.
- Further detailed planning of the five priority areas with particular attention to the Samal and Panglao Island Integrated Resort Estates, Northern Palawan, and in Northern Luzon, planning for the heritage conservation of Vigan, the old capital of the Philippines for a period during the Spanish era.
- Investment promotion activities involving the preparation of suitable brochure and video selling collateral materials and undertaking investment selling missions to Europe.

Other features of the plan are also being implemented according to the schedule of activities set out in the medium-term action programme.

Achievements to Date

To properly evaluate the achievements of the two post-Marcos administrations in the development of tourism in the Philippines, it is necessary to net out the impact of events that were beyond their control. These events include: recessions in the main market areas for the Philippines; natural disasters: overseas conflicts that disrupt the flow of international tourism; and the impact of past repressive policies, inadequate planning and the corrupt practices of the Marcos regime. Only then is it possible to adequately assess the real effect of the post-Marcos administration on the development of tourism in the Philippines.

The condition that confronted Philippine tourism in the period between 1986 and 1993 could not have been worse. The sequence of events was as follows:

- In December 1989, the hard-won democracy of 1986 was at risk when an army rebellion exploded into a full-scale bloody coup attempt involving the hostaging of tourists in their hotels, which virtually shut down the tourism sector for many weeks; then in June 1990, a major earthquake devastated Northern Luzon, destroying over 1,500 hotel and resort rooms.
- In September 1990, the Central Philippines was devastated by super typhoon Ruping, which shut down much of Cebu's tourism plant for several weeks.
- In the first four months of 1991, the Gulf War shut off west–east travel from Europe and dampened international travel overall.
- In June 1991, the eruption of Mt Pinatubo volcano, the largest recorded in the twentieth century, devastated large parts of Central Luzon and with it, a large volume of tourist attractions and accommodations.
- Throughout the latter part of 1992 and all of 1993, crippling power shortages affected the operation of tourist facilities throughout the Philippines, especially in Metro Manila.
- Recession in the main market-generating countries of Japan, Europe and North America.

Together, these events provide the framework within which the development of the tourism sector must be understood and evaluated in the post-Marcos years. In this context, the development of tourism can be reviewed and evaluated in terms of key indicators such as: the flow of tourism and tourism expenditure; market share in the ASEAN region; economic impact including investment activity, and regional distribution effects. As far as possible, the principal developments in each of these factors between 1986 and 1994 is reviewed below, and an assessment made of the extent to which any observed change could be attributed to the policies and programmes of the post-Marcos administrations.

Foreign tourism arrivals and expenditure

With the restoration of democracy, the Philippines quickly reversed the downward trend within the first year of the new administration. However, as is often not appreciated, the policy initiatives of new administrations typically take up to 18 months to manifest themselves (if at all) given the circumstances. Table 12.2 outlines the trends in foreign arrivals and expenditure between the end of 1985 (two months before the Aquino administration assumed office) and the end of 1993, 18 months into the second post-Marcos administration.

The efforts to address the country's poor image as a tourist destination both at home and abroad, the reorganization and streamlining of the Ministry of Tourism and its attached agencies, the implementation of the domestic tourism programme, and the securing of the necessary finance to fund these activities, began to have an effect by 1988, when tourism volumes increased by 31.2 per cent followed by an increase of 14.2 per cent in 1989.

However, as indicated, these growth rates were achieved against the gathering clouds of man-made and natural calamities, most of them beyond the control of the administration. Taken together, these events ensured that any real recovery would be deferred at least until 1994. Nevertheless, and

Table 12.2   Increase in foreign tourist arrivals and expenditure to the Philippines under the post-Marcos era

Year	Foreign arrivals	Increase (%)	Foreign visitor receipts*	Increase (%)
1985	773	Base	–	–
1986	782	1.2	–	–
1987	795	3.8	1,200	base
1988	1,043	31.2	1,301	8.4
1989	1,190	14.1	1,465	12.6
1990	1,025	(13.9)	1,306	(10.9)
1991	951	(7.2)	1,282	(1.9)
1992	1,153	21.1	1,674	30.7
1993	1,372	19.0	2,122	26.8

* Prior to 1987, accurate and reliable data on tourism expenditure were not available.
Source: EIU (1994)

despite the difficult circumstances facing the administration, foreign arrivals in 1992 and 1993 recovered significantly. Even so, the 1993 level of arrivals stood only 15.3 per cent above those achieved in 1989. Thus, a combination of political events and natural disasters conspired to negate much of the hard work of the administration up to 1989 and beyond. Even so, the 1993 performance is impressive as it is only 8.5 per cent below the short-term target set for that year in the Philippine Tourism Master Plan.

Share of ASEAN arrivals

In 1985, even with a declining volume of foreign tourism arrivals, the Philippines still had a small but respectable share of arrivals to the ASEAN region (7.5 per cent). However, the legacy of the Marcos regime was such that the Philippines could not match the tremendous expansion of tourism capacity that took place in Singapore, Bali, Pattaya, Phuket and Penang in the second half of the 1980s. As these destinations took off, the Philippines was left standing without the capacity to compete. Coupled with the many internal problems faced by the administration between late 1989 and 1993, the effect was to reduce the Philippines share of total ASEAN arrivals to 4.8 per cent in 1991, down 34 per cent on the market share in 1985. However, the impact of the post-Marcos administration's programmes in its foreign tourism markets, and in generating investment activity in new hotels and to a lesser extent in resorts, during 1987 to 1991, appears to have reversed the downward trend. The trend of the market share claimed by the Philippines in terms of international tourism arrivals, compared with the total ASEAN complex between 1985 and 1993, is depicted in Table 12.3.

Economic impact

The economic impact of tourism on the economy was first measured using input output analysis in 1987 (AIT, 1987). This study was reviewed in 1990 and 1991 as part of the Philippine Tourism Master Plan project (McCann, 1991). This resulted in an improved estimation methodology that has been used up to the time of writing. Table 12.4 compares the performance of

Table 12.3 Philippine market share of foreign arrivals in ASEAN

Year	Total ASEAN Arrivals	Total Philippine Arrivals	Market Share %
1985	10,640,000	773,100	7.3
1988	14,640,000	1,043,100	7.1
1989	17,000,000	1,190,000	7.0
1990	21,300,000	1,024,500	4.8
1991	19,965,000	951,000	4.8
1992	21,850,000	1,153,000	5.3
1993	23,660,000	1,372,100	5.8

Source: ASEAN Tourism information Center (Industry Reports 1991, 1992 and 1993)

234 Ludwig G. Rieder

Table 12.4 Impact of international and domestic tourism expenditure

Year	Gross receipts (P Billions)	GDP contribution (P Billions)	GDP Contribution (%)	Net Foreign exchange earnings (P Billions)	Estimated number employed	Approved capital invested (P Billions)
1987	na	na	na	na	na	0.34
1988	na	na	na	na	na	2.50
1989	51.0	44.0	4.5	26.0	690,000	20.47
1990	60.0	52.0	4.9	25.0	660,000	9.52
1991	62.0	53.7	5.0	na	630,000	7.10
1992	83.5	72.2	5.0	na	680,000	4.8
1993	91.4	79.0	5.3	44.6	757,000	4.24

Source: Department of Tourism

tourism in the post-Marcos era in terms of total gross receipts, Gross Domestic Product (GDP) contribution, net foreign exchange earnings, employment generated, and DOT approved capital investment.

The impact of the debilitating events of late 1989 to 1993 are clearly discernible in: the flattening of receipts between 1990 and 1991; the flattening of GDP contribution between 1990 and 1993; the decline in employment between 1990 and 1991; and the significant decline in approved capital investment activity from 1990 onwards. Based on the bullish outlook in early 1989, a number of major investment decisions were made, which included the construction of the Makati and Edsa Shangri-la hotels, the New World Hotel and the Diamond Hotel. However, any enthusiasm for further investment quickly evaporated as fast as adverse events appeared. Indeed, had it not been for the strength of the domestic market, the position would have been considerably worse than it was (Table 12.5).

Clearly, the domestic tourism market took up a large proportion of the slack left by the foreign tourism market in 1990 and 1991, thus vindicating the MOTs/DOT programme to promote the development of domestic tourism between 1987 and 1990.

Conclusion: Prospects for the Future

Given the extraordinary degree of uncertainty associated with the development of tourism in the Philippines, it is difficult to be firm about the prospects for tourism in the country. There are still many obstacles in the path of more

Table 12.5 Impact of domestic tourism expenditure

Year	Gross receipts (P Billions)	GDP contributions (P Billions)	GDP Contributions %	Net Foreign exchange earnings (P Billions)	Estimated number employed
1989	10.0	9.0	0.9	–	190,000
1990	21.0	19.0	1.8	–	260,000

Source: UNDP/WTO (1991a)

rapid development. The most important of these include: the readiness with which government and legislators are prepared to trade-off increased foreign and domestic tourism access to and within the Philippines arising from a more flexible approach to aviation policy for the interests of specific and slower growing groups such as the national carrier; the ability to deliver the needed infrastructure (especially the international and domestic airports; transportation, power, water and telecommunications) to secure the development of competitive resort and other tourist facilities; the ability to secure the safety and security of tourists in an environment of rising criminality; the extent to which environmental degradation can be stopped and reversed; the priority that tourism is afforded in the national economy, and the consistency with which tourism officials stick to the implementation of the Tourism Master Plan or the danger of powerful pressure groups prevailing upon the president to move away from his policy of organizational streamlining, deregulation and liberalization; the degree to which the funding of the needed development, promotion and training activities is secured; and above all, the many unforeseen environmental and man-made hazards yet to challenge the Philippine tourism industry.

Nevertheless, as judged from the point of view of the Tourism Master Plan, the potential of the Philippine tourism sector is considerable. With careful management of the obstacles outlined above, a little more luck than experienced in the past five years, and continuation of the current economic growth surge, the Philippines for the first time has a good chance of developing a robust and highly productive tourism industry in the years to come.

Bibliography

Asian Institute of Tourism (1987) Impact of Tourism on the Philippine economy. Manila: AIT, 1–26.

ASEAN Tourism Information Center (1991) *ASEAN Tourism Industry Report, 1991*. Kuala Lumpur: ATIC, 13–15.

ASEAN Tourism Information Center (1992) *ASEAN Tourism Industry Report, 1992*. Kuala Lumpur ATIC, 13–15.

ASEAN Tourism Information Center (1994) *ASEAN Tourism Industry Report, 1993*. Kuala Lumpur: ATIC, 30–2.

Economic Intelligence Unit (EIU) (1994) Philippines. *International Tourism Reports*, No 3.

Lim, N.Z. (1992) Women and cultural tourism: the Philippine experience: enriching or degrading culture? *Proceedings of the International Conference on Cultural Tourism*. Yogyakarta: Gadjah Mada University, 87–90

McCann, R. (1991) The economic impact of tourism in the Philippines. *Tourism Master Plan*, Republic of the Philippines, PH1/88/036 Technical Papers, Vol.2. Madrid: WTO, 15–28.

Department of Tourism (Bureau of International Marketing) (1987a, unpublished) *Tourism Marketing Plan*, Manila, 1–12.

Department of Tourism (Office of Tourism Development Planning) (1987b, unpublished), *National Tourism Plan*, Manila.

Department of Tourism (Office of the Secretary for Tourism) (1992a, unpublished)
Organizational Transition Report, 1986–1992. Manila, 34–5, 83–109.

Department of Tourism (Office of the Secretary for Tourism) (1992b, unpublished)
Social Tourism Program. Manila, 1–7.

Department of Tourism (Office of Tourism Department Planning) (1994a, unpublished) *Statistical Report on Travel and Tourism for 1993*. Manila.

Department of Tourism (Office of Tourism Development Planning) (1994b, unpublished) Economic impact tourism. Manila.

Richter, L.K. (1989) The Philippines: the politicization of tourism. *The Politics of
Tourism in Asia*. Honolulu: University of Hawaii Press, 51–81.

UNDP/WTO (1991a), *Tourism Master Plan, Republic of the Philippines, PH1/88/036 Final
Report*. Madrid: WTO, 43–5, 180–267.

UNDP/WTO (1991b) *Tourism Master Plan, Republic of the Philippines, PH1/88/036
Technical Papers*. Madrid: WTO.

13

Singapore: Development of gateway tourism

LINDA LOW
TOH MUN HENG

Introduction

The tourism industry has undergone a transformation that has, put simply, been from mass tourism to new tourism. This new tourism involves new consumers, changed lifestyles and workstyles, values, changed demographics and income patterns on the demand side; on the supply side are new technologies, new production practices and management techniques, more countries tapping tourism as a growth pole and a conscious, rational concern of sustainable tourism and the environment.

This chapter aims to review the role and prospects of Singapore's tourism industry under both a more competitive and a more challenging environment. As a city state with limited natural resources but highly globalized in business and services such as communication, telecommunication and information technology, Singapore has a unique role as a gateway. This is for all sorts of economic activities where its focal position, beyond the limits of its geographical location and concentration of such networks, constitutes a comparative advantage. Like Hong Kong, Singapore thrives on its cosmopolitan, intelligent city image, the only difference being that Singapore is the gateway to South-east Asia (Naisbitt 1994: 134), given its dominant Chinese base and multi-ethnic cultural potpourri, whilst Hong Kong is more for North-east Asia.

There will be a brief but necessary overview of the transformation from mass tourism to new tourism. This is followed by another background on the main characteristics and profile of the tourism industry in Singapore. These global and local trends are then put together to understand and analyse how urban tourism centres like Singapore can thrive in the coming decades. The summary draws together the conclusions and policy implications in the context of Singapore's regional and global roles.

Transformation from Mass Tourism to New Tourism

The transformation can be discussed in terms of the evolving concept of tourism, the new demand factors and supply factors. The concept of a tourist is changing. The World Tourism Organization's (WTO) definition is someone who moves away from home on a temporary or short-term basis for at least 24 hours, whether travelling in his or her own country (domestic tourism) or going to another country (international tourism). But this excludes day-trippers or excursionists. A broader concept uses the term 'visitor' to cover the overnight stayer and daytripper. In fact, the literature has a classification of travellers by scope, international/domestic, overnight stayer/daytripper, primary and secondary activities (see Metelka, 1981).

The types of visitors include leisure seekers for holidays crudely divided into: sunlust (conditioned by weather) and wanderlust (psychological, value and lifestyle) (Gray, 1970); pleasure seekers as in visits to friends and relatives; and other personal business as well as businessmen involved in buying and selling goods and services, management functions, conferences and exhibitions (Law, 1993: 9–11). A combination of these is increasingly observed.

The forces of mass tourism in contrast with new tourism from the demand side lie fundamentally in their definitions. Mass tourism is defined as a phenomenon of large-scale packaging of standardized leisure services at fixed prices for sale to a mass clientele as prevailed in the 1960s to 1980s (Poon, 1993: 32). New tourism is defined as a phenomenon of large-scale packaging of non-standardized leisure services at competitive prices to suit the demands of tourists as well as the economic, socio-environmental needs of destinations (Poon, 1993: 85). Leisure time is increasing and incomes are growing all over the world; value structures, workstyles and lifestyles are changing. There is also the product cycle effect on tourism.

A simple comparison of old versus young tourists, for instance, would show their differences in mentality and goal. The young visitors seek adventure, want to be in charge and have fun but are conscious of not destroying the environment. They are a hybrid of more daring but budget conscious consumers. In contrast, the old are more cautious, seek comfort and the sun, follow the mass, have already been and seen places. While more homogenous as a group, they have greater affordability in both time and funds. Generally, consumer affluence, expectations, lifestyle, demographics, family-based activities and the demonstration effect blend together with corporate-paid incentive and business-cum-pleasure holidays.

Responding to such demand changes, competitive tourism strategies stress putting consumers first, being a leader in quality, developing radical innovations and strengthening firms' strategic positions within the value chain. The concern to segment consumers along demographic (age, income, educational attainment, where they live) and psychological lines means a high touch (high quality and personal touch) delivery. For instance, German and Swiss visitors are like the Japanese preferring high quality, high price tourism, while British and American visitors generally opt for low price and low quality tourism. But a broad reflection is that Japanese visitors have switched from high quality, high price to high quality, medium price tourism.

On the supply side, the tourism system can be divided as follows (Gilbert, 1990;Poon, 1993):

- producers: airlines, holiday-makers, hoteliers, on-site providers;
- distributors: incoming agents, tour operators, travel agents;
- facilitators: financial service suppliers.

There is integration that can be vertical, horizontal and diagonal. The backbone for diagonal integration is lower costs of production made possible by economies of scope, gains and synergies from the systems as in travel plus insurance plus holiday plus personal banking. It is a phenomenon of the service industry, created by information technology. Travel and leisure become blurred as an industry and competition will come from outside the industry.

The industry value chain has primary activities in transportation, services on site, wholesale and packaging, marketing and sales, retail distribution and customer services and support activities in firm infrastructure, human resource development, product and service development, technology and systems development and procurement. It has nine players with airlines, holidaymakers, hotels, on-site providers, incoming agents, tour operators, financial service suppliers and travel agents as the producers of travel and tourism services and the ninth player is the consumer.

Technology as in jet aircraft, auxiliary land transport, computer reservations, accounting systems, telecommunication, information technology, credit cards is a key stimulant on both the demand and supply sides. Technology is partially responsible for the abundant supply and production of services with cheap oil, charter flights, packaged tours, hotel overbuilding and mass production. Rising competition has led to management in economies of scale, hotel chains and franchizing, hotel and holiday branding, promotional airfares, mass marketing. But overriding the demand and supply factors are the frame conditions in post-war peace and prosperity, population boom, deregulation of air travel and air transportation, tertiarization or growth of service industries including tourism and opening up of destinations as in economies in transition, like China and Africa, and geopolitical restructuring.

Condensing the above forces in a triangular diagram, one possibility of mass tourism is created as in Figure 13.1. Probably, more or less the same forces can explain new tourism though certain characterizations, like packaged tours, may have to change to more tailored packages.

Singapore Tourism Industry

Past Performance

A brief overview of tourist arrivals in Singapore is germane. With a balance of travel (overseas net of Singaporeans travelling abroad) in 1995 of S$4.4 billion or 3.6 per cent of Gross Domestic Products, the industry is an important source of growth. Tourism receipts for 1995 increased by 6.6 per cent to S$11.7 billion. As an open economy and society, Singaporeans are affected by all the supply and demand factors discussed earlier with respect to travel. Hence, more travel abroad is expected.

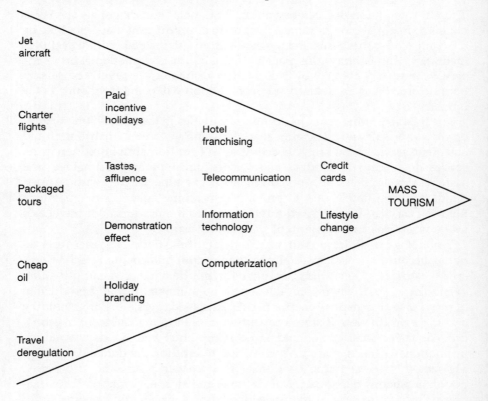

Figure 13.1 Mass tourism forces.
Source: Adapted from Poon (1993).

The tourist industry achieved a total number of 7,137.3 thousand visitors in 1995 (Table 13.1). Holiday visitors comprised the bulk (55.6 per cent) of total arrivals, followed by business travellers (14.1 per cent) and those in transit (10.0 per cent). But the growth in business visitors (8.7 per cent) was in contrast to the drop in holidaymakers (−1.5 per cent). Male visitors formed 61 per cent of total arrivals and about half of all visitors were between 25 and 44 years old in 1995.

The average age of all visitors was 37.9 years in 1993. About 40 per cent of them were here for the first time, 53 per cent on repeat visits and 30 per cent on package group tours. About 73 per cent arrived by air and 62 per cent are free independent travellers (FIT). The largest market was ASEAN accounting for a share of 30.2 per cent of total arrivals followed by Japan (15.6 per cent), Taiwan (6.6 per cent), Australia (5.7 per cent), UK (4.8 per cent) and the US (4.8 per cent) in 1993. Most of these markets achieved good growth except the UK, Japan and Australia. But visitors from China increased by 142.9 per cent to become the eighth largest market in 1993.

Since 1981, tourist arrivals have more than doubled but the largest category by purpose for holiday has fallen, though the share by business travellers has risen over the period. Six of Singapore's top ten markets have experienced large reductions, the most significant being the Indian market while the Japanese market has stagnated since 1993. Besides China, other emerging markets are South Korea, Taiwan and Hong Kong.

Business-cum-vacation travellers have dropped in number, with those in transit (those staying a day or less) remaining quite stable. More disturbing is, however, the steadily declining average length of stay to only 3.6 days in 1993, falling expenditure per capita and reduction in first-time visitors. Such trends may not be very healthy as they reflect how Singapore is losing its attraction as a holiday resort and combining business with pleasure does not appeal as much. The constant share by transit travellers means that Singapore remains a convenient stopover. Also, the observation of a jump in the share of the 'other' category attributable possibly to educational and training purposes, may mean another potential source of longer-term visitors for Singapore.

Table 13.1 Tourist arrivals by purpose (000s)

Year	Total	Holiday	Business	Business/ vacation	Transit	Others
1985	3030.9	1904.3	395.7	162.4	293.0	275.5
1990	5322.8	3312.4	691.5	214.3	481.2	623.4
1995	7137.3	3965.4	1010.8	212.4	714.6	1234.1
Percentage distribution (per cent)						
1985	100.0	62.8	13.1	5.4	9.7	9.1
1990	100.0	62.2	13.0	4.0	9.0	11.7
1995	100.0	55.6	14.1	3.0	10.0	17.3

Source: Singapore Department of Statistics (1995)

For many years, Singapore has consistently lost out to Hong Kong as the top destination for visitor arrivals on a global basis in the Asia Pacific region (13.8 per cent versus 16.1 per cent respectively in 1992). They also compete for the same top three markets: for Hong Kong these are Taiwan, Japan and ASEAN and for Singapore these are ASEAN, Japan and Taiwan. Singapore's top visitor-generating markets are exactly the same as Thailand's.

The group of visitors travelling for meetings, incentive, conventions and exhibitions (MICE) is a growing one that suits Singapore's comparative advantage relative to those travelling for holidays. Regional and international meetings have grown from 338 in 1980 to 2,904 in 1991 (or 19.6 per cent per annum) and MICE participants have increased from 115,858 to 303,312 (8.7 per cent per annum) over the same period (Table 13.2).

Incentive group meetings dominated (84.3 per cent) in 1991 (Table 13.2). Those on incentive travel registered the highest growth rate over the period (18.9 per cent). Participants from Asia comprised 82.7 per cent of the total incentive market with Japan contributing the bulk with a 67.3 per cent share. Those from the retail sector (12.7 per cent) formed the largest group. But by number of foreign participants, exhibition participants formed 59.5 per cent, they also stayed the longest days (7.9) and had the highest average expenditure per person (S$2,960). The number of foreign exhibitions have increased at an annual rate of 4.5 per cent while the number of foreign exhibition visitors has increased at 9.3 per cent. In 1991, 55 of the 67 exhibitions had less than 200 exhibitors while 46 per cent had less than 20,000 visitors per exhibition. China, US, ASEAN, UK and Germany contributed the most number of foreign exhibitors while ASEAN, Japan, India, Hong Kong and Australia provided the largest number of foreign exhibition visitors.

Medical and health conventions generated the most foreign participants (6,969) in the conventions category, followed by science and technology (6,123) and trade and industry (4,796). More than half of the conventions had less than 50 participants and Asia contributed 65.3 per cent of the convention

Table 13.2   Number of MICE events and participants

Year	Convention[a]	Exhibition[b]	Incentive	Total
Events				
1980	220	48	70	338
1985	429	58	744	1231
1990	500	64	2144	2708
1991	390	67	2447	2904
Participants				
1980	18734	86624	10500	115858
1985	21009	123390	33853	178252
1991	38176	180755	84381	303312

a. Convention participants include delegates and accompanying spouses.
b. Exhibition participants include foreign exhibitors and visitors.
Source: STPB (1993b)

participants. ASEAN, the USA, Australia, Japan, India and UK were the top participant-generating countries.

Table 13.3 shows that whereas Singapore was the top Asian city for conventions in 1991, it was in the seventh position globally but ahead of Hong Kong in the international arena.

Global Prospects

We consider two sources of forecasts of global tourism. First, in the global context, the Economist Intelligence Unit (EIU) (Edwards, 1992) has trends and projections that are more optimistic for the world as a whole after 1995 to 2000. All trips will grow by 5.1 per cent per annum and nights spent abroad will reach 4.7 nights. Long trips grow at a faster rate than short trips. Real tourist expenditure will grow by 5.6 per cent. Growth per annum in trips by country of origin improves strongly to 6.6 per cent from 1995 to 2000 compared with − 1.2 from 1989 to 1995. Trips originating from Europe and the Mediterranean improves, those from North America deteriorate. By tourist spending, Japan will be number one in 2005 and the USA drops to third place. Germany, the UK and France maintain their second, fourth and fifth positions respectively in 2005 and Belgium and Saudi Arabia improve their rankings. Europe will generate the bulk of trips, spending and nights abroad from 1995 to 2000. It is followed by North America except where Asia catches up in terms of spending probably due to Japan's dominance in the region.

Table 13.3 International and regional convention cities ranking 1991

Rank	International city	Meetings	Rank	Asian city	Meetings
1	Paris	349	1	Singapore	110
2	London	244	2	Hong Kong	102
3	Vienna	230	3	Tokyo	84
4	Brussels	184	4	Bangkok	51
5	Geneva	178	5	Beijing	46
6	Berlin	166	6	New Delhi	37
7	Singapore	110	7	Manila	33
8	Strasbourg	107	8	Jerusalem	32
9	Amsterdam	106	9	Kuala Lumpur	32
10	Hong Kong	102	10	Seoul	30
11	Madrid	100			
12	Copenhagen	89			
13	Washington	86			
14	Tokyo	84			
15	Budapest	82			
16	Barcelona	77			
17	Rome	66			
18	Prague	60			
19	Helsinki	60			
20	Oslo	53			

Source: Union of International Associations

The WTO predicts that worldwide arrivals will increase from 449 million in 1991 to 637 million in 2000. The share of arrivals for Asia Pacific will increase from 11 per cent to 18 per cent during the period and it will be the fastest growing region in generating and receiving arrivals. Visitor arrivals to ASEAN exceeded 30 million by 1995 with tourism receipts of more than US $25 billion.

Singapore's prospects

The Singapore Tourist Promotion Board (STPB) had its own targets under its Strategic Plan for Growth, 1993–95. The target of the STPB for 1995 was to have 6.8 million visitor arrivals. This has been achieved. In more specific terms, the six objectives under STPB, Strategic Plan for Growth, 1993–95 were:

1. Boost tourism receipts by 10 per cent per annum from $7.8 billion in 1991 to $11.4 billion by end of 1995.
2. Achieve an annual target of 25 million visitor-days and maintain the 1992 average length of stay of 3.7 days by end of 1995.
3. Improve Singapore's position to be the sixth top convention city.
4. Establish Singapore as a venue with worldclass events.
5. Establish Singapore as the major cruise hub in Asia Pacific.
6. Enhance the quality of the tourism experience.

Arrivals from the Asian markets will expand at a faster rate than those from America, Europe and Oceania. Apart from ASEAN, Taiwan, South Korea and Hong Kong, the emerging markets include China, South Africa, South America and the Middle East countries. These changing market shares will affect the types of services and accommodation given cultural and idiosyncratic features.

According to Visa Travel Barometer, October 1992, Singapore is cheaper than Tokyo, Taipei and Hong Kong. Its strategic location gives it a catchment of some 241 million potential visitors within a three-hour flight radius and 1.3 billion potential visitors if expanded to five hours (Table 13.4). Liberalization in transport regulation and improvement in aircraft technology will widen the tourist hinterland with higher transport efficiency.

In the light of such opportunities and challenges, the STPB has mapped out the following strategies:

● Increase market share in existing key markets.
● More strategic alliances with airlines in new routes, collaboration with other countries such as ASEAN and national travel organizations as well as with

Table 13.4 Catchment of population in terms of flying time

Flying times (hrs)	1	2	3	4	5	6	7
Population (million)	25	125	241	754	1277	2393	2800

Source: STPB (1993a)

industry members like the Singapore Hotel Association, National Association of Travel Agents of Singapore, Singapore Retailers Association, Registered Tourist Guides Association of Singapore.

- Capture niche market segments such as cruises, family travel and other special interest groups.
- Tap new markets, China, Eastern Europe, South Africa and Latin America.
- Intensify convention promotion.
- Develop worldclass events.
- New directions in product development as in four focal zones (Civic District, Singapore River, Orchard Spring and Southern Island) and 11 themes.
- Improving services in terms of workforce, STPB service to industry, rewarding performers, protecting visitors and educating Singaporeans.

Niche markets include catering to special events, study missions like eco-tourism, sports and leisure like the jetset golfers and tapping the youth travel market in educational and cross-country exposure trips. Greater sensitivity or attention can be paid to other special groups like those on honeymoon, those in Singapore for medical and dental treatment or the more elderly, 'silver' visitors.

For instance, the growing trend of visitors who travel alone or as students, warrants some attention and special packaging. In this respect, the availability of a safe, homely environment and accommodation would be better appreciated. It would be better if some local interactive sponsors, whether individuals, families or community groups and associations, can be encouraged to play a role as host or buddy to such single visitors.

The STPB has identified the cruise market as another potential niche. Table 13.5 shows the growing trend there. Cruise passengers will, however, not require hotel accommodation. But they could still use other services like food and entertainment.

A process of reinvention and revitalization has also begun since 1994 and a resulting strategy called 'Tourism Unlimited' aims to tap opportunities beyond the geographical boundaries of Singapore. The complementary appeal of neghbouring countries will be used to create a more sophisticated and attractive tourism product.

City State as Gateway

To examine Singapore as a gateway to tourism, in particular to South-east Asia (Naisbitt, 1994: 134), we examine the generic conditions that a gateway should have and Singapore's prospects as an urban tourist attraction.

Table 13.5 The cruise market

Year	1986	1987	1988	1989	1990	1991	1992
No. of passengers	34,540	59,730	64,153	59,078	62,585	131,491	190,000

Source: STPB (1993a)

Conditions as a gateway

There are no stated, formal conditions as a gateway to tourism, although it is logical to surmize at least two. One set of conditions would definitely concern what Singapore can offer in terms of its infrastructure, including communication and telecommunication facilities, accommodation, entertainment and recreation and others, such as its manpower support and conducive socio-political environment for foreign visitors. In these respects, the foregoing should be sufficiently convincing that Singapore has the basic prerequisites and is in fact continuously improving upon them in innovative ways.

A second set of conditions inevitably concerns how the neighbouring countries in South-east Asia are willing to accept Singapore as a gateway. The gateway concept is very much a spoke-and-hub idea where the hub or gateway radiates or fans out to a number of destinations that appeal to the visitors. Singapore essentially becomes a 'one-stop hub', organizing and facilitating the needs and preferences of the visitors. However, if the other destinations, like Kuala Lumpur for instance, also wishes to be the magnet to draw international visitors and organize packages around the region, there may be one hub too many. All ASEAN and South-east Asian economies obviously have the same target groups by source and interests and it is very competitive to attract visitors when the offerings are quite similar except for individual historical and cultural content. The point, however, is that Singapore as a gateway depends on the hubbing concept being acceptable by other economies.

Consider the possibility of dehubbing. This means Singapore is not necessarily the collecting point for visitors but another location like Kuala Lumpur may enjoy this advantage too. It may also be a consequence of the industry's market structure, which could turn oligopolistic and have a few major chains monopolizing the travel market. Or it could even be the new tourist who is highly individualistic and wanting to do things on his or her own. The airline industry may make more flights available to more cities in the region especially when air rights are traded so sensitively by governments and airlines. Any of these events could lead to dehubbing and Singapore losing its importance as a gateway no matter how efficient and competitive it may be.

Urban tourism

Next, we examine the broad issues of urban tourism. Urban tourism or city tourism is a special product line. Urban or metropolitan areas can be destinations in and of themselves, part of a tour or a stopover to break a long trip, for example. For some cities, urban tourism is part of the urban regeneration and redevelopment prime markets (Law, 1993). Business travellers, conference and exhibition delegates, short-break holidaymakers, day-trippers, visitors to friends and relatives, long holidaymakers on tour, all use the city as a gateway to the surrounding areas.

The following is a possible list of why people visit cities (Denver Convention and Visitors Bureau, 1991):

- unique and interesting (urban experience, lots to see, unique)
- popular
- entertainment (exciting nightlife, excellent shopping, live music, theatre and arts, festivals and events)
- cultural attractions and sightseeing (architecture, history, landmarks, local people, different cultures and ways of life, museums and galleries, local customs and traditions)
- scenery
- food and accommodation (sophisticated restaurants, unique dishes and cooking, first-class hotels and resorts)
- family and atmosphere
- sun and sand
- hospitability
- travel costs.

Singapore is deficient in natural resources and historical and cultural heritages and may be comparatively disadvantaged in attracting adventurous travellers interested in outdoor activities. Its strength is being attractive and accessible as a city state with a service-oriented and safe environment. Travellers' comfort in affordable accommodation, strategic location and hub at the crossroads of international air and sea transport, and communications for business visitors are Singapore's attributes to position itself in the growing Asia Pacific economies and business world.

Issues and prospects

The emerging trends discussed above offer both threats and opportunities. On the pessimistic side, changing economic conditions have led to a fall in share of tourist arrivals from America, Europe and Japan but a rise from Asia. But Asians are generally more budget conscious and they tend to travel in groups and package tours. This trend augurs well only for lower star hotels but would affect those in the upper market end adversely. From the ASEAN market, their restrictive travel policy in exit taxes, limits on shopping expenditure and import of certain goods and foreign exchange control are also impediments.

Even for the traditionally less price sensitive markets, until the USA and European economies rebound significantly or corporate travel improves, the performance of higher-end hotels in Singapore will remain poor. The recovery in tourist arrivals has not been broad-based and too much reliance on one region is not healthy.

While the strength of the Singapore dollar could be at its peak and may depreciate in the late 1990s, it has worsened the general price of accommodation, food and beverage and retail prices. With the tax on goods and services (GST) implemented in April 1994, an initial impact on inflation can be expected. Even if the tourists are specifically exempted in certain designated activities, like accommodation and expenses in tourist establishments and shopping, both the administrative and indirect profiteering tendencies would pose difficulties. Psychologically, tourists would associate the GST with higher costs no matter how careful the government is in offsetting the real impact.

The long-term worry is the attractiveness of other regional destinations and their affordability, made worse by a continuing war in airfares and the impending increase in supply of hotel rooms by 1995. Lower airfares can benefit as well as hurt Singapore. Lower fares from Europe for instance, would induce European arrivals but they could equally induce Asians to switch to other alternative, non-traditional destinations. Higher oil prices might raise air fares though airlines are engaged in price wars to stay competitive or maintain market shares.

Similarly, a possible switch from 'overseas travel' to 'internal or inbound travel' such as within Europe after the single European Community, would reduce European visitors to the region. Poorer economic recovery in Japan may mean more internal than overseas travel or an increasing attraction to China, which is a place of curiosity for both business and recreation. Also the labour shortage problem for a highly service-oriented industry is further exacerbated by Singapore's industrial restructuring into higher technology and value-added activities. There may be an unconscious preference for higher technology and skill-intensive careers for the younger Singaporeans.

In a survey and report by the STPB (1992), covering the hotel, restaurant, retail and travel agent sectors, the hotel sector was the larger employer of full-time and part-time workers on a per establishment basis. The majority of full-time workers in the tourism industry are Singaporeans (85.7 per cent) with the largest proportion (39.6 per cent) in the age group 20–29 followed by those in the age group 30–39 (29.8 per cent). The average age is 33 in the industry with 62.2 per cent with secondary education and even 12 per cent with post-secondary education. The industry has several organizations providing manpower training such as the Singapore Hotel Association Training and Educational Centre (SHATEC), Centre of Tourism Related Studies (CTRS), Institute for Retailing (IR) and Restaurant Association of Singapore Training Centre (RASTC), the Singapore Institute of Human Resource Management (SIHRM) and the Singapore Institute of Management (SIM). For generic skills, there is the government's National Productivity Board (NPB). Skilled workers are most in demand but there is a high turnover of chambermaids and in other menial jobs.

On the other hand, work attitude and dedication to service in the tourist industry are more crucial than mere academic qualifications and intelligence. This pride in service has to be more intensively cultivated in human resource development and management education and training as it is presently relatively shallow compared to the emphasis on high technology and productivity measured in tangible material terms. The flair and finesse for quality service need another way of looking at productivity in the service sectors such as tourism.

On the optimistic side, rising disposable income and per capita GDP in the region enable a higher propensity for travel among Asians. With development, there is more leisure time, higher expectations and a higher quality of life. The rapid expansion and transformation of travel pattern in countries like Korea and China may have some compensating effects though their spending power may be noted.

As Japan is the single largest market, the following trends as its outward-bound market matures in the 1990s are worth noting:

- Single women in their 20s will continue to be a major segment.
- More young adults will travel with their families.
- The silver market will gain greater importance.
- More will seek relaxing experiences as opposed to shopping.
- Cost consciousness in choice of destination will increase.
- Higher demand for quality of service and value for money.
- More sophisticated and adventurous travellers less inclined toward multi-country package tours.
- Shift toward FIT travel will continue tending towards minimally structured tours, allowing more freedom of independent movement.

As noted, business or MICE travel presents an exciting potential especially with Singapore at the heart of the Asia Pacific region with emerging economies such as ASEAN, Indo-China and China at its doorstep. Its regionalization efforts to sprout a 'second wing' or external economy, coupled with corporate globalization, means that Singapore has a good position for enhancing business travel. Though business travel is consolidating as companies rationalize on costs or relocate to other centres, the number of FIT and corporate travellers from outside the Asian region could increase. There are signs of improved conditions in Japan, Australia and America. Regional development of marinas, golf courses and beach resorts will help Singapore to take advantage of package tours from long-haul markets. This would require more intensive marketing and promotion strategies to encourage convention, exhibition and corporate travel.

With the high rate of growth and development in the construction sector, it is both a matter of business opportunities and promotional activities to synchronize supply and demand for hotel accommodation. Inbound tourism and alternative uses in times of slack or some flexibility in switching over from less profitable uses would help the matching process. Over and above the number of hotel rooms, the range in terms of price and quality, variety to suit different needs especially of niche markets and overall flexibility should be stressed. Thus, even large hoteliers or developers have plans to build budget and boutique hotels.

Together with the international business hub strategy, the new creative service sector that Singapore is promoting, which includes entertainment and recreation as well as thriving, existing service sectors in communication and telecommunication, can all provide the synergy. For instance, the Michael Jackson concert and the South-east Asian Sea Games in 1993 boosted the airline, tourism and telecommunication sectors jointly.

The supply of rooms in Singapore is growing, reflecting the industry's optimism and sustainability. But with tourist arrivals growing at 5 per cent to 6 per cent, the impending increase in supply of hotel rooms, especially at the upmarket end, in 1995 will mean acute competition. Room rates will be squeezed further to maintain occupancy levels though there will be no fierce price war like that in the period 1983 to 1985. As hotels aim for an average occupancy rate of 80 per cent, they have to resort to price reductions and special packages especially among the large and very large hotels.

Competition is keen, especially for the upper end of the market. The sensitivity of individual hotels to reductions in room rates varies with their standards and main markets. Lower-class hotels and those catering more for Asian markets could be more resilient. Diversity is another important factor and those that rely solely on hotel business will fare worst. As a destination, Singapore is losing appeal for holiday purposes and prices have generally increased, especially for shopping, which used to be a pull factor. The competition is from other cheaper and more attractive neighbouring destinations. The industry has underperformed on the whole, also due to an acute changing tourist profile and strong Singapore dollar.

Other destinations like Australia, Indonesia, Malaysia and Thailand will sap some demand away from Singapore, especially due to a strong Singapore dollar and lower airfares. These ASEAN countries are equally intense in promoting their tourist sectors. The falling percentage of visitors on vacation, though not significant, may be an early indication of future trends. Thus, the mix between travellers who cannot afford to travel or have tighter budgets and those who are being attracted elsewhere will keep the pressure on the hotel sector in 1993. While MICE is a market segment that Singapore enjoys at a comparative advantage as the top convention centre in Asia, it will have another 13,600 sq ft of convention space from Suntec City in 1995. This together with the supply of new hotel rooms poses a formidable challenge for the industry to fill them up.

In one survey on market segmentation, the responses of 194 respondents, (who were mainly American, British or Australian based in one hotel in Singapore catering primarily to individual travellers not connected with group travel) on 26 key attributes in selecting a hotel are worth noting (Mehta and Vera, 1990). The important choice attributes were in cleanliness, security, location, overall service (particularly check-in), housekeeping and food and room service. Ease of making reservations, furnishing and decor and room size were also important factors. These findings are clearly relevant for luxury hotels catering to frequent travellers.

In particular, it was also found that while corporate customers are most important for profitability, group travellers generate revenue because of their high occupancy though smallest revenue contribution per customer. Lower income travellers have higher expectations of hotel attributes compared to higher income travellers. All those who pay on their own expenses would have a higher demand for value for money. Business travellers may have a lower importance in rating to many of the hotel attributes compared to those on holiday, but they expect better telephone and business-centre services. Those who generally rate hotels favourably include: frequent travellers more than corporate travellers because they would enjoy special privileges and service; group inclusive travellers who generally pay less; and the British more than the Americans and Australians.

These findings have important marketing implications for hotels that generally have to pursue different market segments by offering different packages to suit various segments and target markets. Only the smallest and most focused hotels can afford to adopt a narrow niche and concentrate on a single market segment.

Conclusions and Policy Implications

Tourism has come a long way since initial doubts of whether it is a 'proper' industry, given the low pay, low skills, seasonal and dubious nature of activities (Williams and Shaw, 1988). It is possible to make profits when personal services are provided with a genuine aim to achieve standards and quality in comfort and convenience. Tourism underwent a 'golden age' until the 1973–74 oil crisis, the 1980–81 mild global recession and the more severe 1991 Gulf War incident. A crisis in mass tourism may be sensed with change and uncertainty, technology, more experienced consumers and overall global economic restructuring. Mass tourism has social, cultural, economic and environmental implications. Winning means having to lead and more competitive strategies have evolved in the tourism industry.

Some limits to growth are also imminent as the environmental-intensive pattern of tourism faces constraints. Mass methods of production and consumption are losing ground to the new tourism also labelled soft tourism, eco-tourism, sustainable tourism, responsible tourism or environmentally sound tourism. All these are not a fad but a real way of life. The greening of private sector efforts signals a new approach as tourism fatigue, environmental degradation, airport congestion and noise pollution, cultural intrusion, and negative socio-economic consequences encroach. Future prospects are clear about a slowing rate of growth, a shift in distribution of growth and a change in direction of growth.

While technology in telecommunication, transport and tourism have merged and converged, they are very information intensive requiring speed and efficiency integrating all players from travel agents, airlines and hotels. Information technology has changed the rules of the game, being noted as the fifth wave powered by microelectronics and Japan, in contrast to cotton and coal led by Britain in the first and second waves respectively, steel led by Germany in the third wave and oil led by the USA in the fourth wave (Freeman and Perez, 1988).

New tourism and best practice includes flexibility and specialization, niche markets and customization, human resource development, just-in-time stock inventory, zero defects and zero rejects, innovation, material and energy-saving, and information intensivity. The new product cycle for new tourism as old tourism expires is based on new technology, new consumers, new lifestyles and sustainable development.

For Singapore as a tourism gateway, this chapter has noted threats and opportunities. The success as a gateway is highly contingent on Singapore's attractions as a facilitator and organizer, and also an urban tourist centre that it can influence. But it also requires other countries to accept its role as a hub, which is beyond its control. This is a matter of economic cooperation and political goodwill, and also other destinations not seeing Singapore as an unnecessary middleman.

While the STPB and the government have tried to overcome the natural constraints of land and labour resources, Singapore is quite clear that there are some activities where its best policy is to facilitate visitors into more resource-abundant locations than to try to compete in only man-made facilities. With no mega projects like a Disney attraction as yet, its zoological and botanical gardens, bird park and other theme parks can appeal to family-based excursions to some extent. Worldclass mega tourist attractions need a steady demand and sufficient land and manpower resources to justify their location. Singapore's ultimate comparative advantage may well be as an international business and service centre. New potential may be emerging with its accumulated experience in education and human resource development just as at one time, its export of medical facilities drew in some tourist dollars.

The MICE subsector is another promising area that suits Singapore's globalization and regionalization strategies as noted for other business hubs (Go, 1991). The STPB and those in the industry would have to liaise more closely with the changing needs of such visitors. To begin with, more studies and analyses on economic and business conditions to understand the pattern of who goes where, when, how and why, are needed to throw more light on the requirements of MICE visitors. Innovative packaging and marketing to stretch the urge to travel as well as making it wholesome and dignified would be vital for a gateway like Singapore.

Increasingly, the tourism industry also needs to collaborate with public sector organizations because of the infrastructural and externality effects, including research and development, human resource development and marketing. It is for these reasons that revenue from a cess collected from tourism establishments is earmarked for the STPB. For a city state thriving on urban tourism, the cooperation between the private and public sectors is probably more important and urgent given competing land use and the public sector with a monopoly in land ownership.

This collaboration extends beyond Singapore's territorial area as noted. As a gateway, it must have the cooperation and support of nearby destinations. Technology may have the capability and capacity to connect and link in order to move and expedite visitors. But the political and social barriers may not be as porous and some political investment is as necessary as infrastructural investment. All ASEAN countries are competing for visitors, who are inevitably from Japan, the North-east Asian economies, the American and European continents and Australasia. Inbound or domestic visitors among ASEAN are also targets for competition. Unlike direct foreign investment in the manufacturing industries, there is no distinction between high technology or low technology attributes such that ASEAN economies may not be wooing the same type of investments. In tourism, there is no distinction, making the competition more intense.

However, the rivalry can be turned into a complementary and supplementary effort. The growth triangles that are thriving are in the making and ASEAN has a very strong tourism potential. In the spirit of ASEAN cooperation and solidarity, tourism can be made complementary rather than competitive. Whether Singapore can play its gateway role meaningfully is, however, strongly dependent on this vital cooperative spirit. While it enjoys the comparative advantage in infrastructural and organizational ability and efficiency, its ASEAN neighbours are improving in their uptake of management and best practices as well as in technology innovations. An issue of not falling behind in complacency is also another implication for Singaporeans in the tourism industry.

Finally, the Singapore society has to be educated to consider visitors in a positive light and not just as a source of employment and revenue. Dignified tourism goes both ways, for the tourist centre and the visitors. In its bid to become a global business and service centre that suits its comparative advantage more than manufacturing activities, Singapore must develop high value-added and innovative tourist services. A larger part of this lies in its people. Having a unique blend of Chinese, Malay and Indian connections as well as Western education, which makes most Singaporeans fluent in English and other European and Asian languages, this education process should not be difficult. That the government is willing to give tourism a big hand is another advantage.

Bibliography

Edwards, Anthony (1992) *International Tourism Forecasts to 2005*. Economist Intelligence Unit Special Report No. 2454, June.

Freeman, C. and Perez, C. (1988) 'Structural crisis of adjustment'. Business cycles and investment behaviour'. In Dosi, G. *et al.* (eds) *Technical Change and Economic Theory*. London: Pinter.

Go, F. (1991) The international conventions and meetings market. In Hawkins, D.E., Ritchie, J.R.B., Go, F. and Frechtling, D. (eds) *World Travel and Tourism Review*, Vol. 1. Wallingford: C.A.B. International.

Gray, H.P. (1970) *International Travel-International Trade*. Lexington: Heath Lexington.

Law, C.M. (1993) *Urban Tourism: Attracting Visitors to Large Cities*. London: Mansell Publishing.

Mehta, S.C. and Vera, A. (1990) Segmentation in Singapore. *The Cornell HRA Quarterly*, May, 80–87.

Metelka, Charles (ed.) (1981) *The Dictionary of Tourism*. New York: Morton House.

Naisbitt, J. (1994) *Global Paradox: The Bigger the World Economy, the More Powerful the Smallest Players*. New York: William Morrow & Co.

Poon, A. (1993) *Tourism, Technology and Competitive Strategies*. Wallingford: C.A.B. International.

Singapore Department of Statistics, *Yearbook of Statistics 1995*.

Singapore Tourism Promotion Board, *Survey of Overseas Visitors*, various years.

Singapore Tourism Promotion Board, Industry Services Division (1992a) *Survey of Tourism Manpower Deployment in Singapore, 1992*. Singapore: STPB.

Singapore Tourism Promotion Board (1992b) *Singapore Annual Report on Tourism Statistics, 1992. Singapore: STPB.

Singapore Tourism Promotion Board (1993a), *Strategic Plan for Growth, 1993–1995*. Singapore: STPB.

Singapore Tourism Promotion Board (1993b) *Statistics on the Meetings, Incentive, Convention and Exhibition Industry in Singapore, 1980–1991*. Singapore: STPB.

Williams, A.M. and Shaw, G. (1988) Tourism: candyfloss industry or job creator? *Town Planning Review* 59, 81–103.

14

South Korea: Interaction between inbound and outbound markets

JONG-YUN AHN
STAN MCGAHEY

Introduction

Tourism development in Asia has many fascinating stories to tell. Each country has had its own unique set of external influences and internal nuances, and each has had the development of its tourism industry affected by its own distinct national agenda and history. South Korea, officially named the Republic of Korea (ROK), is no exception; in fact, it is quite an intriguing example.

As we approach the end of this century, Korea has become one of the world's most dynamic international tourism markets. In 1993, Korea accounted for over 5.7 million international tourists. Some 3.3 million foreigners visited Korea, while a little over 2.4 million Koreans travelled abroad (KNTC, 1994). By the year 2000, the combined total is expected to rise to 12 million, almost evenly split between inbound and outbound (Kim, 1990; McGahey, 1994b). Yet a little over a generation ago, Korea was involved in a tragic civil war that left the peninsula divided and in ruins. Even more incredible, everything that Korea has accomplished in terms of international tourism has been achieved since the Korean War Armistice was signed in 1953. The Korean War did not interrupt a tourism industry, nor did World War II, because Korea had no tourism. For centuries, Korea was the 'Hermit Kingdom' until forced from its isolation by Western gunboat diplomacy in the latter part of the nineteenth century. Ineffectively governed by a crumbling dynasty that had ruled since the end of the fourteenth century, Korea eventually fell under the influence of Japan. It was forced to submit to Japanese authority in 1905 and was officially annexed in 1910. The Korean people endured harsh Japanese colonial rule until the end of the World War II (Han, 1970).

In broad terms, the Republic of Korea is known to most people worldwide for one of two things: the Korean War or its economic miracle, which was Korea's recovery from the war. In smaller bursts of attention, South Korea has been noted for its ongoing state of war with North Korea, which occasionally creates an incident worthy of international news coverage, and for its political coups and student riots. South Korea's one shining moment on the world stage was the successful hosting of the 1988 Seoul Olympics. As an export giant, the ROK has also become well known for its manufacturing of consumer goods, particularly appliances and automobiles. Also, in the past few years, many foreign destinations have coveted free-spending Korean tourists. To much of the world, however, Korea still remains an enigma, even to those who are aware that it has become an advanced nation with an affluent, well-educated, globetrotting population.

Korea's century-old saga is, hopefully, about to come full circle. The recent death of North Korean ruler, Kim Il-Sung, has prompted many observers to predict that reunification will begin by the end of the century. Nowhere in the world has a more tense and gripping drama been played out before an international audience of superpower stakeholders and concerned onlookers. Although this scenario goes back a full century, its economic and tourism elements have not surfaced as important factors until the past four decades. Since their introduction, they have each exerted an increasingly strong influence on the direction of events that have taken place on the Korean peninsula. They will undoubtedly play a major role in its ultimate resolution. For these reasons, the story of Korea's economic and tourism development must be told within this historical context.

Inbound and Outbound Tourism (1962–1993)

In 1962, the Korean government launched its First Five-Year Economic Development Plan. The availability of statistics on inbound tourism arrivals and receipts also dates from 1962. In 1962, the total number of tourist arrivals to Korea was 15,000 and the total expenditure only US$4.4 million. During the First Five-Year Economic Development Plan, tourism achieved a robust per annum growth rate of 46.5 per cent to finish with 68,000 arrivals in 1966. During the Second Five-Year Economic Development Plan, Korean inbound achieved an 18 per cent per annum growth rate to finish with 233,000 arrivals in 1971 (KNTC, 1983).

Outbound tourism statistics, on the other hand, are available from 1971, the last year of the Second Economic Development Plan. That year a total of 77,000 departures was recorded. But since arrivals had reached 233,000 a healthy ratio of 3 to 1 inbound over outbound was achieved. More importantly, inbound receipts reached US$52.4 million, greatly outnumbering outbound expenditures of US$14.8 million. This surplus of US$37.6 million contributed to the national balance of payments and assisted Korea in its mammoth task of post-war reconstruction.

Inbound tourism

The significant plateaux of Korean inbound tourism reveals that it first reached the 100,000 mark in 1968. The 500,000 mark was surpassed five years later (1973) when arrivals jumped from 371,000 to 679,000, a one year growth rate of 83.2 per cent. Another five years later (1978), inbound reached the 1 million mark. But the 1.5 million mark was not reached until eight years later (1986). Then the 2 million mark was reached in only two years (1988). The 2.5 million mark was reached in the following year, and the 3 million mark was reached in 1991. The target for Visit Korea Year 1994 was originally set at 4.5 million, but it was scaled back to 4.0 million due to the subsequent tensions involving the construction of North Korean nuclear facilities (Table 14.1).

Outbound tourism

An examination of outbound tourism per the same plateaux reveals that it first reached the 100,000 mark in 1973, five years after inbound. Outbound did not reach the 500,000 mark until 14 years later (1987), and also 14 years after that figure had been reached by inbound. Outbound reached the 1 million mark two years later (1989), the year it was liberalized, and 11 years after inbound. Korean outbound surpassed the 1.5 million mark the very next year (1990), only four years after inbound, and it reached the 2.5 million mark two years later (1992), again four years after inbound. While Korean inbound tourism hopes to reach the 4 million mark in 1994, outbound may leap-frog the 2.5 million mark and seriously challenge the 3 million mark in 1994, which would put it only three years behind inbound at that level (Table 14.2).

As noted, Korean tourism has always recorded more arrivals than departures. In 1988, which was the year of the Seoul Olympics and the year just prior to the complete liberalization of outbound tourism, the inbound surplus reached its zenith at 1.6 million. Although both Korean inbound and outbound tourism continue to grow each year, outbound has been rapidly narrowing the gap on a per head basis since Korea's liberalization in 1989. In 1993, the gap dropped to less than 1 million (KNTC, 1994). Unfortunately, however, for Korean tourism planners, inbound receipts have not always topped outbound expenditures. And, to the ROK government, the former is the figure that really counts.

Tourism balance of payments

The first time that a tourism deficit occurred in Korea was in 1979, when a shortfall of US$79 million was recorded. The second time was in 1982, with a deficit of US$130 million. After three years of only modest surpluses (1983–85), the succeeding three years (1986–88) produced substantial surpluses of US$935 million, US$1.594 million, and US$1.911 million respectively. This period began with the 1986 Asian Games and ended with the 1988 Seoul Olympics. Consequently, it featured the massive development of tourism infrastructure in Korea and the huge expansion of international air service in terms of new carriers, new destinations and increased frequencies, as well as the regional and worldwide media coverage of Korea in the run-up to and the actual staging of both of these sports mega-events.

With outbound tourism unleashed in 1989, the tourism surplus for the year was less than half of the previous year's record total. The surplus was more

Table 14.1   Korean tourism inbound and outbound pax totals 1962–93

Year	Inbound pax	Outbound pax	Total pax	Surplus inbound
1962	15148	–	–	–
1963	22061	–	–	–
1964	24953	–	–	–
1965	33464	–	–	–
1966	67965	–	–	–
1967	84216	–	–	–
1968	102748	–	–	–
1969	126686	–	–	–
1970	173335	–	–	–
1971	232795	76701	309496	156094
1972	370656	84245	450901	286411
1973	679221	101295	780516	577926
1974	517590	121573	639163	396017
1975	632846	129378	762224	503468
1976	834239	164727	998966	669512
1977	949666	209698	1159364	739968
1978	1079396	259578	1338974	819818
1979	1126100	295546	1421646	830554
1980	976415	338840	1315255	637575
1981	1093214	436025	1529239	657575
1982	1145044	499707	1644751	645337
1983	1194551	493461	1688012	701090
1984	1297318	493108	1790426	804210
1985	1426045	484155	1910200	941890
1986	1659972	454974	2114946	1204998
1987	1874501	510538	2385039	1363963
1988	2340462	725176	3065638	1615286
1989	2728054	1213112	3941166	1514942
1990	2958839	1560923	4519762	1397916
1991	3196340	1856018	5052358	1340332
1992	3231081	2043299	5274380	1187782
1993	3330226	2419930	5751156	911296

Source: Korea National Tourism Corporation (Adapted from *Annual Statistical Reports* 1983 and 1993)

than halved again in 1990. This is in despite of the strong halo effect of the Seoul Olympics on inbound tourism (Hyun, 1990b). The cause was simple: the per capita receipts of foreign inbound tourists were much less than the per capita expenditures of Korea's free-spending and inexperienced outbound tourists.

Mounting tourism deficits of US$358 million, US$523 million, and US$595 million were recorded in the following three years (1991–93) (Table 14.3). Initially, as the trend became obvious, the ROK government tried a number of subtle and not so subtle direct and indirect means of stemming the flow of hard currency from its national treasury (Yarmy and McGahey, 1993). These tactics succeeded in slowing the tourism deficit, but they also damaged the reputation of the Korean tourism industry within the international tourism community.

Table 14.2 Korean tourism inbound and outbound pax growth rates 1962–93

Year	Inbound pax	Growth rate	Outbound pax	Growth rate	Total pax	Growth rate
1962	15184	–	–	–	–	–
1963	22061	45.3%	–	–	–	–
1964	24953	13.1%	–	–	–	–
1965	33464	34.1%	–	–	–	–
1966	67965	103.1%	–	–	–	–
1967	84216	23.9%	–	–	–	–
1968	102748	22.0%	–	–	–	–
1969	126686	23.3%	–	–	–	–
1970	173335	36.8%	–	–	–	–
1971	232795	34.3%l	76701	–	–	–
1972	370656	59.2%	84245	9.8%	450901	45.7%
1973	679221	83.2%	101295	20.3%	780516	73.1%
1974	571590	– 23.8%	121573	20.0%	639163	– 18.1%
1975	632846	22.3%	129378	6.4%	762224	19.3%
1976	834239	31.8%	164727	27.3%	998966	31.0%
1977	949666	13.8%	209698	27.3%	1159364	16.1%
1978	1079396	13.7%	259578	23.8%	1338974	15.4%
1979	1126100	4.3%	295546	13.9%	1421646	6.2%
1980	976415	– 13.3%	338840	14.7%	1315255	– 7.5%
1981	1093214	12.0%	436025	28.7%	1529239	21.4%
1982	1145044	4.7%	499707	14.6%	1644751	11.6%
1983	1194551	4.3%	493461	– 1.2%	1688012	2.6%
1984	1297318	8.6%	493108	– .1%	1790426	6.1%
1985	1426045	9.9%	484155	– 1.8%	1910200	6.7%
1986	1659972	16.4%	454974	– 6.0%	2114946	10.7%
1987	1874501	12.9%	510538	12.2%	2385039	12.8%
1988	2340462	24.9%	725176	42.0%	3065638	28.5%
1989	2728054	16.6%	1213112	67.3%	3941166	28.6%
1990	2958839	8.5%	1560923	28.7%	4519762	14.7%
1991	3196340	8.0%	1856018	18.9%	5052358	11.8%
1992	3231081	1.1%	2043299	10.1%	5274380	4.4%
1993	3331226	3.1%	2419930	18.4%	5751156	9.0%

Source: Korea National Tourism Corporation (Adapted from *Annual Statistical Reports* for 1983 and 1993)

Factors that have Influenced Korean Inbound Tourism

Tourism is a delicate industry. The success of inbound tourism depends on many inter-connected elements. Among the most important ones are proper infrastructure, interesting attractions, a receptive host community, a positive destination image and supportive government policies. The absence or weakness of any of these elements seriously impedes the development of a country's inbound tourism sector.

For a decade following the Korean War, inbound tourism was impossible. The Republic of Korea was busy rebuilding its most basic infrastructure and public services. Statistics show that in 1962 only 15,000 foreigners visited Korea. Not only was the country still in bad shape but its international image was one of a military-ruled, war-torn nation sharing a divided peninsula with a hostile adversary that might invade again at any time – not at all appealing to mainstream tourists.

Table 14.3   Korean tourism receipts and expenditures 1962–93 (US$1,000)

Year	Receipts	Growth rate	Expenditures	Growth rate	Balance
1962	4362	242.3%	–	–	–
1963	5212	12.5%	–	–	–
1964	15704	201.3%	–	–	–
1965	20798	32.4%	–	–	–
1966	32494	56.2%	–	–	–
1967	33817	4.1%	–	–	–
1968	35454	4.8%	–	–	–
1969	32809	-7.5%	–	–	–
1970	46772	42.6%	–	–	–
1971	52383	12.0%	14808	19.2%	37575
1972	83011	58.5%	12570	−15.1%	70441
1973	269434	224.6%	16894	35.1%	252450
1974	158571	−41.1%	27618	62.6%	130953
1975	140627	−11.1%	30790	11.2%	109918
1976	275011	95.6%	46234	50.6%	228777
1977	370030	34.6%	102714	122.2%	267316
1978	408106	10.3%	208019	102.5%	200087
1979	326006	−20.1%	405284	94.8%	−79278
1980	369265	13.3%	349557	−13.8%	19708
1981	447640	21.2%	439029	25.6%	8611
1982	502318	12.2%	632177	44.0%	−129859
1983	569245	18.7%	555401	−12.1%	40844
1984	673355	12.9%	576250	3.8%	97105
1985	784312	16.5%	605973	5.2%	178339
1986	1547502	97.3%	612969	1.2%	934533
1987	2299156	48.6%	704201	14.9%	1594955
1988	3265232	42.0%	1353891	92.3%	1911341
1989	3556279	8.9%	2601532	92.2%	945747
1990	3558666	0.1%	3165623	21.7%	393043
1991	3426416	−3.7%	3784304	19.5%	−357888
1992	3271524	−4.5%	3794490	.3%	−522885
1993	3510240	7.3%	4104807	8.2%	−594567

Source: Korea National Tourism Corporation (adapted from *Annual Statistical Reports* for 1983 and 1993)

The creation in 1962 of a national tourism organization, which later came to be known as the Korea National Tourism Corporation, was a major step in launching Korea's inbound tourism industry. One of KNTC's early contributions to inbound tourism was the development and management of key services companies. In the 1960s and early 1970s, KNTC operated numerous profit-making subsidiaries, including up to a dozen tourist hotels, and also a travel agency, a shopping mall, and even a taxi service for foreigners (KNTC, 1992). By the mid-1970s, when these companies were firmly established, they were sold to the private sector.

In the 1970s, KNTC began to shift its emphasis to marketing. It actively promoted Korea abroad by setting up overseas branch and public relations offices. In order to improve Korea's tourism product, KNTC took the lead in the development of resorts that capitalized on the country's rich natural and cultural resources. These developments were also designed to disperse tourists from Seoul, the country's main international gateway, and spread the benefits of economic development through tourism to other parts of Korea. Among KNTC's major projects were Pomun Lake in Kyongju and Cheju Island. Tourism's labour-intensive nature, particularly in regards to entry-level positions, created numerous employment opportunities and introduced many Koreans to the newly emerging services sector. KNTC was also assigned the task of providing tourism industry training, and licensing personnel and companies in order to achieve an acceptable international standard of service (KNTC, 1983).

The development of tourist-class hotels was initially a necessity for attracting and accommodating foreign business travellers. These business travellers were more than just ordinary visitors. They were the people capable of providing the funds and expertise that made Korea's economic miracle possible. A strong national flag-carrier able to provide air service for business travellers and transport export cargo to distant markets was another component vital to Korea's overall economic growth. Inbound tourism growth was necessary to extend routes and attract additional airlines that would connect Korea to additional overseas markets. The requisite government support was provided to both the hotel and airline industries. KNTC operated hotels, and Korean Air began as a national airline. It was privatized under the Hanjin Group in 1969 and now ranks as one of the world's most powerful and profitable airlines.

During the 1960s, the main source of arrivals, with a 40 per cent market share, was the United States; overseas Koreans ranked second. Thus, the main purposes for visiting Korea were for business and visiting friends and relatives (KNTC, 1984b). A major shift in the dominant inbound market took place in the 1970s, however. Japan, which had officially colonized Korea from 1910–45, began the restoration of its relations with Korea in the mid-1960s. By 1971, Japan had taken over as the number one source of inbound tourists, with 41.5 per cent, and by 1963 that figure had reached 69.9 per cent (KNTC,

1984a). Korea was close and convenient for Japanese tourists, and they were familiar enough with the country and the people to accept or ignore conditions, including media reports, that kept other tourists from visiting.

In 1993, Japan was responsible for 44.8 per cent of all international tourist arrivals (KNTC, 1994). This figure was bolstered by the granting of a visa-waiver, ostensibly to facilitate Japanese tourists interested in visiting the Taejon International Exposition, which took place from 7 August to 7 November. In reality it rescued a dismal inbound year and allowed a modest inbound increase of 3.3 per cent to be recorded (KNTC, 1994). Korean authorities eventually decided to extend the visa-waiver for the entire next year to encourage Japanese arrivals during Visit Korea Year 1994.

Taiwan (ROC) and China (PRC)

Like the Korean government, the Government of Taiwan, formally known as the Republic of China (ROC), also placed outbound travel restrictions on its citizens during a period of economic recovery and concern for national security. The restrictions were lifted in 1978, and Korea, its close neighbour to the north, was one of the main beneficiaries. By mid-1992, Taiwan ranked equal with the United States as Korea's second most important inbound and outbound markets (KNTC, 1993). In August of 1992, however, the Republic of Korea and the People's Republic of China (PRC) abruptly announced that they had established diplomatic relations. Taiwan immediately severed its diplomatic ties with Korea, as well as with the air service of its national flag carriers. Korea responded by doing the same. Thus, the bottom fell out of this thriving two-way tourism market (McGahey, 1992a). Alternate means have kept those markets alive but with much less vigour. By the end of 1994, the previous systems should be re-instituted, but it will take some time before the markets regain their former strength (McGahey, 1994). Korea's reasons for re-establishing relations with the PRC, at the expense of its existing relations with the ROC, revert to its concerns over economic growth and national security. China not only holds great promise as the world's largest consumer market and a country that needs access to Korea's technological expertise, investment capital and international distribution systems, but it also maintains tremendous influence over the political and military aspirations of North Korea.

As a result of their renewed diplomatic ties, Mainland Chinese travellers have been visiting Korea in large numbers, mainly by utilizing the inexpensive ferry transportation across the Yellow Sea from several ports into Inchon. From there, many of them link up with long-lost relatives or with employers and stay several months (often beyond the allotted three) in order to accumulate a small fortune by their own standards. Many of the women also find a husband, particularly among the farmers who have difficulty convincing the well-educated and upwardly mobile native-born Korean women of the virtues of rural life. Meanwhile Korean outbound to the PRC grew to 200,000 in 1993, and permission for Korean citizens to visit China for the purpose of pleasure was not even granted until April 1994 and an aviation agreement between the two countries that established regular air service was not even signed until late July. Korean sightseers poured into China during the remainder of 1994, making it the second most visited destination in Asia for Korean outbound during that period (McGahey, 1994a).

The Seoul Olympics

The single most important factor in Korean inbound tourism over the past 15 years has been the 1988 Seoul Olympics. From the moment the International Olympic Committee announced that Seoul would host the XXIV Olympiad in Baden-Baden, Germany, on 30 September 1981, until the Closing Ceremonies in Seoul on 2 October, 1988, the entire population of the Republic of Korea devoted itself to preparation (Ricquart, 1988). The opportunity to host the Olympics was not only perceived by the Korean people as a big honour, but also as a golden chance to showcase their famous 'economic miracle' and 'can do spirit' to the whole world. The Korean government was also determined to make the Olympics Korea's coming out party, its entry onto the world stage as a developing nation. The Olympics was Korea's opportunity to shed its Third World image and impress an international audience of billions with its unique culture and heritage, natural beauty, world-class sporting facilities and modern tourism infrastructure.

Prior to the Olympics, a number of foreign airlines established new routes to Seoul, and a number of international chain hotels constructed properties in Seoul. The Olympics was a huge catalyst for inbound tourism development that would be a permanent legacy to its glory (Ahn *et al.*, 1987). The sporting and cultural events that made up the Seoul Olympics were perfectly orchestrated, and Korea proved its point to the world. In addition to the substantial physical legacy of the Seoul Olympics, the image enhancement achieved by the performance of Seoul as the host city and Korea as the host country were of inestimable value.

The halo effect of the Seoul Olympics produced significant inbound benefits for Korean tourism for the next few years. Today, the main Olympic venues – the Seoul Sports Complex and the Olympic Park – are still popular tourist attractions. And the part of Seoul where they are located is a boom area of considerable affluence.

The hosting of the 1988 Summer Olympics is just one of the sporting mega-events that have been held or will be held in Korea. Actually, the 1986 Asian Games, which served as a dress rehearsal for the Olympics, was a huge success in both sporting and tourism terms. It introduced Seoul as a beautiful modern city to a large portion of the Asian community just at the time when intra-Asian travel was beginning to blossom. The accompanying launching of new air routes to Seoul from other Asian cities at about the same time resulted in a sharp increase in tourism packages to Korea and publicity on Korea as a desirable tourist destination.

Korea is set to host the 1997 Winter University Games in Muju Valley Ski Resort south of Taejon, a city which in 1993 was the site of a BIE (Bureau of International Expositions) sanctioned event. The Taejon Expo featured pavilions sponsored by more than 100 countries (a BIE record) and attracted more than 14 million visitors, including 670,000 foreigners in only 93 days (KNTC, 1994). Korea will also be hosting the 1998 East Asia Games in Pusan and the 1999 Asian Winter Games in Yongpyong (Dragon Valley) Resort. In addition, Korea also hopes to host the 2001 Summer University Games, the 2002 Asian Games in Pusan, the 2002 World Cup, and one of the upcoming Winter Olympics.

Negative developments

On the negative side, Korea's sudden rise to affluence has caused the cost of labour and commodities to increase dramatically. Seoul is now considered one of Asia's most expensive cities. Until recently Korea was known as a shoppers' paradise, but higher operating costs and a crack down on counterfeit goods has substantially diminished this attraction. In short, Korea is no longer considered a bargain destination. As a result, Korea must reposition itself in overseas markets, offer more value for the money, and diversify its tourism products to include lower-budget tourists.

Korean tourism authorities must also improve tourism infrastructure, facilities, and information systems in the provincial areas where more affordable tourism experiences can be found. These improvements would also encourage visitors to extend their stay and return to see more. This is especially important for the lucrative Japanese and Taiwanese markets that have potential for repeat visitation. A major concern, even in rural areas, is traffic congestion that can hinder tourists' mobility. This becomes more acute each year as domestic tourism increases.

Factors that have Influenced Korean Outbound Tourism

The history of Korean outbound tourism is much shorter and more concise than inbound. However, the same two prominent factors that influenced inbound have also influenced outbound: the national balance of payments and national security. This has produced the classic interaction between inbound and outbound markets that has influenced the development of Korea's tourism industry as a whole, including how both the government and the public view tourism as a social phenomenon and as an industry.

While inbound statistics were not disclosed prior to 1962, outbound statistics were not disclosed until 1971. Prior to 1983, there were virtually no Korean outbound tourists, at least not in the classic sense of travelling abroad purely for pleasure. Foreign exchange was too valuable to waste on any activity that did not directly contribute to national growth (Hyun, 1990a). The government was also concerned that Korean citizens travelling abroad might be kidnapped, compromised, or otherwise made an agent of North Korea. And, in fact, this has happened quite a number of times.

In the three decades between the end of the Korean War in 1953 and the beginning of limited outbound tourism in 1983, overseas travel was confined to business, study, and other official purposes (KNTC, 1985). One permissible category was overseas labour, and Korea supplied thousands of construction workers, particularly for huge projects in the Middle East. This helped ensure high levels of employment at home as well as generate foreign exchange from both the workers and the Korean construction companies involved. But this facet of Korean outbound had little to do with tourism other than expanding air and cargo service.

Liberalization of outbound

On 1 January 1983, the Korean government allowed citizens 50 years and older to obtain a single-use passport for the purpose of pleasure travel. These were truly the first outbound tourists in Korea's 5,000 years of history. Other restrictions also applied such as only one overseas trip could be taken each year and 2 million Korean won (several thousand US dollars) had to be on deposit in a Korean bank. In a series of steps over the next five years, the age limit was lowered and the other restrictions were eased. This period also corresponded with hefty increases in the tourism balance and the overall national balance of payments, as well as huge differences in the number of foreigners visiting Korea and the number of Koreans travelling abroad. The catalyst for these situations was the 1988 Seoul Olympics (McGahey, 1992b).

Affects of Seoul Olympics

The Seoul Olympics heightened the public's demands for unrestricted overseas travel in several other ways. First, preparations for the Olympics, which began in 1979 when Seoul was selected as the site of the 1988 Summer Olympics, required an immense commitment on behalf of the Korean government. That in turn required an immense sacrifice on behalf of the Korean people. At that point in Korean history, the Korean people were ready and willing to make any sacrifice necessary to better their lives and further national goals. For the next nine years, the Korean people persevered to ready their capital and their nation to host the world's biggest sporting and cultural event. On a personal basis, however, it was a crucial test of national pride and international credibility.

With 161 nations participating, the Seoul Olympics was widely heralded as the most successful Olympics ever to be staged. The Korean government and the Korean people were ecstatic. Korea had been elevated in the eyes of the world, and the Korean people wanted their just rewards as citizens of an advanced country. One of those rewards was the fundamental right to travel abroad. During the presidential campaign in 1987, candidate and eventual President, Roh Tae-Woo had defused a campaign crisis by promising that if elected he would speed up democratic reforms and personal freedoms. Among them was the right to travel abroad. This message had also been reinforced by the Olympic slogan: 'Seoul to the World and the World to Seoul'. To the Korean people, this meant that they would host the world for the Olympics regardless of the sacrifice, but once they accomplished that monumental task, it would be 'pay back time'. Then they would also be free to see the world (McGahey, 1990b).

There was also a considerable amount of pressure exerted on the Korean government by the international airlines that had inaugurated service to Seoul as part of the Olympic build-up and consequent increase in inbound tourism. The airlines insisted on the capability of hauling outbound Koreans, as well as inbound foreigners. The viability of their Korean routes depended on positive load factors both coming and going. International tourism organizations also put pressure on the Korean tourism industry to contribute to a two-way tourism, rather than just asking for inbound from other countries (McGahey, 1990a). Korea had an abundance of affluent citizens eager to travel abroad, but the government forbade them from doing so. At the same time, the Korean government was active in enticing foreign tourists to Korea. Once Korea elevated its international status via the Seoul Olympics, it also had to discard its excuses used to deny outbound tourism. This had been a foregone conclusion. By the summer of 1988, the age restrictions on outbound tourism had been reduced to 30. The Seoul Olympics ended on 2 October, and on 1 January 1989, only three months later, outbound tourism was fully liberalized. The exodus began immediately. In 1989, outbound increased by 67.3 per cent overall, and outbound for pleasure increased by 235 per cent (KNTC, 1990).

Tourism industry changes

With the continuous increase in outbound tourism, additional airlines have inaugurated flights to Korea, and Korean Air now flies to all six continents. The second national carrier, Asiana Airlines, competes with KAL on domestic flights, as well as serving overseas destinations in Japan, China, South-east Asia, Saipan, and the United States. Hundreds of new travel agencies catering to outbound tourists have also opened. Unfortunately, many of them were under-capitalized, inexperienced, get-rich-quick types that offered inferior products at loss-leader rates in order to carve out sufficient market share. This mode of operation has negatively impacted the public's perception of the professionalism of the Korean tourism industry. The industry itself has taken several self-correcting actions to alleviate the problems and restore public confidence.

The removal of age restrictions on Korean tourists as a major aspect of outbound liberalization has created several new segments. Among them are student backpackers, single office ladies and family travel. These segments are particularly conducive to the Korean preference for travelling together in small groups of their own making, as opposed to being thrown in with a larger group of strangers as individuals or couples (Chung, 1990; Yarmy and McGahey, 1993).

The pent-up desire of affluent and well-educated Koreans to see the world was also accompanied by their desire to purchase foreign products, and Korean tourists quickly gained a reputation for being notorious shoppers. These actions were partially motivated by a desire to obtain famous brand-name products not available in Korea due to the tight import policies. Again, this contradicted the philosophy of its own export-oriented manufacturing sector and mirrored its previous tourism policy that had restricted outbound. The government wanted to sell its products all over the world but was unwilling to allow most foreign products to be sold in Korea.

Frugality campaign

Affluent Koreans were also the target of an anti-conspicuous consumption campaign at home. Although they were obviously contributing to economic activity in a free enterprise system, they were chastised for disobeying the Korean traditional virtues of frugality and austerity. Many foreign governments saw these actions as hostility to the introduction of foreign goods that would compete with local brands. Less than a year after outbound tourism was liberalized, there were already campaigns calling for the reimposition of restrictions in order to cut spending and reduce the outflow of foreign exchange. This was the beginning of the infamous 'frugality campaign' that overtly plagued Korean outbound tourism for the next few years (Breen, 1990; Deans, 1990; Lee, 1990; McGahey, 1990a).

Initially, the Korean government said that the frugality campaign was the result of local citizen groups' sincere reactions to the conspicuous consumption both at home and abroad. That contention was soon unmasked, and it became evident that the ROK government had orchestrated the campaign to serve its own means. During the height of the frugality campaign, Korean travel agencies were warned not to develop, promote or operate tours that featured 'luxury activities' or tours to 'luxury destinations'. All tour programmes should consist of basic sightseeing that would be wholesome and educational in nature and to destinations that were reasonably priced (Kim, 1991; Helmer, 1992).

The most often cited examples of a luxury activity was golfing, but fishing, hunting and shopping were also taboo (McGahey, 1991). A large percentage of Korean businessmen and a growing number of Korean housewives enjoy golfing for its exercise, social aspects and stress reduction. Golfing in Korea is extremely expensive and time consuming. Golfing overseas is normally much cheaper, and there is a certain amount of prestige attached to playing a round of golf on a well-known foreign course. So, even though it was much less expensive to golf abroad than at home, it was considered a luxury to do so. The best example of a luxury destination was the US state of Alaska. The ROK government deemed it luxurious to visit Alaska because Korean tourists were hunting, fishing and skiing. In other words, they were enjoying Alaska's famous outdoor recreation activities. To them, having fun was not a proper way to spend an overseas vacation or a proper reason to spend hard currency. Korean tourists were supposed to go sightseeing, learn about foreign cultures, and recuperate so they could be more productive once they returned home to work.

This response revealed the government's ignorance in two ways. One was people learn and relax in a variety of ways, not just in the old-fashioned Korean ways of visiting museums and shrines, hiking in the mountains, going to the beach, or bathing at a hot springs resort. The other was that the real cost of a trip to Alaska was less than a trip to Japan of comparable duration and style. This point was finally driven home when the Tourism Bureau Director of the Ministry of Transportation accepted an invitation to visit Alaska to see for himself. Upon his return, the harassment of those involved in outbound tourism to Alaska ceased.

Globalization

When President Kim Young-Sam succeeded President Roh Tae-Woo in office in February 1993, the frugality campaign began losing steam. By then, it was clear that it would be impossible to suppress the desire of the Korean people to travel abroad, and the advice of the tourism industry that the ROK government should refocus its energies on stimulating inbound rather than trying to suppress outbound started to take hold (McGahey, 1993). In addition, Korean economic planners finally recognized that to continue the nation's strong export economy it needed to adapt to international rules. The old days of playing by Korean rules and receiving special privileges afforded to a Third World country had ended. Now Korea had to compete on a level playing field. To survive, President Kim began the 'globalization' or 'internationalization' campaign. His basic strategy was that business and government leaders must learn how to think and act in a global manner. They needed to gain a mastery of the language of international commerce –

English – and to develop an international mentality. Being confined to the southern half of the Korean peninsula was not conducive to accomplishing any of the above. Thus, Koreans were given permission to remove their Confucian manner and embrace the twenty-first-century style of business. Now travelling abroad, while still not in a spendthrift manner, to learn the ways of the world is viewed as beneficial rather than detrimental.

Korean overseas travel was originally permitted to foster international commerce. Outbound tourism followed as a consequence of those activities. At present, Korea uses outbound tourism to foster international commerce and views it as an ally and component of international commerce. This may be putting a positive spin on what is deemed a necessary evil, but it also represents the practical side of Korean thinking that has been moulded by modern circumstances.

Theoretical Implications

Regardless of their form of government, nations around the world offer a variety of models for tourism policy development. The interest and influence of the public and private sectors vary as do the interest and influence of the different levels of government – national, provincial and city (Edgell, 1987). Most nations embrace tourism for its economic benefit. Hence tourism policy is developed in the manner in which the individual nation administers its overall economic policy. This includes whether the emphasis is placed on public or private sector leadership or whether or not the government is centralized or decentralized and which level of government has the primary responsibility for tourism concerns (Richter, 1993).

When Korean tourism policy was first discussed in 1954, Korea had a strong, authoritarian, military-backed central government. This structure changed little until the late 1980s when the Korean people began demanding more democracy and individual freedom. The inauguration of a civilian president in 1993 has continued this trend, and plans are under way for the decentralization of many government functions and for local elections in 1995.

Korea's strong central government has traditionally passed laws that have regulated tourism policy down to the local level where they have been administered by appointed officials. In doing so, Korean government officials have been able to tightly direct and control tourism's role within its overall economic and political policy. In the early years of Korean tourism development, the ROK government also developed and controlled the tourism resources and facilities for financial reasons through its main tourism agency, the Korea National Tourism Corporation. This role has been gradually taken over by the private sector, although the central government does continue to finance and develop a number of large national projects.

Conclusion

Tourism is a fragmented industry that has been both nurtured and controlled by Korea's strong central government. Thus, tourism has played a prominent, yet widely unrecognized, role in the economic miracle that has enabled Korea to rise from a devastating and divisive civil war and become a respected member of the world community.

Inbound tourism was utilized to earn foreign exchange and to develop the transportation and accommodation networks required for conducting international business. The domestic tourism industry was utilized as a means to further disseminate inbound tourism and to satisfy the travel needs of Korean citizens in order to minimize outbound tourism. Outbound tourism was kept in abeyance and used as an incentive until Korea's major nation-building goals had been achieved. Then it was permitted as an opportunity to see the world and grow into the next century.

The interaction between Korean inbound and outbound tourism has been a metaphor for economic development versus personal sacrifice, for national security versus individual freedom, and for national interests versus international considerations. As more inbound foreign tourists visited Korea and the tourism surplus increased, the call for outbound liberalization grew. As more flights and more airlines brought foreigners to Korea, the louder the call grew to be able to carry Korean tourists abroad. As inbound tourism contributed to the national wealth, the more people wanted to travel abroad and the more foreign destinations wanted them. As Korea's tourism surplus grew in the mid-1980s, the Korean government was forced to view international tourism as a give-and-take proposition. The maturation of inbound tourism dictated the liberalization of outbound, and the Korean government was forced to accept the reality of two-way tourism. Although the interaction between Korean inbound and outbound had previously maintained a strong impact on Korean tourism policy, the time has come when they will now only indirectly impact it in response to international issues.

In its own unique way, the ROK government strategy has succeeded in building a strong nation that attracts considerable numbers of inbound tourists, while at the same time creating an affluent, well-educated population that has the desire and the resources to travel abroad. The Korean government began by supporting the inbound sector, then built up the domestic sector as affluence developed, and finally, and grudgingly, allowed the outbound sector to develop. Tourism development in Korea has been a tool of the state. In the past, inbound and outbound were manipulated to achieve state goals. In the future, its controls will be shared with lower levels of government and the private sector, and a greater impact will be felt from international market influences. Tourism is projected to be one of Korea's major industries in the twenty-first century.

Bibliography

Ahn, J.Y., Var, T. and Kim, Y.K. (1989) An investigation of Olympic tourists' perception of Korea. *Study on Tourism*, Vol. 13. 109–21.

Breen, M. (1990) South Korea's big spenders remain 'conspicuous'. *Asia Travel Trade*, November 5.

Chung, U.S. (1990) Future development in Korea's outbound tourism market. Speech at Korea World Travel Fair, Seoul.

Deans, B. (1990) Have-nots becoming edgy in ROK. *Pacific Stars and Stripes*, 16 May.

Edgell, D. L. (1987) The formulation of tourism policy – a managerial framework. In Ritchie, J.R.B. and Goeldner, C. (eds) *Travel, Tourism and Hospitality Research*. New York: John Wiley & Sons.

Han, W.K. (1970) *The History of Korea*. Seoul: The Eul-Yoo Publishing Company.

Helmer, R. (1992) Frugality campaign. *Korea Herald*, 26 April, 6.

Hyun, J.K. (1990a) An overview of outbound tourism in Korea. Speech at Korea Visit USA Fair & Travel Trade Seminar. Seoul.

Hyun, J.K. (1990b) Inbound Tourism in Korea after 1988 Seoul International Olympics. *Proceedings of Triple T Task Force Hawaii Workshop, Honolulu*. Tokyo: The Japanese National Committee for Pacific Economic Cooperation, 97–103.

Kim, S.S. (1990) The Impact of Socio-Economic Development on Outbound Tourism in Korea. *Tour Times*, No. 10.

Kim, Y.Y. (1991). Conspicuous consumption. *Korea Herald*, 20 September, 1.

Korea National Tourism Corporation (1984a) *Annual Statistics on Tourism – 1983*. Seoul: KNTC.

Korea National Tourism Corporation (1984b) *Korean Tourism Annual Report – 1983*. Seoul: KNTC.

Korea National Tourism Corporation (1985) *Korean Tourism Annual Report – 1984*. Seoul: KNTC.

Korea National Tourism Corporation (1988) *Korean Tourism Annual Report – 1987*. Seoul: KNTC.

Korea National Tourism Corporation (1990) *Annual Statistical Report on Tourism – 1989*. Seoul: KNTC.

Korea National Tourism Corporation (1992) *Korean Tourism Annual Report – 1991*. Seoul: KNTC.

Korea National Tourism Corporation (1993) *Annual Statistical Report on Tourism – 1992*. Seoul: KNTC

Korea National Tourism Corporation (1994) *Annual Statistical Report on Tourism – 1993*. Seoul: KNTC.

Lee, C.N. (1990) Antiluxury campaign. *Korea Herald*, 29 November, 6.

McGahey, S. (1990a) Korea's 'anti-luxury' campaign and the tourism industry. *Travel Trade Journal* 4 (11), 46–9.

McGahey, S. (1990b) South Korea. *The Economist Intelligence Unit, International Tourism Reports*, 2, 22–43.

McGahey, S. (1991) South Korea Outbound. *The Economist Intelligence Unit, Travel & Tourism Analyst*, 6, 45–62.

McGahey, S. (1992a) Changing China partners causes uproar in tourism circles. *Travel Trade Journal* 6 (9), 61–2.

McGahey, S. (1992b) *Tourism Yearbook 1992*. Seoul: Business Korea Company.

McGahey, S. (1993) New administration re-assesses the value of tourism. *Travel Trade Journal* 7 (2), 63–4.

McGahey, S. (1994a) Big brother and little brother intensify their visits. *Travel Trade Journal*, 8, (2).

McGahey, S. (1994b) Korean and Taiwanese outbound tourism, 1989–2000. Speech at PATA Annual Conference, Seoul.

Richter, L. K. (1993) Tourism policy in South-east Asia. In Hitchcock, M., King, V.T. and Parnwell, J.G. (eds) *Tourism in South East Asia*. New York: Routledge, 179–99.

Ricquart, V. J. (1988) *The Games Within The Games*. Seoul: Hantong Books.

Yarmy, W. and McGahey, S. (1993) Prospects and opportunities for U.S. Suppliers in the Korean outbound tourism market. *The Journal of Tourism Studies*, 5, 253–81.

15

Taiwan: Carrying capacity in an industrializing country

IRENE VLITOS ROWE

Introduction

This chapter provides an overview of recent tourism developments in Taiwan from the point of view of the carrying capacity in an industrializing country. In this instance, carrying capacity refers to a technique that is used to measure the maximum number of tourists which can be contained in a specific space or area without excessively altering the environment. Problems exist in implementing such a technique because there is a tendency for the capacity of environments to change significantly over a short period of time. In addition, the type of management system currently in place can have an influence.

The chapter will show that Taiwan's carrying capacity has reached its limit in terms of the detrimental effect that the increased number of visitors, together with rapid industrialization, have had on the environment over the past three decades. It should be pointed out, however, that this detrimental effect has been largely confined to the capital city of Taipei.

Despite this development, it will be shown that opportunities still exist for expanding the country's carrying capacity. Taiwan has many areas of outstanding natural beauty that existing and/or potential visitors are unaware of. This, coupled with its rich history and culture, make the island an interesting destination to explore and one that needs to promote itself more aggressively.

In addition, as the review of the Tourism Bureau's *General Plan for a Recreation/Tourism System in Taiwan* will show, a blueprint for the future development of the national travel and tourism industry has been created. If the Bureau is successful in implementing most of its recommended development strategies, the carrying capacity can realistically be expected to expand within the foreseeable future.

However, as will be shown in this chapter, Taiwan faces some major challenges in not only redesigning its image but also in distributing this image and attracting, retaining and expanding its pool of both foreign and domestic tourists. The key objective of this chapter is to look at the ways in which Taiwan is changing and to draw some conclusions regarding the implications of these changes for tourism and future economic development.

Historical Growth

The economic miracle of this 'tiger' nation has been well documented elsewhere. Suffice it at this point to briefly review the history of Taiwan's growth over recent years and to assess the reasons for this success.

In 1895, China ceded Taiwan to the Japanese who continued to rule it through to 1945. This latter year marked the turning point in the country's fortunes. From 1949 to 1965 American grants, commodities, subsidized loans and technical advice amounted to approximately US$1.5 billion and, it has been argued (Elegant, 1990), laid the foundation for Taiwan's current economic structure. It was during this period that the joint Chinese–American Commission on Rural Reconstruction addressed the major problem confronting the nation – how to modernize the island's outmoded form of agriculture.

It is perhaps land reform that proved to be the most significant change at this time. By distributing land to new owners, the rice industry was given a new lease of life and the original landowners were rewarded with shares in government-owned industries such as the Taiwan Cement Corporation. This development had the effect of improving the general standard of living for most people, who were now in a better position to influence the political and economic direction of the nation.

The following statistics put these changes and growth in perspective. In 1951, the island had less than 8 million inhabitants; its total exports accounted for approximately US$58 million and each individual's nominal share of the Gross National Product (GNP) was US$48. By 1988, total exports accounted for US$60.6 billion, which represented nearly half of the country's GNP. There was a US$10.9 billion excess of exports over imports and, of this total, US$10.4 billion was the surplus in trade with the USA. In that year, each individual's nominal share of GNP was US$6,045. By 1990, per capita GNP had reached nearly US$8,000 and in 1993 Gross Domestic Product (GDP) per head reached a high of US$11,900. Again in 1993, the population totalled 21 million and GNP growth was at 5.9 per cent.

There are, however, signs that this steady growth is beginning to taper off. Although the 1993 GNP growth of 5.9 per cent compares favourably with other countries such as the USA and Japan, it still represents a slight decline in performance from its 1992 growth of 6.1 per cent and compares less favourably with some of Taiwan's neighbours.

Furthermore, Taiwan's export growth is showing signs of decline as this slowed to 4.3 per cent in 1993 after a period of double-digit expansion (*Far Eastern Economic Review*, 1994). At the same time, domestic demand for consumer goods from abroad is increasing faster than exports. The effect of this trend has been a decrease in the trade surplus to US$7.8 billion in 1993. Consideration of the 1987 figure helps to put this development in context, since in that year Taiwan's trade surplus was at its peak and amounted to US$18.7 billion. The Ministry of Finance is predicting that this downward flow will continue to the end of 1994, with Taiwan's total foreign trade surplus accounting for a little under US$5 billion and trade surplus with Hong Kong–China increasing slightly to approximately US$1.8 billion.

This slow down in economic growth is seen by some to be symptomatic of the fact that the country is now in the throes of its second industrial transition – a transition that is being brought about by Taiwan's move from labour-intensive to higher-technology industries. Although this change has been underway since the 1980s, its potential for negative economic effects have been somewhat muted by the fact that two factors have helped to sustain a certain level of growth – government expenditure on public construction and trade with China.

This high spending on infrastructure, however, is not without its problems. The original national development plan consisted of 780 projects that were expected to cost a total of US$300 billion in 1990. Although the government has since scaled down its ambitious programme, the public debt has increased substantially and it is anticipated (*Far Eastern Economic Review*, 1994) that this will reach 35 per cent of GNP in 1995.

Sectoral Contribution to Economic Growth

China–Taiwan trade

It is the current relationship with China that points the way to the future and represents another major development in the history of Taiwan. It could be argued that just as Taiwan's fate was closely linked with the success of the American economy in the early 1960s, a similar situation now exists with China. The latter ranks among Taiwan's major trading partners and is second only to the USA.

Over the past three years Taiwan's exports to China have grown steadily (an increase that has averaged 20 per cent per month) and Taiwan has enjoyed a healthy trade surplus. China is now Taiwan's fastest growing market and the bulk of this two-way trade is conducted with Taiwanese companies based in the mainland – a total of approximately 12,000. There are, however, signs that China's economy is beginning to slow down and this may have a negative impact on Taiwan's economy in the short term.

Taiwan as a 'mature tiger' nation

Looking ahead it is important to realize that Taiwan is now a *mature tiger*. This maturity has important implications for both its future growth and investment incentives. As Taiwan tries to narrow the gap with some of its neighbours and become more proficient in high-technology industries, it is providing a more focused programme of incentives to both locally and foreign-owned companies. This focus is demonstrated, for example, in a more specific and narrower definition of what could be termed acceptable high-technology projects. It is in this way that it will be able to pass through its transition period as quickly as possible.

It is predicted that growth will decline over the next five years as the economy matures (EIU, 1993) and it is anticipated that personal incomes in Taiwan will be similar to those in Hong Kong and Singapore by 1998. As regards a specific breakdown for Taiwan, it is possible to gauge the sectoral contribution to economic development through data supplied by the World Tourism Organization (WTO) and statistics published by the Tourism Bureau of the Ministry of Transportation and Communications.

The WTO data provides details on visitor receipts over a six-year period and, with the exception of 1990, shows a gradual increase in revenue generated from tourism (all figures '000's): 1987 (US$1,619); 1988 (US$2,289); 1989 (US$2,698); 1990 (US$1,740); 1991 (US$2,018); and 1992 (US$2,449).

The Tourism Bureau's 1992 Visitor Expenditure Survey revealed that visitor expenditure amounted to US$174.28 per person per day for that year. This was broken down into: hotel bills (US$48.27 or 27.70 per cent); meals outside hotels (US$17.3 or 9.94 per cent); entertainment (US$15.54 or 8.92 per cent); shopping (US$70.57 or 40.49 per cent); domestic transportation (US$13.95 or 8.00 per cent; and miscellaneous (US$8.62 or 4.95 per cent). The average expenditure per person per trip was estimated to be US$1,307.10 and the total visitor expenditure amounted to US$2,449 million.

This latter figure compares with US$22.9 million for 1988; US$26.98 million for 1989; US$17.4 million for 1990; and US$20.18 million for 1991. The lower 1990 figure correlates to the drop in visitor arrivals for that year and the 1992 figure indicates a more positive trend for the future.

The State of the Taiwanese Travel and Tourism Industry

Although Taiwan is not usually considered to be on the international tourism map in the same way as, say, Thailand or Hong Kong, this destination still attracts many Japanese, Koreans and ethnic Chinese. Once direct air links are established with China, it is likely that there will be a surge in visitors to

Taiwan from the mainland. In the meantime, however, the Taiwanese tourism sector remains underdeveloped.

Visitor arrivals

According to PATA (1993), Taiwan received a total of 1,873,327 visitors that year. Although arrivals increased 1 per cent over 1991, this modest growth was a reflection of the fact that Taiwan was being 'adversely affected by weaknesses in its main markets' of Japan (down by 3.8 per cent) and Korea (down by 1.9 per cent). Conversely, arrivals from South-east Asia were up by 19 per cent.

For the first nine months of 1993, a total of 1,352,474 visitors arrived in Taiwan. This represented a decline of 5.2 per cent on the same period for 1992. Although the number of foreign visitors decreased by 7.1 per cent for this period, the number of overseas Chinese visitors increased by 8.9 per cent.

This gradual decline in visitor numbers over recent years can be partly attributed to both political and economic developments. For example, there have been restrictions on flag carriers serving both China and Taiwan and the price of accommodation in the country (due to the high value of the NT$) has deterred some travellers.

Happily for the industry as a whole, this slow decline in visitor numbers has been partially offset by the fact that those visitors who do come tend to spend more time in the country and, consequently, more money. However, the signs are there that the Taiwanese travel and tourism industry needs to redress the balance if it is to continue to attract tourists and remain competitive. The modest 1992 average hotel occupancy rate (53.19 per cent for both international tourist hotels and tourist hotels) is a case in point as this compares unfavourably with some of Taiwan's neighbours. Taipei, for example, is the only city with a good supply of rooms at the top end of the market – an indication that further regional hotel development is still needed in order to attract and distribute premium/high-spending holiday traffic throughout the country.

Outbound travel

On the other hand, outbound tourism departures have increased noticeably over recent years and, according to PATA (1993), Taiwan was the second largest outbound travel market in Asia in 1992. This growth has been significant – from a total of 1,601,992 in 1988 to a total of 4,214,734 in 1992. For the first ten months of 1993, the number of outbound departures of nationals totalled 4,002,420.

While the strong New Taiwan Dollar has discouraged visitors to Taiwan, it has encouraged the Taiwanese to travel abroad. In addition, a number of new bilateral air traffic agreements have been signed with foreign carriers and these have had the effect of increasing both airline capacity and flight options.

The Tourism Bureau's General Plan for a Recreation/ Tourism System in Taiwan

It now remains to consider the steps Taiwan is taking to develop its travel and tourism industry. As already alluded to above, Taiwan has suffered from a poor tourism image. Over the past 30 years the priority has been economic development but, unfortunately, sometimes at the expense of both its rich culture and natural environment.

The Tourism Bureau's General Plan for a Recreation/Tourism System in Taiwan, however, was published in June 1992. The Plan reinforces the notion that tourism 'has been recognised as a vital part of the national economy by the government'. It is intended to provide both medium to long-term guidelines for development and suggests ways in which the island can promote tourism in the next decade.

Trends in international tourism market development

The plan begins by analysing the nature of tourism demand in Taiwan and predicts that there will be 'steady growth' in the international tourism market through to the year 1996. It confirms the WTO's recent findings regarding future trends in inter-regional versus intra-regional traffic flows, that is intra-regional traffic is already surpassing inter-regional flows and this is a trend that is likely to continue through to the year 2010 (WTO, 1993). The report makes the point that the economic strength of origin markets is the key driver influencing tourism imports and exports.

Trends in domestic tourism demand

As more tourism infrastructure is put into place and attractions and/or resorts developed, it is anticipated that there will be a surge in the level of domestic tourism. This will tend to be mostly family travel and will be encouraged through the greater availability of private cars.

Although the majority of domestic tourism is likely to consist of such traditional activities as picnicking, barbecuing and sightseeing, plans are underway to develop new forms of tourism such as water-skiing, hang-gliding and other forms of adventure pasttimes.

As regards demographic breakdowns, the Tourism Bureau expects the main demand to come from students and teenagers but acknowledges that the 'silver' or retired population provides great potential for the future.

Characteristics of regional demand

It is interesting to note that there are differences in regional demand within Taiwan's 36,000 sq km. The country is divided into four regions: northern, central, southern and eastern.

According to the Tourism Bureau's research, the majority of domestic travellers are from the north, which happens to be the only region where tourist outflow exceeds inflow from other regions. The majority of visitors to the eastern region tend to originate from the north and south while the local residents in the central and southern regions account for the bulk of tourist demand.

Tourism Demand Forecasts

Domestic demand
The Tourism Bureau predicts that once the Six-Year National Development Plan has been completed the average times of domestic travel per capita per annum will be between four and five trips. These trips will also tend to last for longer periods of time and by 1996 should total 100.6 million.

International inbound demand
It is anticipated that the number of visitor arrivals will continue to increase at an annual rate of 4.5 per cent per annum through to 1996. By this year there will be 2.6 to 2.8 million foreign visitors to Taiwan annually.

International outbound demand
It is forecast that by 1996 there will be approximately 4.7 to 5.8 million Taiwan travellers visiting foreign countries each year.

Accommodation demand

These positive predictions for tourism growth both to and within the country imply that the necessary infrastructure will have to be in place to meet this demand. The development of the Taiwanese hotel sector is an example of where the travel and tourism industry is actually helping the local economy as the construction of new hotels has provided employment to various national building firms and, in addition, has offered more opportunities for jobs in the service sector.

The plan reviews two separate categories of accommodation:

1. Tourist Hotels. It is predicted that by 1996 there will be approximately 28,000 to 30,000 tourist hotel rooms. This compares to the 1992 number of 20,000 and, at the time of writing the plan, an additional 4,600 rooms were being added by the end of 1993.
2. General accommodation demand. It is estimated that by 1996 the domestic lodging demand will be 2.28 times the current (1992) lodging demand.

Analysis of Taiwan's recreation resources

The second chapter of the plan addresses the issue of Taiwan's recreation resources and identifies five different types of relevance to the travel and tourism industry. These include: natural resources; cultural resources; industrial resources; amusement resources and service facilities, which cover transportation and accommodation services. In all cases, development strategies to upgrade existing facilites are outlined.

It is interesting to note that in the plan's view industrial resources are clearly linked with the travel and tourism industry. These include recreational agriculture, fishery, mining and local products. The development strategy in this instance recommends that rural tours should be promoted; industrial museums and shopping facilities established; products repackaged; marketing networks established and a distinction created between production and recreational areas. To quote the plan, there should be the 'integration of cultural and industrial recreational resource with tourism development'.

The system planning process

The plan outlines the system planning process which is being shaped by four key development goals, which are:

1. Satisfaction of demands for different population segments.
2. Integration of recreational with industrial development.
3. Achievement of cooperation and balance between recreation development and preservation of the environment.
4. Integration of recreational and spatial development.

It is apparent from the plan that it is the intention to spread the benefits of tourism throughout the country as three types of essential components are identified:

1. Tourism cities including 'regional tourism cities' and 'local tourism communities'.
2. Resorts including 'regional resorts' and 'local resorts'.
3. Service bases. This category includes the provision of general accommodation; mass transit systems and automobile services; local tourism information; general food services; local cultural events and a general communications service.

Identification of recreational systems

Although a total of 36 recreational systems have been identified the plan focuses on eight categories, which are:

1. Urban Systems, including the urban areas of Taipei, Taichung, Kaohsiung, Hsinchu, Ilan, Puli, Tainan and Chiayi. Development will concentrate on cultural, amusement and industrial urban resources.
2. Cross-Island Highways. These include the Northern, Central and Southern Cross-Island highways.

3.   Rugged Terrain.
4.   Touring Corridors.
5.   Coastal Systems.
6.   National Park Systems.
7.   Outlying Islands.
8.   Hua-Tung and Hengchun Systems.

It appears from the above that the Tourism Bureau has a long-term view regarding ways in which to improve and exploit the country's tourism potential. Although new attractions are necessary, these are not being put in place without the introduction of basic services and infrastructure. In addition, it is anticipated that local support for the plan will be forthcoming as all areas of the country are being targeted.

Major Issues in Planning and Development

As intimated above, Taiwan's rapid industrialization has meant that the country's economy has grown considerably over the past few decades – often at the expense of environmental or tourist concerns.

This situation is compounded by the fact that Taiwan is also experiencing the changes brought about by external forces such as the revolution in technology and communications. It is this revolution that is making it easier for companies to move to locations with lower labour costs or more attractive working conditions – a development that could have dire consequences for an island such as Taiwan that cannot rely solely upon its travel and tourism industry for survival.

Taiwan is not alone in its bid to turn the tide in its favour by introducing a long-term plan (the Six-Year National Development Plan) designed to ensure the correct level of infrastructure for the future. As the competition to attract visitors becomes more intense in the region, many countries are re-examining not only the ways in which they promote their destination abroad but are also actively taking steps to improve their existing transport facilities and attractions.

Strategic Place Marketing

A recent publication (Kotler *et al.*, 1993) has examined the issues involved in what has been termed *strategic place marketing* that is the revitalization of towns, cities, regions and nations. It is the central premise of this publication that 'marketplace shifts and changes occur far faster than a community's capacity to react and respond'. If, however, the correct programmes are put in place the chances of achieving these new objectives rapidly improve. It can be argued that this is the situation in which Taiwan now finds itself.

It is important here to distinguish between marketing, promoting and placing a destination. Promotion is a subset of marketing and, as such, does not bring about the needed improvements by itself. On the other hand, place marketing refers to the design of a place in order to satisfy the needs of its target markets, which could potentially include not only tourists but outside investment and export markets, new residents, goods and services producers, corporate headquarters and regional offices.

Place marketing is faced with two major challenges: first, is it capable of strengthening the capacity of communities and regions to adapt to the changes in the marketplace; and, second, can it effectively exploit opportunities for the long term. Kotler *et al.* argue that a long-term solution is only viable if all four major marketing factors found in every community are actually improved upon.

The four factors are of direct relevance to the Taiwanese situation and are:

1. The ability to provide basic services and infrastructure at a standard acceptable to nationals, companies and tourists.
2. The need to create new attractions that will improve the quality of life. Not only will this help to keep alive existing business and public support but will also serve to attract additional investment, companies and/or tourists.
3. The necessity to communicate these new and improved developments through an effective image and communication programme.
4. The requirement to encourage as much support as possible from the main stakeholders, who include residents, political leaders and institutions. It is crucial that these various elements help to foster a climate that attracts new companies, investment and tourists.

The practical implementation of these four factors may include consideration of some or all of the following:

Improved urban design

There are worldwide examples of efforts being made to improve urban design in an attempt to recreate the original character of the city, town or region. In the case of Singapore, for example, its *Strategic Plan for Growth 1993-1995* (STPB, 1995) confirms that the focus of future urban development will be leisure facilities and attractions. The city state believes that developments in the Civic District and the establishment of the Singapore Arts Centre will provide the basis for a wider range of cultural and street activities to encourage visitors to increase their length of stay.

The intention is to concentrate on the development of 4 focal zones and 11 tourism themes. The targeted zones are the Civic District (e.g. upgrade of Merlion Park); the Singapore River (e.g. new private development of warehouses); the Orchard Spring (e.g. this will be a new focal point for tourist information on the region, shopping and an annual spring flower show) and the Southern Islands. Among the tourism themes are 'nostalgic Singapore'; 'nightlife Singapore style' and 'family theme parks'. It is in ways such as these that a place character can be developed and serve as a major incentive for retaining exisiting businesses or attracting new ones.

Infrastructure improvement

Although infrastructure alone cannot ensure a community's continued growth and success, it can help to support economic productivity. What is certain is that its absence, or failure to provide adequate capacity for current and projected use, can prove to be a serious handicap and one that detracts from the attractiveness of a destination.

Taiwan's government is fully aware of the need to improve its infrastructure. As stated in a recent eight-page advertisement, Taiwan's $303 billion Six-Year National Development Plan (proposed in 1990 by Premier Hau Pei-tsun) is intended to provide 'wide-range infrastructural rejuvenation . . . [and] . . . traffic congestion should be materially eased by this step' (*Asia Inc*, 1994a) As part of this plan, construction began on the $18 billion Taipei rapid transit system in 1988. It is expected that when this system is completed in 1999 it will be able to cope with the city's 2.7 million residents and put an end to the traffic congestion.

However, it has been reported (*Asia Inc*, 1994b) that these well-intentioned attempts to improve local transport are not without their hiccups. The construction has been held up for various reasons, which allegedly range from faulty work to corrupt transportation officials. As the situation stands today, Taiwan 'is the only Asian tiger without a subway system'.

Attractions

Although Taiwan tends to be viewed primarily as a business destination, the island has a strong cultural heritage together with areas of outstanding natural beauty – a case calling for what has been termed 'strategic image management' (*Kotler, et al.*, 1993).

In order to get this message across, however, the tourism officials need to find a common ground that will appeal not only to local residents but also to new residents, tourists, companies and investors. As Kotler *et al.* have stated, the challenge of any new image positioning is the ability to create a picture that 'communicates the benefits and unique attributes that make the place stand out among other places' (1993: 153).

Some examples include Spain's 'Rising star of the European Community'; Thailand's 'Tourism haven of the Far East'; and, perhaps one of the most successful of them all, New Zealand's 'The Environmental Destination of the 1990s'. As a result of this campaign, New Zealand has become synonymous with eco-tourism and all that that implies such as fresh air, beautiful and unspoilt landscapes and the peace and quiet of natural surroundings.

So what are the attractions that need to be promoted more aggressively and effectively? Few people know that Taiwan boasts a varied landscape of forests, mountains and long stretches of idyllic beaches in secluded bays. In addition, its rich cultural history means that it can offer the National Palace Museum, the Chiang Kai-shek Memorial Hall and countless temples.

284   Irene Vlitos Rowe

In some respects, Taiwan's travel and tourism industry has been hampered by its image of being one of the key financial centres in South-east Asia. Its ability to change this impression, while still retaining its attraction for business travellers, is a major challenge for the 1990s.

Conclusion

Throughout the different phases of its history, Taiwan has adapted well to change and the signs are there that it will be able to do so yet again in the 1990s. If this is the case, it will be able to expand its carrying capacity and continue its economic success story.

Although there has not been a dramatic growth in the number of visitor arrivals over recent years, the country appears to have the right mechanisms in place to reverse this trend. Both the Six-Year National Development Plan and the *General Plan for a Recreation/Tourism System in Taiwan* are blueprints for the future.

This is not to say, however, that these plans are not without their flaws. The difficulties associated with the construction of the Taipei rapid transit system is a case in point. This system has proved to be far more costly than at first envisaged and it is estimated that by the time it is finally completed it will prove to be the most expensive in the world, that is the cost averages about $205 million per kilometre – one-sixth of which can be attributed to high land acquisition costs (Asia, 1994b). There are also dangers that the recent high spending on infrastructure will push the budget into deficit.

At the end of the day the question is whether Taiwan will be able to sustain a viable travel and tourism industry. As interlinkages exist between this industry and the rest of the economy, the country is well placed to exploit whatever opportunities exist to expand its carrying capacity.

Bibliography

Asia Inc (1994a) Republic of China on Taiwan: young democracy prepares for the future. *Asia Inc* May.

Asia Inc (1994b) Bumpy ride. Taipei's rapid transit system has faced difficulties at every turn. *Asia Inc* March.

EIU (1993) Asia Pacific regional overview. *EIU Country Forecast*, 4th Quarter. London: Economist Intelligence Unit.

Elegant, Robert (1990) *Pacific Destiny. The Rise of the East*. London: Hamish Hamilton.

Far Eastern Economic Review (1994) A difficult age. Taiwan struggles to engineer sustainable growth. *Far Eastern Economic Review* 30 June.

Kotler, P., Haider, D.H. and Rein, I. (1993) Attracting Investment, Industry and Tourism to Cities, States and Nations. *Marketing Places*. New York: The Free Press.

Pacific Asia Travel Association (1993) *Annual Statistical Report 1992* San Francisco: PATA.

Singapore Tourist Promotion Board (1995) *Strategic Plan for Growth: 1993–1995*. STPB.

Tourism Bureau, Ministry of Transportation and Communications (1992) *General Plan for Recreation/Tourism System in Taiwan*. Republic of China.

WTO (1993), *Global Tourism Forecasts to the Year 2000 and Beyond. East Asia and the Pacific*. Madrid: WTO.

16

Thailand: The dynamic growth of Thai tourism

LAN LI
WEI ZHANG

Introduction

The kingdom of Thailand is the largest country in mainland South-east Asia. It lies in the heart of South-east Asia and shares borders with Myanmar to the west and north, Laos to the north-east, Cambodia to the east and Malaysia to the south. Being located between the Indian Ocean and the South China Sea, it has been a hub of the region for both sea and air traffic.

Diversity and contrast characterize both its people and its geography. Within an area of 514,000 sq m, are tropical rain forests, broad alluvial plains, forest-clad hills and beaches. It has a population of 55 million with a rich cultural mix comprising 8 nationalities and a scattering of hilltribes in the north. Before World War II, many countries in South-east Asia were colonized. But Thailand had successfully avoided domination by foreign powers, thus its architecture and local customs have maintained their indigenous features.

Due to its varieties in natural tourist attractions, its culture and strategic position, Thailand has been a principal tourist destination for about 150 years. However, prior to the 1970s, Thai tourism growth had been of a *laisser-faire* nature without appropriate planning. With the fast economic growth in the late 1970s, the Thai government realized the importance of tourism as a means of increasing foreign exchange earnings. Privileged policies were established to facilitate appropriate tourism development. In 1982, the tourism industry became the largest source of foreign exchange for Thailand and a cornerstone of its economy. Since the 1980s, tourism has experienced a rapid growth with the number of international visitors to Thailand increasing from 1.86 million in 1980 to 5.7 million in 1993 (Figure 16.1). Over the

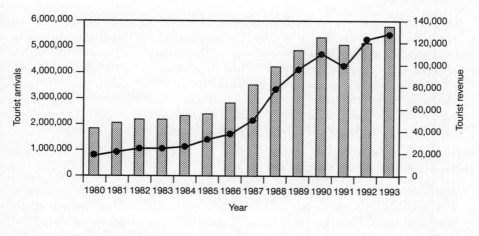

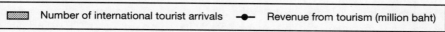

Figure 16.1 International tourist arrivals and revenue from tourism.
Source: TAT (1993a).

same period, tourism receipts increased from 17,765 million baht in 1980 to 127,802 million baht in 1993 (Figure 16.1).

However, the rapid growth without proper control has created a series of obstacles for the further development of Thai tourism. This chapter will review the evolution of Thai tourism, examine the present government tourism policies, and analyse the problems facing Thai tourism and their root-causes. The chapter concludes with a discussion of the future outlook for Thai tourism development.

Evolution of Tourism

Tourism in the nineteenth century

The foundation for international tourism in Thailand was laid in the 1850s when the Thai kings (Rama IV and V) encouraged international trading in Thailand. Foreign trade brought to Thailand not only flows of capital, but also a flow of investors, traders and occasional tourists. The Thai kings in the nineteenth and early twentieth centuries (Rama V, VI and VII) travelled the world on royal visits and improved Thailand's fame as a tourist destination. During overseas visits, the royal family raised curiosity amongst aristocrats who travelled to Thailand on holiday.

In the nineteenth century, the colonial travellers represented another important tourist group. These travellers often used Bangkok as a convenient stop-over en route to the colonized countries including Burma, Malaysia, Laos and Cambodia. Up to World War II, the colonial travellers, especially the French and British, had been the most important foreign tourism source to Thailand. Guest houses and hotels appeared in Thailand during the nineteenth century in response to the demand for lodging. Most of these facilities were small and operated by ethnic Chinese. Several high-class properties were also established by the royal families, including the Paya Thai Place considered then the best such lodging facility in the Far East.

Tourism during the Vietnam War

The Vietnam War (1962–75) had a profound effect on the development of Thai tourism. The presence of US forces inspired the development of an extensive entertainment industry in Thailand. Every American military base in Thailand was surrounded by a 'pleasure-belt' comprised of restaurants, bars, massage parlours, night clubs and brothels. In addition, thousands of American servicemen who were based in Vietnam used Thailand as a destination for their five-day 'Rest and Recreation' (R&R) leave. The R&R servicemen soon became an important part of the growing number of tourist arrivals in Thailand. Their expenditures accounted for one-third of the total revenue from overseas visitors between 1966 to 1971 (Meyer, 1988).

Another war-related effect was the 'sexual paradise' image that is conjured up when Thailand is mentioned. Exotic massage parlours and night clubs started to provide the R&R American soldiers from Vietnam with sex services in order to entertain them. Bangkok received the dubious distinction of being recognized as 'sex capital of the East'. The tourists eagerly followed the soldiers, thus international arrivals increased by 20 per cent annually between 1960 and 1973 (Meyer, 1988), which indicates the pent-up demand for 'sex tourism'. Upon the signing of the armistice in 1975, the soldiers left Thailand, but the image a of 'sexual paradise' remained. The hotel industry also experienced a rapid growth during the war period. The number of rooms increased by an average annual rate of 32 per cent between 1960 and 1968 (Meyer, 1988).

The 1980s tourism boom

The economic value of tourism was recognized by the Thai government in the late 1970s, and tourism was incorporated into the national plan in 1977. A series of tourism promotion campaigns initiated by the Thai government in the 1980s (Table 16.1) were extremely successful. Tourism receipts rose from 17,765 million baht in 1980 to 96,386 million baht in 1989 (TAT, 1990b).

The year of 1982 was a turning point for the Thai tourism industry as tourism revenue became, for the first time, the largest foreign exchange earner (TAT, 1988). Table 16.2 exhibits the importance of foreign exchange

Table 16.1 Major tourism promotion events in the 1980s

Year	Events
1980	The first River Kwai Bridge Week, designed to promote Kanchanaburi
1980	Visit Thailand Year, the Thailand Tourism Festival and Identity Fair has been made an annual event since
1981	Hosted the annual meeting of the Society of American Travel Writers (SATW)
1984	Set up the Thai Convention Promotion Association (TCPA)
1984	Set up Committee for the Promotion of the Restaurants and Food shops
1985	Thailand Travel Scene, a series of sales campaigns
1985	Hosted ASEAN Tourism Forum
1987	The Visit Thailand Year campaign
1987	Celebration of His Majesty the King's 60th Birthday Anniversary
1988	The Longest Reign Celebrations for His Majesty the King of Thailand
1988–89	Thailand Arts and Crafts Year

Source: TAT (1990b)

earnings from the travel industry over other industries. In addition, Figure 16.2 shows the trade deficit balance during 1980 and 1989 and the receipts from the travel industry has helped Thailand reduce its trade deficits.

With the tourism growth in the 1980s, there was a great demand for hotel rooms. The Thai government introduced tax incentive policies to promote hotel construction. Consequently, the hotel industry experienced a boom with 44 per cent room increase between 1986 and 1990 (TAT, 1990b).

Tourism trends in the 1990s

Tourist Market
In the early 1990s, two events hampered the constant growth of Thai tourism – the Persian Gulf War in 1990–91 and Thai's pro-democracy uprising in 1992. In 1991, tourism experienced a 4 per cent decline in international tourist

Table 16.2 Revenue from international tourism and other major exports of Thailand 1981–89 (million baht)

Rank	1981 Export	Value	1983 Export	Value	1985 Export	Value	1987 Export	Value	1989 Export	Value
1	Rice	26,367	Tourism	25,050	Tourism	31,768	Tourism	50,024	Tourism	96,383
2	Tourism	21,455	Rice	20,157	Textile products	23,578	Textile products	48,555	Textile products	74,036
3	Tapioca	16,446	Tapioca	15,387	Rice	22,524	Rice	22,703	Rice	45,462
4	Textile products	12,531	Textile products	14,351	Tapioca	14,969	Tapioca	20,661	Rubber	26,423
5	Rubber	10,840	Rubber	11,787	Rubber	13,567	Rubber	20,539	Tapioca	23,974
6	Sugar	9,571	Maize	8,486	Integrated circuits	8,248	Integrated circuits	15,179	Sugar	19,244
7	Tin	9,091	Sugar	6,338	Maize	7,700	Precious stone	11,550	Integrated circuits	18,424

Source: TAT (1988b)

arrivals and 10 per cent drop in revenue compared with the previous year. However, due to the continuous economic growth of Pacific Asia, Thai tourism recovered in 1993.

In the early 1990s, East Asian countries have become the prime source of Thai tourism while the European and American markets are declining in market share, average tourist expenditure and revenue generation. Table 16.3 exhibits the differences in these respects by regions between 1992 to 1993.

Among the East Asian countries, Malaysia maintained its position as the number one market source to Thailand with 14.4 per cent of total arrivals. A strong economy and currency encouraged Singaporeans travelling abroad, inducing a 12 per cent increase in visitors to Thailand. More growth occurred in both Taiwan and South Korean markets in 1993, an increase of 33 per cent and 29 per cent respectively (TAT, 1993b).

China represents a new market to Thailand. The rapid growth of the Chinese economy and the lifting of travel restrictions by Thai Immigration propelled a meteoric rise in Chinese visitors. In 1993, there were 261,739 Chinese who visited Thailand, ranking China as Thailand's ninth largest market source (TAT, 1993b). Japanese and Hong Kong visitors, Thailand's two traditional markets, contributed little to the country's tourism recovery

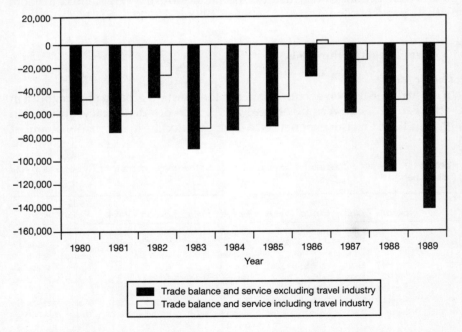

Figure 16.2 Thailand's trade balance with service excluding and including the travel industry 1980–89 (million baht).
Source: TAT (1990b).

Table 16.3 Market share, average expenditure and revenue by regions 1992/93

Region	Market share %			Average expenditure (Person/day)US$			Revenue US$ (million)		
	1992	1993	change	1992	1993	change	1992	1993	change
East Asia	55.78	58.63	2.85	153.35	165.53	7.9%	2262.75	2717.11	20.1%
Europe	25.08	24.49	−0.59	114.89	81.95	−28.7%	1614.82	1291.17	−20.0%
The Americas	6.91	6.24	−0.67	139.31	89.51	−35.8%	365.37	270.16	−26.1%
South Asia	5.39	4.02	−1.37	136.76	191.84	40.3%	240.60	326.54	35.7%
Oceania	4.55	4.14	−0.41	123.80	93.60	−24.4%	198.55	165.01	−16.9%
Middle East	1.53	1.59	0.06	122.90	182.17	48.2%	109.54	175.52	60.2%
Africa	0.76	0.89	0.13	129.46	173.02	33.7%	37.19	68.24	83.5%
Grand Total	100.00	100.00		133.16	125.41	−5.8%	4828.82	5013.80	3.8%

Source: TAT (1993b)

in 1993. Japan had only a slight increase of 2 per cent over 1992 while the number of tourists from Hong Kong was 9 per cent lower than the previous year (TAT, 1993b).

The long-haul travel markets of Europe and the Americas declined in the early 1990s due, in part, to the world economic recession. Though a slight increase in arrivals occurred in 1993, the average expenditures of European travellers decreased by 29 per cent and that of American travellers declined by 37 per cent compared with the previous year. At the same time, revenues from these two markets were also decreased by 20 per cent and 26 per cent respectively (TAT, 1993b).

The South-Asia travel market improved in 1993. Though the number of tourist arrivals was 16 per cent less than 1992, the other three key indicators showed impressive performance: the average length of stay was extended for one more day, the average expenditure increased by 40 per cent, and tourist revenue from this region grew by 36 per cent (TAT, 1993b).

A significant increase in revenue was also achieved from Middle East and Africa source markets in 1993. However, since arrivals from the two regions accounted for only 2 per cent of the grand total they had less impact on Thai tourism.

Tourism to Thailand in the 1990s is leisure dominated according to purpose of visit. Around 90 per cent of all visitors to Thailand cited leisure as the main purpose of the visit (TAT, 1992). Conventions represent an emerging market in the Thai tourism industry with Bangkok, Phuket, Chiang Mai and Pattaya as the major convention destinations.

Travel Related Business
Though land and sea crossings into Thailand are merging as a significant travel trend, tourist arrivals by air continue to be predominant. More than 70 per cent of all visitors arrived by air in 1993 (TAT, 1993b). Bangkok airport is under considerable pressure from overcrowded facilities. At the same time, more than two dozen provincial airports including Phuket, Chiang Mai,

Chiang Rai, Pattaya, Surat Thani and Phitsanulok are undergoing renovation.

In the hotel industry, the boom in the late 1980s has brought about a continuous growth in the supply of hotel rooms in major Thailand destinations, despite the decline in international arrivals in the early 1990s. Table 16.4 exhibits the number of establishments and rooms in the major cities and indicates that the room stock had increased by 43.6 per cent between 1989 and 1993, while hotel occupancies dropped by 14.4 per cent during the same period. Although tourist arrivals picked up again in 1993, the influx of low-yield arrivals to Thailand did little to ease the situation for luxury hotels. The oversupply of hotel rooms has become an obvious problem for luxury hotels in Thailand, which are ill-geared to cater to the new source of tourists from China and other neighbouring countries who demand economy and budget-type accommodations.

The Tour business experienced a tough time in the early 1990s, with more than 20 per cent of operators closing down due to the Gulf War. Most of the Thai tour operations were small-scale companies with 70 per cent having less than 25 employees (Meyer, 1988). The inbound business was concentrated in the hands of 20 leading ground operators, who handled the mass tourism packages and an estimated 70 per cent of the inbound tourism business (Meyer, 1988). Diethelm Travel, a Thai-Swiss joint venture, is the market leader, which handled 20 per cent of all inbound tour business. Other leading

Table 16.4   Number of establishments and rooms in major cities and average occupancy rate

City		1989	1990	1991	1992	1993	Change 89/93 %
Bangkok:*	E	123	131	143	155	210	70.73
	R	27,117	28,845	31,788	34,611	44,245	63.16
	AOR	87.88	78.14	62.44	53.22	56.56	−31.32
Chiang Mai:	E	248	263	274	303	293	18.15
	R	9,474	10,893	11,845	12,057	14,499	53.04
	AOR	56.27	54.08	50.36	41.34	45.95	−10.32
Pattaya:	E	316	324	300	316	310	−1.90
	R	18,097	22,005	24,414	24,957	24,722	36.61
	AOR	58.27	53.60	50.57	45.45	42.49	−15.78
Phuket:	E	203	207	237	261	264	30.05
	R	12,259	13,160	14,912	17,355	17,426	42.15
	AOR	63.08	63.38	57.59	39.63	59.85	−3.23
Hat Yai:	E	79	83	86	88	82	3.80
	R	6,233	7,107	7,501	7,693	7,678	23.18
	AOR	61.25	60.29	55.14	44.14	50.01	−11.24

*Bangkok excluded small size accommodations.
E=Establishments
R=Rooms
AOR=Average Occupancy Rate
Source: TAT (1993b)

agents were Lucky Travel Service, Siam Express, Thaisinn Express, Turismo Thai and World Travel.

Tourism Plans and Organizations

Like any developing country, government support is an important factor for tourism development in Thailand. Thai government involvement in the tourism industry is mainly demonstrated in two areas: tourism planning and the organization of tourism.

Tourism development plan

As the Thai tourism industry developed rapidly in the 1970s, the government realized the benefit of tourism growth to the country's economy. In 1977, tourism was for the first time incorporated into the National Economic and Social Development Plan (NESDP). In the First Five-Year Tourism Development Plan (1977–81), the promotion of tourism was one of the principal measures designed to increase foreign exchange earnings and help reduce the national deficit in the balance of trade and payments (Meyer, 1988).

The encouragement of tourism development by the Thai government also included a budgetary allocation to TAT. The country's tourism revenue grew from 4.6 million baht in 1977 to 21.4 million baht in 1981. This apparent success led the government to aim for projected tourism revenues of 49 million baht at the end of the Second Five-Year Tourism Development Plan period (1982–86). However, this objective was not met. The drop in tourist arrivals in 1983 marked a slowdown in the Thai tourism income growth. By the end of 1986, the tourism revenue barely reached 37 million baht, or 24.5 per cent below the government's projection (Meyer, 1988).

The Third Five-Year Tourism Development Plan (1987–91) was produced under a set of three major economic conditions and problems – namely a balance of trade deficit, unemployment and uneven income distribution. In order to solve such problems, tourism development and promotion were used as major instruments to realize the national development targets. Two courses of action for tourism development were set in the Third Tourism Development Plan.

The first action emphasized marketing, marketing research, advertising and promotion, and public relations. The Plan was to target 'quality tourists', especially European and Japanese tourists, who were perceived as affluent enough to be high spending in Thailand. The second action focused on the development and conservation of tourism resources including the improvement of facilities.

To implement this plan, TAT received budgetary provisions for the development of the tourist destinations for the amount of 20 million baht annually in 1987. The amount was increased to 150 million baht annually during the 1990–91 period. Additional loan projects of 1,544.9 million baht, under the overseas Economic Cooperation's Fund of Japan, were approved by the Thai government in 1988 to improve tourist facilities, preserve the environment and develop convenient transportation routes. A total of 1,310.9 million baht was distributed to 73 tourism development projects in eight geographic areas between 1989 and 1991 (TAT, 1992). The allocation of 73 funded projects by geographic region is detailed in Figure 16.3.

The fourth Five-Year Tourism Development Plan (1992–96) was developed in a crisis environment, and the Plan focused on the renovation, restoration and maintenance of tourism resources. Popular tourist destinations received priority with regard to quality and environmental improvements. In 1993, another 1,445.97 million baht was allocated by OECF Loan to implement 28 sub-projects and a consulting project during 1994–98.

Overall, the four Five-Year Tourism Development Plans provide guidelines for both public and private investments in the tourism industry. The Tourism Authority of Thailand (TAT) and Thai Airways International (THAI) are considered the most important pillars for Thai tourism and the facilitation of the implementation of the national tourism plans.

Tourism Authority of Thailand (TAT)

In order to promote Thailand, the Thai government set up the Tourist Organization of Thailand (TOT) in 1960 (Prachuabmoh, 1990). In 1976, TOT was upgraded and renamed as Tourism Authority of Thailand (TAT), which

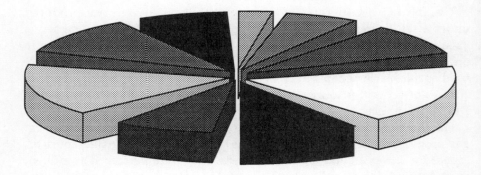

Figure 16.3 Tourism development programme (number of sub-project regions).
Source: TAT (1992).

reported directly to the Prime Minister. With the continuous tourism growth, TAT expanded its authority. The number of TAT employees increased from 52 staff in 1960 to 878 in 1993 (TAT, 1993a) and the TAT has grown into a comprehensive organization encompassing an administrative division, a marketing division and a planning and development division (Figure 16.4), and it has 39 domestic and overseas market promotion offices (TAT, 1993a).

During the period of the First National Tourism Plan (1977–81), TAT had very limited power to manage the tourism industry as a whole, and its major duty was tourism promotion. The limitation of TAT resulted in the lack of macro control in the Thai tourism sector. In the Second National Tourism Plan, TAT was given more authority in tourism development activities (Meyer, 1988). Today, TAT is represented on bodies deciding certain policies such as domestic aviation and transportation, and able to 'push' for solutions through mechanisms such as the Joint Government and Private Sectors Sub-Committee to solve tourism-related problems.

During the Second Five-Year Tourism Plan (1982–86), TAT set its objective to promote Thai tourism, safeguard the overall tourism development, and conduct tourism research (TAT, 1993a). To achieve these objectives, TAT took some major actions in tourism development and promotion.

Tourism Development
The first action was to establish and implement an overall plan for the conservation and development of tourist destinations. In response to tourist demand, public utilities and facilities were developed in selected tourist attractions. The second action for TAT was to constantly strive to raise the quality of services and all facilities, which meant some reorganization of the industry and doing everything possible to protect the welfare of the tourists.

The third action involved the development of tourism personnel. The TAT joined with various educational institutions, government agencies and private companies in producing and developing qualified personnel in the tourism field to meet the demands of the tourism industry.

Tourism Promotion
The first action was to promote leisure tourism in overseas markets. TAT organized sales promotion activities and cooperated with related agencies both in the public and private sectors in advertising and public relations. The second action was to promote Thailand as an international convention destination. In addition, TAT also participated in international meetings,

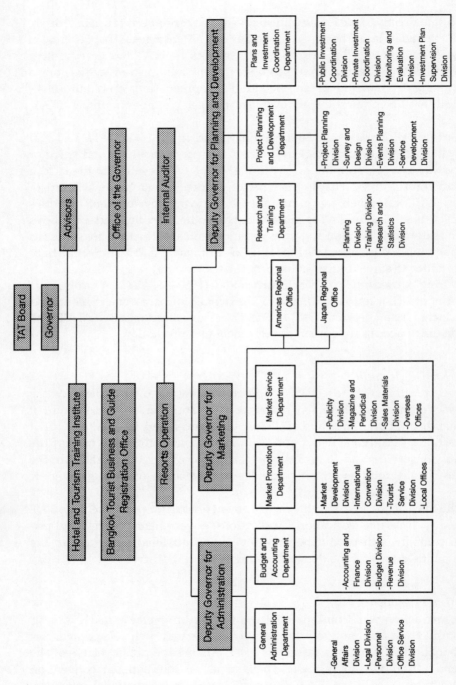

Figure 16.4 Organization chart of Tourism Authority of Thailand.
Source: TAT (1990b).

sales promotion and trade shows to bid for the host of international conventions.

Research and Development
In 1988–89, TAT conducted eight survey and research study projects. The findings of these research projects were used as guidelines for the development of destinations and tourism services (TAT, 1989).

Thai Airways International (THAI)

Thai Airways International Ltd (THAI), the second pillar of Thai tourism, is the national carrier of Thailand and operates international, regional and domestic flights. THAI was founded in August 1959 as a joint venture enterprise with Scandinavian Airlines System (SAS). In 1977, THAI ended the partnership with SAS, and listed its stocks in the Thai stock exchange in 1991. Thai government owned 92 per cent stocks and only floated 8 per cent on the stock market (Jon, 1995).

As THAI is the country's only national carrier, it is financially supported, protected and controlled by the government. One of Thai's objectives is to support Thailand's tourism industry (THAI, 1994). A total of 9.66 billion baht were invested in promoting THAI in 1994 (Muqbil, 1994). In conjunction with TAT, Thai's new advertising campaign – 'Smooth as Silk' – was proved successful and won two awards in the PATA 1993 conference and New York Art Direction Club (THAI, 1994). During the financial year 1993/1994, its net profit reached US$125 million (*Airline Financial News*, 1994). It planned to set up a subsidiary airline in which the private sector would hold a majority stake to handle domestic fights in 1993 (Barnetson, 1993).

Problems in the Thai Tourism Industry

The recent slow growth of Thai's tourism sector could be attributed to the long-term problems that are inherent in Thailand's economy and society. They are the degraded environment, inadequate infrastructure, safety issue and negative image of sex tourism.

Deteriorated environment

The rapid industrialization during the last two decades accelerated the environmental degradation in and around the cities, resorts and beaches of Thailand. Pattaya, billed as the queen of South-east Asia's beach resorts, is presently in serious trouble. Much of the resort's problems stems from its success. Starting as a tiny fishing village, Pattaya has expanded in less than 20 years into a fast-paced pleasure centre attracting nearly 3 million visitors a year (Wedel, 1991). By neglecting the balance between the environment and the economic interests, the overdeveloping resort city lies amid serious pollution today.

Present sewage systems in Pattaya can handle a mere 30 per cent of the raw sewage flowing into the bay (Rolnick, 1994). Local and international publications reported that several Pattaya beaches had coliform bacteria counts of more than 1,600 millilitres – well above the 1,000 mark considered the maximum for safe swimming (Wedel, 1991).

Phuket, another resort area, might turn into a duplicate of Pattaya without a long-term plan and intervention by the local government. Tourist destinations like Chiang Mai and Samui Island in particular also face physical deterioration caused by the destruction of the natural environment and a lack of regulation of land use and constructions.

The Environmental Protection Act was passed in 1989 to protect the environment. The National Environment Board was empowered to designate environmentally protected areas and pollution controlled areas to facilitate conservation (Barnetson, 1993). The first areas to be protected include Phuket and Pattaya.

In addition, Economic Cooperation Fund (OECF) Loan from Japan is being allocated for conservation and preservation of the environment, natural heritage and resources (*PATA Travel News*, 1993). The First Phase loan projects were scattered over Thailand and aimed at improving access to the tourist destinations between 1987 and 1991, and the Second Phase projects (between 1992 and 1995) concentrated on environment improvement in the main tourist clusters of north, north-east and south Thailand.

Inadequate infrastructure

The development of infrastructure services – covering public utilities, amenities, transport, communications and energy services – cannot meet the demand of Thailand's fast growing economy. Traffic in Bangkok has adversely affected the average length of tourist stay, room rates and incomes of hundreds of shops and restaurants, which depend on earning from tourism. Many tourists bypass Bangkok and travel straight to other destinations in South Thailand (Muqbil, 1994).

In addition, the construction of public utilities has slipped so far behind that it may take as long as five years before they can meet the demand from the major tourist cities. For instance, in Pattaya, each hotel with more than 90 rooms must have a water-treatment system (Rolnick, 1994). Due to the insufficient infrastructure, international investors sought alternative countries in South-east Asia for their investments (Chon *et al.*, 1993).

In order to improve the infrastructure and service, the Thai government has taken some positive steps, which include the new Bangkok expressways, an expanded telecommunications network and a new 'state-of-the-art' international airport in Bangkok (Barnetson, 1993). A US$141 million plan was drafted to rescue Pattaya (*Asia Travel Trade*, 1990). The plan included some major projects: US$12 million to build roads, $8 million to build a city drainage system, $5 million to build pavements on the beaches, and $27 million to add a waste-water treatment system (*Asia Travel Trade*, 1990).

Safety issue

Safety is another concern of tourists to Thailand. In 1993, the Royal Plaza Hotel in the north-east city of Korat collapsed, killing more than 130 guests and staff. The disaster was blamed on poor construction methods and the use of cheaper materials in a three-storey extension, which put too much pressure on the foundations. A spokesman for the Bangkok Metropolitan Authority stated 'there are many buildings in Bangkok with illegal extensions including hotels and retail shops'. City and provincial authors released a list of guilty firms and admitted they did know of the infringements for years, but could do nothing about them (Boyd, 1993).

The Government has set up regulations to deal with the safety issue. TAT pledges to conduct a nationwide inspection of hotels for unsafe modifications. The checks will focus on properties built or extended within the last decade, looking at defects from poor design and use of sub-standard materials (Boyd, 1993). Benefits may be available for existing hotels that are willing to spend money on improving their property to cater for higher-yielding visitors (Boyd, 1994).

Negative image of sex tourism

The image of 'sexual paradise' has been affiliated to Thailand since the Vietnam War (1962–75). In the late 1960s, for example, about 40,000 US servicemen were stationed at air bases in Thailand, which conditioned the demand for sex services from local women (Singh *et al.*, 1989). With the withdrawal of American servicemen from Vietnam in the 1970s, sex services remained in Thailand and served the needs of a different category of visitors. An estimated 60 per cent of the 2 million tourists visiting Thailand were allegedly drawn by bargain-priced sex in the 1970s and the early 1980s (Singh *et al.*, 1989).

With the economic development in the 1970s, Thai women migrated to urban areas where there were only limited opportunities to join the industrial workforce and sex tourism provided them with important economic incentives. In 1970, Bangkok with a population of approximately 3 million had an estimated 20,000 prostitutes. Between 1970 and 1977, tourist arrivals in Bangkok almost doubled from 628,700 to 1,22,700, of which two-thirds were males (Singh *et al.*, 1989).

The emergence of AIDS in Thailand coincided with the boom in international tourism during the late 1980s. Thailand found itself facing a 'sexual paradise' image problem connected with AIDs and prostitution. The risk of contracting AIDS discouraged many tourists from visiting Thailand (Chon *et al.*, 1993). Although reported full-blown AIDS cases in Thailand so far only represent a small share of AIDS cases throughout the Asia Pacific region, the nation has still to bear the negative image for its sex trade. Studies showed that more than 300,000 Thais were thought to be HIV positive, and this figure was expected to increase rapidly (Chon *et al.*, 1993). Due to the bad image of the sex trade, many family holiday visitors stay away from Thailand.

TAT has actively campaigned against the sex trade and officially stated 'sex tourists are no longer welcome in Thailand'. In 1992, TAT promoted a 'Women's Visit Thailand Year'. The main objectives were to rectify the negative image of Thai women among foreigners and to attract female tourists from other countries to Thailand (Corben, 1991).

The Root-Causes of Thai Problems and Suggested Solutions

The root-cause of the problems in Thai tourism could be attributed to the lack of government policy enforcement and industry practice. Reports indicated that the Thai tourism industry has developed many plans and regulations, but they have never been adequately enforced (Muqbil, 1993; Barnetson, 1993). The TAT stated that there was a lack of proper public relations activities to promote the plans and regulations (Muqbil, 1993). In Thailand, many public departments are involved in the tourism activities, such as the Board of Investment, Thai Airway International, the State Railways, Ministry of Finance and the Forestry Department. However, there was not enough cooperation, coordination and assistance from the departments concerned. As a result, work plans and projects on development and promotion could not proceed as effectively and timely as desired (TAT, 1991).

A composite body should be developed to provide constructive suggestions. It should act as a discussion forum and jointly determine policies on matters affecting the tourism industry as a whole. TAT should play a major role in the management of the tourism industry and developing the mechanism for policy enforcement.

Research suggested that the future role of TAT should be directed towards developing, conserving and monitoring tourist resources (Muqbil, 1993). A large proportion of the government budget should be reallocated for physical rather than market development. Thailand Development Research Institute (TDRI) suggested that the marketing budget should come from a special tax levied on the tourists sector. For instance, Singapore now levies a 4 per cent tax on tourist hotel rooms so that these special taxes can be used to support activities that directly benefit the tourism industry.

Corruption and a bureaucratic system were also blamed as the root-cause of Thai tourism problems. For instance, the 1979 Building Control Act and its six amendments require all hotels to provide a construction blueprint to the

Bangkok Metropolitan Authority (BMA) for an approval. However, due to the long bureaucratic delays and rampant corruption, many building constructions bypass the regulation through illegal channels, which resulted in the collapse of Royal Plaza Hotel in 1993 and the fire at the First Hotel in 1987.

In Pattaya, officials admitted that the police department was weakened by lucrative pay-offs from go-go bar owners, mini-bus operators and gamblers (Wedel, 1991). Industry investors suggested that the Thai government should 'clean the house' and safeguard the quality of Thai tourism. Disciplinary actions are needed to punish corrupt tourism officials, and the actions must be seen by the public (*Asian Hotelier*, 1993).

Conclusion: Future Outlook for the Thai Tourism Industry

The Thai government has realized the urgency of improving tourism conditions as the industry is important to the nation's economy. Policies and regulations have been developed to improve the quality of tourism infrastructure and service. It is expected that Thailand's infrastructure bottleneck will ease. By 1997, communications are expected to improve when Thailand gets an additional 3-million telephone lines in Bangkok and rural areas as well as the country's first telecommunications satellite (Chon *et al.*, 1993). The second international airport in Bangkok will be capable of handling 20 to 30 million passengers annually by the year 2010, which will relieve the congestion at Bangkok's Don Muang Airport (Chon *et al.*, 1993). However, for future success, both the public and private sectors need to put prime focus on policy enforcement. Government departments need to be well coordinated in order to attain the objectives and targets. Legal actions are needed for corruption and environmental deterioration.

In addition, new markets and a new image need to be developed to maintain tourism growth. Pattaya has tried to reposition itself as a family resort. Tour operators suggested that Pattaya would be a successful destination to inter-Asian travellers as the city provides not only beach but many urban activities. In order to catch the Asian convention market, the National Convention Center in Bangkok was opened to the public four years ago. Thailand has won the bid to host the 1996 annual PATA conference and travel mart, a move that is expected to trigger a major effort to solve the industry's many problems and earn tourism a greater degree of recognition on the national economic agenda.

As Indo-China has gradually opened its market to the outside world, Thailand intends to market itself as a gateway to countries such as Cambodia, Laos and Vietnam. However, it is facing stiff competition from other countries like Singapore. Singapore's unique selling propositions such as safety, cleanliness, strong infrastructure and public convenience, have all marketed the country as a very attractive transit centre for tourists. Singapore will be an important competitor to Thailand, not only on its own merits but also as a gateway to the neighbouring countries.

Thailand's past experiences show that tourism management demands not only planning but also policy enforcement. Whether Thailand can remain as one of Asia's popular holiday destinations will mainly depend on the depth of commitment from government, tourism industry and the lessons learned from the past.

Bibliography

Airline Financial News (1994) Thai looks profitable before Airbus deliveries. *Airline Financial News*, 26 December, 2.

Asian Hotelier (1993) Action now over Korat. *Asian Hotelier*, October, 2.

Asia Travel Trade (1990) Thailand at a glance. *Asia Travel Trade*, November, 56.

Barnetson, W. (1993) Thai me up, Thai me down. *Asia Travel Trade*, November, 31–3.

Boyd, A. (1993) Korat cracks covered up. *Asian Hotelier*, October 1–2.

Boyd, A. (1994) Room glut forces Thai government action. *Asian Hotelier*, October, 1.

Chon, K.S., Amrik, S. and Milula, J. (1993) Thailand's tourism and hotel industry. *The Cornell H.R.A. Quarterly*, **34** (3), 43–9.

Corben, R. (1991) Women's visit Thailand years. *Asia Travel Trade*, November 52–3.

EIU (1992) Thailand. *EIU International Tourism Reports*, No 1. London: The Economist Intelligence Unit.

Jon, A. (1995) Declaration of airfare war on routes to the Far East. *The Times*, 4 January, 3.

Meyer, W. (1988) *Beyond the Mask*. SaarbrÅcken Fort Lauderdale: Verlag Breitenbach Publishers.

Muqbil, A. (1993) The rise and fall of Chatrachai. *PATA Travel News*, September 12–14.

Muqbil, A. (1994) All set for a comeback. *PATA Travel News*, Feburary, 34–9.

PATA Travel News (1993) Upbeat despite problems. *PATA Travel News*, October, 31–4.

Prachuabmoh, D. (1990) Message from Governor. *TAT 30 Years*. TAT, 9.

Rolnick, H. (1994) Dream sinks in a sea of pollution. *Asian Hotelier*, January, 8–9.

Singh, T.V., Theuns, H.L. and Go, F.M. (1989) *Towards Appropriate Tourism: The Case of Developing Countries*. Frankfurt: Peter Lang.

TAT (1988a), *Tourism in Thailand*. Tourism Authority of Thailand.

TAT (1988b), *Annual Reports 1988*. Tourism Authority of Thailand.

TAT (1989) *Annual Report, 1989*. Tourism Authority of Thailand.

TAT (1990a) *Annual Report, 1990*. Tourism Authority of Thailand.

TAT (1990b) *30 Years*. Tourism Authority of Thailand.

TAT (1991) *Tourism Development Plan 1989-1991*. Tourism Authority of Thailand.

TAT (1992) Thailand Tourism Development. *Tourism Development Program Under Economic Cooperation Fund (OECF) Loan Plan Phase I 1988–1993*. Tourism Authority of Thailand.

TAT (1993a), *Annual Report, 1993*. Tourism Authority of Thailand.

TAT (1993b), *Thailand Tourism Statistical Report 1993*. Tourism Authority of Thailand.

THAI (1994). *The Story of THAI – 34 Anniversary*. Tourism Auhtority of Thailand.

Wedel, P. (1991) Rescuing Pattaya. *Asia Travel Trade*, November, 44–7.

17

Vietnam: Tourism in an economy in transition

H. LEO THEUNS

Introduction

The Socialist Republic of Vietnam is situated in South-east Asia and stretches over 1,600 km along the eastern coast of the Indochinese Peninsula. It is bordered to the north by the People's Republic of China, to the west by Laos and Cambodia, to the east by the South China Sea, and to the south by the Gulf of Thailand. The country is S-shaped, broad in the north and south and very narrow in the centre, where at one point it is only 50 km wide. The capital Hanoi, situated in the north on the Red River, 72 km inland from the Gulf of Tonkin, has about 2.1 million inhabitants. Vietnam has three distinct geographical areas: Bac Bo (the north), Trung Bo (the central region) and Nam Bo (the south), which correspond to the French administrative divisions of Tonkin, Annam and Cochinchina (Robinson and Cummings, 1991: 31).

Because of its wide range of latitudes and altitudes Vietnam has a diverse climate. Although the entire country lies in the tropics, local conditions vary from frosty winters in the far northern hills to the year-round equatorial warmth of the Mekong Delta. At sea level, the mean annual temperature is about 27 degrees centigrade in the south, falling to about 21 degrees centigrade in the north. Average humidity in Ho Chi Minh City varies between 70 in the winter months and 84 in summer. As about one-third of Vietnam is more than 500 metres above sea level, much of the country enjoys a subtropical or – above 2000 metres – even a temperate climate. Vietnam lies in the South-east Asian monsoon zone. Between October or November and March the north-east monsoon, which mainly affects Vietnam north of Danang, brings relatively dry weather. Between April or May and October the south-west monsoon brings warm, damp weather to the whole country except for those areas sheltered by mountains. Between July and November, violent and unpredictable typhoons often develop over the ocean east of Vietnam and hit the north and central region.

In 1989 Vietnam's population was 64.4 million (General Statistical Office 1991: 110). For 1992 the UNDP (1993) lists an estimate of about 69.3 million. About 80 per cent of the population live in rural areas. Almost 87 per cent belong to the group of the Khin or ethnic Vietnamese. The official language is Vietnamese, and although some of the older Vietnamese still have a good command of French, the international lingua franca today is English. The principal religion is Buddhism. Since 1976 Vietnam has been a reunified independent state.

In 1990 gross social product (GSP) in constant 1982 prices was 392,665 million Dong. In 1990 a UNDP team led by Van Arkadie concluded that until more work is done, perhaps all that can be said is that the Gross Domestic Product (GDP) per capita lies between US$100 and US$200 (Van Arkadie *et al.*, 1990: 32). Gross National Product (GNP) per capita in 1992 was estimated at US$220 (UNDP, 1993: III). Not surprisingly over 50 per cent of Vietnam's population belong to the group of the poor as defined by the UNDP (*The Economist* 1994: 120). Agriculture, providing almost 72 per cent of total employment, contributed in 1991 to an estimated 39 per cent of GDP, whereas industry, employing only 11 per cent, contributed 29 per cent and services 32 per cent (UNDP, 1993: IV). In January 1993, 28 per cent of the rural workforce were underemployed and 22 per cent of the urban workforce were unemployed (Anon, 1993a: 3,190).

In 1991 Vietnam recorded estimated visible trade deficits of US$200 million in convertible currencies and US$23 million in non-convertible currencies. The current accounts with the convertible and the non-convertible currency countries showed estimated deficits of US$286 and US$154 million respectively (IMF, 1992). In 1992, for the first time since 1976, a visible trade surplus was recorded (Anon, 1993a: 3,190).

Tourism Assets

Vietnam has 3,260 km of coastline, a highly varied climate and topography and a rich history and culture. Numerous beaches, peninsulas and islands can be found along Vietnam's coast. In the interior the landscape is varied and features mountains, lakes, waterfalls, hot springs and passes with magnificent views. In the north, Halong Bay with its 3,000 islands rising from the waters of the Gulf of Tonkin, is one of the natural marvels of Vietnam. The islands spread out over an area of 1,500 sq km and are dotted with innumerable beaches and grottoes. In the centre, the ancient imperial city of Hué comprises palaces, citadels, imperial tombs and pagodas of the kings of the nineteenth century Nguyen dynasty. In the south, a major attraction is the tunnel network of the Cu Chi District, now part of Greater Ho Chi Minh City, which facilitated Viet Cong control of a large rural area 30 km from Saigon.

These few examples give an impression of the varied tourism assets of Vietnam.

Based on an inventory of present assets the two volume 1991 UNDP/WTO tourism sector plan distinguishes four primary tourism destination areas (*pôles de développement*): Hanoi and Halong Bay, Danang and Hué, Dalat and Nha Trang, and Ho Chi Minh City. The main products envisaged in the UNDP/WTO plan are basically of the beach holiday and sea and river cruise types (UNDP/WTO 1991a, and 1991). Experience in Central Europe also indicates that a market for touring holidays exists, which responds to the curiosity motive of Western tourists for travel to countries that, until recently, were behind the iron or bamboo curtain (Theuns and Biernacka, 1994: 6).

Visitor Traffic

Tourism to Vietnam consists predominantly of ethnic traffic, comprising both Vietnamese with a foreign nationality and Vietnamese citizens residing abroad, known as Viet Kieu. Since 1987, however, the share of non-ethnic tourism has significantly increased (Table 17.1).

The 1991 projection of arrivals up to 2005, broken down according to primary destination areas and main type of travel, is given in Table 17.2.

Vietnam Tourism estimated that in 1992 a total of 350,000 arrivals would be realized, whereas according to Saigon Tourism the number of arrivals increased from 110,000 in 1988 to 550,000 in 1992 (EIU 1993: 63). Nguyen Son Tra (1993: 31) mentions 440,000 international tourist arrivals in 1992 and provides a projection for the years up to the year 2000, which is considerably above that given in the UNDP/WTO plan. The diverging data demonstrate the lack of reliable statistical information and therefore the inadequate base for forecasting. The fact that the 1991 UNDP/WTO plan has projected for Dalat/Nha Trang between 1995 and 2005 an increase in leisure tourism of over 500 per cent without any concomitant increase in business tourism – business travel is supposed to stagnate – raises doubts about the validity of the forecasting exercise. In view of the dearth of meaningful and reliable information on tourist arrivals, demand projections made in the 1991 UNDP

Table 17.1   Tourist arrivals by broad categories 1986–89

Category	1986	%	1987	%	1988	%	1989	%
Non-Comecon	4,581	8.4	7,581	10.3	17,865	16.2	40,966	21.8
Comecon	6,300	11.6	6,600	9.0	16,028	14.5	31,723	16.9
Total non-Vietnamese	10,881	20.0	14,181	19.4*	33,893	30.7	72,689	38.8*
Vietnamese (Viet Kieu)	43,472	80.0	59,102	80.6	76,497	69.3	114,844	61.2
Grand total	54,353	100	73,283	100	110,390	100	187,573	100

*Does not add up due to rounding.
Source: Based on UNDP/WTO (1991c)

tourism sector plan are a heroic exercise in planning without facts. Not surprisingly a need was felt for an additional plan. In 1994 a Masterplan for Tourism Development in Vietnam, 1995–2010 has been elaborated. This plan is now under consideration by the Government.

According to an official Vietnam News Agency report, pleasure tourists accounted for only 30 to 40 per cent of the total number of people visiting Vietnam in 1991 (*Bangkok Post*, 1992). The UNDP/WTO projected share for 1992 is 32.5 per cent (Table 7.2). Most tourists used to arrive through Bangkok, where they obtained a visa as part of a group tour arranged by a Bangkok-based travel agent. Now that the regulations for visa and travel permits have been relaxed, Hong Kong and Singapore have also emerged as important gateways.

According to Saigon Tourism in 1992 the major source markets in descending order of importance were Taiwan, Japan, France, South Korea, Singapore, Canada, Germany and the USA. The main change to take place within the past few years is that arrivals from Asian countries, particularly the economic 'tigers' and Japan, have come to dominate in place of visitors from Comecon countries (EIU, 1993: 65). The Institute for Tourism Development Research (ITDR) in a recent interview confirmed that Asian countries are considered to be the major source markets for the development of tourism in Vietnam

Table 17.2 Projection of tourist arrivals up to 2005 for each primary destination area according to main type of travel

Destination area/type of tourism	1992	%	1995	%	2000	%	2005	%
Hanoi/hai Phong								
Leisure	4,538	8.5	24,976	19.5	52,645	14.8	105,680	15.4
Business	49,039	91.5	103,132	80.5	301,944	85.2	580,028	84.6
Total	53,557	100	128,108	100	354,589	100	685,708	100
Da Nang/Hue								
Leisure	17,690	78.9	34,648	68.2	41,577	68.2	48,507	66.7
Business	4,745	21.1	16,133	31.8	19,359	31.8	24,199	33.3
Total	22,435	100	50,781	100	60,936	100	72,706	100
Dalat/Nha Trang								
Leisure	2,607	22.2	28,380	70.4	104,516	89.7	186,285	94.0
Business	9,110	77.8	11,957	29.6	11,957	10.3	11,957	6.0
Total	11,717	100	40,334	100	116,473	100	198,242	100
HCM City/Mekong								
Leisure	28,140	37.5	59,057	26.7	87,156	21.6	128,335	20.1
Business	46,975	62.5	161,804	73.3	316,898	78.4	511,273	79.9
Total	75,115	100	220,861	100	404,054	100	639,608	100
All Vietnam								
Leisure	52,957	32.5	147,061	33.4	285,894	30.5	468,807	29.4
Business	109,869	67.5	293,026	66.6	650,158	69.5	1,127,457	70.6
Total	162,844	100	440,087	100	936,052	100	1,596,264	100

Source: Based on UNDP/WTO/IRDT (1991)

(personal communication by Vu Tuan Canh and Duong Xuan Hoi, Hanoi, August 1994).

Accommodation and Other Tourism Facilities

The information on existing accommodation facilities is also extremely limited. According to the UNDP/WTO study there were 7,477 rooms in hotels and 11,400 rooms in guest-houses in 1989. The Report of a 1990 workshop on Tourism Manpower Development organized by ESCAP (1990: 197) contains higher figures for hotel accommodation: a total of 11,498 rooms, of which 4,995 are of international and 6,503 are of national standard. The broad regional distribution of hotel capacity (Table 17.3) shows that in room capacity the centre of gravity is in the south, even more so for international-oriented capacity, of which more than half is in the south and one-fifth is in Ho Chi Minh City alone. Present-day capacity is much higher. A 1991 source (Le Ngoc Hue, 1991: 155) reports for Ho Chi Minh City 1,382 rooms of international standard, or an increase of 50 per cent since 1989. In Hanoi and Ho Chi Minh City, hotel accommodation is relatively internationally oriented: 74 per cent of capacity caters for foreign tourists as compared to 59 per cent in Vietnam as a whole. Despite this Hanoi is at present confronted by a shortage of international standard hotel rooms, reflected in high average annual occupancy rates of 85–90 per cent, whereas in some other parts of the country average occupancy rates of not more than 20–50 per cent are attained.

Local tour operating is in the hands of official bodies such as Vietnam Tourism, Hanoi Tourism and Saigon Tourism. Recently some small privately owned agencies have emerged. Hanoi has an ample supply of small privately owned art and souvenir shops where good quality art and handicrafts can be bought (silk paintings, silverware, lacquerware, embroidery).

Table 17.3   Regional distribution of hotel room and hotel bed capacity 1989

Region	International standard Rooms	Rooms %	Beds	National standard Rooms	Rooms %	Beds	Total Rooms	Rooms %	Beds
North	1,225	27.8	2,475	1,120	36.4	2,275	2,345	31.4	4,750
of which Hanoi	(479)	(10.9)	(903)	(100)	(3.3)	(200)	(579)	(7.7)	(1,103)
Central	867	19.7	1,780	1,036	33.7	2,114	1,903	25.5	3,894
South	2,312	52.5	4,352	917	29.8	1,179	3,229	43.2	6,131
of which HCM City	(920)	(20.9)	(1,826)	(381)	(12.4)	(542)	(1,301)	(17.4)	(2,368)
Total	4,404	100	8,607	3,073	100*	6,168	7,477	100*	14,775

*Does not add up due to rounding.
Source: Based on UNDP/WTO (1991b)

Transportation

Since almost all international tourists arrive by plane the adequacy of air access facilities is of utmost importance.

The number of internationally scheduled airlines servicing Ho Chi Minh City has increased from 2 in 1987 to 11 in 1989. Mid-1991 Vietnam was served by 12 scheduled international airlines, including Thai International, Air France, Garuda, Aeroflot, and Singapore Airlines operating a joint service with Vietnam Airlines (Hamill, 1991). In December 1991 Hong Kong's Cathay Pacific resumed regular flights to Hanoi and Ho Chi Minh City (Young, 1992). At the end of 1992, a total of 15 scheduled international airlines were flying to Vietnam. The national carrier, Vietnam Airlines, operates scheduled international services to Bangkok, Singapore, Phnom Penh and Vientiane. Its fleet consists of three Ilyushin Il-18, six Tupolev Tu-134 A, two Tu – 134 B, eleven Antonov An-24, three Yak-40, and two An-26. In 1992 the first three Western-built planes were leased. The fleet of ageing Tupolevs is now being phased out.

Vietnam has two international airports: Noi Bai Airport at Hanoi and Tan Son Nhut Airport at Ho Chi Minh City. Danang can also handle international traffic. There are 12 domestic airports. Airport facilities at Ho Chi Minh City are adequate. The terminal building at Hanoi's Noi Bai Airport, which is outdated and not conducive to an orderly circulation of passengers, is in the process of being redeveloped.

Vietnam has about 100,000 km of roads, of which about 11,000 km are sealed. In the north most of the existing roads date back to the French colonial period and are poorly maintained. For example, to travel by road to Dien Bien Phu and Lang Son a four-wheel-drive vehicle is necessary. The roads in the centre and south are from a more recent date, but particularly in the centre they have been damaged by bombings during the Vietnam War. The main link between Hanoi in the north and Ho Chi Minh City in the south – Highway One – is a pot-holed, two-lane road. There is in general an accumulated maintenance backlog, except for a few sections in the south, which covers all aspects of maintenance: resurfacing, pot-hole repair and ditch cleaning. Some roads are rather heavily used: traffic on the Hanoi–Hai Phong and Ho Chi Minh City–Vung Tau routes may amount to 2,500 vehicles a day. Due to the poor road conditions and river crossings, often to be made by ferry boat, an average speed of only about 30 km per hour can be made on many stretches. Hanoi and Ho Chi Minh City used to have few or no taxis, but recently radio-controlled taxis have started operation. For Hanoi this has meant replacing bicycle rickshaws – a revolution in public transportation. For short and long excursions chauffeur-driven cars can be hired.

Vietnam has about 2,600 km of rail with more than 260 stations. Most of the railway track is narrow gauge. Only about 500 km conforms to international standards. The railway covers the whole length of the country and opens up areas that are often inaccessible by road. There are two standard-gauge rail connections from Hanoi with China. One of these is of particular tourism interest because it enables tourists to travel to Peking by train and to continue on the Trans Siberia Express. A 1,726 km metre-gauge track connects Ho Chi Minh City with Hanoi – a journey that normally takes at least three days. A new fast service, twice a week in both directions, is timed to take only 48 hours.

Economic Impact

Thus far tourism has been of a limited, but growing significance to Vietnam's balance of payments. Gross foreign exchange receipts from tourism as a percentage of the value of exports increased from an average of 2.3 in 1975–80 to 5.1 in 1985–89. Foreign currency is desperately needed to buy everything from heavy industrial machinery to medical and educational supplies for children. Tourism is seen as one way of bringing in foreign currency, and the central and provincial governments have therefore started to develop tourist services.

According to the 1991 UNDP/WTO study, turnover in the tourism sector in 1989 amounted to US$140 million. It is not clear whether this amount relates purely to international tourism or includes turnover from domestic tourism as well. Assuming that the US$140 million pertain to international tourists only, average expenditure per foreign tourist in 1989 would have been US$746. In view of the number of ethnic Vietnamese in total foreign tourist arrivals, however, it is likely that the expenditure per foreign tourist is much lower. The UNDP/WTO study states that 40 per cent of turnover is in US dollars. If this is to be considered turnover from foreign tourism, the average expenditure per foreign tourist – including ethnic Vietnamese – amounts to US$299. Another source gives figures of foreign exchange earnings leading to quite different results (Table 17.4).

The fact that there is no plausible explanation for the decreasing receipts per foreign arrival since 1987 casts serious doubts on the reliability of these data on gross foreign exchange earnings. Data on gross foreign exchange earnings provided by the EIU (1993: 63, 66) are unclear and/or inconsistent.

Table 17.4   Foreign exchange earnings from tourism (million US$) 1986–90

Year	Foreign exchange earnings (1)	arrivals (2)	1/2
1986	32	54,353	589
1987	46	73,238	628
1988	64	110,390	580
1989	68	187,573	363
1990	75	250,000	300

Source: Vietnam Tourism (1991)

As far as employment in tourism is concerned the only information available is that for hotels the staff–room ratio is approximately 1.7:1. This implies that the hotel sub-sector employed about 12,700 people in 1989. The Research Institute for Foreign Economic Relations (Le Nhat Thuc, 1992: 19) puts the number of employees in the tourism sector at about 25,000 and expects that employment in the tourism industry and tourism-related jobs shall increase to 123,480 in the year 2005.

Further information on the balance of payments, income, and employment effects of tourism in Vietnam is lacking.

Socio-Cultural Impact/Environmental Impact

Since Vietnamese culture and society have withstood or assimilated many outside influences it may be expected that tourism will pose no serious problems. Positive effects are visible in tourism providing a market for silk paintings, silverware and lacquerware and thus reviving traditional handi-craft skills. Well conceived tourism policies and their monitored implementation are needed and may help to prevent possible adverse effects.

Vietnam has no specific laws pertaining to environmental effects from tourism. There is, however, a growing concern for these effects nowadays. With support from Sweden and the UNDP in 1993 a *National Plan for Environment and Sustainable Development: A Framework for Action* (NPESD) has been drawn up and the government has identified seven priority action areas to address environmental problems. Among these are pollution control and waste management, integrated coastal zone management, and creation of national parks, protected areas and wildlife reserves (UNDP, 1993: 13). Successful coastal zone management is a basic element in sustainable beach tourism development. Also a draft basic law on the environment – supported by Germany – has been completed and is now under consideration by the government. The main subjects covered are: protection of natural resources, prevention of air-, water- and soil-pollution, and the establishment of na-tional parks. Legal action is long overdue. Sewerage has up to now been discharged untreated into the rivers as there is no law prohibiting this. Neither has there been a sanction on littering so far. The Law on Foreign Investment (Socialist Republic of Vietnam, 1991), however, stipulates in Article 34 that enterprises with foreign invested capital shall be liable to take the necessary steps to protect the environment in the course of their opera-tion. As part of an extensive national research programme on the environ-ment, in which 140 scientists participated, technical measures for reducing pollution are being studied. Since there is no government department with a specific responsibility for the environment, the secretariat of the national research programme is at the Centre for Natural Resources Management and Environmental Studies (CRES) of Hanoi University.

Economic Renovation

At the Sixth Party Congress held in December 1986 it was decided to restructure the Vietnamese economy. The programme of economic reform is referred to as *doi moi* (renovation) and is called Vietnam's version of perestroika by some outside observers. *Doi moi* stands for many steps such as liberalization of prices, commercialization and privatization, budgetary discipline, and opening up to the outside world. The transition from a command to a market economy has been rather slow. The slow progress towards reform is *inter alia* due to the lack of cooperation of officials in the implementation of new policies. Every level of the bureaucracy is plagued by functionaries who would like to see the reforms fail. Chairman Vo Van Kiet in his December 1991 speech to the National Assembly recognized that the State apparatus and personnel have not kept pace with the new mechanism, 'Many cadres are falling behind the requirements of their tasks, both in capacity and in virtue' (Council of Ministers, 1991: 4).

The government of Vietnam seems determined to continue the open-door policy and to strive for a market economy. It is devising commensurate measures to streamline the government apparatus and to relieve the government budget from the burden of subsidizing unprofitable state enterprises. Government administration should – in Vo Van Kiet's words – shift its emphasis 'from directly interfering in concrete matters of business and production to regulating production and business activities of all economic sectors, by means of laws and various economic levers' (Council of Ministers, 1991: 23). It is clear that these broad policy objectives in aiming at the elimination of bureaucratization, etatism and market distortions will enhance productive capacities in the Vietnamese economy, and as such will also have a beneficial effect on development in the tourism sector.

Foreign Investment

An important action in converting Vietnam to an international market economy was the passing of the Law on Foreign Investment in December 1987, which was amended and supplemented in June 1990. The Law on Foreign Investment sets forth the provisions concerning investment by foreign enterprises and private persons in the Socialist Republic of Vietnam. Foreign organizations and private persons are welcomed and encouraged to invest capital and technology. The State shall guarantee the ownership of the invested capital and other rights. The law allows the establishment of enterprises with 100 per cent foreign capital. Foreign organizations and private persons may invest in Vietnam in any sector of the economy. The State encourages foreign organizations and private persons to invest in five areas, one of which is the foreign exchange-earning services, such as tourism, ship-repair, airport and seaport services. In joint ventures the foreign contribution to the legal capital shall not be less than 30 per cent. The duration of an enterprise with foreign invested capital shall not exceed 20 years. Where necessary, it may be extended for a longer period. The government of Vietnam shall guarantee fair and equitable treatment to foreign enterprises and private persons investing in Vietnam. The invested capital, property and assets shall not be expropriated or requisitioned by administrative procedures, and the enterprises with foreign-invested capital shall not be nationalized. Foreign enterprises and private persons investing in Vietnam shall have the right to remit abroad:

- their share of the profits accruing from business operations;
- payments due to them for the provision of technology or services;
- the principal and interest due on loans made in the course of business operation;
- their invested capital;
- other sums of money and assets in their legal ownership.

Enterprises with foreign investment are normally subject to corporate income tax from 15 to 25 per cent of the earned profits. For oil and gas companies a higher rate will apply. Withholding tax on remittance of profits abroad is between 5 and 10 per cent. Depending on the sector of investment, the geographical area where the investment is made, the scale of investment, the volume of exports and the like factors, the State Committee for Cooperation and Investment (SCCI) may exempt a joint venture from payment of corporate tax for a maximum period of two years, counting from the year in which the joint venture starts making profit, and grant it a 50 per cent reduction of the same tax for a maximum period of two more years. In the course of its operation, losses incurred by a joint venture in any tax year may be carried over to the next year and made up with the profits of the following years but not exceeding five years.

The SCCI is responsible for all matters related to the investment operations of foreign organizations and private persons in Vietnam. More specifically the SCCI has the following rights and responsibilities:

- To assist and guide potential foreign and Vietnamese partners in the negotiation and conclusion of joint venture and business cooperation contracts; to assist and guide foreign organizations and private persons in the establishment of enterprises with 100 per cent foreign capital and to act as a focal point for settlement of any matters related to foreign investment as may be requested by the foreign investors.
- To examine and approve business cooperation and joint venture contracts, authorize the establishment by foreign organizations and private persons of enterprises with 100 per cent foreign capital, and approve the charters of enterprises with foreign invested capital.
- To decide on and grant preferential conditions to enterprises with foreign invested capital and the foreign partners operating under business cooperation contracts.

- To monitor and supervise the execution of business cooperation and joint venture contracts and the operation of the enterprises with 100 per cent foreign capital.
- To analyse the economic operation of enterprises with foreign invested capital.

Vietnam's Law on Foreign Investment, which is one of the world's most liberal laws of this kind (*The Economist*, 1993a: 24), has led to a considerable number of investment projects. Up to October 1991 the SCCI had licenced 39 projects in the tourism sector, with a total capital amount of US$113.8 million, and a foreign share of 65 per cent. In December 1992 the number of licensed tourism projects had grown to 47, with a total capital amount of US$682 million (EIU, 1993: 64). This leads to the conclusion that the scale of tourism projects has increased considerably. Tourism is, together with oil and gas, one of the two leading sectors in foreign investment. The largest projects measured by the amount of investment are in hotel renovation, such as the renovation of the Metropole Hotel in Hanoi. Only a few joint ventures have been involved thus far in building new hotels. The leading tourism investor in Vietnam is Hong Kong with, up to October 1991, 21 projects and a committed amount at the end of 1992 of US$476 million or almost 70 per cent of the total amount of all licensed tourism projects. It is followed by France, which shows a renewed interest in its former colony (Mallet, 1994). Other Asian sources of investment are Singapore, Japan and Thailand.

Tourism Organization

The orderly development of tourism presupposes the existence of an adequate institutional framework. The government institution at central level responsible for tourism is the Vietnam National Administration of Tourism (VNAT), which is directly accountable to the government. The VNAT comprises two distinct 'branches': Vietnam Tourism and the Institute for Tourism Development Research.

Vietnam Tourism is in charge of international marketing and domestic tours operating at central government level, and operates 13 tourism companies. Country-wide there are 60 companies active in tourism development at different government levels. Hanoi Tourism and Saigon Tourism are well-known examples. The renovation of the Metropole Hotel in Hanoi, for example, is executed by a joint venture between the French Pullman group (30 per cent share) and Hanoi Tourism (70 per cent share).

The Institute for Tourism Development Research is in charge of research, planning and product development, including education and training. Education and training are also offered under the auspices of other institutions such as Hanoi Tourism, Saigon Tourism and the Ministry of Higher Education. The latter has established a college level course in travel economics and tour organization at the University of Economics in Hanoi.

Development Constraints

The development of Vietnam's visitor industry is subject to several constraints:

1. There is a lack of basic statistical information on visitor numbers and characteristics needed for effective policy formulation. The information collected for immigration purposes should be improved and processed for tourism policy purposes.
2. There is a lack of basic statistical information on the economic impact of different types of visitors.
3. There are no adequate hotel statistics. Since these are necessary for both government and potential investors in planning the smooth and profitable development of the hotel industry every hotel should be required to complete a simple form each month providing information on a daily basis about rooms and beds available and occupied.
4. There is a need for reliable and conveniently listed hotel information. In order to be able to provide such information a hotel classification should be made.
5. There is a lack of qualified manpower, particularly on management and entrepreneurial level, both in the hospitality sub-sector and in tourism in general. Existing tourism educational facilities need upgrading and strengthening.
6. Important parts of Vietnam's national heritage have suffered from the war and lack of maintenance over the years and are consequently in a derelict state. Their preservation needs urgent attention.
7. The road infrastructure urgently needs upgrading in order to be able to comply with increased tourist traffic. Vietnam's government, however, is short of funds.
8. The government apparatus responsible for tourism development is not adequately structured. Commercial operations (hotels and tour operating) should be separated from other more classical government tasks in research, statistics, planning, education, product development and marketing.
9. The National Tourism Organization lacks qualified personnel to make a smooth change to a market economy tourism sector. It urgently needs strengthening as far as the classical tasks of the NTO are concerned.
10. Both the divestment of government-owned tourism facilities and the establishment of newly privately owned facilities are hampered by a lack of investment funds in the newly emerging private sector. The establishment of a public development bank, aimed at providing investment loans to the private sector, may help to overcome this constraint.

Conclusion

Vietnam provides a rather atypical example of tourism development in an economy in transition. It differs from countries in Eastern and Central Europe in several respects. Although the Iron Curtain fell in 1989, Vietnam had already embarked upon a policy of economic reform in December 1986. Economic liberalization and the transition from a command to a market economy in Vietnam, however, are not part of a wider change of system extending to the political domain. Such limited liberation entails the risk of obstruction by the communist *nomenklatoera* who tend to defend the status quo to protect their influence and position of relative power. This is confirmed by Vo Van Kiet's 1991 remark that many cadres are falling behind the requirements of their tasks, not only in capacity but also in virtue. Compared to the countries in Eastern Europe, which have decided to pursue a comprehensive liberalization of their social system in both its economic and political dimension, Vietnam is at a disadvantage. It is in an advantageous position, however, in that it has a quite recent experience and knowledge of the requirements for a proper functioning of a market economy in the southern part of the country, which succumbed to communism and a command economy only in 1976. This may explain why Vietnam managed in December 1987, just one year after the Sixth Party Congress decided to restructure the Vietnamese economy, to pass a law on foreign investment which is one of the world's most liberal laws of this kind. It may also explain the Party's clear recognition of the need to regulate economic activities by providing an appropriate legislative framework. This is a definite advantage which Vietname has over the countries in Eastern Europe, where due to the long isolation behind the Iron Curtain, knowledge and experience of the functioning of a market economy have to be built from scratch; and where, consequently, the enactment of a law on tourism, providing a much needed legal framework for the proper functioning of tourism in a market economy, may be equated with the return of Stalinism (Theuns, 1993: 3).

Vietnam is endowed with a variety of tourism assets. It has a highly varied climate and topography, numerous beaches, peninsulas and islands, and a rich history and culture. These assets provide ample opportunities to develop a buoyant tourism sector. Asian countries are considered to be the major source markets. The same Asian countries are also major sources of investment in Vietnam's tourism facilities, providing a commitment to, and a sound basis for, its long-term tourism development.

At present tourism development in Vietnam is still seriously hampered by a number of constraints similar to those to be found not only in other countries in transition, but also in the poorer developing countries. There is, for instance, a general lack of reliable and accurate statistical data and qualified manpower needed to adequately manage and develop tourism in a market environment, and there is a shortage of investment funds for the upgrading and expansion of facilities and infrastucture, and the preservation of assets. The prospects for overcoming these constraints depend to a large extent on the continued pursuance by the Vietnamese government of market economic reforms. If the right entrepreneurial climate is maintained, private (foreign) investment and expertise will be increasingly attracted to the country's tourism sector and official multilateral and bilateral technical assistance will be more likely to come forward to assist in bridging the existing gaps in knowledge and expertise.

Acknowledgement

This chapter is an amended and up-dated version of part of a 1992 report for ESCAP on the possibilities for sustainable tourism development in selected least developed ESCAP countries and Vietnam (ESCAP, 1992).

The author gratefully acknowledges ESCAP's permission to use part of the 1992 report as base material for this article. In addition the author is indebted to Paul J. Theuns for the collection of additional documentation and information during his July/August 1994 holiday in Vietnam.

Bibliography

Anon. (1993a) Viet-Nam. In *The Europa World Year Book 1993*, Volume II. London: Europa Publications Limited.

Bangkok Post (1992) Vietnam tourist arrivals rise 36 percent. *Bangkok Post* 28 January.

Council of Ministers (1991) On the tasks of socio-economic development for 1991–1995 and 1992. Report of the Council of Ministers presented by Chairman Vo Van Kiet at the tenth session of the eighth National Assembly. Hanoi: Vietnam News Agency.

The Economist (1993) South-east Asian economies – dreams of gold. *The Economist* **326** (7803), 21–24.

The Economist (1994) Poorest people. *The Economist* **331** (7869),/20.

Economist Intelligence Unit (EIU). (1993) Indochina – Vietnam, Cambodia & Laos. *EIU International Tourism Reports, 2*, 59–82.

ESCAP (1992) *Possibilities for Sustainable Tourism. Development in Selected Least Developed ESCAP Countries and Viet Nam*. Report to ESCAP by H. L. Theuns. Bangkok: ESCAP.

General Statistical Office (1991) *Statistical Data of the Socialist Republic of Vietnam, 1976–1990*. Hanoi: Statistical Publishing House.

Hamill, Tom (1991) World Airline Directory. *Flight International* **139** (4260), 39–131.

IMF. (1992) Vietnam – Recent Economic Developments. Washington DC: IMF.

Le Ngoc Hue (1991) *Ho Chi Minh City – Reality and Perspective*. Ho Chi Minh City: Statistical Publishing House.

Le Nhat Thuc (1992) Country report for seminar on the promotion of sustainable tourism, Development in Selected Least Developed Countries of the ESCAP Region and Viet Nam, Pattaya, Thailand, 26–30 October. Hanoi: Ministry of Trade and Tourism, Research Institute for Foreign Economic Relations.

Mallet, Victor (1994) France rediscovers Indochina. *Financial Times* 29 July.

Nguyen Son Tra (1993) Investment Opportunities in Vietnam Tourism. In K.S. Chon (ed.) *International Conference 'Tourism Industry in Vietnam: Opportunities for Investment, Development and Marketing', Ho Chi Minh City, Vietnam, April 25–27, 1993; Conference Proceedings*. Las Vegas: Center for Hospitality Research and Development, University of Nevada, 29–31.

Robinson, Daniel and Cummings, Joe (1991) *Vietnam, Laos and Cambodia – A Travel Survival Kit*. Hawthorn, Vic./Berkeley, CA: Lonely Planet Publications.

Socialist Republic of Vietnam (1991) *Law on Foreign Investment in Vietnam*. Hanoi: The Juridical Publishing House.

Theuns, H. Leo (1993) Government intervention in tourism: some fundamental preliminary issues to be addressed. In *Report on the Evaluation and Revision of the Draft Regulation concerning Accommodation, Travel Trade, and Tour Managers and Guides*. Tourism Programme, Institutional Strengthening Working Paper I. Warsaw: Instytut Turystyki.

Theuns, H. Leo and Biernacka, Agnieszka D. (1994) *The Tourism Regions of Poland – A Statistical Analysis*. CEC-PHARE Tourism Programme, Product Development. Working Paper III. Warsaw: Institute of Tourism.

UNDP (1993) *Socialist Republic of Viet Nam – Briefing Note*. Hanoi: United Nations Development Programme.

UNDP/WTO (1991a) *Vietnam. Plan Directeur du Tourisme*. Volume I: Les stratégies de développement. Madrid: World Tourism Organization.

UNDP/WTO (1991b) *Vietnam. Plan Directeur du Tourisme*. Volume II: Partie 1 – L'analyse de la demande, Partie 2 – Le produit touristique du Vietnam. Madrid: WTO.

UNDP/WTO (1991c) *Vietnam. Plan Directeur du Tourisme*. Rapport de Synthèse. Madrid: WTO

UNDP/WTO/IRDT. (1991) *Viet Nam Tourism Development Master Plan – Summary Report*. Madrid: WTO.

Van Arkadie, Brian *et al.* (1990) *Report on the Economy of Vietnam*. Hanoi: State Planning Committee/UNDP

Vietnam Tourism (1991) Country Report Vietnam for seminar on Investment and Economic Co-operation in the Tourism Sector in Developing Asian Countries of the ESCAP Region. Tokyo, 15–20 October 1991.

Young, Denise (1992) Hong Kong sets up as gateway to Vietnam. *Bangkok Post*. 1 February.

PART III

Looking Ahead

18

Alternative paths to sustainable tourism: Problems, prospects, panaceas and pipe-dreams[1]

TONY GRIFFIN
NICOLETTE BOELE

Introduction

Two great movements emerged in the latter half of the twentieth century. The first, tourism, has featured the movement of people within and between nations on an unprecedented scale. Ostensibly, it has been motivated by the pursuit of pleasure and the belief that a temporary change of environment would provide or stimulate those pleasurable experiences. The other, environmentalism, has involved a movement in consciousness, attitudes and values whereby humankind began to question the meaning and nature of its 'progress'. It has drawn strength from the growing acceptance of our role as 'stewards' of the Earth (May, 1991), responsible not only for preserving and protecting its quality for future generations but also for ensuring the survival of other less manipulative and exploitative species.

The strength and nature of these movements made conflict almost inevitable. Tourism has been an agent for spreading and diversifying human impacts on the environment; it has created the need to provide settlements that cater for temporary as well as permanent accommodation, leading to the transformation of formerly pristine environments in some places and intensifying development in others. An added dimension of the conflict is the effect that tourism has had on the ways of life and well-being of host communities. The debate has consequently assumed strong social, cultural and economic dimensions.

Recently the debate has crystallized around the notion of 'sustainability', raising questions about the long-term survival of tourism as an industry. This chapter examines the application of this concept to tourism, particularly the idea that sustainability can be achieved through adopting alternative forms to 'mass' tourism. Despite the laudable aims of alternative tourism, its efficacy, or even desirability, is debatable. Will it really ensure that tourism does not run counter to the objectives of global sustainability? Is it realistic in the light of the projected growth of tourism? Does it represent an appropriate response to the problems generated by tourism? What implications does it have for the tourism industry and the development of tourist destinations? How will it impact on opportunities for people to travel? And, if adopted, would it increase or decrease the net benefits associated with tourism?

It is vital to the future of tourism that greater clarity be sought in relation to these questions. They affect most aspects of tourism, including broad national and international strategies and policies, the planning of individual destinations and developments, the conduct of tour operations, the mix of products available, and even the behaviour of tourists. The most fundamental question is one of focus – should the search for alternative forms of tourism be pursued, or should we accept that mass tourism will continue to grow, and therefore focus rather on finding more sustainable ways to accommodate that growth?

The Meaning of Sustainable Development

The meaning of sustainable development, particularly as it relates to tourism, must first be clarified. The Brundtland Report has provided the most generally accepted definition (Farrell and Runyan, 1991, Hare 1991), that is 'development that meets the needs of the present without compromising the ability of future generations to meet their own needs' (WCED, 1987: 87). Espousing the same general principles but specifically geared to tourism, Globe 90 defined it as 'meeting the needs of present tourists and hosts while protecting and enhancing opportunity for the future' (cited in Sofield, 1991: 68). But the succinct nature of these definitions belies the complexity of their interpretation and the variety of elements that have been associated with their achievement.

Achieving sustainability has been perceived as comprising a number of key elements:

1. Maintaining our current resource base for future generations (McKercher, 1992). This can be interpreted as either maintaining the supply of those resources or their value. If the latter is accepted, the supply can decline provided those fewer resources are more highly priced (Sinclair, 1992).
2. Maintaining the productivity of the resource base. In relation to tourism this is founded on the continued well-being of the physical and social environments (Hall, 1991), particularly those features that attract tourists and contribute to the pleasantness of their experiences. Tourism therefore needs to be environmentally sensitive (May, 1991) and ensure the continuity of culture (Wall, 1992). As it also depends on the hospitality with which residents of a destination receive tourists, it should be mindful of residents' needs (Curry and Morvaridi, 1992).
3. Maintaining biodiversity and avoiding irreversible environmental changes. This is founded on the notion of 'ecological sustainability' rather than

'sustainable development' (McKercher, 1992), although it has been applied to cultural as well as ecological change (Sofield, 1991). Strict adherence to it implies much less tolerance to change and support for more constraints on tourism development.

4. Ensuring equity both within and between generations (WCED, 1987; Cronin, 1990; ESDWG, 1991; Hare, 1991; Sofield, 1991; Curry and Morvaridi, 1992). Excessive depletion or despoliation of resources by tourism in the present may reduce opportunities for tourists, the tourism industry and other users of those resources in the future. The Brundtland Report pointed out that this concern for equity between generations 'must logically be extended to equity within each generation' (WCED, 1987: 87). For tourism this further highlights the need to be sensitive to conflicts between residents and tourists. The implication is that some degree of local control, ranging from participation in planning processes through to ownership and operation of tourism plant, is essential if tourism is to be sustainable (Murphy, 1985; Cronin, 1990; Craik, 1991; ESDWG, 1991; Hall, 1991; Hare, 1991; Ritchie, 1991; Sofield, 1991; Curry and Morvaridi, 1992; Sinclair, 1992).

Alternative Tourism as a Path to Sustainability

Alternative tourism has been proposed as an appropriate panacea to the problem of making tourism more sustainable, despite there being little consensus about its precise meaning and the forms of tourism it encompasses (Weaver, 1991). It is conceived primarily as an alternative to mass tourism, but its evolution has been accompanied by a large number of equivalent terms, including: 'green' (Stevens, 1990), 'soft' (Krippendorf, 1991), 'defensive' (Krippendorf, 1987), 'responsible' (Wheeller, 1991), 'low impact' (Lillywhite and Lillywhite, 1991), 'endemic' (PATA, 1992b), 'progressive' (Wheeller, 1992b), 'appropriate' (Holden, 1989), 'sideline' (Kelly and Dixon, 1991), 'quality' (Craik, 1991; Schmidhauser, 1992) and 'new' tourism (Poon, 1989). It has similarly been equated to a range of more specific forms such as: 'nature' (Long, 1991), 'eco-' (Jansen-Verbeke, 1991), 'ecological' (Farrell and Runyan, 1991), 'cultural' (Dunstan, 1989), and 'heritage' tourism (Hall and Mitchell, 1991), most of which have, themselves, been interpreted in a variety of ways.

There is general agreement about some of its broad characteristics, however. Essentially, it is regarded as alternative to mass tourism or more broadly as 'alternative to something which is exploitive' (Holden, 1989: 5). It has been characterized as involving small-scale, locally controlled development that is based on local nature and culture and pays special attention to environmental and social carrying capacity (Jarviluoma, 1992: 118). Although most commonly discussed in relation to natural settings or to Third World destinations where the physical or cultural environment is particularly fragile and sensitive to change, it has been more broadly applied, even to First World urban settings (Jansen-Verbeke, 1991). It holds instant appeal for those concerned about the impacts of mass tourism, but its potential to solve the problems must be questioned in the light of what is known and understood about tourism and its prospective growth.

Tourism: The State of Development

Growth

Tourism has grown enormously and its influence has spread widely since World War II. Tables 18.1 and 18.2 illustrate the extent of this growth. After the initial surge of the 1950s the growth has been strong and sustained, except for a brief period, 1982–83, when international recession caused a slight decline. Recovery was swift and strong, however, as in 1984 international arrivals grew by nearly 10 per cent (Holecek and van Deijck, 1991). The main impact of economic downturns would therefore appear to be a bottling-up of tourism demand, which is subsequently released as soon as conditions improve.

Of late, the fastest growing destinations have been outside the traditionally strongest continents of Europe and North America. The Continents of Africa, Latin America, Oceania and most parts of Asia have experienced recent rates of growth significantly above the world average (WTO, 1990), albeit from relatively small bases. The magnitude of tourism and its growth is even more

Table 18.1   International arrivals worldwide 1950–90

Year	Arrivals ('000)	Year	Arrivals ('000)
1950	25,282	1984	312,434
1960	69,296	1985	321,240
1970	159,690	1986	330,746
1980	284,841	1987	356,640
1981	288,848	1988	381,824
1982	286,780	1989	415,376
1983	284,173	1990	443,477

Source: *Latham (1992)*

Table 18.2   Rates of growth of international arrivals 1950–90

Year range	Average annual percentage increase
1950–60	10.6
1960–70	8.7
1970–80	6.0
1980–90	4.5
1980–85	2.5
1985–90	6.7

The average percentage increase is calculated as the constant annual percentage increase, which would result in the overall change over the specified period.
Source: *Latham (1992)*

pronounced if domestic flows are included, estimated by the WTO to be ten times those of international (Pearce, 1987b).

Impacts

As it has grown, tourism has generated a broad range of significant impacts on the natural, social, cultural and economic environments of destinations. These have been extensively catalogued (e.g. in Mathieson and Wall, 1982), and there appears to be consensus that while the net economic impact is usually beneficial, the other impacts of tourism are commonly detrimental. In specific cases, the net effect, seriousness or even causal links to tourism may be debated, but it is virtually irrefutable that harmful impacts have arisen and concern is justified. This recognition of tourism's harmful effects is not new. For example, as early as the 1860s Cook's tours were criticized on the basis that 'natural and man-made attractions were being spoilt by the very agency that enable them to be widely appreciated' (Brendon, 1991: 76). However, the rapid growth of tourism has magnified the scale and range of impacts.

The potential for decline

These early concerns expressed about Cook's tours point to the notion that tourism has the potential to cause its own decline by despoiling the attractions on which it is based. The now widely accepted model of the tourist area cycle of evolution (Butler, 1980) suggests that decline may set in if deliberate steps are not taken to manage tourism sensitively. Numerous studies have tested this idea and produced evidence to support it (e.g. Meyer-Arendt, 1985; Cooper and Jackson, 1989). The Coasts in Spain and Pattaya, Thailand stand out as clear examples of the consequences of ignoring cumulative environmental impacts. On the other hand, some doubts have been raised about its universal applicability and practicality (Haywood, 1986; Choy, 1992; Getz, 1992). Many tourist destinations, especially in Europe, have continued to absorb increasing numbers of tourists with few negative impacts or signs of decline, 'particularly where there is a long history of tourism, large population centers to absorb impacts, or concentrated tourist enclaves which are more or less self-contained' (Craik 1991: 118). Places such as Cannes, Nice, San Sebastian, Florence, Interlaken and Lucerne appeared in Thomas Cook brochures over 100 years ago yet they remain significant tourist destinations (Thomas Cook Archives). Decline, therefore, cannot be seen as an inevitable outcome of mass tourism development, but it must be admitted as a possibility. We also cannot assume that tourism will be sustainable without deliberate attempts to make it so. From the tourism industry's perspective, therefore, some level of concern about the implications of tourism's impacts is clearly justified.

Prospects

In all probability tourism will continue to grow strongly. The WTO has prepared a range of forecasts for international visitor arrivals, which are presented in Table 18.3. From a base of 443 million in 1990 (Latham, 1992), international arrivals are predicted to reach between 637 and 956 million by the year 2000. Other estimates range from 532 million (Edgell, 1990) to 746 million (Hiemstra, 1991). Even the most conservative of these estimates predicts growth of at least 20 per cent over the next decade, with proportionately greater growth in Africa, Latin America, Asia and Oceania.

When the factors driving this growth are considered, the case is even stronger. In developed countries the growth of tourism has been fuelled by such factors as rising disposable incomes, increased levels of urbanization, increased mobility, higher levels of education, increases in leisure time (Mathieson and Wall, 1982; Butler, 1990b; Bentley, 1991; Holecek and van Deijck, 1991; Krippendorf, 1991), and a greater global media network that has helped stimulate the desire to travel (Coates, 1991). In the foreseeable future, it is unlikely that any of these factors will change in such a way that they reduce the demand for tourism. Perhaps more significantly tourism has come to be a part of the accepted lifestyle and aspirations of many people in these nations (Mathieson and Wall, 1982; Urry, 1990), making it even more unlikely that aggregate tourist numbers will decline.

The geographical distribution of this growth is somewhat less predictable. Tourist flows are becoming more diffuse, with increasing numbers of visitors travelling to more remote locations (Romeril, 1989b: 106), and some of the new alternative forms of tourism such as green tourism are perceived to be 'demand-led' (Shaw and Williams, 1992: 48), a reflection of the growing sophistication and/or experience of travellers. Tourists from wealthier nations are becoming more aware of environmental issues and increasingly perceptive of and sensitive to environmental hazards in some older, established destinations (Smith and Jenner, 1989). However, there is little evidence

Table 18.3   World Tourism Organization's international tourism forecast by region

Forecast arrivals (millions)

	Based on growth rate 1950–89		Based on growth rate 1960–89	
	1995	2000	1995	2000
World	641	956	515	637
Africa	26	40	23	32
Americas	114	154	103	128
Europe	376	530	294	338
Asia/Oceania	125	232	95	140

Source: World Tourism Organization modified from Holecek and van Deijck (1991)

that they are reducing their absolute amount of travel, even though they may change their destination or be more selective about their choice of product.

The inevitability of the growth of tourism is further supported by the emergence of new nations as significant tourist generators due to economic and/or political impediments to travel being removed. The growth of outbound tourism from the rapidly developing nations of the Asia Pacific region has already been impressive and the prospects for travel from Eastern Europe have been considerably enhanced by the political changes of 1989–90 (Holecek and van Deijck, 1991).

Reconciling impacts and prospects

If tourism is to be sustainable, the evidence on impacts suggests that some basic changes need to be made to the way it has been developed, and corrective action is required to resolve existing problems. However, considering tourism's prospective growth, it is doubtful whether policies based on restraint would be successful. Similarly it is doubtful whether 'alternative tourism,' given its reliance on small-scale development, has any chance of accommodating the projected growth, and there is a growing body of opinion that it may create new problems or exacerbate existing ones. This may seem a somewhat defeatist attitude – tourism policy and planning can be about creating desired futures rather than simply attempting to cope with trends – but in this case the trends may be too strong to counteract. Moreover it is not certain whether restraining tourism, or attempting to steer it in directions that clearly do not appeal to the bulk of travellers, is necessarily desirable. By accepting that mass tourism will continue to be the predominant component of tourism's growth, it would be more realistic and even beneficial to focus on finding means of coping with that growth and making mass tourism less harmful in its impacts. The remaining sections explore these notions in more detail.

Does Alternative Tourism Contribute to Sustainability?

After the initial burst of enthusiasm that greeted alternative tourism, an increasing number of critics have emerged. At best, they have cast doubts on its ability to significantly contribute to the goal of sustainable tourism development, and at worst declared that alternative tourism may run counter to that goal. The major points raised by these critics are reviewed here briefly.

The first and possibly most significant criticism is that alternative tourism may actually spread the influence of mass tourism by seeking out new, more exotic and pristine environments, and thereby establishing a base for others to follow in much greater numbers (Butler, 1990b; Wheeller 1991; Jarviluoma, 1992; Jones, 1992). The initial objectives of alternative tourism in a new destination may be to remain low-key and small-scale but it is difficult to guarantee this once the tourism industry perceives a new product development opportunity and starts to market that opportunity. In the same vein, it has been suggested that alternative tourism, even if it succeeds in restraining numbers, may exacerbate negative social and cultural impacts by intensifying the degree of contact between hosts and tourists (Butler, 1990a; Long, 1991; Jones, 1992).

The proponents of alternative tourism argue that the way to circumvent these problems is to ensure that the control of tourism remains in local hands – that way tourism will develop on a scale and in a manner appropriate to local needs. Critics respond that it is virtually impossible to define what is 'appropriate' and to whom (Butler, 1990a; Wheeller, 1991) and cast doubts on whether local control is realistic in many instances. Achieving consensus in a community is difficult if not impossible, particularly where questions of development and change are involved. There are inevitably trade-offs between economic and social well-being, short-term imperatives and long-term objectives, and there are different perceptions about the desirability of change. It is even more problematic when the supposed costs and benefits of the alternatives must be anticipated rather than experienced. Furthermore, effective local control is unrealistic because: the local community may be in a relatively weak bargaining position (Wheeller, 1991); the prevailing political structures have not devolved decision-making power to the local level (Redclift, 1987); environmental issues are not high on the agenda in poorer destinations where short-term economic imperatives are more compelling (Long, 1991; Cooper and Ozdil, 1992); and the local community does not possess the appropriate capital or technology to ensure environmentally sensitive tourism (Long, 1991).

A third major criticism is that alternative tourism is essentially elitist and supports middle-class values and preferences. It is exclusive in the sense of attracting 'desirable types of visitors' (Long, 1991: 4) and shutting out the 'riff-raff' (Wheeller, 1992b: 105). Those attracted to alternative tourism are likely to be 'highly educated, affluent, mature and probably white' (Butler, 1990a: 43), and there is some empirical evidence to support this contention in relation to nature-oriented tourism at least (Ingram and Durst, 1989).

Alternative tourism has also been criticized for ignoring the preferences of the vast majority of tourists and thereby not being geared to the realities of the market (Butler, 1990a; Wheeller, 1992a). Many people may enjoy the offerings of mass tourism and there are doubts that alternative tourism may be able to generate repeat visits (Butler, 1990a). This has notable implications for the viability of the tourism industry (McKercher, 1992).

Finally, the proponents of alternative tourism seem to place undue faith in the notion that the behaviour of tourists, developers and other industry operators can be modified through education or awareness programmes (Butler, 1990a; Pigram, 1990; Wheeller, 1991,1992a). In recent years there has been a flood of 'codes of ethics' or 'charters' released by a variety of tourism industry groups and environmental organizations (Australian Conservation Foundation, 1992; Australia Tourism Industry Association, 1990; D'Amore, 1992; Ecotourism Association of Australia, 1992; PATA, 1992a; World Wide Fund for Nature/Tourism Concern, 1992). The benefits of raising awareness in this fashion have been tentatively acknowledged (Cooper and Ozdil, 1992; Jarviluoma, 1992), but it remains to be seen whether this results in modified behaviour.

Is Restraint of Tourism Achievable or Desirable?

The above criticisms are manifold and growing, and the place of alternative tourism in the conventional wisdom is likely to be short lived. Of the equivalent terms cited earlier 'sideline tourism' (Kelly and Dixon, 1991) is perhaps the most appropriate, implying as it does that alternative tourism is peripheral to the mainstream (and likely to remain so). 'Sustainability' retains its credence, however, and it is worth examining further implications of this concept, some of which also relate to the more specific notion of alternative tourism. Before imposing further restrictions on tourism development we should be confident that the resultant sacrifices are worth the possible gains.

Suggested restrictions associated with sustainable development and alternative tourism have included both qualitative and quantitative measures, including charging higher prices for access to tourist destinations and attractions (Wanhill, 1980; Sinclair, 1992). Indeed restricting supply would automatically increase the price of tourism products, thereby reducing the opportunities for some prospective tourists. The question is whether this is consistent with the principle of equity embodied in the concept of sustainability. Despite the problems it causes, mass tourism has effectively democratized travel (Urry, 1990), at least for those in the wealthier, developed nations. From this perspective mass tourism has served the cause of equity and restraining it excessively at this point may deny similar opportunities to residents of the newly emerging nations. From an intergenerational perspective the question is, if we are preserving special environments and elements of cultures for future generations, when do we give them the opportunity to enjoy the benefits of access to them? It is possible that support for conservation/preservation causes will wane if the benefits do not become apparent because a 'tomorrow-never-comes' attitude has been adopted. The

Brundtland Report's assertion that sustainable development involves 'extending to all opportunities to satisfy their aspirations for a better life' (WCED, 1987: 88) should be kept in mind.

Adoption of this broader perspective of equity would require a greater recognition of the benefits that arise from being a tourist. This aspect seems to have slipped from the agenda somewhat in recent years when much of the attention has been focused on either the tourism destination's or industry's perspective. There is implicit recognition in both academic studies and marketing analyses that people are motivated by the prospect of perceived benefits, but little attention has been paid to how those benefits manifest themselves during and after a trip. Ironically there has been much official recognition of the benefits to individuals from holidays and travel: the United Nations' Universal Declaration of Human Rights 1948 includes the rights to rest, leisure and paid holidays; many nations have entrenched these rights through legislation; and the Manila Declaration on World Tourism (1980) affirmed the rights to travel and tourism, the need to provide non-discriminatory access to these activities (cited in WTO, 1983), and recognized that modern tourism was born out of considerations of equity and such subsequent social policies (Haulot, 1981). In developed nations, there is some evidence that tourism is regarded as a necessity and that poorer members of the community have limited access to its benefits (Hughes, 1991). Pursuing sustainability through restraint may further limit equity of access.

Broader social benefits, which do not accrue directly to the host community, have also been neglected. The only attempts to seriously discuss such benefits have been couched in terms of tourism's contribution to world peace and international understanding (e.g. Goh, 1988; D'Amore, 1991). While one can be sceptical about such grand claims, they at least place this neglected dimension of tourism on the global balance sheet. As sustainability is ultimately a global concept it is appropriate to include a more complete assessment of tourism's benefits within its framework.

This is not to suggest that the interests of tourists and any subsequent broader social benefits should be paramount, nor that expanding the opportunities for travel should necessarily be the major consideration when dealing with matters of equity. Many international tourist flows involve people from wealthy nations travelling to poor nations where even the poorest tourist would be substantially better off than the bulk of the host population. It certainly does not advance the cause of equity if the bulk of the social costs are borne by the poor while the social benefits are effectively exported. But without an assessment of these so far neglected benefits, the balance sheet is fundamentally incomplete.

There is the added factor that sustainability seems to be interpreted as stability, and stability implies no change. Thus the discussion of many impacts of tourism interprets social and cultural change as inherently bad, particularly in developing nations. This is somewhat ironic given that the major tourist-generating nations appear to value change and cultural diversity: USA, Canada and Australia are multicultural societies; Western Europe is intent on integration; and Japan has been the most dynamic society of all in the post-war period. One nation's progress may be another's cultural imperialism. Social and cultural change is neither inherently good nor bad, and care should be taken with its interpretation. Even some of the concerns expressed earlier about alternative tourism and its spreading and intensification of cultural contacts may, in fact, be misplaced.

Finally, the drive to direct and/or restrain tourism development in the cause of sustainability may ultimately be futile and counter-productive. The evidence presented on the prospective growth of tourism suggests that unless a global approach is adopted, tourism will simply be diverted and any problems it creates transferred to other settings. The likelihood of such a global approach is remote. The desire to travel is strong and the prospect of economic advancement through tourism may be too compelling for a nation or region to resist. Moreover tourism companies are understandably likely to devise creative ways around many restrictions, simply to ensure their own survival. Witness the outcome of currency restrictions imposed in the United Kingdom in the 1950s, 1960s and 1970s. The limits placed on British citizens' expenditure on overseas holidays, coupled with very liberal tourism development policies in Spain, contributed to the evolution of the cheap package tour and the emergence of resorts that epitomize the worst excesses of mass tourism (Pearce, 1987a; Brendon, 1991). The possibility of repeating this scenario should not be neglected when devising strategies for sustainable tourism development.

Towards Strategies for Sustainable Tourism

There is no one 'appropriate' form of tourism or general strategy that will ensure its sustainability. To some extent, different solutions will need to be devised for different nations and for different regions within those nations. However, the following suggestions may offer some points of focus.

Recognize that mass tourism will continue and that this is not necessarily undesirable
This will mean a move away from defining carrying capacities, which has proved fruitless in most cases (Mathieson and Wall, 1982; Pearce, 1989; Romeril, 1989a, b; Butler, 1990b; Farrell and Runyan, 1991), to devising management strategies designed to accommodate growth with minimal adverse impact. Within that framework, however, it may be appropriate to protect some particularly fragile or special places from excessive use or development.

Plan for tourism within the framework of a vision that recognizes the special qualities of a place which need to be sustained
In some instances this may be quite simple, e.g. maintaining beach and water quality, while in others it may involve a more complex mix of culture, architecture and ambience.

Apply environmental impact assessment procedures stringently to tourism development in a way that considers the qualitative impact on that vision
In most developed nations existing procedures are adequate in principle but poorer in application. There are weaknesses in dealing with qualitative issues, cumulative as opposed to project-specific effects, and in identifying social impacts (Grey *et al.*, 1991).

At the national level, aim to provide as wide a range of tourism opportunities as possible
A mix of places that cater to both mass and alternative tourists is likely to be desirable. In this regard, the notion of a 'tourism opportunity spectrum' (Butler and Waldbrook, 1991) has potential for further refinement and application.

Recognize that alternative tourism can make a valuable contribution to filling out the tourism opportunity spectrum but it is not a general solution to the problem of making tourism more sustainable
It caters to a niche market that has some potential to grow, but its very nature suggests that it is the form of tourism where limits to capacity are likely to be most relevant. The maintenance of mass tourism destinations, catering to the majority, may well be vital to the long-term sustainability of alternative tourism.

Place less faith in the notion that community involvement in tourism will contribute significantly to sustainability
It is certainly desirable in principle, and therefore warrants some encouragement, but it is difficult to achieve in practice. Prevailing political and economic structures constrain it in some instances, while in others a community consensus may be a pipe-dream, and the process may be subject to distortions, manipulation or capture by limited interest groups. Views on what is 'appropriate' tourism development may vary widely.

Continue with efforts to raise the environmental consciousness of both the tourism industry and tourists, but recognize that this is a limited and long-term process
From the industry perspective, entry is relatively free and many outside organizations, for example property developers, have only a partial and fleeting interest – they are consequently less likely to be influenced by long-term considerations. Research needs to be conducted into the effectiveness of

environmental codes of ethics and similar educative mechanisms (e.g. Weiler and Johnson, 1992).

Acknowledge the benefits that flow from being a tourist and recognize that they are valid aspects of equity and opportunity, inherent in the concept of sustainability
The industry would seem to have an interest in encouraging more research on this aspect as it is potentially as strong a lobbying point as the more straightforward economic benefits.

Encourage systematic research that identifies 'best practices' in relation to sustainable tourism development
Such studies should aim to identify a variety of practices that are transferable to tourist destinations possessing similar political, economic, social, cultural and physical conditions. Initially the research could focus on destinations that have proved their longevity or been successfully rejuvenated, as these are indicators of sustainability.

Conclusion

Tourism has undoubtedly generated significant environmental and social changes, many of which have been detrimental. However, there is no inherent reason why, having recognized these problems, it cannot become more sustainable. The first step in achieving this is to be realistic in acknowledging that the problem is complex and that any solutions must be founded on the necessity of accommodating further growth. Simplistic, naive or marginal approaches such as an over-reliance on alternative tourism are clearly not the answer. Alternative tourism, as a path to sustainability, is more pipe-dream than panacea.

Note

1 This chapter is a slightly modified version of an article first published in the *American Express Review of Travel* (1993), 2nd edn, New York, American Express Travel Related Services, 13–23.

Bibliography

Australian Conservation Foundation (1992) *Draft ACF Tourism Policy*. Sydney: ACF.
Australian Tourism Industry Association (1990) *Code of Environmental Practice*. Canberra; ATIA.
Bentley, R. (1991) World tourism outlook for the 1990s. In Hawkins, D.E. and Ritchie J.R.B. (eds) *World Travel and Tourism Review*, Vol 1. Oxford: C.A.B. International, 55–8.
Brendon, P. (1991) *Thomas Cook: 150 Years of Popular Tourism*. London: Secker and Warburg.

Butler, R.W. (1980) The concept of a tourist area cycle of evolution: implications for the management of resources. *Canadian Geographer* **24** (1), 5–12.

Butler, R.W. (1990a) Alternative tourism: pious hope or Trojan horse? *Journal of Travel Research* **28** (3), 40–5.

Butler, R.W. (1990b) Development strategies: integrating different approaches. Paper presented to *Pacific Asia Travel Association Annual Conference*. Vancouver, 24 April.

Butler, R.W. and Waldbrook, L.A. (1991) A new planning tool: the tourism opportunity spectrum. *Journal of Tourism Studies* **2** (1), 2–13.

Choy, D.J.L. (1992) Life cycle models for Pacific island destinations. *Journal of Travel Research* **30** (3), 26–31.

Coates, J.F. (1991) Tourism and the environment: realities of the 1990s. In Hawkins, D.E. and Ritchie J.R.B. (eds) *World Travel and Tourism Review*, Vol. 1. Oxford: C.A.B. International, 66–71.

Cooper, C.P. and Jackson, S. (1989) Destination life cycle: The Isle of Man case study. *Annals of Tourism Research* **16** (3), 377–98.

Cooper, C.P. and Ozdil, I. (1992) From mass to 'responsible' tourism: the Turkish experience, *Tourism Management* **13** (4), 377–86.

Craik, J. (1991) *Resorting to Tourism: Cultural Policies for Tourist Development in Australia*. Sydney: Allen and Unwin.

Cronin, L. (1990) A strategy for tourism and sustainable developments. *World Leisure and Recreation Association Journal* **32** (3), 12–18.

Curry, S. and Morvaridi, B. (1992) Sustainable tourism: illustrations from Kenya, Nepal and Jamaica. In Cooper, C.P. and Lockwood, A. (eds) *Progress in Tourism, Recreation and Hospitality Management*, Vol. 4. London: Belhaven Press, 131–9.

D'Amore, L.J. (1991) Sustainable tourism development in the Third World. In Hawkins, D.E. and Ritchie J.R.B. (eds) *World Travel and Tourism Review*, Vol. 1. Oxford: C.A.B. International, 170–2.

D'Amore, L.J. (1992) Promoting sustainable tourism – the Canadian approach. *Tourism Management* **13** (3), 258–62

Dunstan, G. (1989) Sustainable tourism. Paper presented to *Cultural Tourism Seminar*, conducted by Tourism South Australia. Adelaide, 24 June.

Ecologically Sustainable Development Working Groups (ESDWG) (1991) *Final Report – Tourism*. Canberra: Australian Government Publishing Service.

Ecotourism Association of Australia (1992) New ideas in ecotourism. *Newsletter*, **1** (2), 4–5.

Edgell, D.L. (1990) *International Tourism Policy*. New York: Van Nostrand Reinhold.

Farrell, B.H. and Runyan, D. (1991) Ecology and Tourism. *Annals of Tourism Research* **18** (1), 26–40.

Getz, D. (1992) Tourism planning and destination life cycle. *Annals of Tourism Research* **19** (4), 752–70.

Goh, P. (1988) Tourism: a vital force for peace. In *Tourism Research: Expanding Boundaries*. 19th Annual Conference of Travel and Tourism Research Association, Montreal, 19–23 June. 199–208.

Grey, P., Edelmann, K. and Dwyer, L. (1991) *Tourism in Australia: Challenges and Opportunities*. Melbourne: Longman Cheshire.

Hall, C.M. (1991) *Introduction to Tourism in Australia: Impacts, Planning and Development*. Melbourne: Longman Cheshire.

Hall, C.M. and Mitchell, I. (1991) Heritage and ecotourism in New Zealand: towards sustainable development? Paper presented to *Leisure and Tourism Social and Environmental Change*. WLRA World Congress, Sydney, 16–19 July.

Hare, B. (1991) Ecologically sustainable development. *Habitat Australia*. April, 10–12.

Haulot, A. (1981) Social tourism: current dimensions and future developments. *International Journal of Tourism Management* 2 (3), 207–12.

Haywood, M. (1986) Can the tourist-area cycle of evolution be made operational? *Tourism Management* 7 (3), 154–67.

Hiemstra, S.J. (1991) Projections of world tourist arrivals to the year 2000. In Hawkins, D.E. and Ritchie, J.R. (eds) *World Travel and Tourism Review*, Vol. 1., Oxford: Belhaven Press, 59–65.

Holden, P. (1989) Alternative tourism. *NSW Action for World Development Newsletter*. August/September, 5–8.

Holecek, D.F. and van Deijck, C. (1991) International travel and tourism: 1950–2000. *World Leisure and Recreation Association Journal* 33 (1), 21–5.

Hughes, H.L. (1991) Holidays and the economically disadvantaged. *Tourism Management* 12 (3), 193–6.

Ingram, C.D. and Durst, P.B. (1989) Nature-oriented tour operators: travel to developing countries. *Journal of Travel Research* 28 (2), 11–5.

Jansen-Verbeke, M. (1991) Eco-tourism: a challenge for future tourism development. Paper presented to *Leisure and Tourism: Social and Environmental Change*. WLRA World Congress, Sydney, July 16–19.

Jarviluoma, J. (1992) Alternative tourism and the evolution of tourist areas. *Tourism Management* 13 (1), 118–20.

Jones, A. (1992) Is there a real 'alternative' tourism? *Tourism Management* 13 (1), 102–3.

Kelly, I. and Dixon, W. (1991) Sideline tourism. *Journal of Tourism Studies* 2 (1), 21–8.

Krippendorf, J. (1987) *The Holiday Makers: Understanding the Impacts of Leisure and Travel*. London: Heinemann.

Krippendorf, J. (1991) Towards new tourism policies. In Medlik, S. (ed.) *Managing Tourism*. Oxford: Butterworth-Heinemann, 307–17.

Latham, J. (1992) International tourism and statistics. In Cooper, C.P. and Lockwood, A. (eds) *Progress in Tourism. Recreation and Hospitality Management*, Vol. 4. London: Belhaven Press, 269

Lillywhite, M. and Lillywhite, L. (1991) Low impact tourism. In Hawkins, D.E. and Ritchie, J.R. (eds) *World Travel and Tourism Review* Vol. 1. Oxford: C.A.B. International 162–9.

Long, V.H. (1991) Nature tourism: environmental stress or environmental salvation? Paper presented to *Leisure and Tourism: Social and Environmental Change*. WLRA World Congress, Sydney, 16–19 July.

Mathieson, A. and Wall, G. (1982) *Tourism: Economic, Physical and Social Impacts*. London: Longman.

May, V. (1991) Tourism, environment and development: values, sustainability and stewardship. *Tourism Management* 12 (2), 112–8.

McKercher, B. (1992) The unrecognized threat to tourism: can tourism survive sustainability'? In Weiler, B. (ed) *Ecotourism Incorporating the Global Classroom*. Canberra: Bureau of Tourism Research, 134–9.

Meyer-Arendt, K. (1985) The Grand Isle, Louisiana resort cycle. *Annals of Tourism Research* **2** (3), 449–66.

Murphy, P.E. (1985) *Tourism: A Community Approach.* London: Methuen.

Pacific Asia Travel Association (PATA) (1992a) *Code For Environmentally Responsible Tourism.* San Francisco: PATA.

Pacific Asia Travel Association (1992b) *Endemic Tourism: A Profitable Industry in a Sustainable Environment.* San Francisco: PATA.

Pearce, D.G. (1987a) Spatial patterns of package tourism in Europe. *Annals of Tourism Research* **14** (2), 183–201.

Pearce, D.G. (1987b) *Tourism Today: A Geographical Analysis.* London: Longman.

Pearce, D.G. (1989) *Tourism Development,* (2nd edn.) London: Longman.

Pigram, J.J. (1990) Sustainable tourism – policy considerations. *Journal of Tourism Studies* **1** (2), 2–9.

Poon, A. (1989) Competitive strategies for a 'new tourism'. In Cooper, C.P. (ed.) *Progress in Tourism. Recreation and Hospitality Management,* Vol. 1. London: Belhaven Press, 91–102.

Redclift, M. (1987) *Sustainable Development: Exploring the Contradictions.* London: Methuen.

Ritchie, J.R.B. (1991) Global tourism policy issues: an agenda for the 1990s. In Hawkins, D.E. and Ritchie, J.R. (eds) *World Travel and Tourism Review,* Vol. 1. Oxford: Belhaven Press, 149–58.

Romeril, M. (1989a) Tourism and the environment – accord or discord? *Tourism Management* September, 204–8.

Romeril, M. (1989b) Tourism – the environmental dimensions. In Cooper, C.P. (ed.) *Progress in Tourism. Recreation and Hospitality Management,* Vol. 1. London: Belhaven Press, 103–13.

Schmidhauser, H.P. (1992) Quality tourism. *Annals of Tourism Research* **19** (3), 574–5.

Shaw, G. and Williams, A. (1992) Tourism, development and the environment: the eternal triangle. In Cooper, C.P. and Lockwood, A. (eds) *Progress in Tourism. Recreation and Hospitality Management,* Vol. 4. London: Belhaven Press, 47–58.

Sinclair, M.T. (1992) Tourism, economic development and the environment; problems and policies. In Cooper, C.P. and Lockwood, A. *Progress in Tourism. Recreation and Hospitality Management,* 75–81.

Smith, C. and Jenner, P. (1989) Tourism and the environment. *EIU Travel and Tourism Analyst.* No. 5, 69–86.

Sofield, T.H.B. (1991) Sustainable ethnic tourism in the South Pacific: some principles. *Journal of Tourism Studies* **2** (1), 56–72.

Stevens, T. (1990) Greener than green. *Leisure Management* September, 64–6.

Thomas Cook Archives, various brochures.

Urry, J. (1990) *The Tourist Gaze* London: Sage.

Wall, G. (1992) Bali sustainable development project. *Annals of Tourism Research* **19** (3), 569–71.

Wanhill, S.R.C. (1980) Charging for congestion at tourist attractions, *International Journal of Tourism Management* **1** (3), 168–74.

Weaver, D.B. (1991) Alternative to mass tourism in Dominica. *Annals of Tourism Research* **18** (3), 414–32.

Wheeller, B. (1991) Tourism's troubled times: responsible tourism is not the answer. *Tourism Management* **12** (2), 91–6.

Wheeller, B. (1992a) Alternative tourism – a deceptive ploy. In Cooper, C.P. and Lockwood, A. *Progress in Tourism. Recreation and Hospitality Management*, Vol. 4. London: Belhaven Press, 140–5.

Wheeller, B. (1992b) Is progressive tourism appropriate? *Tourism Management* **13** (1), 104–5.

Weiler, B. and Johnson, T. (1992) Nature based tour operators: are they environmentally friendly or are they faking it? In Institute of Industrial Economics, *The Benefits and Costs of Tourism: Proceedings of a National Tourism Research Conference.* 1 February, 15–126.

World Commission on Environment and Development (WCED) (1987) *Our Common Future.* (The Brundtland Commission Report, Australian edn.) Melbourne: Oxford University Press

World Tourism Organisation (WTO) (1983) *Development of Leisure Time and the Right To Holidays.* Madrid: WTO.

World Tourism Organisation (1990) *Yearbook of Tourism Statistics – 1989.* 42nd edn., Vol. 1. Madrid: WTO.

World Wide Fund For Nature/Tourism Concern (1992) Business charter on sustainable tourism. *Development – Journal of STD* 2, 65.

19

Education and Indigenization

CATHERINE ROBINSON
JORDAN G. YEE

Introduction

The purpose of this chapter is to focus on the education and training that is currently being provided for people who will take potential jobs in the tourism industry, particularly those regarded as 'front-line' workers. It examines education and training programmes in the region and generates some questions about the nature and purpose of these. Education and training for jobs in the tourism industry involves adolescents and adults and consequently is generally considered to be *vocational* in nature. People receive their vocational education and training *after* they have completed compulsory schooling. The quality of the skills and knowledge they bring to their vocational training will reflect the quality of any compulsory education they may have undertaken, and this will vary between each country in the region. Questions will be raised about what 'counts' as tourism knowledge, and the ways in which we think about and structure, vocational education. Most importantly, because these (Western) perceptions are being exported to developing destinations within the region, the issue of their impact will be examined. We are still learning about the very different cultural dimensions that shape the perceptions of students, and the potential employees. How comfortably does Western vocational education fit into their lives and culture? In the light of what we know, does vocational education empower and enrich people, or prepare them for a predetermined place in society?

Copra and Bentley write that

> Vocational education's focus on preparation for dealing effectively with the practical problems of work and family has challenged its subject matter to be under continual development and renewal in order to be relevant to the needs of this changing society and make best use of knowledge developed from

research and practice. While all of education prepares for work and family responsibilities in some measure, directness toward learning that enhances effectiveness in addressing work and family responsibilities is a unique contribution and challenging mission for vocational education. (1992: 891)

John Dewey was writing about vocational education as far back as 1916 in his book *Democracy and Education*. He believed that: 'An occupation is a continuous activity having a purpose. Education through occupations consequently combines within itself more of the factors conducive to learning than any other method'. As to what a vocation actually is, he makes the point that 'The dominant vocation of all human beings at all times is living – intellectual and moral growth'.

Tourism: Can We Define It?

Society has a need to understand itself, and we do this by extracting and examining component parts (which we label as subjects or disciplines or practices). Ideally, we then try to put the parts together again and see society as an integrated whole. So, should we throw a net around anything that involves people moving around for business or pleasure, capture 'it' in specialized vocabulary and package 'it' as a subject? To do this, we have to assume that 'it' is discoverable. How are we discovering, and defining the 'it' that we think of as tourism?

Obviously, before we look at tourism as vocational education and training, we need to know how people define tourism itself. During the past two decades, educators have tried to construct a curriculum for tourism education, without any consensus as to what tourism, as a subject, discipline or practice actually is. When tourism first moved into educational institutes, there were not, nor are there now, any clear boundaries around 'what counts and what does not count as tourism'. There are as many definitions of tourism.

In 1981, Jafari and Ritchie wrote: 'Unless the contextual boundaries and concerns of tourism are known, it is difficult to even suggest what tourism education involves and what should be studied' (Jafari and Ritchie, 1981: 14). Murphy (1981: 98) expressed the view that the first task was to define a subject area, not only to explain what the course actually is, but 'to illustrate what it is not'. He felt that since most people had experienced tourism, as a tourist, they became instant experts and gave simple descriptions of the industry as a definition of tourism. A definition of tourism that includes such a description might be 'Tourism denotes the temporary, short-term movement of people to destinations outside the places where they normally live and work and their activities during the stay at these destinations' (Burkart and Medlik, 1974: v). Jafari extended the industrial description to place it within a conceptual framework: 'Tourism is a study of man away from his usual habitat, of the industry which responds to his needs, and of the impacts that both he and the industry have on the host socio-cultural, economic and physical environments'(1977: 8).

More recently, it has been observed that tourism might never become a 'single discipline' as such, and consequently it has begun to be conceptualized as multi-disciplinary, in that more than one discipline is needed to understand the phenomenon that we label 'tourism'.

Pearce classifies tourism as a 'specialism' rather than a discipline. Disciplines have 'a history of scholarship, international scholarly communities, established publication outlets, wide-spread systematic University recognition in the form of departments ... disciplinary "heroes" or "heroines" and professional societies as social and prestige reference systems' (1991: 298). Pearce contends that specialisms share only some of these features, and may or may not mature into disciplines. He cites Graburn and Jafari as stating 'No single discipline alone can accommodate, treat or understand tourism: it can be studied only if disciplinary boundaries are crossed'(1991: 7). Research into tourism then, comes from many disciplines whose ways of looking at problems differ widely. Economics, anthropology, geography, science, psychology are some examples. In a multi-disciplinary approach, the knowledge generated is likely to be 'owned' by the parent discipline, rather than the offspring specialism. Who gets access to this knowledge, and the ways in which it is disseminated, will determine whether it becomes knowledge about tourism or remains knowledge about, say, anthropology.

Now, the focus is on an inter-disciplinary approach, which adds something extra to the multidisciplinary perspective. An inter-disciplinary approach deliberately sets out to synthesize the philosophies and techniques of the separate disciplines into the framework of 'tourism'. In this way we frame the problem as a tourism problem in its own right, rather than an economic or an anthropological problem brought about by, or impacting on, tourism. The solution, resolution, answer, understanding or knowledge then belongs to 'tourism', and not to the parent discipline.

In fact, there might be no discernible 'it' out there, which we are trying to locate and identify as tourism and attempting to establish as an entity in its own right that is worthy of study. Tourism might consist of a myriad experts who are creating conflicting sets of discourses, and technologies (systems and scientific hardware) that we have put together and come to know as tourism.

Constructing the Knowledge

Research and Practice

It is reasonable to ask '*how* do we know?' as well as '*what* do we know?' about tourism. *How* we know that there is some phenomenon labelled tourism, emanates from two sources - research and practice. Research and practice provide us with *what* we know – the knowledge we call 'tourism'. This 'body of knowledge' gives rise to the curriculum, or course of work to be followed by students. Unfortunately, as we shall see, this is not a simple and un-complicated process.

Firstly, there are many types of research that will give different and conflicting 'knowledge', all of which will be 'true' to some extent, especially in a subject conceptualized as multi- or inter-disciplinary. Secondly, when we observe *practices* – what people actually do, and then try to draw some conclusions and insights from this – we are observing something that has already been artificially constructed. Initially, much of the knowledge la-belled tourism came from observing and asking people in the industry what they did in their jobs and what they would have liked to have known about before they started work (Airey and Nightingale, 1981).

But 'job' is a construct; a job has no existence of its own. The boundaries of what people do and do not do in a particular job have been determined for reasons that have been historically and politically determined. For example, in its early days, nursing carried with it a range of responsibilities including ward cleaning, cooking, sewing and so on, all of which are now someone else's job. Observing a nurse in the nineteenth century would give a set of practices – and knowledge about nursing – different from those derived from observing a nurse today.

The tourism curriculum: where does it come from?

The tourism curriculum – including decisions about 'what counts as tourism knowledge and what does not' – originates from the research of many disciplines and the practices of a number of groups. In particular, 'the industry' (a loose and problematic term in the tourism field) and educational institutes in both the public and private sector contribute to the knowledge, which is then shaped into the curriculum. Influences on the curriculum come from other sources. A major influence is government, both local and central, which may have developed policies to promote tourism as a source of overseas revenue, and to generate employment. Another influence is the international tourism bodies – The International Hotel Association, the World Tourism Organization and bodies such as ASEAN and the Pacific Asia Travel Association (PATA). There are many local industry bodies, commit-tees and councils, such as the Australian Tourism Industry Association, the Tourism Authority of Thailand, who make recommendations that influence and shape the way in which we think about education and training in tourism.

Nowadays, curriculum is conceptualized as more than 'a list of content'. It is a dynamic and fluid process involving interactions between teachers and students; at its best, education - especially post-compulsory education – is a *process* that results from the curriculum, transforms people, and thus enables them to grow intellectually. In this way, they can critique and contribute to their society in a thinking and productive manner. Harvey (cited in Horsburgh and Robinson, 1994) states that 'the critical test of higher education is whether it can develop and disseminate knowledge that enables all of us to deal with an ever-changing world'(1994: 5). The Copra and Bentley (1992) view of vocational education supports this in that the challenge of vocational education is that it should be 'relevant to the needs of this changing society'. In 1916, Dewey was writing that we should avoid limited conceptions of vocation, and not assume one occupation per lifetime, since 'any one occupation loses its meaning and becomes a routine'.

Does the tourism curriculum, as demanded by the industry and presented by trainers and educators, encourage people to transform, and to live and work in an ever changing world? Or does it intentionally direct them into low paying, menial jobs? Where there are many educational options resulting in highly paid jobs, well informed students do sometimes choose not to enter tourism education programmes. The largest National Training Organization in the region, Singapore, claims that the tourism industry is experiencing difficulties (ASEAN, 1991: 4) in recruiting labour because it faces competition from other industries. A survey in 1988 found that 'the industry has a poor image as an employer' (ASEAN, 1991: 5). Whether this image is justified or not is beyond the scope of this chapter. However, as we shall see, industry groups are often in the driver's seat in respect of 'what counts as knowledge', and they do this from their role and practices as employers.

The tourism curriculum: what is its intention?

As yet, we have no clear statements about the intention of tourism curriculum in the region, other than its role as a tool to alleviate the problem of training large numbers of people fairly quickly. Go (1993) analyses the problem, using projected figures from *Gearing Up For Growth*, published by the World Travel and Tourism Council in 1993. The Council projects that by 2005, the industry in the Asia Pacific region will require an additional 72 million workers. Though these workers have different education and training needs, three key categories are identified: 5 per cent of the total projected jobs will be senior executive or management positions; supervisors or middle management will make up 20 per cent of the jobs, whilst front-line workers will make up the remaining 75 per cent of jobs. That is to say, 800,000 senior executives/managers, 3.4 million supervisory staff and 12.8 million front-line/technical workers have to be trained and educated over the next ten years. As we move towards the year 2005, how are the industry and education providers approaching this task?

Personnel Education and Training

Management training: a brief look

It has been estimated that 800,000 senior executive positions will be generated by the increase in demand for tourism in the region. Torrington *et al.* (1989) identify substantive differences in the types of jobs performed by managers at various levels, and by supervisors.

They claim that top-level managers spend most of their time outside the company with peers and are relatively detached, in terms of responsibilities, from their organizations, whereas second-level managers are concerned with policy formulation and implementation. According to Go' s estimates, only 5 per cent of the positions will be in the top/second-level management area. However, their education and training needs will be different, even though both come under the heading of 'senior management' positions.

Middle management and supervisory positions are estimated to be 20 per cent of the positions generated. Middle managers tend to be concerned with making the organization work. Torrington *et al.* express some concern that middle managers, for example, tend to go in for 'management development' in order to make sense of the job, which is often a ramshackle collection of humdrum tasks that any literate school-leaver could easily accomplish. The constant stream of books, lectures, seminars and symposia from the behavioural science entrepreneurs offer neat packages of answers, rapidly replacing one management myth with another, and the clientele for such placebos is almost exclusively middle managers (1989: 34). In fact, they see the number of middle-management posts in organizations *decreasing* in the future due to the growing sophistication of information technology available to senior managers in developed countries.

Supervisors: career culmination?

Supervisors are generally drawn 'from the ranks', and a supervisory position is often the career culmination for people who start in an operative post. Thus, a waiter might become a head waiter, a secretary in a travel business might become an office manager and so on. Torrington *et al.* believe that it is rare for people to work their way up from supervisory positions. They draw attention to the fact that 'there is a dearth of recent studies of supervisors' (1989: 37). In 1977, Drucker expressed the belief that supervisors were seeing their role shrinking in status, in importance and in esteem. Drucker believes that supervisors act as buffers between management, unions and workers and that their main function might well be 'to take the blows' (1977: 36).

The conventional wisdom is that front-line work leads to middle-management and supervisory positions, which are routes to the 'top'. This view is reinforced by advertising material *Careers in Tourism* put out by the Alberta Tourism Education Council in Canada. 'Susan' is described as a busperson – 'I carry dishes to the kitchen' – who becomes, through a series of steps, the owner and manager of a restaurant; 'Robert' also begins as a busperson and ends up as 'the general manager of a fine hotel'. It might be that some people in the tourist industry, if they have the time and resources to take on further education during their careers (both Susan and Robert did this) are able to progress 'up the ladder'. But it is far from proven that all front-line people have these opportunities.

This might be more true in developing countries where there is a shortage of highly trained people at management level, but it should not be taken for granted that progression up the hierarchy 'automatically' occurs for most people who enter at the operative level. Research into management and supervisory career paths needs to be done in the newer destinations to establish what the trends are, and whether they differ from those in established destinations.

In themselves, management and supervisory positions might well represent interesting, and relatively well-paid jobs for some people who do not aspire to move up in the hierarchy. However, we should be cautious of claims that jobs in tourism, at the operative level, are the beginning of some sort of a career path which includes an executive, decision-making role at its culmination. Notwithstanding the success of Susan and Robert, it is unlikely that guides in National Parks ever actually end up running them, whichever country we are talking about. Or that housekeeping room attendants in motels end up as managers through promotion or training schemes, though they might end up supervising other housekeeping room attendants. The management training needs of middle managers and of supervisors in countries at different stages of their development are overwhelmingly different. We need to ask how well education programmes in the region make allowances for these differences.

Executives and managers do not need to be trained exclusively for jobs in the tourism industry. In many developed countries, they can take commerce, management or other degrees and diplomas (which sometimes have a tourism 'option') and their knowledge is transferable to management in the tourism industry or any other industry. Ironically, at this level, they will have little day-to-day interaction with tourists anyway. What is often overlooked is that many successful businesses in the industry were simply set up by entrepreneurs with little or no business or tourism education/training but with lots of energy and ideas. Moreover, it is far from clear that tourism management training *per se* has brought about improvement and innovation in the industry in the more developed destinations in the region.

Front-line workers: people who interact with tourists

Most of the education and training programmes reviewed in this chapter are, in fact, at the craft level. The programmes are provided to the front-line or technical workers who actually interact with the tourists. An estimated 12.8 million front-line workers are needed to fulfil 75 per cent of potential vacancies in the region. It is the training programmes for these people – they tend to be referred to as training rather than education programmes – that this chapter will focus on. These programmes are being exported from the developed destinations to the less developed ones, as a quick and handy answer to the massive and complicated human resources problem. It is critical to identify who are front-line workers since training programmes written for Western front-line workers have become models for other areas in the region.

In Canada, Withey *et al.* (1991: 286) note that

> Profiles of front line employees indicate that low literacy levels ... plague the industry. Often staff are recruited from the ranks of the high school drop outs and many have had negative experiences with traditional education systems ... the tourism/hospitality industry has traditionally utilised a readily available labour pool of women and youth. (1991: 286)

In Australia and New Zealand, the tourism industry provides a source of short-term jobs for students who are paying their way through university, although the tourism industry in Australia is trying to phase out casual workers (Commonwealth Department of Tourism, 1993). For these casual workers, jobs are obviously not intended to lead to careers in the industry. Front-line workers in developed destinations are, thus, a diverse group of people with special vocational educational needs that might go beyond mere training.

This is where we experience difficulties when exporting training to other countries. Blanton writes that

> Tourism training in developing countries has almost exclusively centred on vocational and technical skills. Little thought has been given as to how this education relates to the existing social and cultural framework of the host country, to the problems of communication between guest and host, or to the demands and stresses placed upon those in the front-lines of the industry, whose potential for 'culture shock: far exceeds that of their foreign guests'.(1981: 117)

This view is supported by Bruner who examined the advertising literature of travel agencies that promised to transform the tourist, so that they would be forever changed. He found naive promises of 'a complete change occurring within the tourist self, in a brief 3-week period' whilst at the same time, the underlying assumption was that there was no change in the front-line people who interacted with tourists. The 'native self' was assumed to remain the same, despite 'industrial revolution, colonialism, wars of independence, nationalism, the rise of new nations, economic development, tourism and the entire production of modern technology, including automobiles, television, Sony radios and Casio watches' (1991: 239). In contrast to the profile of the Western front-line worker, Blanton points out that it is not safe to assume that the front-line worker is a 'marginal' person (1981: 120). They are fully functioning members of their own society, and not drop-outs. But, traditional societies in the region do not have a cultural frame of reference for tourism. 'Experience with travel is extremely limited ... concept of a vacation is virtually unknown' (1981: 121), as is the notion of saving money in order to get away from it all. There are traditional concepts of leisure, ceremony, celebration, as well as travel and hospitality. People who have no notion of 'service' in the Western sense, let alone 'quality service', might not make the distinction between service and subservience. This is especially true if the incoming tourist interacts with them from a frame of reference that perceives porters and housekeeping room attendants as lowly occupations, as they are perceived in their own countries.

In the publication *Preparing for ASEAN Tourism: Training Needs*, ASEAN points out that there is a high labour turnover in the sector, and that 'The 15–24 age group provides the core recruitment pool and this age group is expected to decline steadily in the region after 1990' (1991). The question to ask is 'who, or what, is at the centre of any training programme – what exactly is it that should drive it?' Is it the needs of the tourist, the needs of trainees who become front-line workers, the teachers, the employers, the government, industry profits? Some combination, or something else?

Expansion in the Region: The Challenge ...

Tourism in the Asia Pacific region has grown at a tremendous rate. International visitor arrivals between 1983 and 1990 increased from 9.8 million to 21,698 million, an increase of 121 per cent (ASEAN, 1991: 1). This growth is likely to continue and the region could well be the focal point of future world tourism development. As ASEAN has pointed out (ASEAN, 1991), it is the quality of service that visitors associate with an area which gives it a major competitive advantage. In order to maintain this service advantage in the region, sufficient numbers of people must be educated and trained to work in the industry. This is an expensive and complicated undertaking for all the countries in the region.

Education and training schemes for the industry in the region range from long-established government and industry education and training programmes, to situations where governments and industry are scrambling to meet the human resources challenge. The education and training issues confronting the industry reflect the same diversity, contrasts and challenges as the make-up of the industry as a whole.

A PATA (Yee, 1992) overview on the human resources situation in the region and the World Travel and Tourism Council survey report, *Gearing up for Growth* (Go, 1993b) both identified the lack of tourism education facilities as a key issue for the area. Tourism education requires qualified teachers who must be recruited, usually from the industry, and who need teacher education programmes to enable them to pass on their knowledge effectively. The issue of 'lack of tourism education' is a complex one, and involves strategies that take into account the needs of all the stakeholders. Ideally, industry and higher education should work together to identify needs and to develop programmes to reflect the complexity and diversity of educational needs for a huge range of occupations within the industry.

This complexity is highlighted by Withey *et al.* in their study of front-line staff training in the hospitality industry (the occupation of server) in Canada. They note that 'A number of factors impact the industry's ability to provide quality service', and in particular draw links between poor or non-existent training of managers in the 'vast majority of these businesses, 85 per cent [which are] small or medium sized enterprises, many of which are struggling for survival' (1991: 286). Managers in these types of enterprises are concerned with the immediate running of the business, and for them, acquiring further training is a low priority. Human resources planning and training – their own as well as that of their staff – has insufficient attention. In the region, ASEAN reports that tourism is a 'small business industry' and that many small businesses exist on the fringes of tourism.

Notwithstanding this difficulty, Withey *et al.* identify the ideal educator for front-line workers as the managers of the enterprises in which they work. They believe that the venue for education and training should be the place of work, to ensure that it is relevant and delivered in the context of the work environment. Education and training about methods of training their own employees should be given to managers. In this way, both managers and front-line workers are developed simultaneously.

Better Quality of Staff: . . . But Is It True?

There are many reasons why a tourist chooses to travel to a particular destination, and it is too simplistic to claim that if only there were more people giving quality service in the industry, then more people would travel there. The human resources issue needs to be viewed in the wider context of the infrastructure, culture and politics of a particular country. For example, visa requirements, whether independent travel is allowed, and how safe it is, airport facilities, banking, transport, availability of hotels or guest houses, hygiene standards, faith in the local police and so on are all considerations for people thinking of travel. Terrorism activities, internal wars and strife are a great deterrent, no matter how good the weather or how polite the waiters are. The Minister of Culture and Tourism of Pakistan noted that 'The most important lesson of the eighties is that tourism as an industry prospers only in peaceful conditions' and commented euphemistically about the 'protracted period of disturbance' in the region that took a high toll on tourism activities (WTO, 1992).

In addition, in many under-developed countries, there is a lack of higher education facilities, and a culture with no history of ever having felt the need for vocational education. There is often geographic isolation. How are the locals of the hill tribes of Thailand expected to understand that tourists from France wish to 'visit' them? With no access to television, films, books or formal education, how are they expected to even know about Europe and the 'leisure needs' of its people? Is preparing them to receive 'visitors' in fact educating them? The question of whose interests are being served is an ethical question that should not be overlooked if we believe the local people benefit from 'transmitting their cultural legacies'.

In countries like Australia, New Zealand, Hong Kong and Singapore the stability and wealth of the countries enabled the industry to tap into, and use confidently the well established infrastructures. As tourism developed, these were already present. There were polytechnics, technical colleges and universities with good reputations already established, and which were able to offer courses in tourism within an existing system. The local populations, many of whom are travellers themselves, have a ready-made awareness of the needs and expectations of tourists.

However, some of the newest destinations in the region have difficulty because they must develop their economies so that they can afford to provide both the infrastructures and tourism educational programmes at the same time. Countries such as Vietnam, Laos and Myanmar are aiming at the international tourism market again (ESCAP, 1993). It is estimated that the current tourism industry in Vietnam employs about 25,000 people. Most of these workers have learned from the on-job training. But, 'by the year 2005, the work force involved in the tourism industry and in tourism related jobs will reach 123,480' (ESCAP, 1993: 85).

In Papua New Guinea, 1993 was seen as the first time that the image of PNG has been promoted ' . . . in an organised and directional manner in the international market' (WTO Technical Paper 1994: 6). Human resources training has a very high priority in the Tourist Promotion Authority's development strategy. All parts of the sector are at a rudimentary level, but considerable attention has been placed on implementing training programmes for staff. The paper stated that 'A small hospitality training facility exists, offering basic certificate courses in tourism, in addition to basic food training'.

Educational and Occupational Standards: A View of People and Jobs

In this chapter, we are examining the question of 'What is the knowledge – about tourism and about people – that the tourism curriculum is based upon?' Furthermore, we are trying to determine where the ideas for the 'stuff' to be learned by the various groups of front-line workers actually comes from. In addition, we want to know the processes by which students are expected to absorb this knowledge, and consequently become citizens who can live, work and contribute to our ever changing world.

Ask any industry group to determine what they require in an employee, and they will inevitably come up with a list of standards and/or competencies (Robinson and Yeilder, 1995). If these lists do not result in 'quality' workers, then the industries construct another set, using sharper, clearer, more focused language, with different systems for ensuring that quality will result. Are they doing what Miller and Rose (1993) identify as 'reforming reality'? This is defined as being eternally optimistic that if some aspect of life could be better, more effectively administered, all will be well. Failure of one set of policies brings about the need to devise another policy or set of guidelines which will, of course, work this time.

In effect, the groups who draw up lists of competencies prejudge the key questions about vocational education to be those about how education can best serve industry in the least expensive way. In examining the various committees and commissions that were charged with making government policy about vocational training in Australia, Kaye (1992) wanted to know 'what informed' the members of these groups? In other words, what was the basis for their knowledge, what were the arguments or philosophies that shaped their views? He was sceptical of their efforts to keep on redefining and refining lists of competencies, believing that they had a narrow, economically driven view of the world.

The difficulty is to determine whether lists of competencies or worker profiles in practice, generate stereotypes – newer versions as well as the old familiar versions. Certainly, they appear to promote the conventional assumptions of social class. University graduate profiles generally include 'personal autonomy' and 'acceptance of responsibility towards others' (Wilson, 1993), because these are seen as professional attributes that people of high intellectual ability should be encouraged to develop. However, these types of competencies (sometimes known as 'capabilities' in the context of university graduates) are generally omitted from lists of competencies for front-line workers; they cannot be adequately standardized and measured.

In many parts of the Western world, the prevailing idea as far as vocational education is concerned, is to 'categorise and standardise minimum skills groupings required for performance of specific industry positions' (Burns, 1988). Jobs such as those performed by front-line workers are conceptualized, not holistically, but as a number of tasks to be performed. Each of these tasks is reduced to a set of discrete skills that must be performed in the same way by all potential employees.

The vocational education world is awash with recognizable performance standards, levels of learning, criteria, measurable outcomes and behaviours. The prevailing idea is that vocational education qualifications must be standardized. The assumption that underpins this idea is that 'standardization = consistency = quality'. When we examine the various training programmes in the region, we can see that such training activities in the tourism industry are actively promoted as the way in which to meet the human resources needs of the industry. Such a form of training brings about the need for a standardized system for administering it, for controlling it to ensure consistency and therefore, according to the rationale, assuring quality. Let us examine the mechanics of one such system in the region and consider the implications and expense for implementing such a system in the newer destinations.

Setting up Systems: The Context

Freedoms and frameworks

As Western governments such as the United States and the United Kingdom became committed to monetarism and moved towards economic liberalization, higher and vocational education came to be viewed as commodities able to be purchased by anyone, provided they have the money to pay for them. Post-compulsory education is purchased, then, because of its job potential. The acquisition of further education leads to well-paid jobs. The more qualifications a person can accumulate, the more employable he or she is supposed to become, generating positive spin-offs for the economy (Fitzsimons and Peters, 1994). Economic liberalization by Western governments has provided a global context for reforms in higher and vocational education in countries such as Australia and New Zealand.

The consequent freeing up of the economy has meant that anyone can set up an educational institution to educate and train students to meet the demand for places. Not surprisingly, this proliferation of providers seems to have generated a need for 'proof' of graduate competency and quality of teachers, facilities and courses. The paradox is that with the 'freedom' to provide a diverse range of vocational education programmes, has come the industry's response for 'the necessary institutional frameworks for tourism training ... training boards within national training councils, trade testing and certification ... apprenticeship schemes' (TCSP, 1991). Frameworks and other mechanisms, in practice, act as control mechanisms – they bring all education providers into line, and define what is to be 'counted' as tourism education and training. They generate the need for 'experts', expert systems, administrators, consultants, and electronic technology. Who will pay for this?

Setting up the necessary institutional frameworks and organizing advisory groups like Tourism Training Organizations, National Training Councils, Lead Bodies (The National Council of Vocational Qualifications in the UK is advised by 140 Lead Bodies) and so on, is an expensive business for both education providers and the industry. It creates a bureaucratic revolution.

New Zealand: a qualifications framework for vocational training

In New Zealand, the Education Amendment Act (EAA) 1990 provided for higher education institutions to have 'as much independence and freedom to make academic, operational and management decisions as is consistent with the nature of the services they provide, the efficient use of resources, the national interest, and the demands of accountability' (Fitzsimons, 1994: 5).

The EAA 1990 established a National Qualifications Authority, along the lines of the UK National Council of Vocational Qualifications. The New Zealand Qualifications Authority (NZQA) administers the New Zealand system for both school and vocational qualifications. Any group wishing to gain NZQA accreditation must develop courses that satisfy NZQA criteria. The NZQA facilitates groups from industry – National Standards Bodies – to formulate criteria for vocational qualifications. So, to be effective and enforceable, frameworks must be firmly situated within the laws of the land; they do not just appear.

National standards bodies: their role

There are over 70 National Standards Bodies (NSBs) in New Zealand. Their major role is to devise criteria for measuring the competence of employees in a particular field. NSBs are comprised of individuals who represent the various industry groups, for example the tourism industry, or professional bodies, government departments and major businesses that are connected to the industry or the occupation. In 1992 there were 202,143 students enrolled in post-compulsory education and training (Prime Ministerial Task Force on Employment, 1994). Therefore there is one Standards Body for approximately 2,800 students.

In New Zealand, Standards Bodies meet regularly. They set and review the standards, because each standard has a 'use by date' and must be reviewed so that it will not become obsolete. If the skills or knowledge become obsolete before the 'use by date', all stakeholders are to be contacted to make sure that the skills or knowledge are obsolete and a new standard is then written. This process takes up to two years.

New Zealand Qualifications Authority: its role

The role of the NZQA is to approve qualifications, and their stamp of approval indicates that the holder has attained a predetermined level of knowledge, skill and understanding of a certain subject. Vocational certificates or diplomas are not awarded by the NZQA as such, but by the institutions offering NZQA approved courses.

To be approved by the NZQA, qualifications have to be competence-based. This means that the training undertaken must contribute directly to a person's ability to complete a job. Courses need to cover all the 'elements of competence' associated with a specific type of work. NSBs provide much of the expertise, in determining what the elements of competence are for a particular job. Elements of competence are descriptions of actions, behaviours, outcomes or knowledge of what is, or should be done in a workplace situation. These elements are then collected into 'unit standards' that form the basis for a NZQA recognized award. Each unit standard is accompanied by 'performance criteria', that is, definitions of what trainees should be able to do on completion of the training.

In New Zealand, the universities have chosen to operate outside of the NZQA system. Institutions that choose to operate outside the system take the risk that their qualifications will not be 'recognized', whereas those within the framework are recognized as having fulfilled the quality requirements. What this means in practice is not clear. Various degrees in tourism and numerous degrees with tourism options are available at universities and degree-granting polytechnics. Whilst it is acknowledged that front-line worker qualifications are different, as yet, there is no information to suggest that only a graduate with a 'recognized' qualification, that is, a non-university degree, is more acceptable to the industry (and therefore gets the job).

In similar forms, this type of competence-based model and the system for administering it is being used in the developed countries in the region as a way of managing vocational education. It is not clear where the wealth or funding comes from to enable people to spend their time in this sort of exercise. Do front-line workers perform their jobs more efficiently and effectively, so that service improves because of the increase in bureaucracy and control mechanisms that exist for certification? The jury is still out.

A qualifications framework, then, sets parameters around what is, and is not counted as vocational education/training. What is counted is that which is measurable by outcomes to be achieved. Time is an element and the faster a student can complete the outcomes, the more efficient the provider is supposed to be.

Fitzsimons (1994: 7) argues

that the wealth of the nation is measured by the attainment of certificates by the human capital. The logic seems to be that more certificates is equivalent to more successful participation [in vocational training], more participation is equivalent to more skills, more skills is equivalent to the enhanced value of the human capital and more human capital is equivalent to more wealth. The possession of paper makes us wealthy! One difficulty with this approach is that the attainment of certificates is not identical with skill formation nor is it identical with economic recovery. We can see here the belief that equity comes from the production of certificates, the 'paperisation' of society where every movement and situation is documented in the form of performance-based documentation.

Vocational Education: A Set of Skills?

For some graduates about to enter the professions (for example the medical or legal professions) vocational education is often interpreted to include wide general knowledge about society, ways in which society operates, ways of thinking about this and ways of critiquing the conventional wisdom within the discipline. In addition, specific skills training required to perform certain aspects of the job are a complementary part of the curriculum. However, a different perspective of professional or vocational training exists in the types of jobs we are discussing – guides of various kinds, front desk agents, bartenders, tourism/visitor information counsellors, reservation sales agents, housekeeping room attendants, servers and other front-line workers. Vocational training for these people has evolved through the apprenticeship tradition in what Schrag describes as the passing on of 'know-how'.

> Under the apprenticeship system, the know-how of the master crafts person is analysed into sub tasks. These tasks are identified with various stages of training. The apprentice first learns the most rudimentary and least rewarding parts of the occupation, moves on to the more engaging and skilled aspects and ultimately acquires the secrets of the guild. (1992: 269)

For front-line workers, though, there may not be too many engaging and skilled aspects, or secrets of the guild available to them. These are more difficult to measure, and therefore do not fit easily into the competence-based model.

Where vocational education is seen as being synonymous with 'training for a specific job' it does not usually incorporate a professional dimension or broader concepts of education. Students learn only diminished 'trade', a discrete and measurable set of skills, and it is not intended that they become poets, commentators on society or autonomous master craftsmen or craftswomen; these are not criteria that can be clearly and objectively measured, nor are they generally identified by the industry as directly relevant for the job. Vocational education then, is 'knowledge about skills and (sometimes) why they are performed'.

Put simply, and into the training context for front-line workers, when we apply this view of training to tourism and to people, we must ask:

1. Can knowledge be identified only by certain people in the industry, from their analysis of their present and future needs, and the jobs people are currently engaged in? In addition, can it be constructed into lists of competencies, using standardised, objective language so that all stakeholders are able to construct the same meaning. 'Here is a list of what we want an employee to be able to do ...'
2. Are educators or trainers able to package knowledge in such a way that the learning activities achieve the pre-prescribed outcomes, which can be assessed by observation? Will all packages be consistent so that 'quality' is assured? Will employers know exactly what employees can and cannot do? 'Here is a certificate which guarantees everything we say that this potential employee can do ...'
3. Will the knowledge up-skill, or enhance trainees/potential employees because as they collect increments of knowledge and skills, they become more employable and therefore more valuable to society? As a person becomes more skilled and knowledgeable as, say, a recreation camp attendant, is there an increase in the number of jobs available to them? Will they command higher wages, therefore receiving direct financial rewards, and consequently paying more tax? But, in this way they will contribute to the economic well being of society as a whole, as well as to their own economic well being. 'Here is a certificate which guarantees me a better income than before I had it ...'

This rational view – that everyone seeks to increase only their economic well-being – dominates the discourse. The industry benefits economically because the workforce is skilled, bringing about greater customer satisfaction and therefore higher profits. The worker benefits because up-skilling increases the chances of a better-paid job. The competence-based, or standards model, is able to be efficiently administered, since we have developed the electronic technology to collect information about qualifications and the standard or level at which a student is able to perform. Economic growth is all set to take place, and the industry's human resources problem has been solved ...

The Industry: Diversity and Inflexibility

The standards model has its adherents in many developed countries in the region. As we examine some of the training programmes offered in places such as Australia, an underlying belief is clear that the knowledge, skills and dispositions for most vocational and professional occupations within the tourism industry can be identified, classified, placed on a hierarchy (simple to difficult) and described in an objective language. It is important to acknowledge that the systems designed to administer the standards-based model of vocational qualifications are not neutral; they have shaped the way in which education and training will take place.

As yet, the industry has accepted uncritically beliefs about the nature and purpose of vocational education for its front-line workers. If we accept Pearce's (1991) view that tourism is a specialism and not yet a serious discipline in its own right, we can accept that tourism is still evolving and the possible 'body of knowledge' upon which it is based has not yet settled, or been entirely agreed upon by all of the stakeholders. There might never be a settled 'body of knowledge'. So, when trying to face the reality of lack of training for millions of potential workers in the industry, the 'questions to ask' about this are difficult to formulate – who will ask them? Which of the stakeholder's perceptions of training will be privileged? Is it possible for the industry to move beyond simple skills training and to incorporate competencies into a new model for technical training, which acknowledges the learner and the needs of his or her community at the centre of the curriculum? In this way the individual can become fully competent in a given job, but also live in such a way as to enhance his or her community. It is only when we understand our own cultural heritage that we appreciate why others might also find it interesting. A front-line worker, who is confident and exudes knowledge and self-esteem, is a far more gracious host than one who conceptualizes him or herself as a servant. Preserving a 'cultural heritage' means more than displays of traditional dancing every night after dinner in a five-star hotel. One of the positive spin-offs of tourism is that it has encouraged the preservation of unique buildings and land. We need now to learn how to nurture the uniqueness of those people who, daily, interact with tourists.

Degrees in tourism acknowledge the need for the learner to widen his or her perspective beyond the immediate industry requirements of the 'now'. The challenge is to find a way of liberalizing technical training so that it liberates the learner and still meets the requirements of the industry now. Or, maybe it is much easier to look for quick, simple and ready-made solutions.

There is a paradox in that the industry, whilst acknowledging and celebrating its own diversity and innovations, has assumed conventional beliefs and ways of thinking about vocational education. It is uncritically locking itself into established, inflexible systems in an effort to meet the training needs of its potential workforce.

It is important to remember that this belief about vocational education is being exported to many of the newer destinations that are entering the market, along with the more tangible technology required for implementing the systems. Notions of rigid forms of vocational education seem invariably to reinforce the social stratification within society and within the world. Remember that this is training for the people who directly interact with foreign tourists, but always on unequal terms. Along with the training comes messages, implicit as well as explicit, that shape the nature of the relationship between the server and the served. Both know that their roles will never be reversed in some future personal interaction; the status quo remains intact. We can see this belief about vocational education 'in action' as we examine the practices of some of the developed countries within the region.

Australia: A Plethora of Standards

In Australia, Tourism Training Australia (TTA) had set one of its objectives as 'to establish agreed national training standards with associated portability of qualifications'. In 1990, Australia established the National Training Board, and Tourism Training Australia was recognized as the Competency Standards Body for the hospitality industry for a number of areas. The first set of standards that received approval from the National Training Board were those for Food and Beverage. These standards were placed at four levels from 'Introductory and Basic Skills' at level 1 to 'Supervisory' at level 4. This conforms to a traditional hierarchical view of vocational education, which identifies simple skill training at the first level and works through to more complex skills at higher levels.

According to Rein (1991; personal communication)

> All major occupations are covered with the system identifying both common skills across occupations at different levels and occupational specific skills ... the system is designed to provide flexibility in specific job design. The system provides information at a number of levels: occupation skill profiles which identify core and job-related duties and the associate skills/training modules; competency standards for each unit of competency; training specifications and short-form curricula which provide guidance to training providers.

'The system' appears to be of paramount importance. All major occupations are covered by the system: the system identifies ... the system is designed to ... the system provides information ... etc. The skill profiles, standards and training specifications resulted from CODAP (Comprehensive Occupational Data Analysis Programme) methodology, which is described as an 'internationally known methodology'.

Within the framework of the hospitality industry, the standards relate to some 60 occupations and standards being developed that relate to approximately 80 occupations. For travel-related sectors the standards' salient features are said to be modularity, flexibility, universality and include both vocational front-line worker skills and senior management education. However, Tourism Training Australia has not developed their standards to a high level of specific detail. This was because 'In many occupational areas, there already exists a long tradition and shared understandings of acceptable standards' (Rein, 1991). This highlights a paradox. Fundamental to the perception that education can be standardized and systemized is the belief that all we have to do is find the correct objective language to describe the standard. Language is the tool and shared understandings will automatically result if we use the tool correctly. Shared understandings mean that all stakeholders act consistently. But, where a long tradition and 'shared understandings' already exist, it is too difficult to capture them by writing them down. Language, as a tool for describing existing traditions and shared meanings proves to be inadequate; however, polished, sharpened and fine tuned, we can use it for establishing and describing future traditions and shared meanings.

According to Rein, TTA found that the more detailed the standards were, the less likely they were to be used in the work place. It was more difficult to judge overall performance, especially the ability to apply a range of skills in different situations to satisfy customer needs, 'Instead, we decided on a simpler format for the standards with detailed back up material available ... and training programmes on how to interpret and use the standards' (ibid.). Once students have passed all the training modules required at a particular level, they receive an official certificate, diploma or degree that lists the modules successfully completed. The ways in which this can be achieved are flexible – through training programmes, distance learning, 'skills assessment' (which tests whether experienced people can achieve the module outcomes without having to work through the module), or some combination of these.

Keeping Australians in the tourism industry once they have been trained is sometimes a problem. In 1993 the Commonwealth Department of Tourism reported that 'a factor which contributes significantly to job satisfaction and job performance is identification with available career pathways. Until quite recently, such career pathways in the tourism industry from various points of entry have not been identified' (36).

Competent Communication

By examining one of the competencies, the ability to communicate which is on almost every list in some form or another, we can see how difficult it is to interpret the meaning of a phrase like communication skills, not only in a country such as Australia, but in less developed destinations.

'Ability to communicate' is generally regarded as a generic transferable competency. It is often broken into a number of component skills, which are taught separately, and somehow come together as 'ability to communicate'. According to Kaye (1992) there is, as yet, no absolute consensus as to which of these skills are marginal and which are central. He believes that people who have not seriously studied the field of communication see it as the simple act of individuals exchanging messages. With this over-simplistic notion of communication, they draw up a rag-bag of micro skills that can be assessed in a simple way to certify that someone has the ability to communicate.

Kaye identifies some of the component skills from the wide field of Communication Studies, which are far from simple: listening, assertiveness, expression and interpretation of non-verbal cues, negotiation, conflict resolution, overcoming communication apprehension and questioning. In order to communicate, he writes, people need higher order abilities such as accuracy in person perception and attribution or intent, impression formation and management, social-perspective taking, effective use of language in inter-personal settings and the construction and coordination of meanings in intercultural settings. In addition, he introduces the Constructivist view, which is that communication is the reciprocal construction of meaning. And, communicative effectiveness depends, he states, on the degree to which individuals are able to differentiate information and to think in abstractions. Effective communicators are able to construct meanings from a variety of perspectives and have the ability to make predictions, explain the behaviour of others and to reduce uncertainty. These, he says, are all part of the repertoire of ingredients that collectively constitute 'communicative compet-ence' (1992).

How do we train people in, say, Papua New Guinea, where 'only 7 per cent are so far integrated into the money economy', to communicate effectively with tourists? (Tourism in Papua New Guinea, 1994: 1). As far as training is concerned, staff are to be given training programmes 'to build – and then transfer – multiple skills in marketing and tourism promotion'. Short-term 'experienced consultants are to provide on-job training and leadership trans-ference' (Ibid: 6). As there are no indigenous people to act as consultants, presumably they will be brought in from abroad. How will these consultants interpret and adapt the critical competency 'ability to communicate', to take into account the Papua New Guinean's varied views of foreigners? In effect, assuming that Papua New Guineans are a homogeneous group is problem-atic, since the country is comprised of different tribal groups with different colonial histories (Bruner, 1991).

The idea that generic skills can be easily transferred is an integral part of the competency movement. The Tourism Authority of Thailand aims at developing a pool of trained tourism instructors (McNabb, 1990), and estab-lishes national training standards based on what they identify as Core and Generic Tourism Skills. Core skills are to be covered in the first few lessons. Customer relations and service, communication and cross-cultural skills will be covered as well. Materials will be imported and translated with 'support' from the industry.

Portability and Mobility

Portability is seen, commendably, as a key equity issue. The idea is that if qualifications are endorsed by a responsible national authority, holders of these qualifications should be able to move from job to job, and from country to country, and their qualifications will be recognized as quality training for a particular job. Certificates and Diplomas therefore empower their holders whilst ensuring employers of the performance level and quality of the prospective employee. Theoretically, and notwithstanding the work permit situation, the holder of a Bartenders Certificate, issued by the relevant credentialling authority in say, Indonesia, is able to get a job in Sydney,

Australia, and obtain higher pay than an Australian who does not hold a certificate. As yet it is not clear how the standardizing of qualifications in the tourism, or other industries, works in practice. Convincing evidence that the theory works is lacking. However, The Alberta Tourism Education Council in its *Careers in Tourism* leaflet cheerfully tells us that, in tourism, all the skills and knowledge 'travel with you wherever you go. Whether you move ... your work experience could be the springboard to a new job. New restaurants, hotels and resorts continue to open and expand across our province. Not to mention – the world beyond'.

Is training itself portable? There seems to be an assumption that it is. The standards-based model is being adopted in other countries in the region. Many of the developed countries 'export' higher education to less developed countries, or 'donate' it in the form of aid. For example, Australia gives three-quarters of its assistance to the educational sector in developing countries in the form of higher education (Byrne, 1994). Education and training consists of ideas, values, beliefs, ways of looking at the world and methods of administering it, as well as the 'knowledge' itself. It is not able to be exported or donated devoid of the set of values that underpin it. Social and cultural beliefs cannot be arbitrarily split off from education and training as though they were all separate entities. Education and training are transmitted by individuals to other quite different individuals, and (like tourism) are not of themselves, uncomplicated separate entities. An examination of how individual developing countries are trying to address their human resources dilemma highlights the way in which the prevailing western belief about the nature of vocational education and training has spread.

Education and Training in Developing Countries

Malaysia

In Malaysia, under the ASEAN Sub-Committee on Tourism (ASEAN-SCOT), a set of national craft standards was recently completed. The work of ASEAN-SCOT has resulted in the creation and development of Tourism Occupational Skill Standards. The ASEAN Training Directory states: 'The aim of the standards is to identify the tasks performed and the skills required by personnel in all sectors with reference to the specific job title' (1992). The standard is of an international level based on the tasks-approach developed by the International Labour Organisation. Each standard contains a definition of the skill. Though part of the standard can be used for the training of one job, certification can be granted only when all parts have been understood and tested. Some dubious claims are made:

> What is required is more bottom-up training so that all entrants to the industry will have certificates for basic training, opening up career paths for them. We are establishing regional and national training standards at craft level and are establishing regional and national training councils so that standards in schools

will be industry-led and employees will have skill certificates, and pride in their jobs. (ibid.)

Given the standards or competence-based model, the regional and national training council would have a role similar to that of a Lead Body, or Industry Training Organization. It will have the responsibility for setting the performance criteria for the student.

In Malaysia, the main training activity of the Malaysian Tourism Promotion Board is to train the tourist guides. Training is conducted in collaboration with Malaysian Association of Tour and Travel Agents (MATTA) and the Malaysian Tourist Guides Council (MTGC). They are the state organizations. The Malaysian Tourism Promotion Board recently formed a National Tourism Training Council in conjunction with the private sector. This body is for coordinating all tourism training, occupational standards and certification procedures as well as human resource issues. The Hotel Management National Productivity Corporation, which was founded in the early 1970s, is likely to become the certification and the curricular Validation Body for Malaysia's hospitality industry.

Macau

In Macau, the Department of Training plans to develop examination programmes to certify qualifications in the hotel industry and in the Food and Beverage area. This programme is based on identical programmes in Portugal and Canada (Direccao dos Servios de Turismo, 1992).

Korea

In Korea there is strict government regulation of tourism industry personnel which is achieved through government conducted eligibility examinations (KNTC Annual Report, 1992). Whether this is to ensure 'quality service' or has some other political rationale is difficult to ascertain.

However, the government encourages practical training and internships. The KNTC (1992): 'In general, most travel companies are too restricted in financial resources to conduct their own in-house training courses and therefore have to rely on organised courses from outside ... The Korea National Tourism Corporation runs two training centres responsible for the education of prospective workers'. As in most parts of the world, 'The public organizations subsidise educational and training programmes for the private sector'. However, students majoring in tourism management 'are provided with chances to apply and practise their theoretical knowledge as part of an on-job training programme prior to their entry into the travel industry'.

People's Republic of China

China's travel industry is developing rapidly and has become a key industry, while tourism education has also 'grown to a fairly large scale since . . . 1978' (Xu Fan, 1994: 2). However, the Chinese experience shows the difficulty in managing such a diverse and growing industry at the same time as educating people how to operate it. According to Xu Fan, the National Tourism Administration of the PRC recognizes that

> Personnel training is out of step with the tourism trade . . . at present . . . tourism colleges and schools have not been recognised as the principal source of new employees for the country' s tourism industry . . . there is a lack of an explicit stipulation of the requirements for qualifications for every kind of work in the tourism industry, and a certain degree of dislocation between personnel training and personnel employment. As a solution, emphasis will be shifted to the development of vocational and technical education. (ibid.)

Other problems are said to be the lack of centralized management of tourism education and a 'certain rashness in building tourism schools'. The teaching quality in tourism schools is not yet satisfactory to employers because graduates show 'an inferior political-ideological quality and competence in work'. It is seen as important to train tourism professionals to be 'of fine moral quality and high proficiency'. It is also important to standardize teaching and teaching programmes to 'unify the most fundamental teaching content and time allotment' (ibid.) But, in spite of doubts, 'National or regional training centres such as the Tianjin Institute of Tourism Management are being built at an accelerated pace. Tourism administration at all levels . . . are taking numerous forms to train workers at varying levels'.

Qualifications are important. For example, Tourist Guide qualification tests were introduced in 1989, and more that 40,000 persons have taken the examinations since then. As a solution to some of its problems, the China National Tourism Administration has signed an agreement to acquire tourism training services from the Australian Department of Tourism. Given the standards approach in Australia, it is likely that this method of training and certifying students will be exported to China.

The South Pacific

The United Nations Development Programme's 1988 report of the South Pacific found that 'the need for the training and registration of tour guides' and 'trade testing and certification' is a recurring theme common to all nine countries (Burns, 1988: 3).

In discussing projected human resources needs for the sector, an article in *TCSP Tourism Topics* noted that it is necessary for most TCSP member countries to set up the necessary institutional frameworks for tourism training, such as hotel and catering training boards within national training councils, trade testing and certification schemes, apprenticeship schemes (TCSP, 1991).

Burns' report the South Pacific tourism development planning and training recommended developing training-the-trainer programmes: 'A prerequisite to the successful implementation of any vocational training plan is the establishment of a cadre of trainers of tourism skills in the country ... A trainer training strategy ... will contain: how to identify a potential trainer, developing basic trainer skills [defined as instructing and demonstrating], identifying training needs ... etc.' (1988: 70). It is not clear who will train the trainers. Historically, Australia and New Zealand have strong links with the South Pacific, so it is likely that training packages, and beliefs about vocational education and frameworks, will be part of any potential advice in this regard.

However, it is recommended that future UNDP/WTO training assistance should work on creating and developing an environment conducive to encouraging local tourism training initiatives. This includes establishing the institutional framework for tourism training in each country and developing what they describe as the optimal method for creating, at a national level, 'trainer trainers'.

Standards and Standardization

Freedom: a problem for the industry?

A number of countries in the region do not have standardized, controlled programmes for students who want to work in the tourism industry. This is perceived as a problem by ASEAN.

The Philippines Tourism Manpower Survey Final Report conducted by the World Tourism Organization for the United Nations Development Programme recommends efforts to 'establish and introduce a structured vocational training scheme for the industry, with certification and appropriate standards' (UNDP, 1990). The standards referred to are aimed at the vocational and skills training courses offered by institutions that do not have accreditation or approval from either the Philippine Department of Education, Culture and Sports (DECS) or the Department of Tourism (DOT).

The institutions that have not been accredited to offer courses are free from the control of the DECS and the DOT. The quality of their facilities, teaching, staff training and the training programme as a whole are neither controlled nor standardized. This lack of control is viewed by the ASEAN as a problem. They recommend efforts to bring these training courses into the control of the Tourism Board Foundation Inc. This tri-sectorial body was created to meet the requirements of the Labour Code and to 'ensure that manpower of the right quality is made available at the right time and in the right quantity' (ASEAN, 1992). They report that the TBFI is 'Aware of the need to set minimum standards for training centres, training programmes and trainers ... [they have] already formulated standards which are currently being used for accreditation by the DOT ... eight national standards developed under the ASEAN agreement are presently being used in the design of tourism training programmes' (ASEAN, 1992).

Recognized qualifications: what difference do they make?

So, what difference does a 'recognized' certificate or diploma for a front-line or craft-level job make to the student, the potential employee? What are the benefits to be gained from enrolling and paying fees to an accredited institution, and completing a narrowly defined, standardized course of work, leading only to a specific job? Can students feel confident that, at the end of a training course, they will be able to deal effectively with change and the practical problems of life and work? Or should this confidence be developed elsewhere?

As we have seen, fundamental to the notion of standardization is the idea of a recognized, quality assured and therefore portable certificate, accepted on both a local and international level. A prospective employer is assured that the holder is able to perform a series of tasks at some prescribed standard. For the holder, this is supposed to guarantee a job at a higher level of pay, as compared with someone who does not hold the certificate, otherwise, what is the point of training?

It is not yet clear how this actually works in practice. Does it depend on the nature of the business? Foreign hotel chains employ qualified staff, but most of the work available is not in foreign hotels. Are people with certificates in Food and Beverage who work in back-street cafes paid more than people without a certificate who are doing the same work? Do certificates and diplomas enhance mobility when there is a decrease in demand for labour in one's own locality?

And what is the advantage to local employers in employing someone with a certificate or diploma? Are they willing or able to pay more? As yet, we have no evidence to be able to claim for example, that a guide in the Cook Islands with, say, a Cook Islands Guide Certificate (which enables him or her to take tourists reef-walking) is able to get a well-paid position in Hawaii doing a similar job. In the Cook Islands, the people who currently do this sort of job are self-employed, work concurrently in a number of tourism-related jobs and have loose flexible arrangements with hotels and tourists. What is the rationale for the UNDP claim that in the South Pacific 'the need for the training and registration of tour guides' is an issue? An issue for whom?

The industry: on-the-job training

Where the industry is directly involved in training, for example in on-the-job or in-service training, it tends to follow the assumptions already outlined – that increments of skills and knowledge enhance a person to the extent that they are able to perform better. So, on-the-job training tends to be packaged 'education' and training. It is substantially the same as the packages, or units of work, or modules, presented by education providers. For example, in the countries served by the Tourism Council of the South Pacific

> The TCSP publishes a wide range of training manuals which assist employers with staff training. The manuals are aimed at the hotel and catering professions and emphasise the need for good operational skill and are intended for use in on-job training situations or personal development. The manuals are presented as a series of short modules or study units each taking from 30 minutes to one hour to complete. (Tourism Council of the South Pacific, 1991)

Conclusion

There are two notions of tourism education and training that have run through this chapter. First, we have education for people who might or might not work in the industry, but who study tourism at a university as some sort of entity that exists in its own right.

This is where the 'battle of the definitions' is situated. The definition gives rise to the subject of tourism, which is then moulded into the curriculum. Because there is no consensus about what counts as tourism, there are many definitions, and consequently, many curricula.

These programmes are largely academic courses. Students study tourism in much the same way as they study history or literature; the curriculum in these subjects is not designed to make students employable in the history industry or as writers of great novels. The scholarly literature about tourism education is generally about the best way to view tourism so that students can conceptualize 'it' and understand where 'it' fits into society. However, some of these programmes *are* designed to educate personnel for the industry, at management level, or for government, at policy level, and they incorporate a broad understanding of principles and sometimes a critical approach to tourism. But they are not usually designed for people who will interact daily with tourists.

Generally, the discussion appears to centre around ensuring that vocational education in universities is wide and liberal, as well as skills forming. Academics are there to see that this happens, because universities have a culture of their own that nurtures scholarship and encourages critical thought. The fact that there are many diverse views of tourism can only add to the debate and make us think more creatively. It also fits the model of the tourist industry: diverse, dynamic, willing to adapt and change, and welcoming of new-comers with ideas to add to this image.

Secondly, there is the notion of tourism education and training, as one meant to equip people to bring about tourism. There could be no tourism industry without these people, yet, on the whole, they are overlooked as the key element that enables the industry to function because the focus is on the tourist and on managing the tourist experience. Front-line workers are seen as 'labour', and hopefully 'labour at affordable costs' (ASEAN, 1991: 4), or 'software' – the human element that marks this region apart, or a part of an innovative product. They are perceived as being the human resources problem. Actually, they are people with the same needs, not only for a well-paid job, but one that is interesting, enriching, challenging – just like people who are in a position to enroll for programmes in tourism at universities.

There are, then, two types of curriculum for people in the tourism industry, and they are vastly different in their beliefs about the nature and purpose of education. The challenge is to think creatively about technical vocational education, which is becoming both controlled and controlling. It is the industry, not the academics who watch over this type of education. Which industries have been known to nurture scholarship and critical thought in their labour force?

Whilst graduates from tourism programmes in universities are supposed to have gained some conceptual understanding of tourism, trainees from certificate courses (if they are lucky) get 'orientation to the industry'.

What is the purpose of this distinction? Ideally, graduates from universities will have grown personally as well as learned knowledge and skills to equip them for a professional occupation. This is because the university environment is seen holistically as enriching and challenging and it actively sets up opportunities for personal growth.

How can training be turned into an holistic experience, so that graduates from training courses develop as individuals as well as competent professionals? Front-line workers are the unique, indigenous individuals with whom tourists interact the most. Tourists are drawn to places to experience cultural difference, but want to feel welcomed and safe, and they appreciate quality service.

What is the difference between quality service and quality subservice? How can we ensure that quality service is not construed solely in terms of its Western understanding? Does the standardization of service bring about the standardization of indigenous people? Ivan Illich claims that 'Certification constitutes a form of market manipulation' (Illich, 1971: 15).

In the current rush to have every individual certificated, who is being manipulated by whom? Illich goes on to say that opportunities for skill-learning can be vastly multiplied if we open the 'market', which he admits is 'subversive blasphemy to the orthodox educator' because it promotes both unlicensed learning and unlicensed teaching (ibid.).

Is it possible to free training from its tight and often superficial lists of skills and ensure that potential employees can do the job with greater efficiency and pride? How? Can this be accomplished within the bureaucratic frameworks that have been put into place to control learning and teaching? The industry has the enormous responsibility of identifying the training and education needs of its workforce both now and in the future. What they do affects the total life experience of each individual in the workforce. Dewey wrote that no one is a worker and nothing else. 'A person must have experience, he must live, if his artistry is to be more than a technical accomplishment'.

How can industry and education work together to promote deeper and clearer insights into each others contribution to the well being of all individuals for whom they are responsible? How can the community and the individuals themselves be given a voice? ASEAN suggests that tourists remember 'Attentive service and friendliness/hospitality long after the memory of shops, hotels and sights have faded' (1991: 7). The other side of this is 'What will the front line worker remember, long after the memory of the tourist has faded?'

Bibliography

Airey, D. and Nightingale, M. (1981) Tourism occupation. Career profiles and knowledge. *Annals of Tourism Research* **VIII** (1), 52–68.

Alberta Tourism Education Council (undated) *Careers in Tourism*. Edmonton, Alberta, Canada.

ASEAN (1991) *Preparing for ASEAN Tourism: Training Needs*. ASEAN/Manpower.

Blanton, D. (1981) Tourism training in developing countries: the social and cultural dimension. *Annals of Tourism Research* **VIII** (1).

Bruner, E. M. (1991) Transformation of self in tourism. *Annals of Tourism Research* **18** (2), 238–50.

Burkart, A.J. and Medlik, S. (1974) *Tourism: Past, Present and Future*. London: Heinemann.

Burns, P. (1988) Study of regional strategy for tourism training in the South Pacific. *United Nations Development Programme* (RAS/86/134). New York: United Nations.

Byrne, A. (1994) Australia's programme of educational assistance to developing countries: the place of basic education. *International Review of Education* **40** (6), 455–68.

Commonwealth Department of Tourism (1993) Tourism: Australia's passport to growth. *Implementation Progress Report* No. 1. Canberra: CDT.

Copra, G. H. and Bentley C.B. (1992) Vocational education. In Jackson P.W. (ed.) *Handbook of Research on Curriculum*. New York: American Educational Research Association Macmillan Publishing Co.

Dewey, J. (1968) [1916] *Democracy and Education: An Introduction to the Philosophy of Education*. New York: Macmillan.

Drucker, P.F. (1977) *Management*. London: Pan Books.

ESCAP (1993) Tourism development in selected least developed countries and Vietnam. *ESCAP Tourism Review* No. 10 New York: United Nations.

Fitzsimmons, P. (1994) The management of tertiary educational institutions in New Zealand. Paper prepared for *Foucault: The Legacy* Conference, Surfer's Paradise, Australia, 4-6 July.

Fitzsimons, P. and Peters, M. (1994), Human capital theory and the industry training strategy in New Zealand. *Journal of Education Policy* Paper 10001 6.

Go, F. (1993) Creating global travel and tourism competitiveness through human resource development. Presented at *PATA/WTO Human Resources for Tourism Conference*. Bali, Indonesia, 4–6 October.

Harvey, L. (1994) Continuous quality improvement: a system-wide view of quality in higher education. In Knight, P. (ed.) *System-Wide Curriculum Change*. Buckingham: SEDA/OU Press.

Illich, I. (1971) *Deschooling Society*. London: Calder & Boyars.

Jafari, J. (1977) Editor's page. *Annals of Tourism Research* **V** (6), 11.

Jafari, J. and Ritchie, B. J.R (1981) Towards a framework for tourism education: problems and prospects: *Annals of Tourism Research* **VIII** (1), 13–34.

Kaye, M. (1992) Adult communication management in adult vocational education: a contemporary Australian perspective. Paper presented to the International Communication Association Annual Conference. Miami, Florida, 21–25 May.

McNabb, P. (1990) *Tourism Personnel Development Project (Thailand)*. New Zealand: Peak Tourism International Ltd.

Miller, P. and Rose, N. (1993) Governing economic life. In Gane, M. and Johnson, T. (eds) *Foucault's New Domains*. London: Routledge.

Murphy, P.E. (1981), Tourism course proposal for a social science curriculum. *Annals of Tourism Research* **VIII** (1).

Pearce, P. L. (1991) Locating tourism studies in the landscape of knowledge. Paper presented at the *New Horizons in Tourism and Hospitality Education, Training and Research Conference*. Alberta, Canada.

Prime Ministerial Task Force on Employment (1994) *Employment: Facing New Zealand's Biggest Challenge*. Wellington, New Zealand.

Rein, A. (1991) Chief Executive: Tourism Training Australia (PO Box K743, Haymarket, NSW 2000) Interdata.

Rein, A. (1994) Personal correspondence with Yee, J.

Robinson, C., Yielder, J. and Associates (1995) Levels of learning: an examination of the use of 'Levels of Learning' in New Zealand Polytechnics. Report to the New Zealand Qualifications Authority, Wellington, New Zealand.

Schrag, F. (1992) Conceptions of knowledge. In Jackson, P.W. (ed.) *Handbook of Research on Curriculum*. New York: American Educational Research Association, Macmillan Publishing Co.

Torrington, D., Weightman, J., Johns, K. (1989) *Effective Management: People and Organization*. Prentice Hall International.

Tourism Council of the South Pacific (1991) *TCSP Tourism Topics* July/August No. 28.

Tourism In Papua New Guinea (1994) World Tourism Association Technical Paper.

UNDP (1990) Philippines Tourism Manpower Survey Final Report. *United Nations Development Programme* (PH1/88/036). New York: United Nations.

Wilson, P. (1993) Beyond 'A Basis for Credit?' Developing The Technical Specifications For A National Credit Framework. Unpublished paper. Commissioned by the Further Education Unit, UK.

Withey, M., Gorman, G. and Dicks, J. (1991) Investing in people: an evaluation of a pilot project for training front-line staff in the hospitality industry. Presented at *New Horizons in Tourism and Hospitality Education, Training and Research*, Conference. Calgary, Alberta, Canada, 2–5 July.

World Tourism Organization News (1992) *Pakistan: Tourism to the year 2000 – The South Asian Perspective*. January, No.1.

World Travel and Tourism Council (1993) *Gearing up for Growth: A Study of Education and Training for Careers in Asia–Pacific Travel and Tourism*. Brussels: WTTC.

Xu Fan (1994) Division of Market Research, National Tourism Administration of the People's Republic of China Tourism Education. Personal communication with Yee, J.

Yee, J. G. (1992) *Human Resources Development for the Travel, Tourism and the Hospitality Industry in the Pacific Asia Region: A Preliminary Overview*. San Francisco: Pacific Asia Travel Association.

Index